a Mother's Journal

BOOK ONE:

Let My Children Go!

a Mother's Journal

BOOK ONE:

Let My Children Go!

*My true story about my daughters' sexual abuse,
the refusal of the Cobb County, Georgia, Superior Court
to protect them, and my long fight to free them
from the grip of their abusive father.*

WENDY TITELMAN

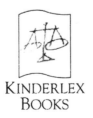

KINDERLEX
BOOKS

Serving Children in the Legal System
New Orleans, Louisiana

A MOTHER'S JOURNAL
BOOK ONE:
LET MY CHILDREN GO!

Published by Kinderlex Books

For further information or to order additional books write to:

Kinderlex Books, Inc.
P.O. Box 531883
New Orleans, Louisiana 70153-1883

Library of Congress Cataloging-in-Publication Data

Titelman, Wendy, 1952-
  Let my children go! : a mother's journal / Wendy Titelman.
      p. cm.
  ISBN 0-9729025-0-3 (pbk.)
1. Sexually abused children--Georgia--Cobb County. 2. Sexually abused children--Legal status, laws, etc.--Georgia--Cobb County. 3. Mothers of sexually abused children--Georgia--Cobb County. 4. Trials (Child sexual abuse)--Georgia--Cobb County. I. Title.
  HV6570.4.G4T58 2003
  364.15'554'092--dc21

                                                                    2003004418

Cover design by Jeanne Ducote. The heart on the cover was painted by Amanda Titelman and made into a card. She and her sister, Jessica, gave it to their mother in April, 2000.

Printed by Hauser Printing Co., Inc. in Harahan, Louisiana

Everything I share with you in this book is true and happened as described. My daughters and I have been targets for destruction by individuals in the court system, my ex-husband, and his family. We have been targets because we have exposed these people for who they really are and what they have done.

The old expression, "You can't judge a book by its cover," is ever so true with people as well. The external cover of education, dress and livelihood cannot reveal what is in the depths of the heart of a man. There are, however, behaviors that will give us clues to his deep inner thoughts.

The names of the individuals involved are accurate. However, the names of my two innocent children and friends who are worried about retribution have been changed to protect their privacy. The altered names, Amanda Titelman, Jessica Titelman, Gail Vernon, Michael Vernon, Rick Thompson, Mary Thompson, and Janice Morgan, were chosen at random without knowing if there are others with the same name.

There are many who have encouraged me, held my arms up when I was too tired, and helped me to stand steady and strong. With deepest gratitude, I want to thank Nadine Youngblood, Susan Ibarra, Peggy Carlson, Doreen Buben, and others who have consistently supported me and the girls in organized intercessory prayer for several years. Dan and Jeanette Adkins, Cathy and Dave Dishman, Gail and Michael Vernon, Rick and Mary Thompson, Denise and Wayne Savely, Darlene Simmons, Lynn and Jim Palmer, Deana and Lynn Williams, Lisa Curtis, Vicky Rivet, and many others have been of immense help also through the giving of their talents, prayer and resources. I am grateful to Jeanne Ducote for her creativity and compassion. I especially want to recognize Nadine and Bill Youngblood, Jan and Jerry Geiger, and my mother, Frances Evans, for their abundant gifts and financial support. Particularly, my mother has given all that she has to help her granddaughters and me. These and many others, too numerous to name, have also consistently worked to get the system to examine its errors and hopefully bring protection to my girls. They all have shed their tears along with mine.

In December, 2000, I was given a lovely diary entitled, "A Mother's Journal," to record my thoughts and feelings. I shared a small portion of my diary with my friend, Garland Waller, who is a writer. She gave me the confidence that I could write my story in a way that could be understood and felt by others. Hence, this book is borne.

This book is dedicated to my beautiful children, whom I love more than anything or anyone else in the world, and for whom I would give my life over and over again.

Amanda and Jessica, December, 1995

FOREWORD ONE

This book is an extraordinary document which, once again, clearly indicts the justice system, this time in Georgia. We now have on record many, many cases of women and children who have been misused, abused, undermined, and treated badly by the lawyers, the judges, and the guardians.

The extraordinary way in which Wendy Titelman and her family were dealt with needs to be shared with all. What has been done has led to a heavy accumulation of information about the misuse of the courts and the horrible injustices created by the judge and other court officials.

I strongly endorse that this is an important book for people to read because without a doubt, it provides an extensive demonstration of the corruption in the courts, particularly concerning women and children. The PAS is junk science and the resulting misuse of women and children in the courts is outrageous.

Paul Jay Fink, M.D.

Dr. Fink, a prominent psychiatrist, psychoanalyst, and speaker, a past-president of the American Psychiatric Association, and the founder and current president of the Leadership Council for Mental Health, Justice, and the Media.

Dr. Fink is a Professor of Psychiatry at Temple University School of Medicine and Chairman of the American Psychiatric Association's Task Force on Psychiatric Aspects of Violence. He has extensive leadership experience and is considered an expert in program development and enhancement. Dr. Fink has served as the president of numerous organizations including the American Psychiatric Association (APA), the American College of Psychiatrists, the National Association for Psychiatric Healthcare Systems, the Philadelphia County Medical Society, and the American Association of Chairmen of Departments of Psychiatry. He served as both Chairman of the Department of Psychiatry at Albert Einstein Medical Center and Associate Vice President of the Albert Einstein Healthcare Network. He founded and directed the Einstein Center for the Study of Violence and is a co-founder and past president of the Greater Philadelphia Health Care Congress.

Dr. Fink currently serves on a variety of committees having to do with issues of youth violence. He chairs the Youth Homicide Subcommittee of the Philadelphia Youth Fatality Review Team, and he serves on the Board of the Philadelphia Health Management Corporation, and was, for five years, on the Philadelphia Board of Health.

Dr. Fink is co-editor of the books, *The Stigma of Mental Illness* (American Psychiatric Press, 1992) and *Misinformation Concerning Child Sexual Abuse and Adult Survivors* (Haworth Press, 2002), and has authored over 190 articles. He has been the recipient of a number of national awards including the APA's Vestermark Award and the Francis J. Braceland Award for Public Service. In 1999, the Philadelphia County Medical Society selected Dr. Fink as Physician of the Year.

FOREWORD TWO

Let My Children Go! is a moving account of the failure of a system that is supposed to be protecting children.

Wendy Titelman's voice needs to be heard by as many people as possible. Perhaps it will be heard by someone who will have the power to change what is wrong with the way the "system" approaches these matters.

Every social worker, law enforcement investigator, judge, custody evaluator, family court investigator, child's attorney, and family lawyer in the country should receive a copy of this book in order that they may see, first hand, the results of "system failure."

In much the same way that Wendy describes her life, both in the marriage and afterward, too many children and mothers in this country have experienced the wrath of an abusive father. I hope that the pages in this book help to reflect light into the dark corners of systemic failure, illuminating and enlightening those who see its glow.

Seth L. Goldstein,
Attorney and Counselor at Law

Mr. Goldstein is the Executive Director of the Child Abuse Forensic Institute, which he founded in 1992. The Institute assists parents in Family Law, Juvenile, and Personal Injury matters wherein child abuse allegations have arisen.

Prior to founding the Child Abuse Forensic Institute he was the investigator and Project Director for the Child Abuse Vertical Prosecution Unit of the Napa County District Attorney, Napa, California. He also worked as an investigator with the Santa Clara County District Attorney, San Jose, California, and was a special prosecutor for the San Benito County District Attorney, Hollister, California.

Prior to obtaining his law degree from the Oakland College of Law, Mr. Goldstein was a police officer. He worked for the Berkeley, California, Police Department for thirteen years. He served in the Patrol, Service, and Detective Divisions of the police department, including two years as a Juvenile Officer. During this time he served as the Chairman of the Northern California Juvenile Officers Association Committee on Sexual Abuse and Sexual Exploitation of Children and also has served as the Association's President and editor of its newsletter.

Mr. Goldstein has presented at seminars and workshops throughout the country and in Europe, including the FBI Academy at Quantico, Va. He is certified as a Criminal Investigation Instructor by the Robert Presley Institute for Criminal Investigation, and has testified as an expert witness in court, including a branch of the Florida Supreme Court, as well as numerous California and Federal legislative commissions and committees.

Mr. Goldstein is a former consultant to National Resource Center on Sexual Abuse of Children and the International Association of Chiefs of Police (IACP). He sat on the California Attorney General's Violent Crime Information Systems Advisory Group and was a founding Member of the Board of Directors of the National Center For Missing and Exploited Children. He also sat on the California and United States Department of Justice Committees that created investigative and academy curriculum for investigations of sexual abuse and exploitation of children.

Mr. Goldstein has written several articles on the subject of sexual abuse and exploitation of children which have been published nationally. He is the author of the textbook *The Sexual Exploitation of Children: A Practical Guide to Assessment, Investigation, and Intervention*, 2nd Edition, published by CRC Press.

Mr. Goldstein has received numerous awards for his work, including the American Bar Association's Gavel Award in 1980, the California State Juvenile Officer's Dan Pursuit Award (Officer of the Year) in 1990, and the American Bar Association Child Advocacy Division's National Certificate of Recognition for Significant Legal Contributions Advancing the Welfare of Our Nation's Children in 1997.

FOREWORD THREE

While my position precludes my commenting on the specifics of the case contained within this book, *A Mother's Journal*, I do have some thoughts which I would like to share with you.

First of all, I have a master's degree in social work and was the assistant director of probation in the New Orleans Juvenile Court as I went back to law school in the evening from 1958 through 1962. Upon graduating law school, I practiced law until 1972. Among other things, I was also the attorney for child protective services in Jefferson Parish. In 1972 I was elected Juvenile Court Judge for Jefferson Parish and served there until 1986 when I was elected to the Fifth Circuit Court of Appeal for the State of Louisiana, in which I presently serve. Therefore, over the course of 44 years, as a probation officer in New Orleans, Juvenile Court, an attorney, and Judge, I estimate that I have personally been involved with between two and three thousand cases of child sexual abuse. I have published articles, I am a full professor at the Tulane School of Social Work, and have lectured and taught extensively about various aspects of child sexual abuse, to judges, social workers, psychologists, police and every other group that deals with the problem of child sexual abuse. At the time of writing this, I teach a course called "Defining and Proving Child Sexual Abuse" on the Internet, under the auspices of Tulane School of Social Work, and to the juvenile police throughout the state that meet each year at Louisiana State University in Baton Rouge.

I mention all of the above, to state my experience and knowledge in the field of child sexual abuse. There are very few times in law when you can state anything categorically, but I can certainly say that beyond any doubt whatsoever, the problem expressed by Wendy Titelman in this book is epidemic and widespread, and it has been this way for the forty-four years that I have been involved with the legal system.

In spite of the fact that there are wonderful seminars for judges on this subject, and that I teach at very many of them, it seems that only the knowledgeable judges come to the seminars in the first place. Very similar to the good parents that go to PTA meetings. The ones that need it the most, do not go, and that is why they continue to act out of ignorance. In the judicial field, it is so alarming to see so many judges uninformed and/or misinformed that would rely on such nonsense as the "parental alienation syndrome." I state this categorically and in writing, because I have overwhelming evidence of the nonsense of this notion, and of the harm that it has caused.

In addition to my other activities, I have also been a consultant on behalf of a lawyer in California and an eminent social worker in Michigan who were the victims of this false science. I am happy to say that both of these people ultimately prevailed. I am also aware of many other cases in which "parental alienation syndrome" has been erroneously relied upon by Judges.

Sol Gothard, Judge
Court of Appeal
Fifth Circuit
State of Louisiana

Judge Sol Gothard, JD, MSW, ACSW, was elected to the Fifth Circuit Court of Appeal for the State of Louisiana in 1986, where he continues to serve as Senior Judge. He was formerly Chief Judge of the Juvenile Court, Parish of Jefferson, State of Louisiana, having served there for fourteen years. Before being elected Judge in 1972, he was engaged in the private practice of law for over ten years. Prior to that he was a social worker for sixteen years in a variety of settings. He has a masters degree in social work from Case Western Reserve University, and a JD from Loyola University in New Orleans.

He is married to the former Jacqueline Pressner and they have five children. He is an Honorably Discharged Veteran of the United States Army.

He has participated as lecturer, workshop leader and keynote speaker for numerous international, national and regional conferences and workshops.

His articles have been published in Child Welfare, Social Work, Journal of Independent Social Work, Journal of the National Council of Juvenile and Family Court Judges, The Practicing Law Institute, The American Medical Association, RoundTable, Journal of The American Professional Society on the Abuse of Children, Seattle University Law Review, Louisiana Bar Journal, and other books and publications.

He is Past President of the Louisiana Council of Juvenile Court Judges. He teaches at Tulane University Graduate School of Social Work, where he has the rank of full professor.

In the past, Judge Gothard was selected "Citizen of the Year" by the Louisiana State Chapter of the National Association of Social Workers; he was awarded the Alfred E. Clay award for significant contributions to children by the Children's Bureau of Greater New Orleans; he delivered the commencement address to the graduates of the Tulane University Graduate School of Social Work, and the commencement address to the graduates of Mandel School of Applied Social Sciences of Case Western Reserve University, where he was also honored as "Alumnus of the Year"; he delivered the keynote address at the closing plenary of the 1990 NASW annual conference in Boston, which was attended by approximately 5,000 social workers.

Judge Gothard is a past member of the Board of Directors of numerous organizations, including The American Professional Society On The Abuse of Children (APSAC), The American Humane Association, Children's Division, The National Organization of Forensic Social Work (NOFSW), 2000: Year of the Humane Child, One Voice: The National Alliance for Abuse Awareness, Our Children Our Future Charitable Foundation, and the Louisiana/SPCA. He is currently vice-chairman of the Louisiana Animal Welfare Commission.

His most recent publications include: "The Evolving Law of Alleged Delayed Memories of Childhood Sexual Abuse"; "Therapeutic Jurisprudence In The Appellate Arena - A Louisiana Jurist's Response"; "Truth' versus 'Justice' In The Legal Arena: A Survey of Judges, Lawyers and Mental Health Professionals"; and "Child Abuse/Animal Abuse: Psychological and Legal Implications." He is currently teaching two Internet Courses on "The Social Worker in Court: Playing Ball in an Unfamiliar Ballpark" and "Child Sexual Abuse and the Courts," under the auspices of the Tulane University School of Social Work.

Mommy and Amanda, December, 1992

Mommy and Jessica, October, 1994

CHAPTER ONE

I used to sing all the American patriotic songs with pride celebrating our land of freedom, justice, and government of law. This is America - I thought the courts would protect my children and me from my abusive husband. I was taught to believe that the justice system in the United States would protect each one of us and our children from abusive situations, such as sexual molestation or domestic violence. I was taught that the Constitution of the United States would be upheld in the courtroom. I was taught that court rulings are based on law and evidence and truth. I found that this system doesn't always work, and I found that the family courts of America are often very broken and sometimes corrupt.

It has been another sleepless night, as I have tossed and turned with disturbing thoughts about my daughters, Amanda and Jessica, and the people responsible for harming them. I think of them constantly, whether awake or asleep, unable to reconcile the events that have taken place in our lives over the past few years.

More than two years have passed since I last saw or talked with my daughters, and more than three years have gone by since Amanda and Jessica shared with me and others that their father was sexually molesting them. No words can describe the intense emotions and grief that a mother feels upon finding that her children have been harmed so badly. I had committed my life to protect, nourish, and raise them to be physically, emotionally, spiritually and intellectually healthy and fit.

Why would a competent, loving mother lose custody of her children to a man the family court knew to be harmful? Why would a court of law prevent visitation or communication between a loving mother and her young children when they desperately want to see each other, when there are findings that the children's father is molesting them, and the mother has appropriately responded to the abuse?

It has now been over two years since the Cobb County Superior Court in Georgia, through an "ex-parte" or one-sided order entered by Judge James Bodiford, has allowed me to see or communicate with my two daughters, now ages ten and eight.

1

On June 4, 2001, I went to the Cobb County Magistrate Court in Marietta, Georgia, a suburb just north of Atlanta, to get a warrant for the arrest of my ex-husband, Andrew Titelman, for his crimes. I gave the clerk a packet of information containing abundant evidence of his guilt, much more than is ever required for one's arrest. The clerk gave it back to me, and I was taken to the office of Judge Laura Austin who greeted me with a loud voice and an angry disposition. When she asked me why I was there, I approached her desk to give her the packet of information. She yelled at me to get away from her desk. As I attempted to explain to her my purpose for being there and that the Cobb County Superior Court had given sole custody of my two daughters to their abusive father, she stormed at me questioning, "And why did you lose custody?" There was a long pause as I sat back and looked her squarely in the eyes, and then I spoke very clearly and slowly - "Parental - Alienation - Syndrome."

There was silence, and I saw painful expressions cover her face. "What does Parental Alienation Syndrome mean to you?" I asked. She changed completely and became more soft spoken as she told me that her sister had just lost custody of her children in Texas by the use of Parental Alienation Syndrome. She accepted my packet and listened to my plight. She told me, "You will never win in Georgia. You are dealing with the good 'ole boys who stick together no matter what." She told me my only chance was to go to the media and expose the cover-up.

The evening of June 4 Judge Austin spent several hours reading the evidence of abuse and debating what she should personally do in this situation as the Magistrate Judge. After consideration she called me and told me that I had put her in a very bad position. Instead of stepping up to the plate and doing the right thing, Judge Austin issued no arrest warrant. She attempted to have an investigation of Andrew Titelman opened, but then allowed it to immediately be closed after receiving a phone call from those participating in the cover-up.

"Parental Alienation Syndrome" (PAS) is a pro-pedophile philosophy introduced to judges, attorneys and psychologists by Dr. Richard Gardner in the mid 1980's. PAS is described as a "disorder" that arises in a highly contested divorce and custody dispute in which a child is on a campaign of denigration against a parent, usually the father, because the other parent has put him or her up to it. If a child speaks negatively about his or her father, Gardner states that the mother is to blame and that the solution is to increase the amount of time the child spends with the father. The court is told to ignore the

> If the child continues to speak out against the father, Gardner insists that the mother should be jailed and the child should spend time in a detention center, in order to silence the mother and the child.

child's cries for help and the pleas to remain with the mother who is protecting her. If the child continues to speak out against the father, Gardner insists that the mother should be jailed and the child should spend time in a detention center, in order to silence the mother and the child.

Richard Gardner is a self-published author. His publishing company is called Creative Therapeutics. In several of his books, he expresses that our culture has made adult sex with children taboo, and that we need to be more tolerant of this behavior. He believes that it is not a crime and that it should not be treated punitively. He blames the Jews and the Judeo-Christian principles for the present punitive reaction to pedophilia in our country. Gardner states, "Perhaps she can be helped to appreciate that in the history of the world his behavior has probably been more common than the restrained behavior of those who do not sexually abuse their children."[1]

He further states, "Many of these excessively moralistic individuals are secretly envious of those who can guiltlessly allow themselves such release. They cannot express this directly; in fact, it may be unconscious. In order to protect themselves from the discomforts of their jealousy and the temptation of indulging themselves in the forbidden sexual activities, they embark upon a campaign of denigration, the final goal of which is to expunge entirely those who allow themselves greater freedom of sexual expression."[2]

Gardner believes that we are all pedophiles. He states, "One of the steps that society must take to deal with the present hysteria is to 'come off it' and take a more realistic attitude toward

3

pedophilic behavior...and accept the fact that all of us, to some degree, are pedophilics."[3] Gardner admits, "Sex abuse allegations that arise in the intrafamilial situation have a high likelihood of being valid." "Incest is probably quite common," he says, "especially father (or stepfather) - daughter (or stepdaughter) relations."[4] Yet Gardner teaches that all children lie, and therefore, should not be believed. He says, "...they have little or no guilt over the damage they wreak on the lives of their fathers."[5]

PAS is considered "junk science," and as such, should be inadmissible in all courts. Gardner's theories are pro-pedophile, bizarre, and unaccepted in the competent professional community. PAS has been denounced by the American Psychological Association, the American Psychiatric Association, and the American Bar Association. Many articles have been written about the danger of using these theories. They have been used by "fathers' rights" attorneys to protect child molesters and to help them get custody of children.

Even though courts across America have kicked Dr. Gardner and his theories out, there are other courts that have embraced his theories, ignoring the evidence and the law. "Fathers Rights" groups, masking as children's advocates, propagate Richard Gardner's materials and teach abusive men how to get custody of their kids. This continual barrage of pro-pedophile literature has infiltrated the justice system and is taught by these groups as valid and scientific. As a result, some of our court officials and court appointed representatives have been duped, and our children are suffering the consequences. Others use it to benefit their pocketbooks, and still others use it because of judicial bias favoring abusers.

My experience in the judicial system has been shocking, and neither my children nor I will ever be the same again as a result. The Cobb County Superior Court has not only given my girls to a child molester, but I have been jailed for trying to protect them. I have been stripped of every monetary resource available to me. I keep asking the question, "Why?" Why would they do this?

The stated purpose of our judicial system is to seek the truth. This doesn't always happen. Judges are often relying on guardians *ad litem* - attorneys appointed by the court to make custody recommendations. The courts then ignore all other testimony and evidence outside of the guardian's *ad litem* recommendations. The role of the guardian *ad litem* is unlike any other role in the courtroom. It is poorly defined with few rules, and typically these guardians come up with recommendations that are based solely on the guardian's thoughts and personal biases. However, the judges typically do

> The role of the guardian *ad litem* is unlike any other role in the courtroom. It is poorly defined with few rules, and typically these guardians come up with recommendations that are based solely on the guardian's thoughts and personal biases.

whatever the guardian says because it is expedient. Life decisions have even been determined in the courtroom by the "toss of a coin," making a mockery of the judge's position.

If a woman unknowingly gets involved with an abusive sexual deviant, the family court far too often makes it impossible for her to protect the children. If she reports the abuse, she is likely to lose them to the custody of the abuser. If she doesn't report the abuse and someone else does, she will lose the children due to neglect. When judges allow the use of the dangerous Parental Alienation Syndrome and other junk science into the courtroom, they immediately begin to annihilate women and children. Again, one must question, why are judges doing this? Is there such a great bias in court against women that judges can so frequently harm families?

The American Psychological Association's Presidential Task Force on Violence and the Family stated, "Fathers who battered the mother are twice as likely to seek sole physical custody of their children than are nonviolent fathers."[6] Statistical studies published by the American Judges Association have shown that approximately 70 percent of the men who seek and are given custody of their children are abusive men.[7] Yet the family court continues to give custody of children to abusers. Judges find that mothers are unfit parents by using pedophile friendly propaganda such as "Parental Alienation Syndrome" and "False Memory Syndrome," both of which were used to take my children away from me.

5

The Association of Family and Conciliation Courts Research Unit in Denver, with funding from the National Center on Child Abuse and Neglect has reported that the number of sex abuse charges arising during divorce and/or custody disputes is small, even in the contested cases, with less than two percent having allegations of sexual abuse.[8] This is contrary to what Richard Gardner and his followers teach. Gardner claims that false sexual abuse allegations made by a malicious spouse are common during custody disputes. The report goes on to state that deliberate false allegations made to influence the custody decision or to hurt the ex-spouse do happen, but they are viewed by the knowledgeable professionals as rarities. Gardner says that all children lie, and therefore, should not be believed.

> [D]eliberate false allegations made to influence the custody decision or to hurt the ex-spouse do happen, but they are viewed by the knowledgeable professionals as rarities.

This study confirms what the real experts in child sexual abuse already know, is that the clearest indicator of child sexual abuse is the child's own testimony. The study said there were fewer false allegations across the board in child sexual abuse cases than there are in most criminal reporting of other cases. Other studies have shown as well that false allegations of abuse are rare. It is widely known that a child will more often say that nothing has happened to him when in fact it has. The truth is covered with a lie because the child is afraid he will get in trouble.

Most people don't want to believe that a loving mother can lose custody of her children to an abusive man. They don't want to believe there are ordinary looking, charming men in high positions who molest children.

My story is not unusual. There are many other stories like mine all over the country. Garland Waller, an award-winning producer-writer-director of nationally syndicated documentaries, presented three similar cases in the film, *Small Justice* (2001). There, Dr. Gardner states on camera that if a child reports a father's abuse, the mother must tell her child that he is never to say that again, and that if he does, he will be put in a detention center until he learns not to say it. He goes on to say that if the mother does not cooperate in silencing the child and forcing him to go visit with the father that she should be jailed.

Small Justice was named Best Social Documentary in the New York International Film and Video Festival. Helen Grieco, Executive Director of California NOW says, "There is a crisis in the Family Law Courts in America: perfectly fit mothers are losing custody of their children. Mothers are reporting gender bias, denial of due process, incompetence, corruption and fraud in the family law courts. ...'Small Justice' is ...the first film to break the silence on America's injustice. This documentary will serve to mobilize the movement to save women and children from the hands of the Family Law Courts in America."

The problem should be an alarming call to the American public. We cannot tolerate the destruction of family, women, and children by our family courts.

The words of Judge Laura Austin stay with me, that my only chance to protect my daughters is to expose this through the media. I have sought every resource I know, and thus, I share this Mother's Journal in hope that it will open the public's eyes. I also hope that my children will get word that I love them and have not abandoned them. I have learned through my court hearings that my children are being told by court appointed professionals that I do not want to see them. One day I will personally give them this journal. They will know how much I have fought to see them, to protect them, and how much I love them.

The Superior Court of Cobb County Georgia is holding my children captive. Like Moses before Pharaoh, I am begging the court to let my children go!

CHAPTER TWO

I live in uptown New Orleans in a three-bedroom home that was built in the late 1800's. My home is located just three blocks from St. Charles Avenue, one of the world's most beautiful streets. Along with Tulane and Loyola Universities it is lined with mansions and cathedrals and tall oaks and magnolias that lead into the central business district. Old-time streetcars run down the center of the street called the neutral ground. New Orleans heritage comes mainly from French emigrants. Beginning in the 1800's, the French lived on one side of Canal Street, which also runs through New Orleans, and the Americans lived on the other side. The median between the two was ground that was considered to be owned by neither the French nor the Americans, hence the name "neutral ground" was born. Horse and buggies carry tourists around town and artists and musicians are found on many street corners. New Orleans is a most unusual city filled with lots of history, beautiful old mansions and every style of architecture.

My ceilings are 12 feet high. There are hardwood floors throughout, and there is abundant character. Most of the rooms have fireplaces with beautiful tile and mantles. I have a small courtyard. When you enter through my front door, the warmth is ever present.

Amanda and Jessica's pictures and belongings are in every room. I have a piano in the dining room and all the Suzuki training books and CDs that the girls used once to play the piano. Their books line shelves in my office and in a bedroom upstairs, books such as *Goodnight Moon*, *Barnyard Dance* and *The Napping House*. Their Bibles, unopened for so long, are neatly placed among all the other books. Their Little Tikes kitchen and all their little dishes are a part of my country kitchen dining area. Their computer and computer games are set up in a corner. The mouse pad is a picture of the three of us just a month before they were taken from me. Jessica's ceramic duck sits under a plant on the file cabinet. The bread warmer Amanda made for me hangs over the stove. On the refrigerator are the last pictures I took of them in Alexander Springs, Florida, over two years ago. Preschool crafts cover the side of the refrigerator along with notes that say "I love Mom." A vase holding sunflowers made from Popsicle sticks, construction paper and sunflower seeds is beside the sink. Two wind chimes hang in the window, one with Noah's Ark and one with an angel. Amanda and Jessica's homemade soaps are in a dish in the downstairs bathroom. Macoco, their animated gorilla, sits on my desk, and when I cough or make a loud noise he wildly sings *La Macaraina*. A calendar, a candle, and other items lie about, all of which belong to my children. A closet at the top of the winding stairs holds some of their clothes now long outgrown. Two bedrooms are adorned for two little girls just the way they were when they were with me. Pink and purple butterflies hang from a mobile in a doorway. Art supplies, puppetry, baby dolls, books and games fill the shelves. A small child's table and four small chairs sit waiting to be used again. My bedroom is filled with pictures of Amanda and Jessica when they were little. CD's of children's songs and children's videos fill an entertainment shelf. Hair bows hang on the wall in the bathroom at the end of the long hallway, and little toothbrushes wait on the bathroom counter. Their hand-painted jewelry boxes sit on a shelf next to towels they once used.

Many weekends I walk in the Audubon Park. Even though it is very beautiful and peaceful, I walk with the deep painful thoughts of how much the girls would enjoy riding their bikes here, feeding the ducks and geese, climbing the beautiful oak trees dripping with moss, and visiting the adjacent Audubon zoo.

Often, I thought it was just a matter of a few days before the girls would be returning to me, but those hopes have been dashed over and over again. The torture and devastation have been great, and I have had to learn to cope with the disappointments. Nevertheless, my faith is great and I believe the day will eventually come. Their home is ready for them. They have outgrown most of the things they once enjoyed, but those belongings remain in place for closure's sake before moving on to a future day.

CHAPTER THREE

I brought my precious children into this world with the greatest love. Like any mother, my desire to protect them was powerful. I didn't know at the time that I would have to protect them from their own father.

Amanda and Jessica's father, Andrew "Andy" Titelman, and I had many problems during our marriage. They all seemed to be focused around his relationship with his daughter, Katie, from his first marriage. Counselors told me that if I could "hang in there" our marriage would improve when Katie went off to college. But no one realized the core or the depth of the problem until Amanda and Jessica began to tell what their father was doing to them.

My awareness of incest in our home was a slow and disturbing process lasting about seven years. As I look back, and knowing what I now know, it should have been obvious.

My family and friends began telling me that I should be highly concerned that Andy was molesting Katie and that my children would be next. There was every objective indication that was happening, but I didn't know for sure. However, in 1998, when my brother and sister-and-law took me aside to say that they didn't want to hurt me but that it was obvious to my family that Andy's relationship with Katie was sexual, I knew in my heart they were right.

Around the same time two friends intervened and took me to lunch. They also told me I was in denial, and that the signs indicated that Andy was molesting Katie. They, too, warned me that when Katie went off to college my daughters would be next. They listed behaviors in the family on a sheet of paper. Like a connect-the-dot picture, not knowing what the picture would be until finished, I was floored by the ugly truth.

Several months later, another friend who had child abuse training and who was totally unaware of my concerns at home, told me that she believed Jessica was being sexually abused. She had seen symptoms while Jessica was in her care.

The dynamics of the relationships in our home during the marriage were always disturbing and serious. My instincts had been to preserve the marriage and to keep an intact family for my children. Andy's conduct was of such concern, however, that we continued in counseling throughout our marriage.

As I look back now, I see how blind I was. Being involved in an abusive relationship is like being lost at sea in the midst of a terrible storm. You know there is safe ground somewhere out there, but you can't see it, and you don't know in what direction to turn or how to get there. Every Mayday you send dies unheard, and it feels there is no help anywhere around. It was important to me to make the marriage work, and I was willing to do just about anything before I knew the full picture.

Sexualized and incestuous behaviors were present from the very beginning. I continually passed it off as emotional problems stemming from Andy's difficult divorce and custody battle with his first wife, Sydney. As time progressed, my concerns and fears increased. My brother, Mark, sent me a book by Dr. Patricia Love called *The Emotional Incest Syndrome*. The picture it painted mirrored what I was experiencing in my home. Andy agreed with me that the behaviors were present. Therapists told us that Andy's relationship with Katie was unhealthy and termed it as "emotional enmeshment."

Katie vied for my position as Andy's wife and lady of the house, and Andy treated her as though she were. He expected me to be subservient to the two of them. There was a power struggle, and Andy was enraged with me if I didn't do as Katie desired. He lavished her with gifts and luxury while Amanda, Jessica and I went without. Whatever Katie requested, she received.

Andy warred with me on a daily basis about Katie's unhappiness with me and with Amanda and Jessica, but he never was able to tell me anything specific. He simply said that Katie was unhappy and that it was my fault. Andy and Katie treated Amanda and Jessica as intrusions in their lives, and they blamed me for every ill feeling. The tension in our home while Katie was there was so overwhelming. I never knew when or why Amanda and Jessica or I would be attacked.

Andy claimed that Katie's mother, Sydney, had affairs throughout their marriage and that for the last four years that they lived separately in one home. She would leave the house in the afternoon and go out to bars at night, leaving Andy with total responsibility for Katie. This reportedly began when Katie was five and lasted four years. Andy told me terrible things about Sydney, and I believed everything he told me. However, based on what Andy has done to me, I now wonder how much of it was true. Some truth mixed with a lot of deception becomes a very dangerous weapon, a weapon I learned the Titelmans use regularly.

Andy and Sydney fought for custody, and even though Katie requested to live with her mother, Andy was given full custody of Katie when they divorced. Andy continuously told Katie and me that it was in Katie's best interest that she see her mom as little as possible because she behaved inappropriately and was dangerous. Whenever Katie received a note or a phone call from Sydney, Andy made derogatory remarks about her, saying "she is stupid," "her voice is whiny," and "she dresses like a child." He made it perfectly clear that Katie was not allowed to visit her mother beyond what the court had ordered, and there were many disturbing times because Katie craved contact with her mom. Katie spent most of her time in her room on the phone with her. It appeared her mom yearned to be with Katie, too.

CHAPTER FOUR

One would never know from the derision hurled at me in family court that my background demonstrates competence and ample maturity. In every job I ever held, I was quickly given great responsibility as my abilities were recognized. I think it is important that this story be viewed in the context of my entire life.

I was very busy and productive prior to marriage. I enjoyed life and poured all my energy into what I believed was good. The transition from career woman to stay at home mom was easy for me, as I just changed my goal to raising my children.

God blessed me with a bright and energetic spirit, and a desire to make a difference in the world. During my school years my classmates selected me as a "class superlative" and described me as "happy go lucky." I was co-captain of the cheerleaders, a basketball player, a state-level gold medal gymnast, class officer, queen of the senior prom, first runner up in the homecoming court, and participated in many clubs. As a young adult I volunteered as a youth minister for Skyland United Methodist Church in Atlanta. I sang and performed in a small group called Friends, and we even cut a record. I was selected by a Nautilus Athletic Center in downtown Atlanta for their magazine and television advertisements. My body strength and form were excellent. The company trained the Atlanta Falcons at the time, and they used me to pace the players weekly in a seven minute mile run.

In the early 1980's the desire to be financially independent burned in me, and I began to pursue a viable career. After investigating my options, it seemed I was best suited for sales. I was bright, multi-talented and had a lot of interests, but I was a master of nothing. I read an ad in the Atlanta Journal Constitution for an outside sales representative position for investment gemstones. I though it would be fascinating and fun to be surrounded by top quality diamonds, emeralds, rubies, and tourmalines. I began my career with this small company. I started contacting everyone I knew, set up displays at conferences and trade shows, and I enrolled in a school to become a gemologist. I absolutely loved what I was doing and began my own investment portfolio.

Another sales rep, Marie Haver, became a close friend. She was 23 years old, and a beautiful vibrant young woman. Marie had a quiet, gentle, independent and free spirit. She had a way of attracting interesting people and opportunities. We went to Ted Turner's parties in Atlanta. We rode around town in a Rolls Royce and presented our gemstones to the Falcons. We had luncheons and dinners in business clubs around the city with rich and influential people.

I began to really enjoy the investment aspect of the business and wanted to expand the options for my clients. I also needed to increase my commissions. The perfect opportunity presented itself when a California company opened an office in Atlanta, looking for people to train as financial planners. I loved them, and they loved me. So I began my training. I worked and studied from 5:00 a.m. until 11:00 p.m. until I earned licenses required for the job. I completed Xerox Sales Training. I received licenses in the Series 7 and Series 63 for the Securities and Exchange Commission and National Association for Securities Dealers. I also received my Georgia insurance license. Unfortunately, the day after I received all the necessary licenses, the company announced that they were closing their Atlanta office.

During my studies for the Securities 7 licensing test, I met Bill Mize, who was working with the Hugh Bowman Company. He was such an unassuming and quiet man, one I would never have guessed to be as financially successful as I later found him to be. He convinced me to come to work with him. The company was affiliated with Financial Services Corporation and located in downtown Atlanta in the Hilton high-rise. The company provided no leads and very little guidance and assistance. I was on my own but too green to be a success in this environment. I did continue though to study various investments and attended all the presentations around the country on various products.

One night I left one of these presentations about 10:30 p.m. I walked alone to my car, which was parked in a poorly lit, small-unattended downtown parking lot. When I arrived at my car, I found a broken back left window. A large bag of groceries of coffee and canned goods was missing from the back seat. Books were still all over the seat, but I was very alarmed at what else might be missing. I also had in my car over a million dollars of gemstones that I had shown to a prospective buyer that afternoon. In my trunk were hundreds of dollars worth of clothing I was returning to an exclusive salon. The clothes were on loan from the night before for the Atlanta Ski Club fashion show. I was one of the models. What a night to be robbed! My car was loaded, and I didn't know if some villain was still lurking in the darkness. I was petrified as I opened the glove compartment first to search for the gemstones. They were all still there! I couldn't believe my luck. I opened the trunk and there were the clothes. Thank God! The thief never knew what he overlooked.

One evening after returning home from working and studying all day, I received a message that my best friend, Marie, died in a tragic accident. I learned that she had been driving on I-285 during the afternoon business hours traveling only 25 m.p.h. to deliver a diamond to someone on the northeast side of town. A truck preceding her lost an unsecured ladder. Marie tried to avoid the ladder and threw her wheel hard to the left toward the median. She lost control of her car when she overcorrected. Marie's windows were open and her seatbelt was not fastened. The car flipped over and she was thrown out. The car rolled over on her and killed her instantly. I couldn't believe that her life was over and that my dear friend was gone. She was too young and had so much to offer the world. Her mother requested me to be a pallbearer at her closed casket funeral. Next to her casket was Marie's picture of her in a fur coat, dolled up, spunky and with a twinkle in her eyes, now snuffed out by death. The loss I felt was so great. I would never be able to talk to my friend again. I could never tell her what a wonderful and talented and spunky woman she was, and I could never tell her how much I admired her.

Just a couple of months prior to this I lost another very close friend, Sandy Jones. Sandy was in her mid-forties. She suffered a very slow and painful death from a battle with cancer. Five years prior she had bled from one of her nipples, a warning sign of cancer. An Emory University physician treated her for several months with antibiotics, dismissing cancer as a concern. When Sandy finally went to another doctor, the cancer had already spread to her lymph nodes and to her liver. She sued the doctor and won a million-dollar lawsuit prior to her death, which gave her some relief that her four children, the youngest of whom was seven, would be taken care of financially. Sandy never gave up hope for a miracle, and she would be healed. She tried everything possible. The cancer spread to her brain and to her bones. The pain became so great that even in a state of unconsciousness, when Sandy was turned in bed, her eyes bulged from their sockets as she screamed in pain. I no longer could bear to visit Sandy and see her like this. It was just a few days after my last visit that she died.

Around the time of my grief, I joined Toastmasters to become a better presenter and sales person. I found that I loved speaking to groups. One year later, the group appointed me to represent them as a member of the Georgia Speaker's Bureau. Optimist Clubs and Kiwanis Clubs invited me to speak to their groups about any subject I chose.

I became overwhelmed in my new career with all the information from the many different companies and types of investments presented through Financial Services Corporation. I realized that without a superior who could help me discern these companies and products and guide me, I was not going to make it in the business. Around the same time, Bill informed me that he had started a new company venture in the health care industry and needed someone with a medical background to help him sell the service and product. He knew I had worked with a surgeon for five years prior to going into sales. He thought I could have the best of both worlds, calling on doctors providing both medical and financial investment sales. What an opportunity! I immediately jumped on board. This would help me hold on to what I had worked so hard to achieve. I could work in both the investment and the medical fields, which I loved, and also earn more.

I began to learn about holter monitoring, electrocardiograms, monitoring and defibrillation and began working with cardiologists and their patients. I loved it. After several months one of the three partners became angry and took an axe to the office one night and hit everything in sight. The partnership and the business dissolved. However, it also left a new product line open for another manufacturing representative, an innovative product made by R2 for heart monitoring and defibrillation. The more I studied the product and its life saving benefits the more passionate I became about selling it. I continued to sell the devices for one month, even though Bill and his partners were no longer distributors. At the end of the month I called R2 and told them that I was interested in taking the line over as their manufacturing rep for Georgia. I was told, "No way!" Because I did not have experience as a manufacturer's rep they did not want to give the line to me. I told them that I was the one who had been selling it in Georgia anyway. I told them how much business I had produced that month, and that if they wanted the business they would have to give me the line. R2's national sales manager came to Atlanta and spent a week with me. I worked him from 6:00 a.m. until midnight every day calling on doctors and hospitals around the city. After one week, he was exhausted, and R2 accepted me as their manufacturer's rep for Georgia. We celebrated at one of the finest restaurants in Atlanta and toasted our success with Dom Perrignon.

I began paramedic training so that I could learn emergency procedures, especially cardiac care. I learned how to read electrocardiograms, and I received Advanced Cardiac Tech Certification. I rode in ambulances assisting and teaching emergency personnel how to use the R2 product. I worked with leading cardiologists, emergency room physicians, nurses and operating room staff and observed open-heart surgery. Later that year, the Chairman of the Board of R2 came to Atlanta and invited me to be their Southeastern Regional Sales Manager covering seven states. I accepted and successfully set up and trained distributors throughout the region.

I began establishing scientific studies in major hospitals. I was so impassioned for the product. I believed that R2 defibrillator pads saved lives when nothing else would. The studies demonstrated that there was much less heart damage from the use of R2 pads than from conventional paddles, since a lower current was required to change the heart rhythm.

I had worked and studied very hard to be successful with R2, and my future with them looked promising. Eventually, however, the company took on new management, went direct, and all the regional sales managers were laid off. There I was without a job, and the newspapers didn't hold much promise of my finding anything significant any time soon. I looked for medical sales, then for any kind of sales positions. I had been inactive with financial planning for quite some time and had let my securities licenses expire. I didn't know what to do.

Northwest Orient Airlines was hiring for flight attendants, and on a fluke I decided to interview for the job. I began to think it might be nice to take a break and just travel the world. So that is what I did. I became a flight attendant based in Minneapolis. This was the first time I had lived outside of the metropolitan Atlanta area. It was a great and welcomed adventure. I stayed on call for whatever flight they needed me to take, usually on very short notice. I traveled to Japan, England, Germany, Scotland, Ireland, Alaska, Hawaii, Canada, and across the United States.

I had been a flight attendant for only a few months, but desired to do more and grow with the company. An opportunity arose to become an in-flight supervisor. I interviewed for the position and was accepted. There were flight attendants who at first were disgruntled that someone who had been a flight attendant for such a short time was being assigned to critique their skills and to offer and teach better service. Most of these people learned quickly that I was not a threat to them, but was helpful and knew my stuff.

About four months later, Northwest Orient merged with Republic Airlines and became Northwest Airlines. The company grew significantly taking on new ground bases. The Detroit Republic flight attendant base would immediately expand to include Northwest flight attendants as well and needed ground management personnel. I sought a position as a Base Administrative Supervisor and was accepted. I immediately transferred to Detroit.

The company suffered from the merger and the Detroit base manager had her hands full. Several months later, she was terminated. I interviewed for the open position, which was several position levels up from where I was. I was told that they were giving me a courtesy interview, but that I really didn't have a chance. I traveled to Minneapolis and interviewed with the Executive Director and the Executive Vice President. A few days later I was told that I knocked them off their feet, and they had selected me as their new base manager.

I went to work immediately to improve the base, to make it more productive and to increase the suffering morale of the employees. Only those who have been through mergers of such a magnitude can begin to understand the stress and distress a company experiences trying to bring two cultures together and working with several different unions. There was a great display of hatred by many of the Republic employees toward Northwest as their name became a thing of the past, and their way of doing things changed. It was common to find a pilot's hat or a coat cut up and other such behaviors. I was understaffed, with a freeze on hiring, was not computerized and had a base of twenty-four hundred flight attendants. The stress on the management, particularly in Detroit, was horrendous.

Early one August evening in 1987, I was standing outside near the airport with Kay Dacko who worked with me as a base administrator. Within half a mile from where we were standing, one of Northwest Airlines planes had just taken off and couldn't reach its proper altitude. At 45 feet above the ground and traveling 222 miles per hour, the plane hit two light poles, then crashed into a concrete embankment on a two-lane road and into I-98 Freeway. We heard a loud explosion, and it burst into flames before our eyes.

"Oh my God," is all we said as we jumped into my car and quickly drove back to the airport just a minute away. It was confirmed by the control tower that it was a Northwest plane, Flight 255, headed for Phoenix carrying 155 passengers, flight attendants and pilots. It was later confirmed that all were killed with the exception of a four-year-old little girl whose mother had wrapped herself around her child to protect her. The child suffered broken bones and second and third degree burns on her arms and legs. Her mother saved her life when all else perished. I immediately called the Minneapolis home office to tell them about the disaster.

The next morning I was on an early morning flight to Phoenix. I was to accompany grieving and distraught families of passengers and flight attendants to Detroit to identify their loved ones. A temporary morgue had been set up in a warehouse close to the crash site. Identification was frequently made from a piece of jewelry or clothing worn by the victim. When a plane crashes with such great force, bodies become unrecognizable. Sometimes the only way to confirm that a person was actually on that flight is by a finger with an identified ring. As these families went into the makeshift morgue, they went up and down several aisles of jewelry, luggage, purses and other belongings. As the items were claimed, they were tagged, and identified to confirm the death of a passenger who was thought to be on board.

One of the people I brought back to Detroit was the husband of a pregnant flight attendant. She was found with her unborn baby separated from her and lying under her body. Her husband requested that he be allowed to walk the crash site, which was totally against Federal Aviation Administration rules. As expected he was extremely emotional. With his insistence, the FAA made an exception and allowed me to escort him onto the crash site. The plane had disintegrated and the debris spanned a large area. It was shocking to see glass bottles of liquor and other items still totally intact among so much brokenness. Remnants of human tissue and body parts were strewn all over the ground and covered with flies. The bodies had already been removed. As we walked through the rummage, this young man saw a flight attendant jacket. He reached down and picked it up. He looked at the nametag on the jacket and burst into tears as he read his wife's name.

Things began to get more difficult at Northwest. I often had to stay in the airport Marriott to be quickly available.

I witnessed another plane crash outside my office window. A small plane holding about 18 passengers hit the end of a concourse on landing, flipped over, and burst into flames. I ran out onto the runway to help emergency personnel. I talked to one of the passengers who had been on board the plane. She was sitting on the back of an ambulance being treated for burns. She told me the passenger sitting next to her could not unfasten his seatbelt, and she, too, failed to free him. He did not get out of the plane.

We experienced a flight attendant strike. Employees were not paid on time because of computer glitches in merging two systems together. Anger continued to build with the employees as we tried to resolve problems from the merger. We could not stay on top of the crises. A Teamsters Union representative came regularly to my office issuing loud hostile threats in what appeared to be staged productions for the flight attendants.

Our working conditions worsened. Our offices were under the concourse and in the mornings we found black smut on our desks. We reported seeing mice run across our office floors, and then we suffered the disgusting smell of dead mice in the walls for weeks.

I became exhausted and feverish day after day. One day, I awoke four hours later than I normally did, and found I could not get out of bed. After a couple of days of rest, I returned to work and several months later I chose to no longer tolerate the stress.

My secretary, Jan Buccirrosso, and her family had become my dear friends. Her husband, Vince, was President of the Washtenaw County United Way in Ann Arbor and had asked me several times to come and work with him. I wrote several letters to the upper management of Northwest and met with the President of the company. The abuse by management during this time was very great, and I wanted him to know it was intolerable. I requested a year leave of absence and received it. I went to work with United Way on a one-year non-contractual basis responsible for three divisions, Marketing, Government Relations, and Endowments.

I kept a low-grade fever for many months, but health finally returned during the year I worked with United Way. Years later during my pregnancy with Amanda, I learned that at some point in my life I had contracted Epstein Bar Virus, a cousin to mononucleosis, and that was most likely what I had suffered during the months of illness while working with Northwest Airlines. During my pregnancy, I had a relapse of the virus, and then later it became dormant again. Once the virus gets into one's system, it usually remains in a dormant state but can become active again.

My experience with United Way was filled with more education and was very rewarding. I became very involved with the community at large and made some lifelong friends. I wrote the first marketing plan that Washtenaw United Way ever had and established a volunteer group composed of the most respected marketing executives in the area. The University of Michigan invited me to be a guest lecturer for their MBA students. I also chartered and recruited members for the first Kiwanis Club in Manchester, Michigan.

I purchased a 1910 home in Manchester Village and restored much of the beautiful oak cabinetry and acorn trim to its original

21

wood. The kitchen stove was very old and full of grease in every little crevice. One day I began scraping and cleaning and taking it apart to make it presentable. Then all of a sudden smoke began to pour out of the stove and flames appeared. My heart and mind raced. There was no cord that I could pull. It was wired in. I dialed 911 and ran outside. I was fearful my home was going to burn to the ground. Twelve volunteer firemen on their red fire truck responded very quickly. They went to the basement, pulled the power fuse and took the stove to the street for me. They just laughed and winked at me.

Manchester Village is very small, and everyone knows each other and looks out for each other. I never worried about locking my door, and neighbors sometimes just walked in. That's just what they did, and that was fine with me. My next door neighbors, Jane and James Reibel, had become good friends, and I became God-mother to their youngest daughter, Becky. They knew all the people in town, and heard all the gossip. They still share with me years later that the firemen who came to my home still laugh and talk about the woman that lived in the house at 310 E. Duncan whose stove caught on fire.

Don Parker, a distributor I had set up in Georgia to sell R2, called me and told me he was opening a human tissue bank. He wanted me to come back to Georgia and lead his new company. My year was about to expire with United Way, and I was offered a permanent position. My year leave of absence with Northwest Airlines was also coming to an end, and management was asking me when I was coming back. I made the decision to resign from Northwest, finish my responsibilities with United Way, and take the opportunity back in Georgia.

Don and I were excited about the possibilities the company had. I began setting up operations and developing marketing materials for this brand new company, and I assisted Don in establishing the by-laws, filing of the 501(c)3 tax-exempt status and other organizational development. I educated hospital professionals and support staff about the importance of tissue donation to enhance the quality of life for many. I spoke on a radio talk show to educate the public about tissue donation. We hired a team of people to retrieve tissue and a surgeon skilled in this area. We worked very closely with Cryolife, a company who preserves human tissues. We studied at Emory University. Using cadavers donated to science, we learned the surgical procedures used to harvest heart valves, saphenous veins, bone and other tissues. We then began our endeavors as a company. However, within a year the company began to fold from inadequate funding, and I began my search for another job.

This time I put an ad in the paper advertising myself. I got a call from a start-up company, DSI, who needed an operations manager to help get them established in prestigious Buckhead offices. I enjoyed helping them get their business started, purchasing equipment, working with vendors, and hiring personnel. It was while I was working with them that I met Andy, fell in love and got married.

CHAPTER FIVE

All of my life, more than anything, I wanted to have children, a dozen of them. As I grew older, I found I had spent most of my time in business and in travel. I began to worry that I would never marry and would miss out on having children. My biological clock was about to expire and any opportunity to bear children would be gone.

At 38 years of age I didn't know where to go to meet single men, so I joined Great Expectations Dating Service. I was generally disappointed in the men I met through the service. There were control freaks, men who needed the coddling of a mother and intensive psychotherapy, and some who were nice but with interests and goals different from mine. I determined I just wasn't going to get married. I felt very sad, but I was tired of going out with these kinds of men. I was looking for a self-assured guy with a zest for life who was kind, sensitive, and wanted children. I wanted a relationship where we could enjoy and raise each other to higher levels of being through support and encouragement.

Just when I was going to remove my name from the Great Expectations profile book, I met Andy. He told me almost immediately that I was the woman he was going to marry. He treated me like a queen and pampered my mother. He liked everything I liked, and his goals were the same as mine. He joined me in my activities and went to church with me every Sunday morning. We attended the symphony, played volleyball and games with my friends, danced to classical music, and spent a lot of romantic time alone.

I was 38 years old, and we both desperately wanted children, so we were married after only seven months. We wasted no time in having babies - Amanda was born 13 months later.

I quickly learned that I had married into a very peculiar family, and quite honestly I didn't know what to make of them.

Andy's mother and father eloped when they were teenagers, were first cousins, a Titelman marrying a Titelman, and had a long marriage till the death of Mr. Titelman who was in his 70's. They raised their three sons and one daughter in the mountains of Altoona, Pennsylvania.

Mr. Titelman worked for his father in a textile business manufacturing men and women's clothing, brand names like White Stag and Van Heussen. At some point after the death of Andy's grandfather, and after Andy had gone off to college, the business was sold. The Titelmans moved to Atlanta and opened a very successful franchised AAMCO Transmission shop in Marietta. Eventually, Andy left his job with Sears as a shoe salesman and manager, and moved with his wife, Sydney, from California to Atlanta to work with his father in the transmission business. Andy told me the Titelmans had art that was being circulated and displayed in museums around the world. Andy used to brag about a picture that hung on our walls, which he said belonged to Katie, an inheritance from her grandmother. It was an Andy Warhol picture of butterflies and at that time was valued around forty to sixty thousand dollars.

I never could determine exactly how Andy's brothers and sister made a living. Anne is a jet setter who travels the world and lives in Park Place on Peachtree Road in Atlanta among millionaires like Elton John.

Andy and I learned early during my pregnancy that our baby was a girl, and we chose the name Amanda for her. When I shared this with Mrs. Titelman, she commented that it was Anne's favorite name. She said Anne wanted to name her baby Amanda if she ever had children. Anne was not married and was not sure she wanted children, but I was told that Anne might have a problem with it. During the next family gathering I was sitting in a room with both of my sisters-in-law, Anne and Donna. I told them that Andy and I loved the name Amanda and would like to name our baby this. I turned to Anne and asked her if she had any problem with our using the name. Anne told me, "No," that if she got married, she would have a different last name anyway. So Andy and I chose to name our baby Amanda.

Joy is the only way I know to describe the way I felt when I found out I was pregnant. There was life in me, the life of a baby forming and growing, and that life was my child. I could see her perfect form on the sonograms, her arms and legs, hands and feet, nose and eyes and mouth. I could see her heart beat. She sucked her thumb and did somersaults in my womb. I began to nurture her from the moment I was aware of her presence. I talked to her and sang to her and rocked her, and I called my baby by her name. She was Amanda.

Unknown to me, there was a stirring of dissent in the family because of the name Andy and I chose. Andy told me many months later that the family was angry with me. They said I had no right to name my child Amanda, that the name was reserved for Anne's future child. I asked, "If there was a problem, why didn't Anne tell me when I asked?" It would have been easy to find another name at that time, but for months I had been calling my child by her name, and Amanda is who she was. I was told I should have read between the lines and known that it was not okay, and that Anne could not answer me honestly because I had asked her in front of Donna.

Andy told me I needed to find another name for our daughter. I thought the whole thing was ridiculous, and I was not about to be bullied by these controlling people. They had an opportunity to voice their thoughts, and they did. I considered what they said to be the truth, and I made a decision based on that. It caused a lot of friction between the family and me and Andy and me because I was not doing what Anne wanted me to do now.

All the while, Mrs. Titelman was telling me she wanted me to name the baby "Anne" after her daughter. Anne is now 45 years old. She was married two years ago, and has never had children.

I don't know what Andy's brother, Jack, did with his time. He just seemed to mill around here and there. He became very involved in the Sterling Club of Relationships, organized and run by Justin Sterling who advocates for the oppression of women. Jack and his brother David became disciples of Sterling, recruiting Andy, and others. The club maintains secrecy for what they learn and do.

Our friend, Lisa Curtis, and I began to research what my husband had gotten involved in and what the secrecy was all about. I found a lot of information that made me sick. I learned while at these "workshops" that the men "strip naked and chant and dance, as a sort of male bonding." They are videotaped. Waivers are signed that everything that goes on at the workshop will remain secret and that the videos may be used at their discretion. It was also reported that for five minutes they would walk around the room and repeat, "fuck you, you fucking bitch." Other chants were incorporated in the weekend like, "I'm a fucking jerk." Sleep deprivation, chanting, lack of regular meal breaks and intimidation were a normal part of the weekend.[9]

Sterling teaches that women are sex objects and are to be used by men for their pleasure, discarded at any time. He describes that a good short term recreational relationship is "If she gives good head," "If she swallows," "If she takes it up the ass." Sterling says, "Pussy costs money," and "You should never get involved in a long term committed relationship until you are totally self-sufficient which means you can go without pussy. You should never get involved in a long term committed relationship until you have succeeded in short term recreational relationships."[10]

I also discovered that Justin Sterling, alias Michael Santangelo, whose birth name is Arthur Kasarjian, is a pornography producer who loves to star in his own porno films. Those in the pornography business consider him to be the "Baron of Balls" and a "porn visionary," who leans toward the "artsy hardcore nasty sex."[11]

In 1994 Justin Sterling was investigated by the Oakland police and Children's Protective Services when his seven-year-old daughter told that her father had sexually abused her. The Alameda County district attorney did not press charges.

Andy refused to tell me what he was doing or where he was going while involved with the Sterling Club. He would stay out until 1:00 a.m. a couple of times a week and tell me it was a secret. Andy began to lock a bedroom door while he watched videos and then began to state to me that I needed to watch XXX movies.

Later during court proceedings, I shared this information with attorney Diane Woods, the guardian *ad litem* appointed by the court supposedly to represent the best interests of Amanda and Jessica. She said she was very familiar with Justin Sterling and his club, and she saw nothing wrong with it.

Jack introduced a friend of his, an artist, to Andy. Andy purchased one of his pictures, an eight-foot pornographic production. An artist friend of mine who examined it named it aptly, "orgasm." It is three dimensional with white and cream splashes against black, skeletons all over it, and at least three real-life pictures showing a sexual orgy and oral sex. I learned that the people in the picture are friends of Jack and Donna, Jack's wife. Andy and I fought for five years about this picture hanging on the wall above our bed. A realtor who sold our first home questioned our moral character after seeing the picture on the wall. It was greatly degrading. Andy insisted that the picture was not pornographic and saw nothing wrong with it hanging in our home in full view of our children.

Andy's brother David lived in the Maharishi Center in Ohio and spent much of his day in meditation. He prided himself in "levitation." I rarely saw him and was glad of it, as I found him to be extremely overbearing and abusive. He was very active with his brother, Jack, in the Sterling Club of Relationships. My understanding is that he was born with or developed epilepsy at a young age, and Mr. & Mrs. Titelman gave him about $35,000 a year to live on, although, I never saw him as disabled. He seemed to function as well as anyone else, and seizures were controlled by medication. During the last year of my marriage to Andy, David purchased a cigar shop in Ohio and began to manage it.

The Titelmans seemed to be a close family getting together frequently, making each occasion festive, many times catered with foods from the finest restaurants in town. I was never able to get close to anyone in Andy's family. I have never known anyone so long who failed to ask me any personal questions except the Titelmans. Mrs. Titelman, as I explain a bit later, was different. The Titelmans had no interest in my past, my present, my beliefs, my thoughts, or my future. I recall only a few instances of receiving a compliment from one of them. Once when unaware my leg and hip were totally exposed while sitting on the floor, and Jack and Donna commented that they liked it. I had a terrible feeling there was something very wrong and deviant in the manner in which they commented.

I also sensed there was unkind mumbling about me going on behind my back. I always felt like a foreign object that they wanted to expel along with anything that had anything to do with me, including Amanda and Jessica. Sydney had expressed a similar concern with the Titelmans, saying they saw her as a brown shoe and themselves as black patent leather shoes.

Mrs. Titelman on the other hand was friendly and wanted to know what was going on. She talked at great length about her concerns about Andy's unhealthy relationship with Katie and the family's hatred for Sydney. She shared with me that they wished they had hired a hit man instead of paying out $150,000 in divorce fees. She was proud that she knew how to get information out of Katie about her mother, Sydney, "by playing dumb and friendly" with Katie. Consequently, her friendliness toward me was suspect as my marriage to Andy disintegrated.

Mr. Titelman became ill with Alzheimer's disease, which I noticed early in our marriage. He quickly deteriorated, rendering conversation very difficult as he was very confused, and then thoughts and words were not recognizable. Eventually, he was put in a nursing home where he remained until his death over a year ago.

During our first few years of marriage Andy talked a great deal about his father's verbal abuse of him. There was a deep hurt and anger toward his dad, and he cried when he told me how his dad wished he were like the boy down the street. He said his dad always called him stupid and told him he could never do anything right.

The entire family seemed to be angry with Mr. Titelman. Mrs. Titelman said if anyone had reason to divorce someone, she did. I was able to observe Mr. Titelman's temper from time to time, especially during gift-giving occasions, of which he wanted no part.

The Titelmans' home was filled with expensive art and furnishings. During the times we visited, it was difficult to have two small children there for several hours and expect them to touch nothing and to sit still. When they became active or touched any of the many expensive articles, they received a verbal tirade from both Mr. and Mrs. Titelman.

CHAPTER SIX

Even though the Titelmans had a Jewish heritage, no one practiced any religion. I gave them the first Passover dinner they had ever experienced. I researched Passover, talked to Jewish friends, and purchased special dishes, books, and music. I prepared an outstanding meal totally in the tradition of Passover. I cooked a large leg of lamb using fresh herbs. It was so delicious that everyone was picking at the bone and the platter when it was gone. I have tried to cook lamb like this since, but I have never tasted any better lamb than we savored that night. It was a wonderful experience for all.

A picture of Jesus sat on a table in Mrs. Titelman's den, "For good luck," she said. I always had a secret hope that she would begin to understand who Jesus really was, and that she would begin to love Him.

Andy attended my church with me from the time he met me until the latter part of our marriage, each year demanding that we go less and less. Initially we attended Sunday School and worship service every Sunday morning. During the course of a year prior to filing for divorce, we attended church together about a dozen times. Andy called this obsessive and bitterly complained. He did not want me to go to church unless he went with me, but he refused to go when asked. After Andy filed for divorce I told him the children and I would be attending church regularly each Sunday morning, and I welcomed him to go with us if he liked. He called me defiant. The family seemed to have a tolerance for all religions but any commitment to the beliefs of any religion was not tolerable, as I later learned.

I am a member of Mt. Paran Church of God in Atlanta, which has a membership of over 12,000 people. It is an unusual church in that it is somewhat of a melting pot of Methodists, Presbyterians, Catholics and other Christian denominations and unlike most "Church of God" churches. It is a happy church filled with joyful praise and worship. The singing is robust, spiritual, and sensitizing to the soul. Many raise their hands to praise the Lord, and they gently sway side to side in rhythm with the music. It is not uncommon to hear a prayer spoken in tongues and then translated by someone else. The teaching is excellent and when the service is over, you wish there were more. These practices seem curious and strange, though, to those who have never experienced them and to unbelievers. This is the church Andy attended with me before we were ever married, and it is the church he said he enjoyed.

Football games are filled with people full of expression, clapping, cheering, chanting, and cooperatively doing "the wave." Sometimes people become so excited, they jump out of their seats, screaming out in their excitement. Sometimes they beat their chairs with objects and stomp their feet to make noise. God made us to be expressive. Yet, there are many who find worshiping God with expression of movement and praise to be repugnant. They go so far as to say it is a sign of mental illness or weakness. These people, obviously, are spiritually dead. You cannot know God without wanting to respond to Him.

I am very conservative. I do not speak out in church, and I do not pound on bleachers. But I find those who criticize others for expressing love of God to be very shallow and empty.

Andy attended a Methodist boarding school in Mercersburg, Pennsylvania, during his high school years. He told me that Bible class was his favorite class, even though he said he doesn't believe in the Bible. I guess it was historical fiction to him and sport to study. He was the only one of his siblings to go to boarding school, and I've never known why.

Andy knew my commitment to Christ before we ever became seriously involved. His not being a Christian was the factor that concerned me the most in considering marriage, but he told me that my spirituality is what he loved most about me. He convinced me from the very beginning that he loved attending church and worshiping with me. He sang all the songs and prayed the prayers and even partook of Holy Communion. Even though I knew he had not accepted Christ as his savior, I wondered if he was considering it. Prior to our marriage we agreed that any children we had would be raised Christian. Andy willingly married me in my Christian church and readily accompanied me to Christian premarital counseling. The children were christened in the church when they were babies, and Andy took an oath that he would teach them in the ways of Christ.

31

Amanda and Jessica went to a Methodist preschool program and learned a prayer they sang at snack time. Each evening as we began our dinner the girls delighted in taking turns singing this short blessing. Andy was respectful until Katie began to voice criticism of having any prayer. During the blessing Katie began to make disgruntled sounds and then stared coldly. Then Andy began to get up and pinch the girls and throw small pieces of food at them. Giggling and rambunctiousness would follow.

When Amanda was three years old and Jessica was one, I learned that Mt. Paran was offering an intensive Bible study every Monday night. I had never participated in a study like this before, studying the Bible from cover to cover. I was very interested in it. I sought Andy's permission to attend with the understanding that it meant seven to eight hours of homework per week. My attendance on Monday evening meant he would have to care for the babies during that time. He agreed. However, the first night of class, I came home, and Andy expressed his anger. He wanted to know if I sat next to a man. He stated it was wrong that he should have to "babysit" Amanda and Jessica. He said Jessica had taken her diaper off and urinated in the crib, and that it was he who had to change the sheets. I dug my heels in and told him that I would continue in this class that there was no reason he could not contribute to the care of Amanda and Jessica. I had paid the costs and had committed myself to the class after receiving his permission to do so. I was not going to quit now.

I usually studied while Andy was at work for less than an hour a day. It never ceased to amaze me that every time I sat down to study, the children would awake, and my study time would be cut very short. There were times Andy charmingly asked me about my classes and I cheerfully shared what I was studying. A couple of times he asked me if he could help me memorize concept cards. Afterwards, Andy attacked me saying I devoted too much time to study, that all of it was obsessive, that he had to clean the house in my absence, babysit the kids, eat out, and rearrange schedules to accommodate me. Yet, the only inconvenience to Andy was that I was not present on Monday night to clean the dinner dishes or to care for our children during this time.

Andy "revealed" at Dr. William Van Horn's Wednesday night group of about 50 others that he had received Christ during an Easter presentation at the church in 1997 called *The Choice*. He did not want his family to know, however. But there was no change in him evidencing such an epiphany. All the while, he had an unspoken antagonism toward me, and I felt it piercingly. It was much later that Andy admitted he only pretended to receive Christ to "fit in" with the Van Horn group we were attending to try to improve our marriage. He asserted that I was trying to make him something that he wasn't. He insulted my raising my arms in church. He said I and my friends were "on tilt."

In the last couple of years of our marriage Andy called me and the children names, proclaiming that I was "out to lunch" for believing in the Bible. He and his mother began to call the children stupid for singing Christian songs and participating in Christian training. Attending church, praying, singing Christian music, reading the Bible, or speaking the name of Jesus or God, unless used in profanity, was unacceptable to Andy.

CHAPTER SEVEN

There were red flags even before we were married. Andy always explained them away, and that was good enough for me at the time, because he seemed genuine, gentle, and kind. Sometimes I thought he was naive. Many times I thought he had his head in the clouds and was just really clueless, but I always had an unsettled and troubling feeling in my gut about the behaviors I was witnessing. I think some of us, when we get uncomfortable with something and we know something's wrong, are afraid to find out what it is. We would have to make consequential decisions once we do know the full truth. Therefore, we choose to ignore it. That's what I did.

There were enough disturbances that I mentioned a couple of them to Dr. Paul Walker, our minister, during our premarital counseling. I told him about an oriental rug that Andy and I had bought together and an occasion when we were eating on it with Katie. I had asked Katie to stop wiggling a TV tray table with her foot. Instead Katie stared me cold and defiantly tipped the table over, spilling her chocolate milk onto the carpet. I patiently cleaned it up and asked Andy if we could make a rule that we no longer ate on this carpet. He agreed, but I later found out that the rule only applied if I were present. He told Katie that she could do whatever she wanted when I was not around. Dr. Walker told me at that time that I needed to call this wedding off. Andy profusely apologized for making me out to be a monster with Katie and for other behaviors he had with her. He said that he would change, so we went forward with our wedding plans. To say that it was the biggest mistake I have ever made in my life is an understatement.

Shortly after Andy and I were married, he began to make excuses for our not getting together with my friends or my family, pushing them further and further away from us. I had been playing sand volleyball every week with a great group of people and getting together with a group of adults to play Pictionary, Boggle, and Charades. This all ended very soon after our wedding. Also, slowly, I began to realize that all the things I enjoyed in life were really not his cup of tea. My leaving the house became taboo and friends were not welcome in our home. It seemed that nothing was acceptable outside of Andy's own family. Likewise, Katie rarely had playmates and refused to get to know any of the children in the neighborhood. Her father was her only playmate and any attempts I made to change that brought hostile reactions from both of them.

Katie was just a month shy of being 10 years old when Andy and I married. I read several books on stepfamilies and step parenting and knew that it was not going to be easy. I was trying to follow all the suggestions, to love Katie and to be a good friend. But it seemed that Andy undermined me in everything I did and purposefully tried to divide Katie and me.

I began to pick Katie up from school in the afternoon on my way home from work. The first few times I was greeted with her screaming at me, "Where is my father?" When we walked through the door of our home each day, Katie threw her coat on the floor in front of the door. I asked Andy if we could begin to give Katie an allowance and to give her responsibilities, like hanging up her coat when she came home. Andy agreed until he talked with Katie. Then he insisted that it was my responsibility to pick up the coat - not Katie's.

I know children need boundaries and responsibilities to grow up emotionally healthy, and Katie had none. Andy refused to instill any form of discipline, expectations, or boundaries on Katie, and we all suffered greatly as a result. He said that it was unloving to discipline a child.

Imagine what it is like to live in a home where you are glared at with cold stares all the time, where whatever you say is said to be stupid, to exhibit joy or laughter is huffed at, to have a friend over is treated with disdain, to be made to feel that if you express yourself in any way you are interfering or disturbing or not maintaining the household - expressions such as singing, playing the piano, listening to music, reading books, talking on the phone, or using the computer! I lived with this almost my entire marriage to Andy.

My existence in that home so greatly disturbed Katie and resulted in tremendous conflict and strife. No matter what I did, Katie found it to be bothersome. Andy would panic with her each frequent mood shift or complaint. Then he would begin a tirade of accusations toward me and call me names. Andy catered to every whim and demand that Katie made. "Dad will do whatever I ask him to do," she said to me once. She was right.

I found that when Katie was absent from our home to visit her mother, Andy was loving and there was peace. He participated in activities with me and Amanda and Jessica during these times. But as soon as Katie came home, the craziness and rejection would begin, and the accusations would fly.

I was deeply alone - married to a man who only wanted me to cook, clean, take his daughter back and forth to school, watch her when he wasn't there and free the two of them from responsibility in the home. They just wanted to play, watch TV together, go for walks, and play with the dogs. Andy didn't do anything with me unless Katie was gone.

I married Andy for companionship, love, and children. I wanted someone with whom I could share my deepest secrets and my greatest dreams, someone I could lean on when I needed help and someone who could lean on me when he needed help. I believe Andy wanted to love me, but there was a war going on in him that kept him actively sabotaging any closeness we may have had.

I expressed a desire for him to call me loving names such as honey, darling, baby, and sweetheart. But Andy refused and replied to me, "It is not appropriate." He also said he could not tell Katie that he loved me because it hurt her and just caused conflict!

When Andy called home in the afternoon, he only talked to Katie. He would ask if she needed anything from the store and would let her know when he was going to be home late from work. He rarely considered talking to me because he said, "Katie didn't like it." Many times dinner was ready, but no one had told me that Andy would not be home at the usual time.

I witnessed Andy dressing Katie for bed when she was almost 10 years old, even putting her panties on her. After I told him she needed her privacy and that it was totally inappropriate, he continued to dress her night after night. I became angry with him and told him I was concerned about what was in his mind. This is one of the things I brought to the attention of Dr. Paul Walker at our premarital counseling. After that I never saw him dress her again. From that time on Andy angrily said that I called him a child molester.

After Andy stopped dressing Katie at night, Katie, at ten years old, began to come downstairs after her bath with a towel wrapped around her. She would stop in the middle of the staircase. In our full view, she would then drop her towel from her body, and with it draped over her arms, she would stand there like a naked model. This occurred several nights in a row, and each time I told her to go get her clothes on. She stopped only when I insisted that she was to never do this again. Andy just looked and never said a word.

One afternoon Katie and Andy each showered and agreed to meet in the kitchen for a doughnut before getting dressed. They each had a towel wrapped around them. Andy didn't own a robe or any pajamas. Katie did. So I purchased Andy a robe as a gift after this incident. This made him angry.

We also disagreed about Katie dressing with us almost every morning. Andy was not concerned with nudity around his daughter and said that he had a "very natural relationship" with her. He became more and more defensive with me, as I voiced my concerns regarding what I was witnessing.

One night while watching television, Andy was lying on the floor and Katie was sitting straddled over his back. I looked over and saw Katie moving her hips back and forth in what looked like masturbation. I told no one about this for years, but it alarmed me. It was after Amanda and Jessica told about their father's abuse that I was able to understand and qualify all the troubling behaviors that for years I had witnessed.

Anytime Andy engaged in conversation with me, Katie was an expert at diverting his attention away from me to her. If I had my hand on Andy, Katie would slip her hand under mine, pushing mine away. I was shut out and that was okay with Andy.

During the summer right after our marriage, Andy, Katie, and I went to an Atlanta Braves game. The temperature was around 100 degrees, a miserable day for watching a ball game outside. When we arrived at the stadium, Andy and Katie got out of the car and began walking away hand in hand. They left me carrying a cooler of drinks and a bag of food behind them. Katie sat between the two of us with her legs draped over her father's legs and her arms around his right arm. This had become the norm. The stress of our relationship had become so great in such a short period of time:

Silently, at the game, the tears flowed down my face stinging my hot and sweaty neck. Andy and Katie were in their own little world and neither of them allowed me to enter it. I was a newlywed, and all my dreams about love, romance and marriage were shattered. I sat alone crying the entire game. That week I spent a lot of time sitting on the driveway at night looking up at the stars, crying and thinking I was going to have to share with my family and my friends that my marriage was a disaster and a mistake. I felt lonely and ashamed.

Shortly thereafter I learned I was pregnant with Amanda, and I became ecstatic.

During our first year of marriage, each night Katie would awaken us at least two to three times on the intercom saying she couldn't sleep or that a dog was barking. This continued for several months, along with severe stomachaches and flatulence every day. She had stomachaches since I had met Andy, and they never seemed to subside. It was obvious that Katie was disturbed; she had physical manifestations and emotional difficulties. I thought we needed to get professional help.

Dr. Walker suggested we see Dr. Shirley Parsons whom he greatly respected, but Andy and his mother were adamant that their family friend, Dr. Frank Pittman, was the person we needed to see. So we set up an appointment with him. He asked that Katie's mom, Sydney, also meet with Katie and Andy and me. So all of us met together several times over six months.

He gave Katie the assignment of asking her parents what caused the divorce. In a meeting with Dr. Pittman and all of us except Sydney, Dr. Pittman told Katie that it was not good for her to be with her mother, and that is why her father would not allow any more contact than necessary. He told her that her stomachaches were self-seeking attention. After that Katie never complained of another stomachache. Eventually she stopped waking us in the middle of the night, but other manifestations of disturbance arose.

Sydney seemed to feel empowered in our home and began calling over and over again every day, from the time Katie got home from school until late at night. I stopped answering the phone and let Katie answer it because it was nearly always Sydney. I later learned that when I received a call from my family and friends,

Katie told them that she was on the phone and that she would give me a message. But I never got the messages.

I had expressed in a fax to Dr. Pittman prior to our ever seeing him that I was concerned with behaviors between Andy and Katie, the issues of nudity, Andy dressing her, Katie clinging to her father and his being her only playmate, etc. I was not happy with the results of Dr. Pittman's meetings. We had been seeing him for six months, had met with him about eight times, and things had progressively become worse. I thought Dr. Pittman made some weird statements during the sessions. After we talked with him about a vacation Andy, Katie and I took together and the horrendous treatment I received by the two of them, Dr. Pittman told me that the problem was that I was a jealous woman. I decided he was not the counselor that we should have. Our problems were much deeper than my being a "jealous wife." I told Andy I would not go back, and I didn't until six years later, following the divorce papers being filed. Then, I only wanted to confront Dr. Pittman with statements that he made about me to Andy.

I was seven months pregnant when I terminated my relationship with Dr. Pittman. I went to our pediatrician, Dr. Stephen King, to prepare for Amanda's birth and care. As I talked with him, I broke into tears and began to share what was happening in my home. He listened and responded that the behaviors between Andy and Katie were very harmful and wrong, and that the stress it caused me could be harmful to Amanda as well.

The need to help Katie shifted to the need to help our marriage. Very soon after that I made an appointment with Dr. Shirley Parsons, and Andy and I saw her together regularly for the next four and a half years. I always made the appointments for us. We would go in, talk, and come home with Andy profusely apologizing to me saying he was going to change. Things would be better for a short period of time, and then snap right back to the way it was before. I was shocked to learn in 2002, when I actually counted the visits, that over these years the number of times we saw Dr. Parsons was 93 visits.

Our counseling with Dr. Parsons ended when she felt she could not help us and that possibly a program called "Getting The Love That You Want" might work instead. She referred us to Dr. Louis

McCloud who ran the program. There were some good aspects to his program designed to uncover hidden sources of pain. However, he failed to deal with destructive behaviors in the now and present and it proved useless.

If Dr. Parsons, or Dr. McCloud, or I had known at the time that the children were being molested or being set up to be harmed, counseling or dealing with hidden sources of pain would not have been considered. The only remedy to something so serious as this is separation of the children from the abuser. But none of us knew this was happening.

Katie's hatred for me increased to the level that even suggesting we see a movie together was punishment to Katie. I had long past stopped trying to hug her because she pushed me away every time. She began calling me "bitch" and said she would like to "slap my face and spit on me." Her mother told Katie, "Tell her to stuff it up her ass," and "I'll come over and slam her face into the wall." This was after I told Katie that she needed to clean up her room.

Mealtime at our home was always very stressful. Katie, as always, constantly hung on Andy at the dinner table. Drinks were spilled, and I worried about why she was so insecure. The first year of our marriage, Andy and Katie treated me as though I wasn't even there, and when I attempted to contribute to the conversation, Katie would call me "stupid." There was never any correction; Andy said nothing. To survive Andy's scorn I had learned to remain silent.

After Amanda was born, Andy did divert some of his attention away from Katie. Twenty-two months later Jessica was born, and there was more activity at the table. I joyfully interacted with my children. I loved them, and they loved me. Katie, in response, ate in silence with her head hung, refused to talk, and occasionally glared at me. For years it was as though she was trying to have a stare-down with me, and she would only stop when I asked her why she was staring. Anytime I attempted conversation with Katie, I was met with anger and as few words as possible. I always tried to maintain a pleasant attitude and came to the table with a smile on my face. But it was very difficult to ever enjoy a family meal because of the strife.

Katie was a beautiful and bright girl at the age of 14, but on the chunky side. Her friends wrote in her school annual rude comments about her "big butt." She started losing weight over a period of time and trimmed down beautifully, but then she continued to lose weight rather quickly and became too thin. I began to express concern to Andy and to his mother, but no one seemed worried except me. I spoke of it frequently, even pointing out to Andy how the bone of her rear was so prominent. It was like an old woman who was ready to die. I felt certain that something was wrong. I was not trying to be rude, but I was frankly concerned for her health. She was even losing hair. Months went by before Andy finally took Katie to Dr. King, the pediatrician. He diagnosed her with anorexia and told her she would be put in the hospital if she lost another pound. At that point Katie weighed 78 pounds and was 5'5". Dr. King arranged for Katie to see a psychiatrist, a psychologist and a nutritionist for long term treatment.

Katie would sit at the table and refuse to eat, and Andy began to say I served bad food. I asked him many times what he didn't like and what he wanted me to serve. I never got an answer, just insults that the food was bad and that I didn't serve what Katie wanted. Andy had always expected the finest of foods and the best and most expensive cuts of meats. We always had fresh vegetables and fruits and salads. Now Katie refused to eat any of it, and Andy blamed me. One night we had steak, and Katie refused it saying she didn't eat meat anymore. I learned then that she liked salmon, which Andy did not like. The next night I made dinner for all of us and served salmon to Katie and another meat for the rest of the family. Katie was furious that she was the only one served salmon, and she refused to eat it.

It got to the point that Katie refused to eat anything that I bought at the grocery store. Andy began shopping himself saying Katie didn't like the orange juice I selected, or Katie didn't like the turkey, the apples, the bread, or anything else. I asked what exactly they wanted me to buy, and I would be happy to do it. I never got an answer. When Andy began shopping, Katie then refused to eat anything that I cooked. Andy asked if he could cook, and then he began to declare that I wasn't doing my job, that I was forcing him to have to shop and cook because I wouldn't buy the foods or cook the way that Katie wanted. To this day I still don't know what, if anything, would have satisfied them.

Katie never accepted Amanda and Jessica as part of her family and wanted nothing to do with them. My mother commented that she witnessed on a number of occasions that all Katie had to do was say to Andy that one of them was bothering her. Usually it was Amanda, and then Andy would go into a tirade with her and put her in her room holding the door closed. When she tried to open the door, Andy would yell at her. Then he would allow the door to slam open. Then he would hit her, leaving marks, and put her back in the room again. I was always having to defend my children against Katie's unhappiness and Andy's warped brutality. Andy would say I was interfering and reinforcing inappropriate behaviors.

On Amanda's second birthday we gave her a tricycle. We were sitting in our sunroom at the time. Amanda got on the tricycle and honked the little horn on the handlebars. Katie whined to her father, "Tell her to stop." Andy immediately yelled at Amanda to get off the bike and to be quiet.

Others outside the family noticed Katie's distance from the children as well. As a teenager, Katie's friend, Lisa, told her mother, how sad it was that Katie would have nothing to do with Amanda and Jessica. Lisa had two half-siblings whom she adored and with whom she spent a great deal of time.

Nonetheless, Amanda and Jessica loved Katie and were always happy to see her. It used to grieve me so, when in the morning Katie left for school she would walk down the hall and out the door with two little kids running behind her saying, "Bye, Katie, Bye Katie" over and over again. Katie would usually just keep on walking, never look at them, and walk right out the door without saying a word. Occasionally, she said, "toodle-loo," as she closed the door. When she came home in the afternoon she went straight to her room and stayed there with the door closed until it was dinnertime, never interacting with Amanda, Jessica, or me.

We went on two family cruises during our marriage. While on one of these cruises, we stopped on an island to do some shopping. Andy and Katie were interested in the jewelry shops, and I soon discovered why as Andy was getting his credit card out. I didn't know it, but Andy had agreed with Katie to buy her a ring. I was shocked at what Katie was picking out. She was 15 years old and had chosen a very large and expensive emerald and diamond ring. I told her that was the kind of ring a husband would buy for his wife, and she turned to me, smiled, and smugly said, "I know." I told Andy that it was out of the question. Andy did buy Katie a beautiful emerald and diamond ring, but one a little more appropriate for a 15-year-old daughter.

On another cruise we took on the Big Red Boat, Andy invited Katie to gamble with us each night on the ship. Katie won more than $100. The crew was very clear about the age restriction and the penalty violation. However, Andy chose to ignore them, because he wanted Katie to be with him, and it was fun for her.

While on the same trip, we traveled on a small boat to an island. There was a live band, and many of the people including the children sang and danced and had a great time. Amanda and Jessica and I learned to dance to *La Macaraina* on the boat. I tried to ignore Katie's hateful stares and just have a good time with my children. A woman came up to me and asked who Katie was. I told her she was my stepdaughter. She said that she had been watching us and had recognized the cold hatred coming from her stares toward me. She said she, too, had a hateful stepdaughter who caused great difficulty in her marriage. She knew the look ever too well.

At some point during our marriage, the washing and caring for Katie's clothes became Katie's responsibility at Dr. Shirley Parsons suggestion. Katie was happy about that, as she did not want me to touch her things. However, we continually had problems with clothes remaining in the washer and dryer or not being put away out of the laundry room. Andy always reminded me that Katie did not want me to touch her clothes, and if I moved anything from its position, war was declared.

One day I asked Andy to please have Katie finish her clothes. There were wet towels in the washer, clothes in the dryer and clothes on the folding table, and I could not do the family's wash. I talked to Andy about it daily, and the clothes sat there. On the sixth day, I took the mildewed towels and put them on Katie's laundry basket and took the clean clothes and put them on Katie's

43

bed. Shortly after Katie came home from school that afternoon, I received a phone call from Andy. "How could you hurt my daughter like that?" he demanded angrily. He told me I had no right to touch her things. The fury was horrendous for months and months to come because of this incidence of Katie's clothes being touched by me.

One morning I awoke and went out to the laundry room where I found some of Katie's clean clothes sitting on top of the dryer. Our cat, Maggie, had obviously been on these clothes as I could see cat hair on them. I was on the cordless phone and went back through my bedroom and into my bathroom to brush my hair as I talked on the phone. As I came out of the bathroom and back through the bedroom there at the doorway on the floor was a hunk of cat feces, and feces had been smeared down the side of the doorframe. Katie was walking down the hall away from my bedroom at the time. I said nothing to her, but it was obvious she had done this. I called Andy, who was at work, and talked to him about it. He declared war again and said, "How dare you accuse Katie." He began to blame Amanda saying she took her own "poop" and smeared it on the door. This surfaced over and over again, with Andy attacking me saying I "accused" Katie.

It seemed like Andy was always trying to pick a fight with me. He spoke to me as though he were crazy. One night as we were driving, I asked Andy to please slow down since he was going much too fast. I told him the speed limit was 45 mph, but he said that he was fine because he was going over that. The sign was clearly a "Speed Limit" sign and not a "Minimum Speed" sign. I told him that was the limit, and he said that it meant that was the slowest one could go. We constantly had conversations like this. Most of the time I tried to let it go, but sometimes he kept pushing and pushing until we would end up in a fight. He always drove so fast and so recklessly that it frightened me. On one occasion he turned so quickly out of a street that he took the back light off a car passing. He thought it was really funny.

Dr. Mark Crawford, a counselor Shirley Parsons thought would be good for Katie, suggested that Andy spend one night a week alone with Katie doing something just the two of them wanted to do. I began having a problem with it when they came home from major shopping sprees together having spent hundreds of dollars on unnecessary and excessive things. I was buying Amanda and Jessica used clothing, and buying nothing for myself because of our large debts. Then one night Andy fought with me and demanded that I take the girls and leave the house. He wanted to spend his alone time with Katie at the house. He said the children and I couldn't be there. I was furious. We fought, and I left and drove around until Amanda and Jessica were asleep in their car seats. I then drove back to the house, put them to bed and went to bed myself.

I later found out that Andy had written a letter to Dr. Crawford expressing outright lies about me such as that I had been fired from all of my jobs. Andy gave me the letter, well after the fact, probably in an attempt to hurt me. I asked, "Why would you lie about me like this?" He angrily said, "Because that is the way I feel."

Nothing was ever perfect enough. The house could be spotless, and Andy would say it was filthy. I found myself frantic in the afternoon picking up the little ones' toys off the floor before Andy walked in the door, making sure nothing was out of its place. As soon as the children pulled out something else, I was putting it up so that things could be perfect for Andy when he came in the house.

We lived on five acres, and yet he screamed at the kids for walking on the grass, saying they were damaging it. It was absolutely crazy, and we would fight about it. Finally he gave up the fight and said nothing more when the children and I walked around the yard. If I allowed them to play in the sandbox barefoot, I was told I was a bad parent. He would yell at the girls to put on their shoes and socks and not take them off again.

All attempts I made to participate in activities or friendships separate from him were met with great criticism. He said I was "acting like a single woman," and that activities outside the home took me away from my responsibilities of cleaning the house and caring for the kids. He said my friends were "out to lunch," just like me and were not welcome in our home. He said Amanda and Jessica's friends tore up our home and they were not welcome either.

Andy did not want the couple friendships either. When we were with others, he seemed to like them and have a good time, but as soon as they were gone he began criticizing them and making sarcastic remarks. His infamous frequent statement about the involvement of other people in our lives was, "Who needs them." Andy constantly criticized my family, my friends and others I knew, disapproving of every one. If I spoke with a man with any friendliness, Andy accused him of being my boyfriend. He told Amanda and Jessica on a number of occasions that the salesman at the Chrysler Dealership where I bought my car was my boyfriend.

If I wasn't at home during the day when Andy called he became disturbed wanting to know where I was. I began to call him every time I left the house to do anything, feeling like I had to have his permission. He then bought a telephone for my car so that he could call me when I was out. He said he never knew where I was.

Even though Andy always wanted to know where I was and what I was doing, he was emotionally disconnected from me. He wanted to control my every move. He focused and centered his life on Katie and on satisfying her wants and desires at the expense of all else. He devalued me as a wife, as a member of the family, as a stepmother, as a mother, and as a member of society.

My anger built to where I started reacting to Andy with screaming and yelling, and the two of us would shout it out. Andy would purposefully push my buttons, and I would react. Every night we went through the same scenarios of his accusing me of being "mean and hateful" to Katie. Every night I would ask how I was being "mean and hateful," and I was always told, "You just are."

One night I left the bedroom around midnight and went to the living room with a book and began to read. After about a half an hour Andy came out attacking me again. I always asked him to tell me just exactly how I was mean and hateful, and I always got the same answer, the same repeated accusation, "You are just mean and hateful." "You have a vendetta against Katie," he would say. I demanded, "What did I do today that was mean or hateful?" This time Andy responded and said I was mean this day by not asking Katie what she wanted at the grocery store. I couldn't believe it.

This was his reasoning for attacking me and causing such division and grief?

During the preparation for dinner that evening I found I was out of soy sauce and needed to go to the store to finish cooking. Through the intercom I called up to Katie, who was in her room, and told her I was going to the grocery and would be back in a few minutes. There had been numerous times I had asked Katie if she needed anything while I was out. One hundred percent of the time, I was told, "No." She always had her father get whatever she wanted.

When Andy made this statement, I told him that I would be packing my bags in the morning and would be leaving. I was sick of his attacks on me. There was nothing that I was doing that should have offended Katie in any way, and I wasn't going to put up with Andy's continual assault on me, and especially for such a ridiculous reason.

The next morning we went to our neighbor's wedding at her home across the street. When I came home, I packed my bags, and prior to leaving went into the kitchen to clean a pan that had been left in the sink. Katie was standing at the refrigerator, looking very self-assured and victorious. As I walked behind her she threw her rear end out and bumped me into the counter. I said nothing. Andy came in and began to fight. I was in the middle of washing an aluminum bowl, and in anger I took the bowl and threw it straight down on the floor as I yelled back at him. As I picked the bowl up and saw I had bent it, I began to sob. Katie walked up the stairs smiling. I yelled at her for the first time ever - "Excuse me for not asking you what you wanted at the grocery store."

I put my suitcases and Amanda and Jessica in the car. Andy followed me and continued to call me names. I left the house and went to my mom's. Along the way I stopped and held my children as I cried, and I told them how much I love them and how sorry I was.

My anger had been building. It appeared Andy was purposely provoking me. For nine months we had been yelling at each other, and now I lost my temper and threw a pan on the floor. I sought help from a counselor, Dr. William Van Horn, a Christian counselor who had an unusual way of dealing with his patients. He held group workshops and taught principles to help people reorganize their thinking and begin a healing process. He taught us that anger is a thought, and that thought labels physical feelings. When I recognized that, I realized you can control what you do with your thoughts and change the way you respond to situations, and I began to stop reacting to Andy with yelling. Andy, in what I sincerely thought to be an effort to save our family agreed to participate with Dr. Van Horn. He forced Katie into the program as well.

Dr. Van Horn's goal was to teach people to reach a higher level of love and intimacy. People participated in the process either because they had difficulties in their personal lives and/or relationships, or because although they had reasonably good lives and relationships they believed that they could attain something greater, something deeper to experience more of what God intended for them.

He taught us that we are spiritual beings, and each of us comes into the world with an empty vessel that is meant to be filled up with God's love. Usually our parents are the primary channels of God's love to us, but none of us is capable of loving the way God fully loves. Therefore, we all have fallen short of giving the love needed to our children or receiving love from our parents as God fully intended. He said we will experience our spiritual emptiness to the extent that our vessel is not filled up with God's love. To the extent that our vessel is empty, we will hurt, and we will seek to fill that emptiness or cover it up with something else. Our covers may be in the form of an "ugly cover" such as drinking or pornography. Or they may be "pretty covers" such as excessive working or studying or doing mission work. But the more we cover up the less sensitive we are to the spiritual realm, and while those covers block out the pain or some of the pain they also block out God's love. Dr. Van Horn's program was created to help us go back to the source of the pain, to remove those covers in order to get to the sensitive spiritual being, and to experience God's love where we can grow and mature spiritually as God intended.

Dr. Van Horn asked program participants to write letters to our mothers and fathers and others who have "hurt" us in any way. The letters are not intended to be given to the individuals to whom they are addressed but are used only in a group setting to read out loud in order to grieve while in the presence of loving people. The purpose of the letter writing is not to rehash or to blame. The purpose is to help people get back to that sensitive vulnerable hurting state and to do so this time around in an environment of God's love where that hurt can be healed.

In working with couples, Dr. Van Horn had each spouse write a letter to the other saying "how I perceived you hurt or failed me." That was intended to be a one time deal to "clear the table," and from that time on, each person was to ask for forgiveness. You might still hurt when you thought about those incidents, but you would give up the right to blame the other person for your hurting.

Dr. Van Horn recognized that it is human nature to avoid pain, and that people are motivated by one of three things, movement toward pleasure, movement away from pain, or the Holy Spirit. Unfortunately, none of us is so spiritually mature as to be motivated 100% of the time by the Holy Spirit. Our humanity gets in the way. Because of that, it is important to have other people in our lives who are committed to real love, who will hold us accountable to the goals that we set for ourselves to help us experience what God intends for us.

I went through Dr. Van Horn's workshop and found much of what he taught to be good. The three of us spent a very intensive four-day weekend along with others learning these and other principles.

Each person wrote three-page letters to our moms and dads. We wrote one-page letters about the five most painful experiences that happened in our lives, and we wrote one-page letters for the three ugliest things we had ever done. We were directed to write these letters focusing on all the sadness. The letter was to begin and to repeat with something like, "I was a sweet, sensitive, vulnerable little boy/girl who desperately needed a mommy/daddy's love and you hurt me terribly when you . . . "

Each person was asked to read at least a couple of his/her letters before the group, and everyone did except Katie. She had written some of her letters, but refused to read them. As each person shared about the pain in his or her life everyone else had their heads bowed and their eyes closed. Most people, surprising themselves, became very sensitive and began to cry as they talked about a painful experience. The group listened and then loved them and accepted them for the person for who they really are in Christ - a beautiful, wonderful child of God. Through love and forgiveness and the loving grace of God that flows through people, we can begin to heal through this process and respond to life differently. We can then begin to experience the joy of the Lord.

Dr. Van Horn's methods were far different from any other form of counseling we had received. He not only dealt with hidden sources of pain that might cause one to react to situations irrationally, but also included systems of accountability for one's behaviors. Many who participated in his program benefited.

During the period Andy and I attended Dr. Van Horn's groups, we were encouraged to write as many letters as we could to express pain in our lives. I wrote letters to my mom and dad and others, and I wrote a letter to Jesus. The letter which began, "Dear Jesus," expressed the sorrow and desire for forgiveness for my family for the many behaviors that were destroying our lives. The prayer was taken from a book called *Prayer Portions* by Sylvia Gunter and is used by intercessory prayer groups in churches all over the world. The book describes different kinds of spirits that can be present in spiritual warfare, like that of biblical characters, Jezebel, Ahab and Saul. I copied the parts of the book that were like my family and put the names in where appropriate. I asked God for His mercy and His forgiveness and for His healing hand upon our family.

I never read the letter to the group and eventually, I threw it away. Andy must have taken the letter from the trash and given it to Diane Woods, the guardian *ad litem*. In the final custodial and divorce hearing, Ms. Woods said this prayer was proof that I am mentally ill. All the other letters I wrote were taken by Andy as well and used in court in an attempt to discredit me, and to discredit my mother and father as abusive. Yet every letter that was written by the Van Horn group participants, including Andy, was written in such a way that one would come to that conclusion with every person. One cannot understand the meaning behind these letters without understanding the nature of the assignment and its purpose.

When I left Andy, the girls and I stayed with my mother for seven weeks. During that time Andy begged me to come home. He said Katie was cooking his meals and serving him wine each night, and that it wasn't right.

One afternoon he made plans to come see me and Amanda and Jessica. Andy told Katie he was taking her to her grandmother's house, and on the way she learned he was going to see me. She became so disturbed about it that she attempted to jump from his moving truck.

Toward the end of seven weeks of separation, Jessica became very ill with a high fever. During the middle of the night I took her to the children's hospital emergency room, concerned with her rising fever. She was examined, and we found that the fever had caused her to develop a heart murmur. She was diagnosed with a virus, and we were sent home with treatment instructions.

The next morning I decided to take my children back to their home, where Jessica could sleep in her own crib and be in her normal surroundings. I called Andy and told him that I was going back to the house, and that if he and Katie didn't like it they could leave until we could work things out. Andy wanted me back until he talked to Katie, and then he told me to leave the house because Katie didn't want me there. I refused to leave, and Katie refused to stay. She moved in with her grandmother, and Andy blamed me for his daughter leaving him. Katie remained with her grandmother for several months, and then returned when the new school year began.

Andy and I were still involved with Dr. Van Horn's group. He invited us to attend his personal support group, which included worship, grieving by reading letters, and measures of accountability. Dr. Van Horn suggested that Katie live with her grandmother. He said she was the most manipulative child he had ever met, and that if she remained in our home, she would sabotage our marriage. Andy was furious that I agreed.

The process of accountability was set up so that the parameters are increasingly narrowed. Andy constantly complained to the group that I was "mean and hateful" to Katie and that I cooked "bad food." Andy was asked to give specifics of what he meant, but he never was able to be specific. So Dr. Van Horn gave him an assignment: for one week he was to document every time he saw me do something that he didn't like and then come back to the group and share it.

Andy had complained about me for months to the group, and now he was at the point he was about to be found out, like a vise being tightened, he couldn't worm his way out any more. A good liar cannot get away in this process of accountability. Andy could not have stayed in the support group without being discovered. It was also during this period of time that Andy had become involved in the Sterling Club. And I was sharing with the group about Andy's participation in this secret organization and about the secret phone calls he was receiving from other Sterling members.

Andy never returned to the group. Instead, he wrote one of his infamous letters he had written to other counselors stating he could not come back to the group because of me. He told them what a terrible person I am, how mean and hateful I am, and how I was pulling the wool over their eyes.

Katie began dating the son of one of our friends. They had been dating for at least two or three months when Rob invited her to a concert. Andy called the family and told Rob's mom that Katie would not be going to the concert, and that she didn't want to date Rob any more. Everyone found it strange that it was Andy who was calling.

One night Andy went into the bathroom where Amanda and Jessica were bathing. Amanda's soiled panties she had just taken off were on the floor next to the tub. She had been having a great deal of difficulty with her bowels for a number of months. She had complained of pain while trying to have bowel movements, then became impacted from holding it. A watery seepage would then occur around the impaction, and would soil her clothing. While she had this problem, it was usual for her to have to change her clothing two or three times a day. Dr. Stephen King suggested giving her mineral oil, which helped her significantly.

Anything Andy could criticize, he did, and this didn't pass without his criticism either. He constantly attacked me and the children saying I didn't teach my children proper bathroom habits and that they were "filthy" and "smelled like latrines."

When Andy saw the panties, he took Amanda, who was then six years old, out of the tub and told her to spread her legs and bend over so that he could see if she was clean. I told him that was totally inappropriate. She was in the tub and washing herself. He began yelling at me, that it was wrong for me to say that in front of the children. He said, "This is what a good parent does."

When Amanda was about four years old, she had a bladder infection, which the doctor explained to me is highly unusual for a child her age. Outpatient hospital procedures were done to make sure that this was not a developmental problem. That was ruled out. I have since learned that impacted bowels and bladder infections may be signs of sexual abuse.

The sexual impropriety throughout the marriage seemed to worsen as time went by and became overwhelming. Andy had a proclivity toward pornographic art and pornographic videos and television. In a deposition when he was questioned about credit card purchases at an adult store, he claimed to have bought some pornographic videos for one of his employees. Andy was involved with the Sterling Club, which teaches men to hate women and treat them as sex objects. It is run by a man who produces pornographic films. For the first two years of our marriage, Andy and I had sexual relations only when Katie was away from our home. That is the only time Andy had any sexual interest in me. Then he became obsessive for the six years that followed, constantly pawing at my body in a way that was neither loving nor arousing. He had a lack of and rebellious refusal to put into place healthy sexual boundaries with the children. He allowed Katie to watch R-rated videos at age 10 and X-rated videos at age 15 with her boyfriend. Secrets were a major issue in our home, and during the last year of our marriage prior to the filing for divorce, Andy went to Katie's room each night and stayed behind closed doors for about 30 minutes, and always dening that the door was closed. There were a couple of occasions I walked into a room where Andy was standing behind Katie with his hand on her rear. When he saw me, he immediately dropped his hand and changed his posture. Within the first three months of our marriage Andy brought a XXX video downstairs and put it in the VCR and asked me to watch it with him. He said he found it in his son's room. We watched the first minute of the video, and I told him I didn't want filth like that in our home. I asked him to remove it.

Andy began to talk about getting a divorce about a year and a half before the divorce was filed. Around the time he began talking about it, he took over the finances and emptied our house of all our financial records and his and Katie's personal files. He forbade me to open any of the bills unless they were in my name. I received his wrath one day after opening the mortgage statement even though the house was in my name as well. During this time he continued to say he wanted the marriage to work. One day he would say he didn't want a divorce and a few days later he wanted a divorce, yo-yoing back and forth.

In the last couple of years of our marriage Katie expressed that when her father married me, he abandoned her, and she repeatedly made statements about how much she hated me and wanted me to hurt. She began to give Andy ultimatums of, "It is either her or me." Katie left our home when I returned from a separation with Andy. She returned to the home several months later, and then left again when the school year ended. Andy blamed me for Katie not living with him anymore and told me he wanted me to hurt as much as Katie wanted me to hurt. A month later, in July, 1998, he filed for divorce. Amanda was 6 and Jessica was 4.

I had quickly jumped into the relationship with Andy at a very vulnerable time in my life. Even though life was difficult in this marriage, I somehow saw redeeming traits in Andy and kept hoping that he would change. I also was greatly encouraged by counselors to hold on until Katie went off to college since they believed that things would turn around for us then. I had two children with Andy, and I desperately wanted to have an intact family for them, both a father and a mother. I admired and agreed with Dr. Laura Schlessinger that parents need to stay together for the sake of their children, and maturely endure the unpleasant parts of their marriage. The driving force to remain and fight for what could be was greater than my temptation to leave the marriage. I foolishly and blindly stayed, hoping and praying all the while for change. As bad as things were, I never wanted to end the marriage until Jessica shared with me about a "secret" bath her father took with her, a bath she detailed as deviant and abusive. Andy had filed for divorce

> Domestic violence isn't just hitting or other physical abuse. It is a chronic abuse of power.

months before, but when he found out that I knew about the bath, he asked me if we could stop the divorce. I said, "No."

Domestic violence isn't just hitting or other physical abuse. It is a chronic abuse of power. The abuser uses intimidation and calculated threats to torture and control others, and even though these things are legal acts, they many times lead to physical violence. The ABA Commission on Domestic Violence, as well as domestic violence councils across the country, include the following descriptions and more in defining domestic violence: calling the other names; degrading or belittling the other; making someone feel bad about him or herself; humiliating the other; accusing one of being stupid, unattractive, or a bad parent; unfaithful or any other similar fault; playing mind games; making the other think he or she is crazy; making the other feel guilty; demanding sex when you are sick, tired or sleeping; being the one to define the role of each person; using one's economic power to control another; preventing someone from getting or keeping a job; making a partner ask for money; not letting a partner know about or have access to family income; controlling others through coercion and threats; threatening to report someone to the authorities; controlling through intimidation; making someone afraid by using looks, gestures, or actions; abusing pets; controlling others through the children; using visitation to harass a partner; threatening to take the children away; controlling others through isolation; controlling what a person does, who he or she sees and talks to, what he or she reads and where he or she goes; limiting others outside involvement; using jealousy to justify one's actions; controlling another through minimizing, denying and blaming; not letting your partner sleep at night; constantly calling and checking up on one; making light of the abuse and not taking the other persons concerns about it seriously; saying the abuse didn't happen; shifting responsibility for abusive behavior; saying "He or she caused it." ALL of these things I experienced with Andy and still am suffering.

Counselors must be trained about the effects of domestic violence so they can recognize the signs and be willing to aggressively uncover the truth and assist the victims to a place of safety. When one is involved in such abuse, it is very difficult to know the right thing to do, especially when children are involved.

I was afraid for my girls, yet knew that I could not totally protect them from their father. Andy had exhibited every one of these behaviors. There was nothing that was criminal that I knew at the time even as damaging as they were. Other than his pushing me across a room and both of us pushing each other into a door, he was not physically violent. However, I saw a frighteningly murderous look in his eyes like I had never seen before, as he stood several feet from me with fisted hands and tensed jaw and arms when I expressed my anger about the bath he had taken with Jessica. At the time we were living separated but in the same home.

I sometimes think about that look remembering his nature and covert and manipulative ways of hurting others. It frightens me for my children. I also sometimes think about a night after he filed for divorce when he gently took my hands into his and gazing into my eyes like a man who was in love with his wife, he smiled and softly said, "I am going to prove you are mentally out to lunch. I hate to say it, Wendy, but you are just plain stupid."

CHAPTER EIGHT

During the first couple years of our marriage, Andy and I purchased five acres of land, had it partially cleared and built a large home. A year later we added a swimming pool. Amanda was 18 months old, and I was five months pregnant with Jessica when we moved into the house. I was very sick in my pregnancy, but I managed to pack the entire house except for Andy's garage items and the belongings of Andy's 23 year old son, Bob.

Bob was a university student and was home for his Christmas holiday break. I kept telling Bob when the movers were coming and that he needed to box his things up. He had put many things in our basement including an aquarium and aquarium supplies, all kinds of mixed drink bar equipment, blender and glasses, clothes, and a number of other things that were not ready for moving. The day of the move, nothing had been boxed, and he started washing and drying clothes in the washer and dryer that were to be moved. I went to his room, knocked at his closed door, and told him the movers were there and that he needed to get his items in his room and in the basement boxed up for the movers. He did not even respond. I called Andy at work and explained to him what was occurring. He talked to Bob and then called me back. Andy was furious saying I had hurt Bob's feelings, and that I should have packed his things up myself.

I was on the floor on my pregnant belly helping the movers get the dolly over door guards and protecting the chandelier and other large pieces of furniture from damage. We had used a very inexpensive moving service, one we later regretted having used. I had an 18-month-old child, I was five months pregnant and sick, and I needed help with this move. Andy refused to come home, and Bob, who was a strong strapping young man, refused to help as well.

I stayed very ill during my pregnancy with Jessica. My body felt extremely toxic. During the last seven or eight weeks I began to express deep concerns with my doctor about the illness I was experiencing. I also had begun to vomit and lost a significant amount of weight. Amanda was about 22 months old and needed constant attention and care. Andy was furious that I was not as attentive in my household chores and caring for everyone as well as

I normally did. He refused to help me with Amanda or with anything else.

The illness became so bad that upon waking one morning, I called my mother and asked her to please help me. She and Alton Davis, my mother's dear friend who is like a stepfather to me and the children's "Poppy," came and took me to the hospital where they began to monitor Jessica and do tests on me. Finding nothing of major concern, they were ready to send me home. I told my doctor I didn't feel I could go another day. Then she said, "let's do some blood work before you go and make sure everything is okay." Within a short period of time, more blood was taken to repeat the test, because they hoped there was a gross error in the previous test. There was no error, though, and within a matter of minutes of the second blood test, I was being induced into labor.

The blood tests revealed that I had a very seriously high liver enzyme level that could take Jessica's and my life at any time, something they called HELLP Syndrome which occurs in a small number of pregnancies. When Jessica was delivered there was an abnormal gush of blood, and Dr. Cook found the placenta had already started separating from the uterus and that Jessica would not have survived from that alone. It was explained to me that had the pregnancy continued for another day that we would probably both be dead. They continued to test my blood repeatedly throughout the day and night. After Jessica was born, my doctor, Nancy Cook, sat beside me during the night in the absence of my husband. The cure for HELLP Syndrome is termination of pregnancy. Jessica and I were fortunate. She was fine, and I immediately began to improve upon her delivery.

Amanda was delighted to have a new baby sister. She had watched Jessica grow in my belly, felt her kick and move, and kissed her on my tummy over and over again, calling her by name. After Jessica was born, Amanda loved holding and touching her and was found climbing into Jessica's crib on many occasions. The two became very close and loved being together.

The girls enjoyed sharing a bedroom and were afraid to sleep alone. When they were about three and five years of age, Andy said that it was "improper" for them to share a room and insisted they sleep in separate rooms. We went in circles over the issue. I found him to be impossible and insane, and he told me I was a "bad parent" and "out to lunch," and that it was "inappropriate for them to share a room." To maintain some semblance of peace I told the girls if they could each sleep in separate rooms for a month, I would reward them with a gift of their choice. They were happy to try in order to get the gift, but they expressed fear. I thought that it was just a matter of their getting used to it and that a month would create a habit and comfort of sleeping alone.

Amanda had been moved to an upstairs bedroom next to Katie's room. Andy began to go upstairs after Amanda was tucked into bed, had said goodnight to all, and the lights had been turned off. He would turn the lights on and read to Amanda for long periods of time, keeping her awake until late into the night. After a few days, he closed her door after reading to her for a while. Andy and I argued about his reading to Amanda after she was in bed ready for sleep. Then we argued about his keeping her awake until late hours. When he began to shut the door, I opened it, and then we argued about that. I told him there was no reason that he needed to shut himself and Amanda behind closed doors.

Amanda and Jessica did not like being alone and continued to be afraid. They wanted to sleep in the same room together. All the while, Andy was making comments to Jessica saying Amanda kicked her in the middle of the night, and she shouldn't sleep with her sister, that it was wrong. He tried to divide the two of them. Amanda and Jessica were both very young. They shed tears to share the same room again.

I was glad when they joined each other again in the bedroom across the hall from our bedroom. They both had nightmares, and Amanda had night terrors most every night. She also had nasal congestion due to allergies and had difficulty breathing. Having them both close to me instead of one upstairs and one downstairs made it easier for me to care for them and help them during the night. Andy was furious and insulted them and me regularly about their sharing a room together.

I wanted my children to know how to swim as soon as possible, as I was fearful of the dangers of a pool in the back yard with small children. Every week I went to water babies swimming classes at Health Place in Marietta to teach my children to love the water. I enjoyed the interaction with other moms and kids. We played water games like Humpty-Dumpty sat on a wall, and when Humpty-Dumpty had a great fall, the babies would come off the side of the pool and splash into the water and scream with glee. We sang and played games and got to the point that we would go underwater with our babies. Eventually, we let go of them and then we brought them back into our arms. They loved the water and always looked forward to our swimming days.

When the girls were older, I enrolled them in classes at the Cobb County Aquatic Center. Amanda was swimming like a fish by the time she was three years old. When Jessica was two she was not yet able to swim without support, but loved the water. When swimming at home I would put a float on her that was built into a swimsuit that gave her great freedom to splash and play in the pool, yet be very safe.

One day after spending the morning swimming in our home pool, I took the girls in for lunch. I took the float off Jessica, dried both girls off and fed them in the enclosed sunroom which was right next to the pool. I had planted a beautiful assortment of perennials and annuals around the pool, mixed with evergreens and rosebushes. There were Peach Bearded Irises, Moonbeam Coreopsis, Veronica, butterfly bushes, Phlox, Patrinia, Yellow Blackberry Lily, spirea, Iceplant, Purple Coneflowers, lavender, Mexican Sage, Swamp Sunflower, lantana, laurel, holly bushes, gardenias and roses of every color. There was an entrance to the pool from the driveway with a trellis approximately 20 feet long and 8 feet wide that was covered with rose vines and beautiful roses that bloomed off and on throughout the spring and summer. One of my rosebushes around the pool had died, and I needed to replace it. I thought it was a good time to do that while the girls were eating their lunch. I left them sitting at their little table in the sunroom, which I could see, from the pool through the windows. I opened the door and left it open so that I could hear them, and they could hear me, and I proceeded to dig the old bush out and to put a new bush in. My back was to the door, and in a very short time I heard Amanda ask, "What's Jessica doing?" I turned and saw Jessica floating face down in the middle of the pool. I was terrified and jumped from where I was standing to where she was and immediately pulled her up and out of the pool. She was perfectly fine, but I was not. I was terrified when I saw Jessica in the pool, not knowing if she was okay or not. Also when I jumped, I tore my cruciate ligament away from my left knee. I tenderly held her in my arms until she was ready to run and play. She had inhaled no water and required no special attention.

Jessica had evidently only moments before gone into the pool not realizing she did not have any flotation device around her body. If Amanda had not come out and said something to me, I might never have even noticed her in the pool until it was too late. So many caring, loving parents have lost their children to accidents like this, and I cringe each time I think about it. Most husbands would have sympathized and consoled their wives, but Andy instead began a campaign saying to others that I did not ever watch the children and almost drowned Jessica.

I had to have surgery on my knee to replace my cruciate ligament. Without the surgery I could not stand on my left leg without it giving out from underneath me. After the accident I couldn't do yard work for several months, and Andy attacked me for not helping him in the yard. I had complications from the surgery with bleeding and ulcers in my leg. My entire leg from my hip to the tips of my toes were swollen and black and blue. Andy and Katie refused to help me with Amanda and Jessica.

Around this time, Amanda and Jessica began to get curious about what was in Katie's room, as they were not allowed to enter. A child's door guard had been put on Katie's door to keep the girls out, and Amanda figured out how to remove it. This caused a lot of problems, because now Amanda and Jessica were able and did go into Katie's room. When Katie found out the girls had been in her room, she did what she always did - she called her dad. Her dad did what he always did - he called me and chewed me out for "my daughters" destroying Katie's property. The girls had taken a bottle of nail polish to another room in the house and used the polish on their toenails and fingernails.

That night when Andy came home, the table was set and dinner was ready. I called Katie on the intercom. She came down for dinner, and they all sat down to eat. I was serving the plates to each person when Andy's anger toward Amanda broke. He screamed at her and then took her to the bedroom and told her she could not come out. He then held onto the doorknob from the outside of the door, and when Amanda tried to open the door, he would hold it and then let go where it would slam open. Then he began screaming and hitting her. Jessica sat terrified in her chair. Katie sat smugly in her chair. I took Katie's plate to her and put it on the table harder than usual and said, "Thanks a lot, Katie." I left the kitchen and went back to the bedroom. Amanda was hysterical. Andy and I screamed at each other. I screamed at him to stop, and he screamed at me that I was interfering with his disciplining Amanda. He left, and I held and comforted Amanda. She showed me the marks on her hips and legs that her father had caused by hitting her. Andy repeated this behavior with Amanda on other occasions for other perceived wrongdoings. Katie told our neighbor, Debbie Bishop, that I was mean to her and threw her dinner in her lap, totaling misrepresenting what really happened.

One night, Andy's mother and cousins visiting from Denmark came to dinner at our home. I was not well enough from the surgery to cook, so Andy got Chinese take-out to serve the family. On this night Amanda tried to enter Katie's room following behind Katie as she was entering. In Katie's anger, she severely gouged Amanda's finger and hand as she pushed Amanda out of her room. This was the second time in a week Amanda had been physically attacked and hurt by Katie. Later when everyone went home, I went to the kitchen where Katie and Andy were, and said to Katie, "You are going to have to deal with your anger differently. It is one thing to be angry but another to hurt someone because of your anger." Andy immediately jumped all over me, saying Katie had every right to hurt Amanda, that Amanda had no business going into Katie's room.

My condition continued to worsen. I was put on medication for excessive bleeding in my leg, but it caused my stomach and intestinal tract to begin bleeding. I also had fever and had developed cysts in my leg. I lost 10 pounds in a week, and I was in a lot of pain, both my stomach and leg. I was put on strict bed rest for 10 days with frequent icing of my leg, which infuriated Andy. The morning after the incident with Katie, I called my mother to come and get Amanda and Jessica and me because I needed help, and all I had received from Andy was his wrath.

While I was at my mother's, I received a letter from Andy telling me that he was sick and tired of me and that I had made Katie cry. He said prior to our leaving that Amanda had "broken into Katie's room," "vandalized it" and "maliciously destroyed her property," and that I had encouraged Amanda to do so. He went on to say, I had a "bad attitude," I was "inconsiderate," "destructive," "disrespectful," "uncooperative," "not understanding," "on a campaign against Katie," "not fair," "unapologetic," "non sympathetic," "unhelpful," that I had "unbalanced the scales of justice against Katie," I was "mean," "the reason for strife in our home," I was "demeaning," that I "reinforce inappropriate behaviors in Amanda," I was "stubborn," "a dictator," "angry," "a name caller," "immature," "accusatory," and I was not to come home until I could "cooperate and humble myself" to him and Katie. He blamed me for all the stresses in our home, for having to attend functions, for broken things that needed to be repaired, the house that needed to be repainted, flowers that had to be planted, my attending Bethel Bible Study, and his having to watch the kids. He accused me of not having groceries in the house and not keeping the house clean, and not taking care of the "poor animals." He went on to say that Amanda had broken Katie's hair dryer, and he was angry that I had not gone out to buy another hair dryer for Katie. It was abhorrent to me that while I was in bed very sick, I was under the attack of my husband, the man who was supposed to be my friend, my lover, and my helpmate, and I was called every name he could think of and told me I should be out shopping for a hair dryer for his daughter.

My mother helped the girls call Andy each night to say goodnight. She put them on the speaker phone so they could both talk during the same conversation. Andy put Katie on the phone one night and she began to criticize my mother, making fun of her mannerisms when serving family and friends food. Katie knew my mother was present and that the girls were on a speaker phone. Yet she purposefully tried to hurt her. My mother could not hold back her tears as she listened to Katie's rude statements about her.

When Jessica was about two or three years old I left her and Amanda with Andy one Sunday afternoon while I went for a quick trip to the grocery store. Upon my return, Andy was on the John Deer tractor lawnmower cutting the grass in our 300' front yard paying no attention to the children. As I drove up our gravel driveway I saw Jessica standing at the base of a pine tree screaming at the top of her lungs. I ran to her and found her standing in a bed of red ants, and her body was covered with them.

I began ripping her clothes off of her and knocking the ants away. I picked her up and ran inside and put her in a tub filled with water and mixed with a full container of baking soda. I gave her Benadryl. I have heard that small children can die from just a few red ant bites, and I was scared. Astoundingly, Jessica had no reaction to the ant bites and was perfectly fine in a short period of time.

Sometimes I pick up a ballerina teddy bear that sits on Amanda's dresser, a bear I bought for her when she danced in the Nutcracker with Ruth Mitchell Dance Studio. Sitting next to it is another bear in a mouse costume which belongs to Jessica and also represents the Nutcracker. The bears are a reminder of my daughters' love for dance.

Amanda had studied ballet for five years with Ms. Irene before she was old enough to participate in a production of this magnitude. The girls were very active in ballet from the time they were three years old until they were taken from me in February, 2000. Then Andy immediately removed them from dance, as well as all the other activities in which they were involved when he got custody of them, activities like gymnastics, T-ball, soccer and piano.

Both of them were in love with the Nutcracker. We used to watch the Nutcracker video throughout the year and listened to the music on CD. We made up our own dances, laughing and twirling and tiptoeing around the room as we watched the professionals on screen. We read the Nutcracker book from time to time and enjoyed the story along with all the beautiful pictures. Both of the girls had wooden nutcrackers that they carried about the house regularly as reminders. The wooden nutcrackers now sit untouched on a mantle in the upstairs bedroom in my New Orleans home.

Jessica never had the opportunity to perform in the production, and any opportunity for Amanda to perform again was taken from her. A greater loss was the loss of their friends, with whom they had danced for five and three years. Ms. Irene, their dance teacher, had become an integral part of their life too. She made dance so much fun for the girls, using all kinds of imaginary games and of course her imaginary fairy, "Abigail" that was ever present. She, too, no longer sees the girls but still asks about them. Opportunities, dreams, desires - dashed, torn, and shredded.

Music was always such a lovely part of my life. I enjoyed listening to beautiful music, singing, and playing the piano. When the girls were born, I played music often for them, beautiful children's songs, classical music, lullabies at night, and music videos made especially for children. Amanda was singing at six months of age, la la la la la, copying what I was singing to her. She was yodeling, yodel-lo-who-who, before she was even one. I laughed with glee every time she sang it.

Baby Jessica (the name we called her for so long), on the other hand, began singing while she was learning to talk, and I still giggle as I recall the words she sang to "Jesus Loves Me." She sang, "Jesus loves me this I know, for the Bible tells me so. Little ones to Him belong, harry butt, harry butt." The first time I heard her sing this, I choked, became very concerned and upset, thinking someone had taught her to sing this on purpose, and then I died with laughter. She soon learned the correct words, but it was a standing joke for a long time to come. The words she heard and understood, and then spoke were so funny.

While living in Minneapolis years before my marriage, I attended a piano recital of a young girl about seven years old who played the most beautiful classical pieces with great skill. She learned at an early age to play first by listening and then later by reading music. This is called the Suzuki method of study and requires the parents' participation in the child's learning. When Amanda and Jessica were 5 and 3 years of age I remembered the little girl and sought out a Suzuki teacher. I found a wonderful teacher, Robin Blankenship, and I enrolled the girls in lessons. We sat at the piano daily together and listened to the Suzuki CD's. They learned so much and enjoyed their accomplishments. They played songs like Twinkle, Twinkle, Little Star Variations, The Honeybee, Cuckoo, French Children's Song, Mary Had a Little Lamb, Au Clair de la Lune, Good-bye to Winter, Allegro, Musette and more. Part of their learning was to listen to other children play as well and to get involved in group activities with them. They developed friendships along with a development and knowledge about music.

During the summer of 1998, Amanda had the fortunate opportunity of taking a lesson from the world renowned Dr. Haruko Kataoka who is the world's leading pedagogue on the Suzuki Piano Method. She is responsible for implementing Dr. Suzuki's philosophy that all children have musical talent if their natural ability is nurtured in a supportive environment. She is the individual responsible for the Suzuki piano instruction. I was so proud of Amanda, as she went on a performance auditorium stage before a large number of people and sat with this incredible woman who critiqued her piano skills and gave her direction for future growth.

On another occasion both Amanda and Jessica performed on stage at Kennesaw College for the 100th Anniversary of Dr. Suzuki. They were so beautiful as each walked up the stairs and on the stage to play. I was the official photographer for the program and was delighted taking pictures of my own children and, of course, other kids for the newsletter that would follow this program. I was also proud that I was able to support and nurture my children to learn in this manner.

The piano now sits for the most part unused in my home. All the Suzuki books and CD's and their progress charts are here in my home, more reminders of the talents, opportunities and development that have been taken from their lives.

When I sit down to play the piano, I feel very sad, so I just don't play anymore. Christmas before last, I asked a musician to play the piano during a Christmas party in my home. It was wonderful to hear the beautiful music and to sing carols around the piano with others. But every moment the piano played the thoughts of my daughters and their absence filled my heart with emptiness and pain for them and for me. I thought about the years we lived together with Andy and Katie. I thought about how sad it is that while we were together nothing like this could have taken place. Now I was free to enjoy other people, their laughter, their singing and playing the piano, but knowing my children could not, inhibited me from the full joy of this event.

Jessica was our little comedian. When she was two years old, we were sitting at the dinner table, and she passed gas, a little at a time causing a blup, blup, blup, blup, blup sound. When asked playfully, "What's that?", without missing a beat and very serious and matter of factly, she answered, "helicopter." She continued eating while everyone else was bent over laughing.

One of the most favorite things Amanda and Jessica enjoyed playing was dress-up. They loved to put on fancy dresses and shoes and hats and scarves. One Christmas I went to a consignment shop and told the owner that I wanted to put a chest of beautiful clothes together for my daughters for play. She helped me put together a wonderful assortment of gowns, shoes, scarves, bags and even a fur wrap at a special price of $100. It was the best present. Amanda and Jessica and their friends spent hours playing dress-up, having so much fun and really looking beautiful. One day I took Amanda and Jessica and their dear friend Sarah to Olan Mills, put some makeup on them, and had their picture taken in the gowns they chose to wear. It is such a sassy picture of them the way they are sitting, the expressions on their faces, and the gloves on their hands along with their bright purple and gold and black dresses. They were quite stunning, and they had so much fun.

Amanda was 11 months old when she met Sarah at Gymboree Play Center. Several of the moms and I started a small playgroup for the children, and we got together once a week and continued meeting every week for several years. Eventually, the group thinned as people moved or got involved in other activities, but Sarah and Amanda and Jessica continued to see each other every week. They were special friends. But their visits immediately stopped when Andy received custody of the children, and now they have not seen each other in over two years. Andy will not allow Amanda and Jessica to see any of their old friends. He has told the court they are all "troublemakers."

Amanda and Jessica loved baby dolls, especially Amanda. They would love on their babies, dress them, take them for walks, feed them, and put them down for naps. Every time we went into a toy store they begged for more. They had a small collection of dolls in their rooms, none that were just to look at; all were loved, held, fed, washed, and cared for by the girls. I bought them miniature baby strollers for their dolls, just like the ones I used when the girls were very little, and they enjoyed taking their lifelike babies for walks down the street.

They also enjoyed trains and puzzles, water guns and games. They swung on our Rainbow swing set almost every day and played in the sand building castles and burying their hands and feet. They loved to explore the outdoors and eat red raspberries off the vines and throw sticks and rocks into the small creek that ran across the front corner of our yard.

The girls and I planted a vegetable garden and grew tomatoes, okra, squash, green beans, peppers and herbs. In the evening as I cooked dinner, I would send them to the garden to pick the fresh herbs that I needed to cook our meal. They learned to identify basil, parsley, rosemary and thyme. We also planted gourds to use in crafts to make birdhouses, ladles, and musical instruments. We collected two large boxes of gourds, but we never had the opportunity to do anything with them. They sit in a storage area in the back of my home waiting for the day the girls can create with them. Just before the gourds ripened for picking, Andy began to rip the vines out of the ground and throw them away. I argued with him in order to keep the gourds for the girls.

I turned one of the rooms of our family's home into a schoolroom and a playroom. It was painted a bright beautiful aqua trimmed in white, had an alcove with a lowered ceiling and a window box, and on each side of the alcove was a built-in book case. In the center was their little table with four little chairs. It was designed so the girls could curl up in the window with a book and look out at the beautiful five acres and into a 20-acre cow pasture that backed up to our property.

Along two walls I designed an art center with a counter and cabinets filled with paints, markers, crayons, construction paper, stencils, and other arts and crafts. Amanda and Jessica enjoyed creating and designing different things such as Christmas ornaments, pressed flower cards, drawings and paintings, jewelry boxes, and sometimes just a mess. They and their friends spent a lot of time at the art center.

Around Valentine's Day of 1999, Amanda painted a heart of many colors onto a card. It sat in a pile of art supplies until April of 2000 when Amanda wrote a message inside the card and gave it to me. Jessica said the card was from her too. At the time the card was finished and given to me the girls were not allowed to see me but 12 hours a week and under the strict supervision of an agency. The card reads, "I love you. I will always be with you even if you don't see me. Love, Amanda. To Mom." The card now sits on a mantle in my bedroom next to a dog made from a rock by Jessica while in preschool. It is this card's heart that is depicted shattered by the judge's gavel on this book's cover. I could not envision a more singularly apt expression of what the Superior Court has done to my girls.

I put a desk with the family computer and computer games in another small alcove in the room. I hung shelves on two other walls where their dolls and stuffed animals sat. Underneath the shelves of one wall were their kitchen and dishes, and against the other wall were their dress-up clothes, pocketbooks, hats, doll beds and high chair. In the center of the room was an oval carpet they sat on to put puzzles together and to play. It was a wonderful room in a wonderful house on a wonderful property, a haven for any little girl or family.

Early one morning as we looked out the window, we saw three bulls in our back yard. The girls and I jumped into the car and drove to the property that had the cows behind us. Our neighbor was coming out of his pasture and told me he was putting up electrical wiring so that his cattle would not break through the fence after our bulls. When I told him they were not ours and I was looking for the owner, he sent me quite a way to another home that had cattle.

When I located the owner of the bulls, I learned he was an Emergency Room physician at Kennestone Hospital. His wife told me he would be over to my property soon to get the bulls. About an hour later a man with boots, spurs, leather, cowboy hat, and rope came slowing riding up our gravel driveway on his beautiful black horse. I went outside and greeted him and tried to make small conversation. He never looked at me or exchanged any greeting. There on that beautiful horse sat a haughty arrogant man who could not even muster a courtesy greeting. Amanda, Jessica and I watched him round up his bulls as though he was herding hundreds in an old John Wayne movie and then ran them in the direction of his home.

About an hour later, I received a call from his wife asking if we had seen the bulls or the horse. When I told her I didn't understand, she shared that while herding the bulls home, her husband took the horse between two trees and got stuck and couldn't get the horse free. He abandoned the horse and the bulls, walked home and told his wife he had to go to work. He told her that she would have to deal with it. Now the horse and three bulls were missing. I never saw the animals again but learned later that another neighbor found the animals and put them in his fence until the owner was located. Amanda, Jessica and I laughed and laughed as we pictured that arrogant doctor with all his Wild West get-up on stuck between two trees and unable to release his horse.

During Amanda and Jessica's preschool years I met some mothers who were home schooling their children, and I began to learn about the process. I had always thought that parents who kept their children out of the school system were harming their kids by making them socially inept. I also thought that it was not a good form of education. However, the more I was around these families and with their children and the more I learned about home schooling, the more convinced I became that it was an excellent form of education. These kids were more well rounded and well mannered and more social than any of the children I knew who were in the public or private school system. They also were bright, capable and educated. I began to do some investigation on my own, and I was astounded with the results that I found. The Rudner study of 1998[12] shows that the average home school child performs significantly higher than the average public school or private school child. Rudner also found no valid correlation between teacher certification and student achievement. Also home school achievement tends to improve the longer a child has been taught at home. The study states, "Students home schooled their entire academic lives have the highest achievement...suggesting that students who remain in home school throughout their high school years flourish in that environment."

Former Georgia Governor Zell Miller applauded those who home school their children "in their efforts to improve the quality of education." He wrote, "It is a valid educational option, creating students who love learning and young adults who are well prepared for a bright future." He also stated, "Studies indicate that children who are educated at home exhibit self-confidence and good citizenship and are fully prepared academically to meet the challenges of today's society."[13] Some of the prominent Americans who were home educated include George Washington, John Quincy Adams, Abraham Lincoln, Thomas Edison, Robert E. Lee, Booker T. Washington, Helen Keller, and Sandra Day O'Connor.

I wanted the very best for Amanda and Jessica. I wanted them to be afforded the greatest opportunities in life and knew they had to have a very sound foundation to allow for that. The Georgia school system has vacillated back and forth between 49th and 50th as the poorest school system in the country. I had reason to be very concerned about the girl's education.

Andy and I discussed my home schooling the children and we decided that I would home school Amanda for Kindergarten and see how it went. I found a local home school group, enrolled both Amanda and Jessica, ordered the ABeka curriculum and began an earnest endeavor to educate my daughters. As I explain later, I was crucified in a deposition for using this well recognized and accepted curriculum. Home school was everything I had been told it would be. It was wonderful for the girls and wonderful for me and allowed us great flexibility to learn outside of the classroom as well as call on resources of others to learn about many different aspects of life.

Andy took no interest whatsoever in what they were learning or how they were developing. He waged his normal and customary attacks on me, complaining that I spent money on books and cared more about Amanda and Jessica than I did Katie. Near the end of Amanda's Kindergarten year, we talked again, and I expressed to Andy the desire to continue home schooling. After debating the subject, he agreed that I could home school the girls. I enrolled the girls in the group for the following year and ordered the ABeka curriculum.

After a couple of months Andy became combative with me saying that he told me that he did not want the children home schooled but that I was defiantly doing it anyway. I immediately went to Andy's mom and told her that Andy did not want the children home schooled and that even though I had no right to ask for her help in educating my children, I did not want 20 years later to say I wished that I had.

Andy's parents, Joan and Dick Titelman had paid for the private education for both of Andy's older children. They were also paying for private school for her other granddaughter, Gina, who is a year older than Amanda. Andy's mother told me she was more than happy to pay for private school for Amanda and Jessica, that she had done it for all of her other grandchildren, but that she would not do anything that Andy did not want her to do.

Andy told me okay, and I began a search for a school that still had an opening. When I located an excellent school that would enroll Amanda, Andy then refused saying his mother gave him $10,000 to do with as he pleased, and he was going to use it for legal fees in the divorce for which he had just filed. This was so typical of his behavior. He constantly baited, switched, sabotaged and undermined any efforts I put forth in our family or my life. He would say one thing and then declare he said something else. He would do something and say he never did it, and when I would prove he did, he would say he had every right to do it. He would lie to me about something and say he hadn't lied. I would bring out the truth and prove it, and then he would make the issue not that he lied but that I called him a liar. It was crazy making.

I dug my heels in. He had made it very clear throughout our marriage that Amanda, Jessica and I were not important to him. He was unwilling to look out for their best interests, and now he had undermined their enrollment in private school. He filed for divorce in the middle of all of this. Therefore, I declared that I would be home schooling the children, and I did for the following year.

Andy made it as difficult for me as he possibly could. Amanda's schoolbooks began to disappear, so I had to get locks for the cupboards and secure them every day. He continuously called

Amanda and Jessica during the day at home interrupting my teaching. He sometimes just showed up at the house in the middle of the day and took the girls to go play with him for no other reason than disruption.

Just prior to filing for divorce Andy went to his mother's house for a get together with his family. As he had previously done on several occasions during these later months, he told me I was not welcome and neither were Amanda and Jessica. He said the family considered them to be unruly children and that none of his family wanted them around. On this particular occasion, Andy's brother David was in town. He called me and said that the family and Andy had changed their minds about the kids coming over and asked me to bring the girls and leave them. I said absolutely not.

CHAPTER NINE

Andy filed for divorce in July of 1998 after he returned home from a trip to Boston with Katie visiting Tufts University. Katie had moved away from the house again and was living with her grandmother, and Andy was furious and blamed me for her not living with him.

We put the house on the market, and we continued to live in the same house with separate bedrooms until the house was sold. Katie's room was a disaster. I had not touched it for a long time in keeping with Andy and Katie's demand. Now that the house was going to be shown, it had to be cleaned. Andy said Katie had removed everything she wanted, so I went to work. The floor was covered with clothes and trash. I washed 15 loads of clothes. After that, I just hung up the rest. Among the many things that I picked up off the floor were velvet bras, silk underwear, and clothes and shoes in excess, some with the sales tags still attached. I found molded food, three measuring cups, kitchen towels and about eight glasses that had disappeared from the kitchen and never returned. I filled a large computer box full of the paper that had been thrown all over the room and threw away four garden trash bags full of trash. The sheets on the bed were disintegrating from lack of washing. The carpet was stained, and many of the stains remained even after cleaning.

Andy's behavior with Amanda and Jessica had become increasingly alarming. He refused to set any sexual boundaries. He bathed in front of them, urinated in front of them, and brought them into bed with him while he was nude. Amanda was six years old and had begun to grab at his penis, but Andy saw nothing wrong in what he was doing. He defended his continuing to behave in these ways.

Andy told me that Dr. Pittman said that I was a very dangerous woman and that Andy needed to stay married to me to protect our children. Obviously, Andy had been talking with Dr. Pittman on his own. I had not seen him for six and a half years. I later learned that Andy and Katie had talked to a number of counselors around Atlanta, making appointments and building a reputation so that these professionals, who had never met me, talked to me or ever seen me were saying I was dangerous, anti-Semitic, and evil.

I called Dr. Pittman and faced him with these charges. In response, he said, "How dare you try to separate a man from his children. How dare you take your children and put them in a cult and seclude them from the world. What kind of credentials do you think you have to teach your children?" He considered my religious beliefs and home schooling to be harmful and cultic.

I informed him that it had been the decision of both Andy and me to home school our children and that it was just recently that Andy had refused to allow it anymore. I also told him that Andy agreed with me that the children would attend private school if his mom would pay for it. When his mom committed to pay for their education, I found a good school and began the testing and enrollment process. Andy then refused

Dr. Pittman said, "Andy is passive aggressive. I need you both in my office as soon as possible. I do not agree with divorce. It does damage to the children. The legal system is slow, and I'm going to get this turned around."

Andy agreed to see Dr. Pittman with me, and we went to see him right away. Andy began complaining saying I was overly religious. He didn't like the books I read, the videos I watched, prayer, and the reading of the Bible. However, he rarely witnessed me doing any one of these.

Dr. Pittman said, "Being involved with the church is not bad, but religiosity is very bad," and "Milledgeville [mental institution] is full of people with a religiosity problem." When I asked him to define the difference, Dr. Pittman said, "Religiosity is when people think that God only talks through them...They condemn the world...They are the only ones who hear from God...All their sentences include the word 'God,'" he said. "That is not me," I told Dr. Pittman. Dr. Pittman turned to Andy and said, "When she talks like this, just consider her crazy. Why does it have to bother you?" As we left the office, Dr. Pittman turned to Andy and said, "If you think home schooling is damaging to children, divorce is far more damaging."

Five days later we returned to Dr. Pittman's office. In the waiting room Andy picked a fight with me regarding the care of our children that day. Our appointment with Dr. Pittman was at 10:00 a.m. My mother was at Piedmont Hospital following a heart attack and was scheduled for a catherization at 11:00 a.m. to see the extent of damage and where the blockage was. It was to be determined whether they would do angioplasty or open heart surgery that afternoon. I left Amanda and Jessica in the care of Doreen Buben, a good friend who had cared for our children a number of times previously. Doreen is a home school mom with four children, two of whom are the same ages as Amanda and Jessica. She could keep them current with their school lessons, and the children would enjoy their friends. Andy knew Doreen, and he had never objected to her caring for the children before. She offered to keep the girls all day, to feed them dinner and to allow them to spend the night if necessary, so that I could be with my mother.

Andy became furious when he found out where the children were. "You always leave me out of everything," he said. "What if I want to spend time with them?" I told him, "If you want to go pick them up and spend time with them, you are welcome." He said, "You try to cut me out of their lives entirely." I told him, "I am responsible for their care every day. You work at AAMCO every day. You have never taken any initiative in their care. If you want to spend time with them, then take the day off work and go pick them up. I'm not going to sit here and have a fight with you over this." I left the room to get a drink of water. When I returned Andy began his attack on me again.

When we were called into Dr. Pittman's office, Andy angrily said, "I can't believe that I have to fight to see my children. She tries to separate me from my children in every way. I can't have a relationship with them at all. She wants to say I'm a child molester all the time. I can't even go in and help my own children with a dirty bottom." I told Dr. Pittman I wanted some healthy boundaries to be put into place. I had already spoken with Dr. Stephen King who told me that if Andy continued to be nude around the children and to behave in the manner in which he was behaving with them that I should call the authorities and get a court order against him, since it was damaging to the children.

Dr. Pittman said to me, "We need to talk about your problem with nudity." He said, "People grow up in nudist colonies every day and turn out just fine."

All of a sudden Andy brought up the subject of my being "overly religious" again, and Dr. Pittman sat back in his chair, put his finger to his chin and appeared to be thinking, and then said, "Shakespeare is wonderful. But the Bible needs to be taken out of your home and burned. It has caused wars in Ireland. It has caused wars in the Middle East. It has caused wars all around the world."

"Well I won't be removing the Bible or burning it," I said. Andy yelled out, "Defiance! This is what she is always doing - defying me!" I looked at Andy and said, "Have a great life without me, Andy. I won't be burning the Bible." Then all three of us were talking on top of each other, all with great emotion. I was angry. Andy was angry. Dr. Pittman was very dramatic.

Dr. Pittman got on his knees on the floor in front of me and with raised hands and great emphasis said, "You think you have a direct link with God. You see yourself as having no sin. You think you are perfect." "I don't think I'm perfect," I protested. He continued to say, "Yes, you think you are perfect. You don't think you're like the rest of us. You think you have a direct link with God."

While he was saying this, I was responding in anger asking Dr. Pittman, "Do you think it is good for a six year old to lie on her father's naked body? Do you think a father should dress his ten-year-old daughter? If I stripped my clothes off and walked outside nude, do you think anyone would have trouble with nudity?"

At the same time, Andy was spewing lewd statements about sexuality, such as, "You fondle them while they are sleeping," and "Yeah, they get in bed with me and lay on my hard penis."

Dr. Pittman got off the floor. I said, "Dr. Pittman, evidently Andy has had conversations with you describing me like a person who either needs to be put in a mental institution or a prison." Dr. Pittman said, "Yes, and we need to set up an appointment for tomorrow and determine which." I told him I would not be returning as I picked up my purse and walked to the door. He followed me saying, "That's right, you think you've got a direct link to God. You don't think you're like the rest of us normal people. You think you're perfect. You've got a direct link to God."

I turned and said, "You're sick!" and I closed his door.

I share this knowing how crazy it sounds, and it was crazy. I immediately documented the meeting. I then called Dr. Shirley Parsons who told me that she had several female patients to whom Dr. Pittman had done great damage. She had heard other crazy stories as well, but she said this took the cake. Later, another therapist shared with me that Dr. Pittman is considered a nut amongst the professionals.

Dr. Pittman has written several books on relationships. I found his views about sex between children and adults to be similar if not the same as Gardner and Underwager, whose views I share later in the book. He writes, "Matings between women who have been around and boys who have not are generally portrayed as acts of generosity and mercy, rather than as child molesting. As long as the older women don't expect the liaison to be permanent, they won't frighten boys who want to be sexual but aren't ready yet to be grown-up."[14]

Dr. Pittman has comments from Warren Farrell, Ph.D., on the cover of one of his books. Farrell is another pro-pedophile whose statements include , "When I get my most glowing positive cases, 6 out of 200, the incest is part of the family's open, sensual style of life, wherein sex is an outgrowth of warmth and affection. It is more likely that the father has good sex with his wife, and his wife is likely to know and approve - and in one or two cases to join in."[15] Frank Pittman has also aligned himself with individuals involved with Ralph Underwager's False Memory Syndrome Foundation. Is it any surprise that the Titelmans befriended this man?

Within a month, Andy declared he was seeking full custody of Amanda and Jessica. It became immediately apparent he was on a fast and furious mission to do everything in his power to discredit me and take the children from me. I had always been the one responsible for every aspect of the girl's lives. Andy was indifferent to their needs and treated them as an intrusion in his and Katie's life for the most part.

All of a sudden Andy began competing with me and wanting the children to be with him. Katie was no longer living with us, and food was no longer an issue. He wanted to buy the groceries and cook our meals again. He became the girl's greatest playmate and indulged them with candy, gifts, toys, and activities and he began buying them clothes and shoes. He would come home late at night after being out with Katie and would awaken the girls and give them sweet treats. He began whispering with them and having secrets like he did with Katie. There was a forceful, very active undermining going on that was wearing me out physically and emotionally. He requested that a guardian *ad litem* be appointed by the court and an attorney by the name of Diane Woods was selected to represent Amanda and Jessica's "best interest" in the custody case. I would have never imagined when I first heard the name Diane Woods that her "representation" of the "best interest" of my daughters was to be their wholesale devastation. Nor would I have ever guessed that Ms. Woods would be the ignorant and dangerous person she turned out to be.

Andy began telling Amanda and Jessica that I didn't love them. Every time they displayed affection toward me he called them idiots and said I was making them act this way.

I enrolled in a Divorce Care Class at the church that I attended once a week for several weeks. The first time I went Amanda and Jessica followed me to my car saying goodbye over and over and saying they didn't want me to leave. They went back to the house when I closed my car door. As I was backing the car out of the garage, Amanda came running to my car crying, "Daddy called us idiots." I calmed her down and told her goodbye again, and she went back to the door where Andy was now standing. He angrily said something to her. She ran back to me again upset and said, "Daddy called me a tattle-tale and says we talk to you too much." Andy then yelled out angrily at me, "You've brainwashed them." Later Amanda said that Andy called Katie at her grandmother's house and told her the kids were holding onto my car, "acting like idiots," and that I was "turning them into idiots."

Amanda began expressing during the day that she was fearful that her daddy was taping our conversations. She said if Daddy heard her say she wanted to be with me or if she wanted me to hold her, he would get angry with her. Both Amanda and Jessica shared that their father told them he wouldn't love them if they wanted to be with me.

One day while I was at my attorney's office we received a fax from Pam Gray, one of Andy's attorneys. It stated that I was not bathing or cleaning the children and that Andy was having to medicate them for sores caused by poor hygiene. I immediately called the pediatrician's office and asked if I could bring the children in for a physical, that it was important that I come right away. I left my attorney's office, picked up Amanda and Jessica from Doreen's home. I went straight to the doctor's office. It was documented that my children were clean, and without sores caused by uncleanliness or neglect.

Andy and then his attorneys accused me of not cleaning, cooking, or caring for the children and of dressing inappropriately around them. They accused me of teaching my children only religion and claimed they were being neglected in their academics. They said I wasn't giving my children medication or taking them to the doctor when they were sick.

Andy began to call the children constantly throughout the day. Anytime he couldn't reach them on the phone, he got angry saying he was going to have to buy them a pager so that he could know where they were at all times. I saw him developing a very unhealthy, needy, close relationship with Amanda and Jessica like he had with Katie. He would come home from work and tell me to put away the food I was cooking because he was going to cook for the children, that they didn't want what I was cooking.

His behavior became more bizarre than ever. One night I baked a cake and iced it. Andy picked up Amanda and sat her on top of the counter next to the cake. He began to laugh hysterically (like the laugh of Mozart in the movie, Amadeus) as he started beating the cake with his fists and tearing it apart. He got Amanda to do the same until the cake was totally demolished and a huge mess created.

Every night he would do things that would cause damage or great messes in the house, and then he would leave it for me to take care of and clean up. He would take games, puzzles and cards, and he and the children would laugh and run and throw these things in the air everywhere. The house was on the market and being shown regularly, and I was constantly picking up after Andy's deliberate destructive behaviors.

After the children were put to bed, Andy would go in, turn the lights on and start picking up the kids and throwing them in the bed over and over again until the bed linens were torn off. The kids would laugh and become hyperactive, jumping on the bed, yelling, and often times one of them would get hurt and begin crying. Then Andy would leave, and I would have to go back in, settle the girls down and make up the bed and get them ready to sleep again.

During these months Andy volunteered to help in Jessica's classroom at school. Her teacher later shared with me that she would never allow him back because he caused the children to become so riled up, to become loud, disrespectful, and unsettled. Andy also became a volunteer with the Cobb County Juvenile Court with whom Diane Woods was affiliated, and he began training.

During the late fall, Jessica got a large bruise on one of her calves. I asked her how she got it, and she said she didn't know. I had no idea what caused it. It wasn't long after that my attorney received a picture of the bruise from Pam Gray stating that I had beat Jessica with a wooden spoon and left this bruise on her leg. Andy has declared this is one of many bruises I have given the girls from my beating them. This was outrageous. I have never caused one mark on my children.

Amanda came running to me down the hall one night while I was helping Jessica. She was upset and accused me of putting a scratch on her back, saying her dad said I did. I told her I had not put anything on her back. I looked at her, and there was nothing, and I told her. Andy who also had come into the room said, "Amanda, I didn't say that." Amanda cried, "You did too, and you said if I told Mommy I would get in trouble."

My personal files began to disappear. My keys disappeared one day and then appeared two days later in the back of a utility drawer. Other personal items were disappearing as well. One night I entered Andy's car, and I found my address book in his glove compartment.

My first deposition was over the course of two full days and most of it was on the subject of religion and home school. Pam Gray, who represented Andy in all of the out of court activities such as interrogatories, depositions, interactions with other attorneys, and with the guardian *ad litem,* was of small stature and presented herself as a very nasty and angry woman. Her short hair fell onto her forehead, down over her eyes and onto her nose. She frequently threw her head to the side and back to throw the hair out of her face. It always fell right back down over her eyes, and I often thought she was hiding behind her hair. She wore a small cross on a necklace and toyed with it between three fingers as she hypocritically screamed at me about my beliefs in God. Her face and lips were lined with angry determination.

She found it reprehensible that I held God in higher esteem than my husband or my children. In Deuteronomy 6:5-7 God commands from each and every one of us, "Thou shalt love the Lord your God, with all of your heart, with all of your soul, and with all of your strength. And these words which I command you today shall be in your heart. You shall teach them diligently to your children, and shall talk of them when you sit in your house, when you walk by the way, when you lie down, and when you rise up." Those who understand this commandment know that God is love. This is the meaning of the first of the Ten Commandments, "Thou shalt have no other Gods before me." It is when we love God more than anything else that we can truly love and give to others.

Pam Gray was merciless. Everything that had the word God or Jesus on it that my children or I had ever written or read was attacked. She rolled her eyes at me as I responded to her questions, and she continued to ask the same questions over and over again. My attorney, Hylton Dupree, never objected to her hostility and form of questioning nor to her repeated attacks on me.

The ABeka school curriculum I used to educate Amanda, who was then in the first grade, is used by most every Christian school across America and is rated as one of the best programs of study. Studies have shown that children who have been educated by ABeka on a whole score much higher on their SAT's than any other curriculum used in any school setting. ABeka is Christian-based, and therefore, has references to the Bible and to God throughout the reading and writing program.

Ms. Gray was adamant that all I taught my children was religion, that the program had no academic training whatsoever. When she didn't like my answer she answered what she wanted me to say. And I would again answer the truth, and she would reverse it again, like a ping-pong match going back and forth. She so badly wanted to make me out to be a monster who used the face of religion to harm my children, hoping to prove that I was mentally warped in my religious views.

She asked me what kind of music I played for my children who were then six and four, and I answered that they listened to different kinds of music like the Beatles, classical, worship and children's songs. She defiantly sneered as she blurted, what like "Farmer in the Dell," as though this were totally inappropriate. Andy had already complained that he wanted them to be listening to the music that the high school kids at McEachern High School voted "number one," Hootie and the Blowfish. Then Pam huffed and said, "So you consider the Beatles Godly music?" I answered, "Yes, but I do not want my children listening to music that talks about sex, drugs, suicide and death."

I was very concerned about disturbances I was seeing in Amanda and Jessica such as low self-esteem, night terrors, and fear of people. Amanda was having physical distress as well - chronic stomachaches, headaches, sinus congestion and fatigue. I also was concerned with all the allegations that Andy and his attorneys were making. Dr. Stephen King suggested that I have a therapist see Amanda. On the advice of my attorney, I asked psychologists, Dr. Jacqueline Hill and Dr. Lynn Brentnall, to do educational and psychological assessments.

The educational assessments showed my children had benefitted from home school. They were intelligent and performing above average. But there were concerns with the results of the psychological testing. The examinations indicated there was a problem in their relationship with their father. There was possibly abuse occurring, or the children were being set up for abuse. There was also an issue with secrets.

Jessica was four years and eleven months old when she told me that one week prior, her father took a bath with her while I had taken Amanda to Home Depot to get items for a science project due the next day. I was horrified as she described the details of what had happened that night.

Jessica said that her father laid down in the tub on his back, and she jumped off the ledge of the garden tub over and over again onto his tummy. She said her daddy bounced up and down splashing water all over the room. She told me not to worry though that they cleaned it all up before I got home so that I wouldn't know about it. She shared that they got out of the tub and slid all over the floor and then ran through the house naked bringing a vase with flowers back with them to the bathroom. She said the flowers were put beside the tub, and they got back in with Jessica sitting on his tummy and splashing water all over. Jessica said her daddy occasionally picked up the vase of flowers and jumped up in the water exclaiming, "hachueee" loudly. She also said that her daddy was going to give her a gift if she didn't tell Mommy about the bath. She said, "Daddy must have forgotten because he didn't give me a gift."

Dr. Brentnall, Dr. Hill, and I became more alarmed and suspicious of serious abuse when Jessica reported the bizarre bath her father took with her while Amanda and I were gone.

I met with Diane Woods in April, 1999, only one time since her appointment in March, 1999, to the present date, January, 2003. I detailed to her the trauma I had experienced in my marriage with Andy. I gave her a 31 page marital history that I had typed in response to two questions that were asked of me in the interrogatories when the divorce was first filed - what Andy had done and what I had done to cause the divorce and why Andy would not be a good custodial parent for his children.

I told her about the emotional abuse, the rejection, the insults, Andy's possessive behavior, and the crazy making in our home. I told her about Andy's sick relationship with Katie and the bizarre behaviors between the two of them. I told her about the bath he took with Jessica and about what my brothers and friends had said. I told her about the pornography and about the Sterling Club. I told her about Dr. Hill and Dr. Brentnall.

She asked me to tell her the worst thing I had ever done in the marriage. I readily told her that I had recently become so infuriated with Andy because of his continual attack of me regarding Katie, that I walked away from him and said, "Why don't you just go fuck Katie." Ms. Woods said she didn't blame me for saying that. Of course, I said.this to Andy while we were alone far out on our property. No one else heard me, and I'm certainly not proud of it.

When we sold our house, and we began to live in different places, we went to court regarding custody of the children. We learned at that time that Andy had been planning divorce since 1995 yet had only spoke of divorce since 1997. He filed for divorce in 1998. It was during these years that Andy and Katie had been seeing a number of different psychologists and psychiatrists speaking negatively about me to people I had never met or talked with in my life and still to this day have not. Andy reported that these counselors told him that I was anti-Semitic and a very dangerous woman. He said that I hated minorities of any kind.

Also during this time, I received in the mail anti-Semitic hate newspapers addressed to me but never ordered by me. I was aware of Andy writing letters to counselors, Dr. Mark Crawford and Dr. William Van Horn, speaking outright lies about me. I was furious that he would manipulate and distort the truth to discredit me.

Diane Woods' job was to represent the best interests of the children. The judge expected her to investigate and to tell him what to do. Instead, Ms. Woods told my attorney that I was a liar. She received reports from the various doctors. She totally ignored the reports from Dr. Lynn Brentnall and Dr. Jacqueline Hill who told her about the psychological results and that something traumatic had happened to the children. She totally disregarded the report she received from Dr. Shirley Parsons who told her "Andy's behavior was 'off the wall,'" that "he did not realize his behavior was not normal," and that "he could be convincing up front but that his behavior was 'bizarre.'" She totally disregarded the letters of numerous people who knew the children and me and had reported their witness to behaviors in the home and in the community that were of concern.

In the first report Diane Woods wrote to Judge James Bodiford, the judge assigned to our custody case, in May, 1999, she stated that she put most of her emphasis on the information relayed to her by Dr. Frank Pittman, saying that he told her he had seen us for eight years and knew us far better than anyone else. Ms. Woods discounted everything I had given her. She disregarded that Dr. Pittman was a family friend of the Titelman's who had only seen us early in our marriage due to Katie's stomachaches and on two occasions after the divorce was filed. She ignored that Dr. Shirley Parsons had seen us for a number of years for marital counseling.

In her report, she stated that I was trying to "alienate" the children from their father by making up all kinds of accusations against Andy, and that I should have very limited contact with the children. She said that Andy would more likely make the children available to me than I would to him, and that I would cause him to be alienated from his children.

For Ms. Woods to have been so concerned for the children to have access to both parents is cruelly amusing. For over two years, she and Andy have done everything in their power and have been successful in keeping Amanda and Jessica from seeing me or communicating with me.

My attorney, Hylton Dupree, told me that judges 99% of the time will do exactly what the guardian *ad litem* tells them to do. He said it would be very risky to go into court and argue our case, that I should attempt to settle with Andy for 50% temporary custody until we could go in for a final hearing and present our entire case.

I didn't know what to do. All the evidence indicated I had good reason to be concerned that Andy was harming our children and would hurt them much more if he had so much access to them. I listened to Mr. Dupree's warning, and agreed to do what he thought was best. The attorneys worked out a 50/50 custody arrangement where the children would rotate a week with Andy and then a week with me.

During that first week of separation, Andy wouldn't let me talk to the girls. My phone calls were not answered. Amanda and Jessica did not hear my messages, and my pages to Andy were not returned.

Robin Blankenship, their piano teacher, called me concerned. She said that Andy had brought the girls to their piano lesson, but that she felt there was something very wrong. She said they could not concentrate at all, especially Amanda, and that the lesson was a total waste. There was something very unnatural about their relationship with him that alarmed her. She said they were obviously trying very hard to please him.

When I finally saw Amanda and Jessica again, they were stiff as boards. Their bodies did not respond to my hugs. They were withdrawn and unable to focus on anything, and unlike the little girls I had known just a week before. Jessica's eyes were glazed over, and there was seriousness on both Amanda's and Jessica's faces.

I picked the girls up at Andy's house, and as we were about to leave, Amanda told me she woke up in the middle of the night with vomiting and diarrhea. She complained of fleabites. Andy snapped at her saying, "You don't have flea bites." Any time in the past she complained of physical distress, he would tell her it was all in her head. We left his house and Amanda told me she found fleas on her ankles. When we got home, I examined her and counted 73 fleabites and immediately called the pediatrician's office and made an appointment to see the doctor that day. Jessica seemed unaffected and at the most had two or three bites.

The girls informed me that their father had told them I was out of town, didn't care enough about them to even call them all week, and that he didn't know where I was so they couldn't get in touch with me. He told them over and over again that I am stupid. The things Andy was saying to them made me sick.

I was still trying to complete Amanda's home schooling as she had just a few lessons left, but it was impossible. Amanda could no longer even tell me what one plus one equals. Prior to going with her father for a week we were studying tables up to eighteen and counting by twos, threes, fives and tens.

During the week Amanda and Jessica expressed that they did not want to go back to their father. Amanda asked how long it would be before they had to go back. She said she hoped it would be "a hundred billion days." Amanda said she wanted to talk to the judge, and I told her she was not allowed but that she could write Diane Woods and Judge Bodiford a letter. She said she wanted to right away. I told her she should write down everything she would want the judge to know and that she should write down all her feelings and all the things she thought were wrong. I gave her letter to Mr. Dupree. He told me he could not give it to Judge Bodiford or to Diane Woods. This is the letter she wrote. The words and writing are Amanda's. However, I helped her with some of the spelling.

June 1, 1999

Dear Judge Bradford and
Mrs. Woods,

Daddy has us tell lies.
Mommy told us that we can't
come to court and tell you
important things like I really
want to live with mommy.
Shhh I don't want daddy
to hear. He will get angry.
Please write back soon to tell me
that stuff and tell me.
I love Mommy please
believe this letter.

Daddy ruined Jessica's silly songs by telling lies on the recorder. Daddy calls mommy names like stupid and me names like tattel tale and liar. Daddy won't let me call mommy and I really want to live with Mommy.

Sincerely,

Amanda Titelman
Wendy's daughter

The girls went back with their father the following Sunday. I called Sunday night and Monday, but no one answered. On Monday night at 10:05 p.m. Amanda and Jessica called me. Amanda began crying saying she wanted to come home. She said she couldn't see her friends when she was with her daddy. She asked me what day it was and how many days before she could be with me. She asked several times when she was coming home to me.

One more difficult week went by with very little communication until finally I could go get my girls. I pulled up to Andy's house in Sandy Springs on Mt. Vernon Road. The girls were in the yard playing with a little girl who lived next door, and Andy was standing at the door. Amanda and Jessica had the same clothes on that they wore to their fathers the Sunday before, even their dirty underwear. They had not worn any of the clothes that I had sent along with them, and I learned that Andy was telling everyone that I didn't give him any clothes for the girls and that he had to buy all new things for them. Their hair was not brushed and hung tangled in their face. Later when I brushed their hair I found Amanda's hair was broken off in the back. She said, "Daddy rips the ponytail holders out of my hair and hurts me."

When the girls saw me they did not come to me. They went to the door and Andy took them inside. When they came out they hesitantly walked to me. When I hugged them they were like bricks and totally unresponsive. Jessica's eyes were totally glazed over.

After we left Andy's house, the girls began to say how glad they were to see me and to be with me. I asked why they didn't seem happy at first. They both said, "Daddy gets really angry if he thinks we love you."

We went to Old Country Buffet for dinner. Amanda said to me, "I hurt mommy." "Where?" I asked. She pointed to her genital area. She said she had been hurting all week, but when I asked her why she hurt, she told me she didn't know. She complained that her stomach hurt and that it had hurt a lot during the week. I was terrified. I was watching my daughters deteriorate so quickly before my very eyes. At bedtime I sat between the girls in bed and read to them. Amanda began telling me, "Every day Daddy tells us you don't love us." She also said that their father bathed them and would not let them bathe themselves.

Amanda continued to complain of pain the following day and in the evening asked me to examine her. She pointed to her vaginal area when I asked where she hurt. She was red and swollen and her vaginal opening appeared abnormal.

We went into the den where Jessica and their friend, Jenna, were playing. We were temporarily staying with a friend, Zoe Hermanson and her daughter, until our rental house in Kennesaw where we were to live was vacated. While Jessica and Jenna danced to music that was playing, Amanda and I sat on the floor Indian style, facing each other.

Amanda began to tell me things her father was saying to her and Jessica. She said, "Daddy says we are going to have a new mom. He keeps telling us that you don't love us and that he is going to get married again so that we can have a mama who loves us." I told her that I would be the only mother she would ever have, that no one could replace me, but that maybe one day she would have a stepmother, but that was different. We talked at length about my love for her and Jessica. I told her that Daddy did not want them to be with me or for them to love me and that is why he is telling them these things. She kept saying she wanted to live with me and that her father makes her say that she wants to live with him. I asked, "Why would you say you want to live with him if you don't?" She told me that he gets very angry if she says she doesn't. At the same time she put her hands into fists, straightened her arms and body, distorted her face, and shook her arms. Amanda said that her dad would take her outside and make her say things on a recorder that were untrue, things like "I want to live with Daddy," "Mommy beats me," and "Daddy never took a bath with Jessica." She said he would not allow her to come into the house until she said these things. "He keeps saying, say the right thing," she said.

I told Amanda that as long as she was willing to lie that Daddy would use those tapes and that she and Jessica would not live with me, and Daddy would win. She immediately said, "No Mommy, God is going to win, and we will live with you."

I told her that as long as God's children were disobedient to Him, that He could do nothing. I told her she needed to tell the truth about everything, about when Daddy is saying bad things about me and forcing her to lie.

I also told her that she needed to tell if anyone was touching her wrongly. I asked, "Do you know what that means?" She said, "No." I told her it is when someone touches you in your private area. I asked her if anyone was doing that to her. She silently nodded her head yes. I asked who and she said her father. I asked, "What is he doing?" Then she showed me. She began rubbing me between my legs with her hand. I told her it was wrong for Daddy to do that.

The pain of hearing this was so great. Tears were spilling out of my eyes. I dismissed myself saying I was getting a glass of water, and I called my friend, Jan, and poured my heart out to her as I cried. Even though I suspected this, I did not want to believe it. I hoped that it wasn't true.

That night at bedtime I talked with both Amanda and Jessica. Jessica said her father touched her sexually as well, saying it happened "morning, noon, and night." Amanda said that he would tickle her all over making her laugh and then he would begin tickling her "there." She pointed between her legs. She said, "Sometimes he puts his hand inside my clothes and hurts me." They said the little girl they played with that lived next door to Daddy told them she didn't like their father because she didn't like the way he touched her. I told them that daddies should never touch their daughters private areas and that Daddy was doing something very wrong. They said Daddy told them they could not tell anyone, and that I was trying to get him in trouble.

When I knew for sure what Andy was doing, I did everything a mother is supposed to do. I took my daughters to Dr. Brentnall and Dr. Hill. I went to my attorney. I went to the Department of Family and Children's Services (DFACS). I did what my attorney said to do. I did what Dr. Brentnall told me to do. Dr. Brentnall did everything she could to try and protect the girls. She called DFACS and reported the abuse as was required by law. [Her written report may be found in Appendix F, Exhibit A.] She called the guardian *ad litem*, Diane Woods. She called my attorney, Hylton Dupree.

The Department of Family and Children's Services had assigned a social worker to interview Amanda and Jessica.

However, Diane Woods immediately took control. She had a different social worker assigned to the case, Julie Hall. Ms. Woods then called the Kennesaw Police Department and had Detective Amy Henderson assigned to the case. Neither Andy nor I lived in Kennesaw, and by law Kennesaw should not have been involved. This caused a delay of several days. Dr. Brentnall wanted to see the children again to videotape her interview with Amanda, but Diane Woods was adamant that this would not happen. She said she would have it taped at the DFACS office.

On June 23, 1999 Julie Hall and Detective Amy Henderson interviewed Amanda. Jessica shyly refused to talk with them. Diane Woods watched the interview on closed-circuit television. Julie Hall told me that her interview with Amanda was confidential and she could not tell me the content except that Amanda had told them her father was touching her in a sexual way, and therefore, I should not return the children to him for his regular visitation.

Later I asked my attorney about the videotape and asked him to obtain a copy. He told me that would be impossible, that DFACS will not release their records and that a subpoena would not be of any value.

After the abuse was reported, I began to feel relieved that my daughters would be protected. I thought I would no longer have to worry about them being hurt by their father again. The girls and I went to a friends home to stay where Andy couldn't find us. Diane Woods sent a letter to my attorney saying that visitation with their father was suspended pending further investigation. However, Andy and his mother began searching for us and threatening my friends and family. I was very concerned for the girls' safety.

Andy and his attorneys filed a contempt motion against me for not returning the children to Andy for his normal visitation. Over one year later after I obtained my file from Mr. Dupree, I found a letter Andy had written to Diane Woods during the time I was told by Ms. Woods not to return Amanda and Jessica to him. Andy wrote that he took his mother with him to pick up the children *as Diane requested him to do*, but that I had kidnaped the children and that he had filed a police report. I couldn't believe Ms. Woods was telling me not to return them to Andy and telling Andy to take his mom with him and go pick them up.

Diane Woods, who was watching the DFACS interview on a closed-circuit television, told Julie Hall and Amy Henderson that Amanda was not credible and that she was lying. She told Mr. Dupree that because Amanda looked down and away before answering the question of what her father did to her indicated to Ms. Woods that Amanda had to think about what I told her to say. Ms. Woods told everyone that I was a liar who was "willing to win at all costs" in an attempt to separate the father from his children or that I was "delusional and overly obsessed about sexual issues" thereby creating this entire story. Andy even wrote in a statement given to the police, "D. Woods told me that Wendy is the biggest 2nd biggest liar she has ever seen."

We also much later learned from the Kennesaw Police Department Incident Report written by Detective Amy Henderson following her interview with Amanda further evidence that Diane Woods had misled the investigation, thereby successfully railroading any protection for the girls. Detective Henderson wrote,

> After the interviews were completed, myself and Hall met with Diane Woods, the Guardian at Litum [sic], and she provided us with a letter that had been sent to Judge Bodiford in reference to the child custody issues. Woods advised that the family had been to numerous counselors, and none of the counselors had made referrals to DFACS or any local police dept with concerns of molestation. The only referral made was by the current counselor, and the counselor is being paid by Ms Titelman.

And she replied, "They are already damaged kids. What's a little more damage?"

We went to court shortly after the DFACS interview but never went before the judge. Ms. Woods came into a conference room with Mr. Dupree, his paralegal, Kyle Broussard, and me and told us that Andy would be picking the children up at 6:00 p.m. that evening. She had asked Andy's mother to be his supervisor until a polygraph test was completed on both Andy and me. When I told her that it was totally insane to assign Andy's mother as his supervisor, she said Andy deserved to see his kids and could not afford to hire someone, and that was that. She said I would have to be supervised as well because she believed I was coaching the children to make these accusations.

She went on to say that if she heard me say anything bad about Andy that she would take my children away from me and put them in a foster home where I would never see them again. I asked, "How could you hurt my children like that?" And she replied, "They are already damaged kids. What's a little more damage?"

My attorney told me to be quiet that she could and would do it. I knew then I was dealing with someone who had no conscience and was very evil and dangerous.

Lynn and Jim Palmer, with whom the girls and I had been staying, agreed to supervise me during this time. After this meeting when I went back to their home where the children were, I had to tell them that their father would be picking them up that evening at 6:00 p.m. They began crying. Amanda clung to me saying, "No, Mommy, No. Don't make us go with Daddy." Jessica hid behind a wall with fear in her eyes. It was gut wrenching to see my children like this and so sickening and unbelievable that I had been ordered to turn them over to a man who was harming them so badly.

When their father knocked at the door, I opened it, and the children put smiles on their faces as though nothing were wrong. Andy dramatically and in a mocking tone of voice said to them, "Oh, you are terrified." They then went with their father as they were required to do.

When the children returned to me a week later, their bodies again were like bricks. They would not make eye contact, and they were very distressed. They complained to the Palmers and me that both their father and grandmother were screaming at them all week about their having disclosed the abuse. They said their father was still hurting them in the bath, when they got dressed and when they were on the toilet. Amanda complained of headaches and she said her grandmother screamed at her that the only thing wrong with her head was what I had put in it. Andy had promised them toys, and they said they wanted the toys, but they didn't want to go back because they were afraid of him. But each week I had to keep sending them back, and the girls continued to tell us that their father was still molesting them.

On one occasion when Andy came to pick up the children he had left the house and then returned within five minutes. He was pounding on the door and rang the doorbell over and over again and was screaming at the top of his lungs. We heard him throw something and then he screamed all the way back to his car. When we opened the door we found the girls suitcase we had packed with their clothing. He screamed at us from his car and then sped away.

We had videotaped the clothes that were packed in the bags because Andy always claimed that I sent nothing. In his course of interrogating the girls, he found out about the video and returned with the clothes.

The Palmers did not want to put up with his abusive behavior and his harassing phone calls they had been receiving, so they called the police. They said they did not want him returning to their neighborhood or calling them again. The police officer that came said we should not put up with this behavior and that he was going to call Mr. Titelman.

After the officer talked with Andy, he wrote up his report. We learned months later the officer wrote that the Palmers didn't like Andy's phone calls, but that Andy was just a concerned father. The Palmers called the Kennesaw Police Department and asked that the report be amended to reflect what actually happened. They said the officer no longer worked for them, and therefore, the report could not be amended.

Every time I was able to get the girls on the phone per the court order, they told me Daddy told them to hang up. Later they would tell me that he held the phone so that he could hear every word that was said, and he would tell them what to say to me.

During the week of July 6, 1999, while Andy was supposed to be supervised by his mother, Amanda called me. She was whispering to me and then said, "I can't talk, Daddy is coming." I could hear Andy screaming at her. Amanda yelled at him, "The judge said I'm supposed to be able to talk to Mommy without you being here." A moment later Andy was on the phone yelling at me. I said three times, "Get off the phone, I am talking to my daughter." He hung the phone up disconnecting my call.

On July 11th when I called, Andy took the phone from the children and stated to me, "I am going to make things difficult for you."

Lynn and Jim Palmer were told by Mr. Dupree that Diane Woods had left a message with him saying they were not supervising me appropriately. Lynn and Jim both tried calling Diane Woods and left several messages to talk with her about her accusation. One or both of the Palmers were with the children and me at all times, and they wanted to know why Ms. Woods would claim such a thing. Ms. Woods never returned their call.

Ms. Woods ordered a polygraph test to be taken, and Mr. Dupree agreed that I would take the test. He and Ms. Woods also agreed that a certain Mr. Peal would do this test, that he was the only one in the area who was qualified to do a polygraph of this type. When it came time for the test to be given I was told that Diane Woods asked Detective Nix with Cobb County Police Department to administer the test instead. When I questioned why the switch, I was told that Mr. Peal was not available. After the test was given Ms. Woods reported that Andy "passed with flying colors" and that my test was "inconclusive."

> Polygraph testing fails to meet standards for validity for application to child sexual abuse cases.

Although I was highly concerned that individuals had skewed the results of the tests to be in the favor of Andy, I later learned that it is common knowledge among professionals that polygraphs should never be used in assessing allegations of child sexual abuse except to get confessions.

In an article published by the *Journal of Child Sexual Abuse*, A Critique of the Validity of Polygraph Testing in Child Sexual Abuse Cases,[16] Theodore P. Cross and Leonard Saxe report the following:

...[T]he nature of child sexual abuse allegations makes polygraph testing particularly problematic.

The nature of polygraph examinations, and available research on factors influencing the test, suggest that characteristics of the sexual offender, the investigation

97

and the social context of the text make inferences from polygraph tests on child sexual abuse especially prone to error. Among the considerations that could influence test outcomes are sexual offender perception and memory, the emotional arousal engendered by sexual abuse investigations, and the effect of base rates of guilt and innocence in the population of suspected sexual offenders who are tested.

If polygraph examinees ...rationalize that it was not a misdeed, they may not believe they are lying and may not become anxious when asked a relevant question on a polygraph examination.

A number of clinicians have detailed how sexual offenders deny and distort their perception of the abuse. Offender denial can take several forms, including denial of commission of acts, denial of the fantasy and planning leading to the abuse, and denial of responsibility for the abuse. Offenders often rationalize that children are not hurt by the sexual contact but instead consent to it, enjoy it and learn from it. Some offenders may even commit abuse in a partially dissociated state, making it difficult for them to recall the nature of the abuse during normal consciousness. For many offenders, such distortions seem to be important to prevent their own awareness of the consequences of their behavior.

If perpetrators do not consciously believe they committed sexual abuse, they may not become anxious when asked about it on a polygraph test, because they are convinced they are telling the truth. In some cases, they have considerable social support for their denial. Even when perpetrators realize there was a physical encounter, they may rationalize their behavior enough to feel that they are responding truthfully to polygraph questions about abusive incidents.

The fact that sexual offenders' perception of the abuse is often distorted raises concern about the validity of the polygraph. To the extent that perpetrators successfully alter their own understanding of the abuse, they may successfully conceal their deception during a polygraph test.

The use of polygraph tests in child sexual abuse matters raises a number of specific concerns. Offenders who have a distorted understanding of their offense may be especially able to escape detection. Innocent subjects facing an emotionally arousing allegation of child sexual abuse may be falsely judged to be deceptive. Systematic use of polygraph testing may yield unacceptable numbers of false negatives and false positives because of skewed base rates. Polygraph testing fails to meet standards for validity for application to child sexual abuse cases.

Much of the enthusiasm for polygraph testing stems from its effect of frightening subjects and inducing confessions. Such effects, however, exist apart from the test's accuracy.

The Kennesaw Police Department and the Department of Family and Children's Services relied on the polygraph test and closed their investigation due to Andy's purported "passing" of the polygraph test. Studies show that the best proof is the children's testimony. But after that all allegations of abuse past, present and future were disregarded as bogus and as lies told by the children, people in the community, abuse experts, and other medical professionals, supervisors, friends, and me.

We went to court again August 9, 1999. No one testified before Judge Bodiford. He came into the courtroom and stated, "Kennesaw Police Department and the Guardian *ad litem*, everyone agrees, the Department of Children and Family Services, the Kennesaw Police Department, the agency investigating these allegations, and the Guardian *ad litem* agree that there has been no substantiation of sexual abuse, none. All parties are of the same agreement. Allegations made by Mrs. Titelman are not substantiated." He immediately ended supervision and said he would put me in jail if I did not abide by the visitation order. Ms. Woods moved the court to appoint a psychologist to determine the best interests of the children, and it was granted.

I located Mr. Peal, the original polygrapher, and I told him what had happened. He said that he was never contacted by anyone regarding his doing a polygraph on us. He also said that Detective Nix was not qualified to do this type of test and that there had been problems with him in the past. After describing the manner in which my test was administered, he said that the results could not have been anything but inconclusive.

Around the same time, I received a bill from Diane Woods in which she was charging me fifty percent and Andy fifty percent for her time as guardian *ad litem*. The bill reflected that the majority of her time (eighty-seven percent) was spent talking with Andy and his attorneys. The rest of the charges were from talking with others and very little with my attorney. She had spoken to me once and to the children only once. I had called her a number of times and never received a response from her. The guardian *ad litem* who was supposed to represent the children appeared to be representing Andy.

There were very suspicious events that led me to believe that Diane Woods was purposefully covering up the abuse of my children. The social worker at DFACS had been changed, the Kennesaw Police Department had been called even though neither Andy nor I lived in the Kennesaw area at that time, the polygraph examiner had been switched, and my attorney had confirmed with me that Ms. Woods was having *ex parte* communication with Judge Bodiford, everything being determined against me outside of court without representation. *Ex parte* communications, or one-sided contacts with a judge by attorneys are strictly prohibited by the ethics rules for judges and lawyers.

Diane Woods had asked that an independent psychologist be appointed to evaluate the children and the family, and she gave us a choice between Dr. Elizabeth King and Dr. Carol Webb. I had no idea who they were or what they were about. I was told that neither was a good choice but that possibly Dr. King would listen to Dr. Hill and Dr. Brentnall. I later found out that Dr. King and Dr.

Webb are partners, and both use "junk science" to advocate for abusive fathers. Furthermore, both are good friends of Diane Woods.

The children continued to disclose that their father was molesting and threatening them. They had disclosed to me, to Dr. Brentnall and Dr. Hill, to Lynn Palmer, to Julie Hall and Detective Henderson, and to their pediatrician, Dr. Stephen King. Diane Woods refused to talk with Dr. Brentnall and Dr. Hill. She never talked to Dr. Stephen King, Lynn Palmer, or me about these allegations. I was calling Dr. Elizabeth King's office regularly begging for an appointment and was told that she would not see anyone yet.

We kept going back to Dr. Brentnall documenting the children's statements because we didn't know what else to do. She said Diane Woods would not talk with her and Dr. Hill. She suggested that I have someone else evaluate Amanda and Jessica to get another opinion. She felt that Ms. Woods would have to listen if another psychologist substantiated the abuse.

I sought an abuse specialist and found Dr. Diane Pearce in Marietta. She saw the children immediately. She found the abuse to be far worse than what we knew. She told me my attorney was not doing enough, and that she was going to call DFACS to report the abuse. She would not tell me what Amanda and Jessica had shared. She said she didn't want DFACS to say I told the children to say these things.

When we left her office that day, Amanda asked me if Dr. Pearce told me about their visit together. I told her that Dr. Pearce would not tell me details but that she believed them and wanted to help. Amanda seemed relieved that I didn't know the content of the information that she disclosed to Dr. Pearce. I was surprised because Amanda and Jessica and I were very close. I did not realize there was anything they felt they could not tell me. I was relieved though that they were willing to talk with someone who could help us. It was over nine months later, just a day or two before the final hearing when I finally learned what Dr. Pearce had found out.

Dr. Pearce called DFACS and made a report. [Appendix F, Exhibit C] No one did anything. She made repeated phone calls and wrote a letter to the director at DFACS asking that something be done. Still the children were not protected. Diane Woods refused to talk with Dr. Hill, with Dr. Brentnall, and with Dr. Pearce. I couldn't believe it! My children were telling professionals about the terrible things their father was doing to them, and yet the very people who were supposed to protect the children wouldn't do anything to stop it. Instead, they called the girls liars and called me a liar, hysterical, and delusional. I was outraged and full of fear for my children.

DFACS social worker Martin Inman and Detective Amy Henderson went to the school the children had been attending for about a month. In the presence of the school counselor they questioned the girls about their father. Amanda and Jessica later told me that they didn't know any of these people including their counselor. Amanda didn't remember Detective Henderson. And they didn't know Martin Inman, the male stranger asking little girls about sexual matters at school. They thought all the new kids were being called into the office to be questioned. They said they were embarrassed and were afraid that if they told that their father was doing these things to them that they would get in trouble at school. So when they were asked if their father touched them in their private areas, they answered, "No."

These so called "investigators" did nothing more until I told Mr. Inman during a phone call, witnessed by Karen Childs, that I expected him to do his job and talk with the professionals who had seen my children. My friend, Jan Geiger, and I then went and talked to Chief Wilson, the Chief of Police in Kennesaw, and I told him the same.

Later Mr. Inman and Detective Henderson met with me and Jan Geiger at my home. Detective Henderson let me know that she was very angry with me for going to her superior about her. She also indicated she was very busy preparing for her wedding which was to take place in several months and for her move to Jacksonville, Florida. After this Mr. Inman and Detective Henderson arranged a meeting with Andy Titelman, and they made several phone calls.

On a taped interview that Martin Inman and Detective Henderson had with Andy, Detective Henderson complained to Andy that I tried to have her fired by going to her boss. It was quite obvious in the tape that Mr. Inman and Detective Henderson were not serious about their investigation of Andy. They were not interested in any of the reports regarding abuse, even though we had three professionals, one being an abuse specialist, who had substantiated the abuse. It was obvious they were ticked off at me.

A social worker at DFACS later told me that DFACS could make no determination because a psychologist was involved in the case, and it was pending her (Dr. Elizabeth King) investigation.

Amanda was having stomachaches daily and was on medication from the doctor. When Andy picked the girls up one Sunday night, I forgot to send the medicine along. I called Andy and told him Amanda needed her medicine, and I was bringing it over. He hung up on me. When I drove to his house, a car was in the driveway, and lights were on upstairs and downstairs. I rang the doorbell three times. No one came. I called Andy's phone from my cell phone, and no one answered. I waited at the door and then finally left. Later Amanda and Jessica told me that Andy had taken them to a bedroom upstairs and locked them in. They said Bobby, Andy's son, was there too. They said, "Couldn't you hear us, Mommy? We kept screaming for you."

The girls said that all their toys disappeared. They said that their daddy told them the toys belonged to Katie and that other toys had been stolen by me. They were pulling some of their toys and belongings out of the trash and then he would yell at them and throw them away again. Their daddy was screaming at them a lot for telling about what he does to them and they were afraid that he was going to hurt them. I told them to call 911 if they needed help, but they said they couldn't call 911 because he kept only one phone, and it was on top of the refrigerator. They said that Daddy told them if they told anyone about the abuse that they would go to children's jail because no one would believe them and that children who lie go to jail. Amanda complained that he continued to call her "stupid" frequently.

Out of the blue one day, Amanda said her daddy was like "he was cut down the middle." She took her finger from her groin to the top of her head and said, "One side is really nice and fun, and the other side is really mean." A couple of weeks later the girls were telling me their father was yelling and throwing things all week. They said he smashed a pumpkin into the wall and slung papers off a table all over the floor.

An acquaintance witnessed Andy standing on the sidewalk in Marietta, leaning into the backseat of his car yelling at Jessica. She wrote in a letter, "Jessica was cowering trying to get as far away from him as possible. Her facial expression was that of a very upset child, one that was about to cry. ...[M]y witness of this made me believe that he was emotionally and verbally abusing her."

The girls were spending a lot of time with Andy and his girlfriend, Anita Miller, the mother of Katie's boyfriend. They were not getting home many nights until after midnight. The next morning they had to get up and go to school. When they returned to me a week later, they were dirty and said they had not had a bath since they left my home the week before. This happened week after week.

Amanda and Jessica appeared sick. Their eyes were swollen and there were circles under them. The girls said they would lay in bed at night at their father's house and cry because they wanted to be with me. Their teachers told me they were always tired and unkempt while they were with their father.

While having lunch with the girls one afternoon at school, Amanda asked me to come back to her classroom with her because she had something to give to me. She had found in the trash can a picture of us that I had given to her. She said her father had thrown it away. She took it to school but was afraid that he would find it at school and throw it away again.

I asked Jessica how things were, and she buried her face into my chest and said, "Not good." She said her father was still hurting her. I told her she needed to be brave and go to her teacher and talk to her. She said she couldn't. Jessica asked me, "Mommy, what do I do when I get scared?" "Call me," I said. "Daddy won't let me. Tell the judge Daddy won't let me call you," she said.

Amanda said her daddy called her into his bedroom closet while he was looking at something, and when she went in he began to call her and me names like "stupid" and "dummy." The girls expressed numerous times they were afraid that I was going to be hurt, first Jessica, then Amanda. Jessica told me that Anita told them she was going to give me something when the divorce was over, but Jessica didn't know what.

Mr. Dupree who was supposed to help the children and me, told me to be patient and wait for the court appointed psychologist to evaluate the children. Then we would go to court for a final hearing. But thus far Dr. King had refused to see us and the court had not helped. Decisions were being made that made no sense. My children were being tormented, and no one seemed to care. I was being forced to return the girls to their father for visitation. Each time I had to send them back to him, knowing what was happening, a piece of me died.

If I refused to send them back, I would be arrested, and they would be sent back anyway. If I hid them with someone, I would be arrested and not released from jail until they were found, and eventually they would probably be found. If I hid with them, we would always be hiding and not be able to let people get to know us. Eventually we would probably be caught, and I would go to jail and they would have to go back to their dad.

Amanda and Jessica were begging me not to send them back to their father. It was so gut wrenching and excruciatingly painful to see what was happening, how their souls were being destroyed before my very eyes.

The choices were awful. No matter what I chose to do, Amanda and Jessica would be harmed, so I picked what I thought would be the least damaging to them, to do what Mr. Dupree told me to do, as difficult as that was. I believed that eventually the court would see and know the truth and protect my daughters. But the Cobb County Superior Court did not protect them.

Soon after the children saw Dr. Pearce, Dr. King's office called to schedule appointments with my children and me. She had been court appointed the beginning of August, 1999, and had refused to see us until October 21, almost three months later, even though there were substantiated reports of sexual abuse. I also received a letter from Diane Woods ordering that I was not to take the children to anyone other than Elizabeth King, including the police, social workers, or anyone else regarding allegations of abuse. I told Amanda and Jessica that they must tell Dr. King everything that was happening while they were with their father, because she had been picked by Diane Woods to determine what was happening to them. I told them she would help them.

Amanda and Jessica disclosed to Dr. King that their father was sexually abusing them. She did nothing. I was disgusted when I confronted Dr. King and asked why she was not helping my children. She was mandated to report these allegations of abuse, but was refusing to do anything.

Dr. King later sent me a letter and stated, "I can appreciate your anxiety about the children particularly given the comments they are making to you and the changes in behaviors others have noticed. Given my role in the situation, i.e. a custody evaluator, I cannot intervene on their behalf." [Appendix A]

I knew that her response was bogus, and that she was not going to do anything to help my children. I knew that DFACS would do nothing to help as well after being told by a social worker that, because Dr. King was involved in the case, they would have to rely on her findings. I knew I was involved with people who were playing games with my children and me.

I didn't know where to get help. I went to the District Attorney, Patrick Head. I went to the Sheriff's office. I called the Georgia child advocate, DeAlva Sims. I called the Georgia Bureau of Investigators. I called other child advocates. I wept, and I prayed, and I looked for every source of help.

Tom Weathers, Assistant Cobb County District Attorney, called me and told me he had personally examined the investigation records and that "they were all in order," and "there was no substantiation of abuse." We later found in a letter that Diane Woods wrote to Elizabeth King the following statements:

Yesterday I just happened to be sitting in the courtroom waiting for Judge White to appear and Tom Weathers (the Chief Assistant) was also waiting. Tom told me that Wendy Titelman had come to the District Attorney's Office complaining that no one would do anything for her children (particularly me)!

What Tom found interesting was the fact that Ms. Titelman "forgot" in her conversation with him to mention the fact that the police and DFCS had fully investigated the case. Tom explained that the District Attorney's Office would have someone independent of his office complete an investigation into the matter, just to make sure that they had done everything they should. Basically he felt she was pretty much a "nut case".

As soon as I get the information from the Chief of Police in Kennesaw, I will let you know about the altercation in his office. I look forward to seeing you really soon.

I wrote to David Hellwig, Director of the Department of Human Resources. He replied in a letter that there had been a thorough investigation (including DFACS, law enforcement, an evaluation by a psychologist, Dr. King, and a report from the GAL) and all showed there was no finding to substantiate allegations of sexual abuse. Yet, DFACS and law enforcement had relied on Diane Woods and a polygraph test in their initial investigation. Now, they were relying on Dr. King, thereby making no conclusions on their own.

As Amanda lay beside me one night while I was trying to get her to go off to sleep, she reported that she was having the same nightmare over and over again when at her father's house. She said she couldn't remember it but that she was having feelings that reminded her of it. She said she was scared. When she opened her eyes and looked at me, she said, "You look so far away. Please don't leave me, Mommy." When she looked at the fan above us, she said, "It looks so far away." When she looked at the window, she said, "It looks so far away." She said when she closed her eyes she had the same thoughts and feelings and was very scared. She said it made her feel I was so far away she couldn't reach me and again expressed she was scared and asked me not to leave her. I wrote to Dr. King and shared this with her. I didn't understand at that time what this all meant. Now though, as I read my diary, I think about a nightmare that Amanda and Jessica both had the night before I saw them last. Now I understand.

The next night when I tucked the girls in at bedtime, Amanda said she was dizzy and felt like she was going to fall out of the bed.

She said she felt like everything was going around and around and that she had felt like that all of the week before. She had expressed that she was dizzy from time to time for many months. She said her feet and hands were hurting and that her arms and legs were affected as well. She could not stand to feel certain fabrics next to her skin. She said, "My hands feel like they are all scrunched up." They felt dry and appeared wrinkled. She put cream on herself several times a day. Certain sounds were disturbing to her like the rustling of clothes, smoothing sheets on a bed, the sound of a hair dryer, or a knife cutting food. She also complained of being very tired.

One night she woke up screaming and didn't stop until I picked her up. Her arms were extended straight out and stiff as a board. I could not get her to relax them at first. I asked her if she was having a nightmare, and she nodded yes. I asked her several times to tell me about it, but she did not respond. I let her go back to sleep. She awoke three more times within the next hour, disturbed and speaking in her sleep.

Amanda and Jessica both continued to say that they were afraid at their father's house, and they both said they were afraid they would never see me again. They were afraid to sleep alone, but that their father would not let them sleep in the same room. A babysitter once let them go to sleep together in Jessica's bed. Amanda said when her father got home he took her to her bedroom. Jessica said her daddy continued to sexually abuse her, and that Amanda stayed with her in the bathroom when she took her bath so that he wouldn't touch her then.

One night Andy was 20 minutes late picking up the girls. Amanda and Jessica said he told them he might not pick them up because he might go to Boston to see Katie while she was away at college. Then Amanda cheerfully and hopefully said, "Maybe he did go to Boston, and the airplane crashed, and he died, and we won't have to ever see him again."

As we waited that 20 minutes the children told me that Anita told them not to tell anyone about her because she would get in trouble. They also said, "Daddy knows everything we tell Dr. King and he screams and yells at us for talking to her." They said they thought Dr. King was telling him.

Amanda began to tell me that Andy was leaving them alone at the house to go shopping with Katie. She said she put a peppermint between cellophane in the toaster oven and it melted, but that she scrubbed it out before her father got home. Amanda was only seven years old.

Amanda and Jessica said that Andy and Anita were getting an apartment for Katie and Anita's son, Jerry, who was Katie's boyfriend. Katie had attended college at Tufts University for one semester and then decided to quit to come home. Andy was purchasing furniture and furnishings for Katie and Jerry, Amanda reported. She said that Katie went to Hawaii and was going again with Jerry.

Amanda and Jessica continued to tell others about the abuse. One Sunday morning our friend, Lisa Curtis, came to visit. I left the children with her and went to the grocery store to get a few things for us. While I was gone the children, who were close to Lisa, told her that their father was hurting them. Upon careful questioning, Lisa learned that Andy was sexually molesting them.

Lisa had spent some very special time with Amanda and Jessica and had grown to love them very much and they loved her. She introduced Beanie Babies to the girls. She brought her large collection and introduced them one by one in such a way that Beanie Babies took on a special place in our hearts. The girls then began their own collection of Beanie Babies. Since Amanda and Jessica have been gone, Lisa has been keeping them for the girls. She bought them special backpacks in which to carry the Beanie Babies, thinking that the court would protect Amanda and Jessica, and they would be coming home soon. Just recently during a phone conversation, Lisa told me she had cried just the night before because she realized that so much time has gone by, and now the girls have outgrown these things.

After the girls told Lisa that their father was hurting them, she went home and called DFACS, Crimes Against Children, and the Cobb County Police to report the abuse. Diane Woods was furious that Lisa had talked with Amanda and Jessica and said I had disobeyed her order. Lisa insisted that Dr. King see her and talk with her, and Dr. King reluctantly met with her. Many people who knew the children wrote to Dr. King and to Diane Woods telling them what they knew. [A few of these letters may be found in Appendix F, Exhibits D, E, F, G, and H.] Witnesses, to the children's behavior and Andy's conduct, reported information that indicates that their father may be molesting them. But Dr. King and Diane Woods dismissed every report from anyone who knew me, saying that these were friends of mine. Amanda asked me on a day she and Jessica were to go back to her father's house, "Why don't our friends help us? Don't they believe me?"

I kept taking the children back to Dr. King at her request, hoping my assessment was wrong. Unknown to me at the time, Dr. King taped her sessions with the children. We were able to obtain the tapes in later discovery, and learned that when the children tried to talk to Dr. King about the gross behaviors of their father, Dr. King would change the subject and instead try to get them to make disparaging remarks about me.

We also found that Dr. Elizabeth King never followed any approved or nationally accepted protocol to determine whether the allegations of sexual abuse were indeed true. In fact, a documented phone conversation between Elizabeth King and Diane Woods contained in Dr. King's records, revealed that Dr. King would do *no* sexual abuse evaluation but would complete a "straight custody evaluation." It is also documented there that the plan was Dr. King would do interviews and then have an emergency hearing. This phone call occurred prior to Dr. King ever having met with the children or Andy or me. Dr. King testified that she has rarely called for an emergency hearing in her many years of practice, and yet she and Ms. Woods had already determined this is what they would do before any evaluation even took place, before Dr. King had ever even met my children or me.   I discovered this purposeful, malicious, and corrupt act after the final hearing. [Appendix B] Dr. King and Diane Woods were conspiring to ignore all allegations of abuse and to give custody to Andy.

Dr. King conducted psychological testing on Andy and me, including the MMPI-2 and the Rorschach (ink blot). Once I had the files which contained the raw data of these tests, I sent them to an international expert in child sexual abuse, Dr. Joyanna Silberg. I learned that Dr. King completely misrepresented to the court the results of both Andy's and my tests.   Mine were incorrectly "interpreted" as negative, while his were falsely reported to be positive. I also learned that tests like these should not be used to determine custody of children.

Dr. Silberg is the Coordinator of Trauma Disorder Services for Children at Sheppard Pratt Hospital in Baltimore, Maryland, and past president for the International Society for the Study of Dissociation. In addition to her role as a clinician, Dr. Silberg is an associate editor for *The Journal of Trauma and Dissociation*, and sits on the editorial board of the *Journal of Trauma Practice*. She is the recipient of the Walter P. Klopfer Award, 1992, for outstanding research contribution and the Cornelia Wilbur Award, 1997, for clinical excellence. She is the editor of *The Dissociative Child* (Sidran Press, 1996/1998) and co-editor of the book *Misinformation Concerning Child Sexual Abuse and Adult Survivors* (Haworth Press, 2002). She has presented at hundreds of professional conferences and conducts training workshops around the world on the treatment of traumatized and dissociative children. She has authored approximately 20 professional articles and book chapters.

the February 18, 2000, "Emergency" Hearing

In February, 2000, after having *ex-parte* communication with Judge Bodiford, Diane Woods and Dr. Elizabeth King held their emergency hearing just as they recorded they would do almost five months before. My attorney and I received one day's notice that the hearing would take place, but we were not given any reason why. On the day of the hearing, Lisa Curtis and I sat in Mr. Dupree's office waiting for him to return from a meeting with Judge Bodiford, Diane Woods, Elizabeth King and Andy's attorneys. One hour prior to the hearing Mr. Dupree received Dr. King's report upon which the emergency hearing was based. The billing record indicates that Diane Woods

> In February, 2000, after having *ex-parte* communication with Judge Bodiford, Diane Woods and Dr. Elizabeth King held their emergency hearing just as they recorded they would do almost five months before.

and Elizabeth King were in constant communication with Andy and his attorneys prior to this event. We had one hour to prepare. There was no way we could get the testimony of those who had evidenced abuse because the Court would not allow us the time necessary to prepare for the hearing.

While reading the report, we learned that Dr. King had received a videotape "produced" by Andy Titelman in which the children had supposedly recanted their allegations of sexual abuse. This video was never presented to the Court. We later learned, it shows Andy Titelman and his girlfriend, Anita Miller, have a documented history of bullying the children into denying the abuse and claiming that Lynn Palmer, Lisa Curtis and I made the children falsely report the abuse. The tape is clear proof that Andy has coached the children to say they were not abused.

We were shocked that Elizabeth King and Diane Woods relied on this tape to discredit the abuse reports. It further supported that no matter what the evidence showed, they were doing everything they could to cover up the sexual abuse of Amanda and Jessica in order to give Andy custody of them. Additionally, Dr. King used Richard Gardner's bogus Parental Alienation Syndrome and Ralph Underwager's False Memory Syndrome (FMS) to take the girls away from me and give them to their abusive father.

Richard Gardner and Ralph Underwager have published materials advocating that sex between children and adults is okay. Underwager in an interview stated, "Paedophiles can boldly and courageously affirm what they choose. They can say that what they want is to find the best way to love. I am also a theologian, and as a theologian, I believe it is God's will that there be closeness and intimacy, unity of the flesh, between people. A paedophile can say: 'This closeness is possible for me within the choices that I've made.'...Paedophiles are too defensive.... With boldness they can say, 'I believe this is in fact part of God's will.'"[17]

Elizabeth King admitted in her report of February 17, 2000, that PAS is highly controversial yet chose to present this to the court anyway. Judge Bodiford allowed it in his courtroom. I have since learned that Cobb County Superior Court Judge Watson L. White is quoted on a father's rights web site promoting PAS. His statement reads, "There is something bad happening to our children in family courts today that is causing them more harm than drugs, more harm than crime and even more harm than child molestation." Judge White's position is that when a child tells of her molestation by a parent, that is more harmful than the molestation itself. This quote is shown under the title, "Learn About Parental Alienation Syndrome (PAS)."[18]

In advocating PAS, Elizabeth King demonstrated complete incompetence to serve in a case involving child sexual abuse allegations. She negligently and incompetently relied on these bogus, unscientific, and discredited theories to discredit the voluminous evidence of Andrew Titelman's sexual abuse of Amanda and Jessica. Dr. King's subsequent endorsement of such concepts as justification to place the children in their father's custody because they repeatedly report that he is molesting them rendered her involvement a direct and immediate threat to the children's welfare, directly contrary to the purpose of her appointment.

Likewise, Judge Bodiford's acceptance of such foolishness in his courtroom, the use of "junk science" to give custody over to an abusive man, and his participation in *ex parte* communications disregarding constitutional due process renders Judge James "Jim" Bodiford as an unjust judge. His participation in *ex-parte* communication alone shows his gross bias against me and necessitates his removal from participating as a judge in this case. To this day Judge Bodiford has never heard the evidence. All he has heard has been through *ex parte* meetings and an *ex parte* court hearing, yet he has stated in open court that Andy is an "innocent man." This emergency hearing appeared staged, scripted, and set up by Woods, King and Bodiford.

A commission was appointed by the Georgia Supreme Court to determine gender bias in the judicial system. In their report published in 1992 they concluded, that in child custody cases some judges are biased and erroneously believe that women are prone to manufacture false sexual abuse

> The Commission recommended extensive judicial education so that judges will realize that often abusive fathers will seek custody, not because they want custody, but only as a strategic maneuver.

allegations.[19] The Commission recommended extensive judicial education so that judges will realize that often abusive fathers will seek custody, not because they want custody, but only as a strategic maneuver. It was also noted that when fathers do seek custody, mothers are often held to a higher and different standard than are the fathers. The results of this study are similar to the results of The American Psychological Association's Presidential Task Force on Violence and the Family which stated, "Fathers who battered the mother are twice as likely to seek sole custody of their children as are nonviolent fathers."[20] Studies cited by the American Judges Association show approximately 70 percent of the men who seek and are given custody of their children are abusive.[21]

Dr. King testified on February 18, 2000, that Amanda and Jessica were liars, that I had not coached the girls, but that I was mentally ill because I believed my daughters. She could not keep her story straight. Despite the fact that Dr. King said that she could not intervene on behalf of Amanda and Jessica when they were reporting abuse to her, and despite the fact that she testified that I had not coached the girls, the day after the emergency hearing she reported to DFACS that Lynn Palmer and I were abusing the girls by coaching them to make disparaging remarks and sexual abuse allegations against their father. When I went back and examined Dr. King's notes in her phone conversation with Diane Woods documenting what they would do with this case [Appendix B], I found her note which stated, "Amy Henderson the Detective - Warrant for Cruelty to Children." It appears this too was planned in advance.

Dr. King recommended that I be put on supervised visitation immediately. I was put under supervision, and Andy was granted temporary custody even though the girls were telling me, their pediatrician, Dr. Stephen King, and psychologists Dr. Hill, Dr. Brentnall, and Dr. Pearce, and DFACS and the Kennesaw Police Department, friends, and Dr. Elizabeth King that he was molesting them and that they never wanted to see him again. Andy and his family laughed out loud in court finding great pleasure and humor in the situation. Not even one of them had concern for the children.

When this happened, I felt everything was closing in on me, and that it couldn't be real. It had to be a nightmare. I prayed that I would awake and everything would be okay. There is an order to our world, but none of this made any sense. I didn't understand how it could be happening, not in a court of law in America! I was mortified because everything that had happened and what was stated in court went against reasoning and common sense. How could they be doing this? I was shaken to the core.

Children are taught to tell an adult if anyone is touching them in a sexual way. Public schools teach "good touch, bad touch" and ask children if anyone is touching them like this. The law requires one to report to the authorities if a child discloses abuse or appears to be an abused child. Amanda and Jessica were exhibiting many behaviors that indicated they were being sexually abused. They were told to tell if anyone was touching them inappropriately. They were told that they would be protected.

My children told me that their father was touching them "in their privates" and was hurting them. The abuse was substantiated by competent professionals, who called the Department of Family and Children's Services and Diane Woods. Amanda told the police and DFACS social worker that her father was touching her in a sexually abusive way.

I did everything I was supposed to do in a situation like this. Dr. Brentnall did everything she was supposed to do in a situation like this. Dr. Pearce did everything she was supposed to do in a situation like this. Dr. Stephen King did everything he was supposed to do in a situation like this. Friends and acquaintances did everything they were supposed to do in a situation like this. By all common sense Amanda and Jessica should have been protected. But the Cobb County Superior Court (the family court) did not protect the children and instead negligently and fraudulently forced the children into the custody of their abusive father.

It takes a very brave child to report abuse. Not only is it embarrassing and shameful to tell, but also generally a child has been threatened by their abuser that harm will come to them or someone else should they ever tell. Amanda and Jessica revealed that their father told them he would hurt me and they would never see me again if they ever told. He told them they would go to children's jail, because children who lie go to jail, and no one would believe them. Even under this terrible pressure, Amanda and

Jessica continued to share with others that their father was abusing them.

This past September, 2002, I attended the 7th International Domestic Violence Conference in San Diego, which was attended by 1700 people from all over the world. Throughout the entire conference PAS was discussed over and over again as being a "death sentence" to abused children. If a child says anything derogatory about one parent, and the test of PAS is used, in every circumstance the child will be called a liar and will be placed in the custody of the parent the child has accused of harming her.

> If a child says anything derogatory about one parent, and the test of PAS is used, in every circumstance the child will be called a liar and will be placed in the custody of the parent the child has accused of harming her.

I was glad to see at this conference four registered individuals from SafePath, a child advocacy organization in Cobb County where the children's taped interviews occurred. Diane Woods is a member of their Board of Directors Steering Committee. I hope that they learned much from this conference, for many children in Georgia have suffered from lack of protection.

Supervised Visitation

From March, 2000, until July, 2000, I paid approximately $2,000 a month in order to see my children 12 hours a week under supervision. During the course of my supervised visits while the children were living exclusively with their father, the girls continued to complain of their father's abuse. Because of Ms. Woods's determination to suppress the truth, she took the absurd position that the girls' continued reports were the product of inadequate supervision. She then terminated my visits with the girls. One month later in April, 2000, supervised visits were reinstated by Judge Bodiford in an emergency hearing.

I began to see a psychiatrist, Dr. James Cheatham, who had a lot of experience with abuse. I asked him to evaluate me to determine if I was mentally ill as Elizabeth King was declaring. Dr.

Cheatham had a psychologist do an extensive battery of tests on me as well. He met with me numerous times, and he also examined the files, read the reports and listened to phone conversations I was having with my daughters along with their father's interruptions. He determined that I am not mentally ill, but that I am a very intelligent woman under considerable stress and who is deeply concerned about the well being of her children. He also determined that Andy Titelman is unfit to serve as a parent/guardian of the children and that he is a sexual predator. Diane Woods and Elizabeth King were not interested in anything Dr. Cheatham had to say.

While under supervision, the children discussed with the supervisors what was happening in their father's home. [Some of their reports may be found in Appendix F, Exhibit I] On March 5, Supervisor Karyn Covington talked to Jessica who told her she didn't love her father and her father didn't love her. Karyn asked her what is love, and Jessica answered, "Love is when you want to be with someone and take care of them." She said her dad did not want them and didn't want to take care of them.

During our visits, the girls became more antsy than ever unable to sit still for a moment. Amanda and Jessica both had stomachaches with diarrhea routinely. They would change their stained underwear while at my home and say they didn't want Daddy to know. Jessica asked me to help her in the bathroom to help her wipe herself because of diarrhea. She said she needed help but Daddy would get mad if I helped because he didn't want me to wipe her.

On March 30 when it was time to take the children back to their father's, Jessica stood in the middle of the living room. Her face was quite strained, and she was just staring. When I asked if she was okay, she began to cry uncontrollably. I picked her up and rocked her in a chair unable to console her for a long time. She never was able to vocalize her feelings that night. She just cried as she clung to me and did not talk. It was time for the children to be at their father's house. The supervisor demanded that Jessica pull herself together, and we had to take the children back

April 13, I tried to talk to the children on the phone and was hung up on three times by Andy. The girls could not tell me where they were and said Dr. King told them they could not tell me. Our phone conversations were always strained, interrupted and cut short.

On one of the supervised visits, April 24, Jessica told us, "I think Daddy tries to trick us." Amanda said, "Dr. King tries to trick us." Jessica didn't feel well on this visit. During dinner she said, "Mommy, please be with me when I die." They both said they were very unhappy and didn't want to live with their father. Jessica was cold all evening. She wanted to lie down in bed under the covers and was still cold. Both Amanda and Jessica asked if I was going to make them go back to their father's house. When Supervisor Joyce Saye and I took them back, Amanda wouldn't get out of the car. She held on to the seat and said she wasn't going. On another night, May 11, when we returned them, Jessica wouldn't leave the van. She said, "Now you are going to take me home with you to live with you. I'm not going to live here anymore." She had to be physically removed from the van. Andy opened both garage doors and stood in the doorway. Jessica relented then and sadly went into his house.

June 02, the girls told me that during the week when we tried to talk on the phone that their father had taken the phone away from them and wouldn't let them talk to me. The phone just went dead.

The supervisors witnessed the girls on a number of occasions with their hands in their pants. They described again that their father was making them do things they didn't want to do.

We had a final hearing in June of 2000. Judge Bodiford said he had a conflict and called his friend, Judge Jon Bo Wood, to hold the final hearing. We thought this was good because Judge Bodiford was grossly biased and had done so much damage.

Judge Wood limited us to three days, allowing us no more. We told him we needed at least five days but he refused. He listened to the testimony of Andy Titelman and Elizabeth King. Then he heard the testimony of a number of people who had knowledge of the sexual abuse of Amanda and Jessica.

He heard about the psychological reports and abuse documented by Dr. Brentnall and Dr. Hill. Dr. Hill testified that Dr. Brentnall followed an accepted protocol in determining that the children were being abused.

Dr. Pearce told Judge Wood what Amanda had reported to her and what had been kept secret from me for nine months. She said that Amanda told her that her father dressed up in a purple dress and high heeled shoes, a wig, nail polish and makeup. Amanda had drawn pictures for Dr. Pearce, and she explained how Amanda described the pictures. She described the clothing and fingernail polish and what appeared to be three legs. Amanda told her that the middle leg was like a dragon's tail that came out from under the dress in the front. There were also pictures of her and Jessica naked with their clothes lying on the floor. A second drawing showed Jessica in bed and her father with his hand on her privates.

I first learned about this from paralegal Kyle Broussard in Mr. Dupree's office one day prior to the final hearing. I thought Mr. Broussard was joking, and I tried to laugh at what I thought was a sick joke. He responded to me with no humor. He said, "I am serious, Wendy." It was like a slap in the face as I sobered to the realization that he wasn't joking. I was shocked and sickened to realize that Andy would play deviant games like this with our children for his criminal and warped sexual gratification.

The supervisors, Karyn Covington and Joyce Saye, testified how Amanda and Jessica had disclosed abuse to them. Ms. Covington told them that Amanda shared that her father "tickles me in my privates"... "at night - a lot." Ms. Saye reported that Amanda and Jessica told her that their father often made them say untrue things, and that when she asked them for an example, Amanda stated, "like when he touches us wrongly." They also described bruises found on Jessica's arm that were like the imprint of the fingers of a hand, and that Jessica said that her father had done this to her. They told the court their witness of Andy's paranoid and other strange behaviors when they picked up the children and returned the children to him after visitation with me.

Gail Vernon reported to the court that while she was in the waiting area at Ruth Mitchell Ballet, she saw Andy Titelman slide Jessica up and down over his groin with his legs open wide while softly singing, "touching, touching, touching." [Appendix F, Exhibit J]

Dr. Cheatham reported that I was a mentally sound woman and in his opinion Andy Titelman is a sexual predator. [Appendix F, Exhibit K]

> Judge James Bodiford helped them to cover up the abuse, meeting with them outside the presence of counsel and rubber-stamping every request they made without allowing due process of law.

Dr. Elizabeth King told the court that I had a paranoid personality disorder right in keeping with Richard Gardner's teachings that a woman who is guilty of PAS most always has a paranoid personality disorder. She told the court I put the bruises on Jessica's arm, even though I was on supervised visitation and no one had ever seen me be inappropriate with my children in any way. She said that the girls were liars.

Diane Woods said the girls were liars and that Dr. Hill, Dr. Brentnall, Dr. Pearce and Dr. Cheatham were hired guns, paid to say what I wanted them to say. She said that my letter to Jesus that I wrote while participating in the Van Horn group "frightened her as the Guardian *ad litem*." She commented, "If I suspected someone of sexually abusing my stepchildren, I sure wouldn't encourage them to go fuck them ..." She said, "I brought in the best forensic evaluator I know of in the State.." Ms. Woods also said that Dr. King is the only mental health professional who could determine what was in the best interests of the children.

John Mayoue, one of Andy's attorneys, said in his closing statement that the only people whose judgment could be deemed reliable and trustworthy were Diane Woods, Elizabeth King and Judge Bodiford. He also led the court to believe that there had been 14 investigations for the allegations of sexual abuse all proving Andy was innocent of child molestation. Yet there were only two investigations that had taken place by DFACS along with the Kennesaw Police Department, the first of which Diane Woods orchestrated and the second of which was determined by Dr. Elizabeth King under the influence of Diane Woods. All of the other reports made to DFACS, Cobb County Police Department, Kennesaw Police Department, Crimes Against Children, and the Georgia Bureau of Investigation were never investigated. Diane Woods and Dr. Elizabeth King sabotaged all efforts to get protection for the children. All attempted investigations were squelched by them. Judge James Bodiford helped them to cover up the abuse, meeting with them outside the presence of counsel and rubber-stamping every request they made without allowing due process of law. John Mayoue's final words to Judge Bodiford concede the abundant evidence of sexual abuse presented during the trial:

> It is difficult to come in here and have somebody say that everybody is wrong, and I fully accept the premise that no one knows what happens behind closed doors. That is why we have professionals because you weren't there and I wasn't there. And we don't know what to do other than to rely upon those with professional expertise in this area and, you know, lawyers and with all due respect, judges don't have the kind of training that these people have and I am talking about Dr. King and I am talking about Diane and I am talking about DFACS and I think we have to go a tremendous way to say that we are going to substitute our goals and ideas for theirs.

In other words, he urged the Court to ignore the ample evidence of the sexual abuse, and instead to accept the opinions of Diane Woods and Dr. King, despite his own acknowledgment that *"no one knows what happens behind closed doors."* In this case, we do know what happened behind closed doors. Andy Titelman sexually molested the children by fondling their genitalia, as Amanda reported to DFACS, to Dr. Brentnall, and to Dr. Stephen King, and as Amanda and Jessica reported to me, to Dr. Pearce, to other neighbors and family friends, and to Dr. Elizabeth King, and as Jessica reported to Dr. Hill and Dr. Brentnall very early on! John Mayoue "hit the nail on the head" on the inappropriate and dangerous reliance placed on the desires of the untrained and negligent Diane Woods and Elizabeth King.

Judge Wood followed the advice of Diane Woods and Elizabeth King. He totally ignored all the evidence that was presented to him in court. He gave sole custody of Amanda and Jessica to Andy and gave me limited visitation without supervision.

Why would a judge ignore the evidence and the law? Did Judge Wood really think I had the power or capability of fooling all these people or getting them all to lie or that I could pay them to say what they said? Did he really believe that because Diane Woods and Elizabeth King were court appointed that they knew better?

Earlier this year, I learned through the Atlanta Journal Constitution that Attorney McCracken Poston out of Ringgold, Georgia, had filed a motion to recuse Judge Bodiford from a very serious case involving the owner of a crematory who was accused of simply dumping the bodies of several hundred people. The four judges in Walker County, Georgia where this occurred recused themselves because of their close association with various people involved.

One judge who recused himself is Judge Bo Wood. His mother had died and her body was sent to this crematory, thus making him a potential victim.

Mr. Poston was concerned that Judge James Bodiford and Judge Bo Wood are friends who trade cases and do favors for each other. Bodiford on a few occasions during hearings in my case brought up Bo Woods name, once saying "Judge Wood is one of my heroes." He also used Bo Wood's decision in the final hearing to support what he did at an emergency hearing, September 20, 2000. He said, "She hasn't gotten one judge to agree with her yet out of the three that I know of." (The only third judge we had was Judge Teel out of Mississippi who is later discussed and who believed the children were being abused by their father. Judge Bodiford may have been led to believe by Diane Woods during their *ex-parte* communications that Judge Teel was opposed to me when in fact he was trying to protect the children from their father.) At one of the Walker County hearings, Judge Bodiford said that Judge Wood had helped him out in a Cobb County custody case and that he jokingly told the 7th District Administrator, Jody Overcash, that she could have the custody case [Titelman case] if she would give him the Walker County case. He also stated that he owed Judge Wood a personal favor.

Judge Kristina Cook Connelly, one of the four judges in Walker County who eventually recused herself from the other case, became concerned about Judge Bodiford's assignment to it. The media had broken the story that Judge Bodiford, from another circuit, had been assigned to the case, yet Judge Connelly had not yet recused herself at the time and began to question what was going on. She called Jody Overcash and confirmed that Judge Bodiford was already "in place." She was told that Judge Bodiford had requested assignment to the case "because he owed Judge Wood a personal favor." Judge Connelly was concerned and felt that the assignment was "highly inappropriate." Ms. Overcash told her they probably would not remove his assignment. Judge Connelly wrote an affidavit conveying the information she had learned and stated that she did not believe that Judge Bodiford could be fair and impartial.

April 12, 2002, Judge Connelly testified at Bodiford's recusal hearing in Walker County before J. Emory Findley, a Senior Superior Court Judge from South Georgia. Judge Connelly stated to the court, "I felt a responsibility to the citizens of Walker County and to the lawyers and the people involved in this case to convey information that I thought they were entitled and should know, and I did." "We have to maintain our integrity in the Court system, or it is worthless," she said. Judge Findley was very harsh as he berated Judge Connelly for what she had done. Basically, he said, we judges stick together, and that this should have been handled in private.

I, too, testified at this hearing. There were indications that favors were being exchanged. I was concerned that Judge Bodiford talked about the Titelman custody case and commented that he owed Judge Wood a personal favor. I learned that the normal procedure for selecting another judge when one cannot act is that the district administrative judge shall select a judge. In my case Judge Bodiford did not follow this procedure. He directly asked Judge Wood to hear my final hearing. His appointment to the Walker County case was now in question as well.

Approximately a week later Judge Findley issued his ruling. Judge Bodiford was not recused from the crematory case. Attorney McCracken Poston appealed. The appellate court also refused to remove Judge Bodiford.

Georgia is one of the only states that has a discretionary appeal process for custody cases. This means that if the appeals court does not want to hear an appeal for whatever reason, they simply deny the request to appeal. In other words, they do not look at all the evidence. They are not even required to determine if the judge made the right decision. In other states, where the appeal is a right that the parent has, the appellate court will review the evidence and the law and decide whether the judge did the right thing. In Georgia, most cases don't even get that far.

The National Alliance for Family Court Justice (NAFCJ), founded and directed nationally by Elisabeth Richards, has documented the family court system's failure to protect children and the retaliation against women who report abuse. Cindy Ross, the California Director of NAFCJ states, "NAFCJ has identified and documented evidence that PAS not only is the means to conceal a pro-pedophile agenda disguised as 'custody resolution,' it is the basis of a court kickback scheme that calls for misuse/diversion of federal grants, primarily Access to Visitation Enforcement, Child Support Enforcement, Responsible Fatherhood and Temporary Assistance to Needy Family (TANF) Welfare program funds."[22]

"Fathers' rights groups" often use organizations such as The American Association for Matrimonial Law (AAML) and the Association of Family and Conciliation Courts (AFCC) to advance their agenda. Children's Rights Council (CRC), formerly called the National Council for Children's Rights, is essentially the "umbrella" organization of the "fathers' rights" movement. Even though the AAML and AFCC have denounced PAS and other pro-pedophile propaganda, there are groups within these organizations that hold seminars and continuing legal education programs around the country, and through the use of federal monies they and their recruits teach judicial officers, attorneys and psychologists the "Parental Alienation Syndrome" and other pro-pedophile philosophies.

Cindy Ross reports that two individuals behind this agenda are Joan Kelly, the former director of the Northern California Mediation Center in Marin County and one of CRC's founding officials, and Judith Wallerstein, founder of the Center for the Family in Transition also in Marin County. Ms. Ross states, "Largely due to Kelly's and Wallerstein's influence, PAS methodology has become entrenched into federal programs, policy and funding, especially through CRC." CRC officials conceal the fact that many of their "experts" adopt or use pedophile theories and propaganda that promote or excuse incest and deviant sex. Some of these "authorities" include Richard Gardner, who coined the term PAS, John Money, a sexologist affiliated with Johns Hopkins University, Ralph Underwager and Hollida Wakefield of the False Memory Syndrome Foundation and Warren Farrell, a political scientist who advocates "family sex" and "genitally caressing children" in the Penthouse article "Incest, the Last Taboo" (1977).

Insight Magazine published an article in April of 1999 called *Is Justice for Sale in L.A.?*. Kelly Patricia O'Meara reported that there might be "a cozy financial connection between judges, attorneys and some court-appointed professionals in the City of Los Angeles which is affecting the outcome of their cases." She goes on to report that "...Private bank accounts that benefit judges are at the heart of this brewing scandal - one that state and local agencies resolutely have failed to investigate, adding further suspicion. Bank accounts funded in part by fees from local lawyers and others involved in the family-court system are troubling litigants. Many feel it is impossible to know whether they're facing a judge who has benefitted financially from an attorney appearing before the court." It appears that the family court system "purposefully profits off the conflict of the families in litigation." "The entire concept of family law," says Marv Bryer, a grandfather asking for a probe of the system, "is that it is to operate in the best interest of the children. But the fact is that court personnel are making a living by decimating the bank accounts of the litigants, which ultimately destroys the quality of the child's life." He adds, "At each step of the process, both litigants are forced to pay thousands of dollars for the services demanded by the court, not including the fees each side already is paying attorneys. But the child-custody cash register doesn't stop ringing. The system continues to rake in money for its swarm of support personnel long after custody has been awarded."

Diane Woods was president of the Cobb County Bar Association when she became the guardian *ad litem* for Amanda and Jessica. The Court ordered Andy and I to pay her. She has been paid approximately $22,000. She picked her good friend, Dr. Elizabeth King, as the custodial evaluator. The court ordered Andy and I to pay Dr. King. She billed $30,458 through September 29, 2000.

Dr. King's former husband and the father of her children, Barry McGough, is a father's rights attorney. While the two were married Peachtree Psychological Services was established. Mr. McGough uses Dr. King and her associates to get custody of children for fathers who have been accused of domestic violence and sexual abuse.

Diane Woods appointed Lorita Whitaker as the children's therapist, also court ordered. Ms. Whitaker has charged thousands of dollars. She has stated that she is not interested in seeing any information that may indicate that the children are being or have been sexually molested. She says it has nothing to do with her therapy with the children.

John Mayoue is a member of the AAML. Barry McGough is a former partner in John Mayoue's firm. Elizabeth King is a member of the AFCC. Mayoue and McGough were past chairs of the Family Law Section of the Georgia Bar Association. Elizabeth King is the only non-attorney board member of the Family Law Section. John Mayoue is an attorney for the Atlanta Journal Constitution.

Diane Woods helped develop the Cobb County GAL program and works very closely with other GAL's who use the PAS technique in determining custody. Woods says she designed her program using the Kelly/Wallerstein model. Woods is very selective in her choice of court appointed psychologists. In a letter to the court October 8, 2000, she states, "In the last eight years in which I have been doing Guardian ad Litem work for the Court, I have become increasingly selective as to the forensic psychologists that I prefer to utilize. My suggestion is that the Court order the parties to submit themselves to evaluations by one of the following: Nancy McGarrah, Ph.D.; Barrie Alexander, Ph.D.; H. Elizabeth King, Ph.D.; or Carol Webb, Ph.D. I have worked with all four of these individuals on numerous occasions..." These are all "Father's Rights" psychologists who use PAS, FMS and other pro-pedophile philosophies to take children away from loving mothers and put them in the custody of abusive fathers. Woods is also a mediator and a member of the Collaborative Law Institute of Atlanta.

Diane Woods, Elizabeth King, and Judge Bodiford have participated together teaching in continuing legal education programs on custody decisions.

Investigations in other parts of the country have explored very questionable collaborations and financial improprieties in the family courts. Here are a few examples:

Arkansas Lawmakers Indicted in Vast Corruption Case

BY DAVID FIRESTONE -- THE NEW YORK TIMES

LITTLE ROCK, Ark., April 28, 1999 -- A federal grand jury shook the Arkansas political establishment Tuesday with a long list of political corruption indictments that reaches to the apex of the state Legislature.

Ten people, including two well-known state senators, two former state senators, two former top education officials and several lawyers and associates of the legislators, were indicted on a variety of racketeering, mail fraud and money laundering charges.

The ringleader of the group, said U.S. Attorney Paula Casey, was Nick Wilson, the senior state senator and one of the most powerful and feared men in Arkansas politics. Ms. Casey said that Wilson, a Democrat, planned and directed four separate schemes to divert $5 million in state money from child-support enforcement, workers compensation for the state school board and a program to provide legal counsel for children caught up in divorce cases.

In the case of the divorce program, Wilson and his associates "corrupted the legislative process of the Arkansas General Assembly" by establishing a program to provide legal counsel to children in divorce cases with no intention of actually providing the services, the indictment said. Wilson and the other legislators funneled the money to contractors who returned most of it to them, the indictment says.

Wilson's lawyer, Bill Walmsley, said Wilson would plead not guilty to each of the 129 charges against him, and predicted he would be exonerated. Wilson believes the indictment raises serious questions about the independence of the legislative branch from the judiciary, his lawyer said.

The office of the other senator named in the indictment, Michael R. Bearden, 50, said he was unavailable for comment. Both Wilson and Bearden are Democrats.

Ms. Casey's office, along with the FBI, the IRS and the state police, has been investigating the case for 19 months, ever since a weekly newspaper here broke the news about problems with the divorce program. But even though the indictments were long expected, the scope of the corruption charges was greater than any subsequent news accounts had indicated. The suspected pattern of kickbacks and self-dealing clearly surprised the investigators.

Larry Jegley, the district attorney for the Little Rock region, who spent a few weeks investigating the case in 1997 before realizing that it was so big that it should be turned over to the federal government, said: "After I issued subpoenas, I got them back and said, holy cow, what have we got a hold of here. There was something at the end of the tail we've grabbed onto."

Good-government groups in Arkansas had long charged that many members of the part-time state Legislature were benefitting from state contracts, but the full scope of the problem had not been publicly known until the Arkansas Times, a weekly newspaper covering politics and culture, reported in September 1997 that several relatives and friends of legislators were directly benefitting from the divorce program. The early articles barely mentioned Wilson; it appeared that other senators had set up the program and funneled the money.

But as federal and state investigators began to look into the case, they said they discovered a much larger conspiracy. Dozens of state legislators, lawyers and lobbyists were interviewed, and Ms. Casey said that several decided to provide evidence to the government as part of plea agreements and immunity deals.

When the FBI raided Wilson's office in November 1997, it became evident to the public that the investigation had grown substantially, and it began to affect state politics. Gov. Mike Huckabee railed against the legislative branch, although many legislators accused the Republican governor of capitalizing on the fact that all of those under investigation were Democrats. Two of the senators named in Tuesday's indictment, Michael Todd and Steve Bell, decided not to run for re-election, and in the most recent session, the Legislature passed a bill that outlaws a wide variety of practices that allowed lawmakers to benefit from state contracts.

If proved, the accusations against Wilson could end one of the state's longest and most colorful political careers. Wilson, who is 57, entered the Senate in 1971 as a fiery, left-of-center reformer from the northern town of Pocahontas, and frequently clashed with governors of both parties, including Bill Clinton. Once, while

129

Clinton and the lieutenant governor were out of the state, Wilson --
then president pro tem of the Senate -- declared himself acting
governor and temporarily fired Betsy Wright, Clinton's chief of
staff. Many legislators said Wilson, gruff and quick with a profane
quote, essentially ran both houses of the Legislature for years.

"He has been an extremely influential senator," said Roby
Robertson, a public administration professor at the University of
Arkansas at Little Rock. "He came in as a maverick, taking on the
establishment, and has always been one of the brightest people in
state government. I have to admit, I was often very impressed with
him."

But the indictment paints a grim picture of a different kind of
brilliance. Beginning in 1995, it says, Wilson set up a corporation
that received state contracts to collect child-support payments. The
corporation submitted phony billings, and two-thirds of the
$546,000 received from the state was kicked back to Wilson, the
indictment says, while other payments were made to Bearden, a
senator for 13 years.

In addition, it says, a Little Rock insurance company,
Sedgwick James of Arkansas, paid Wilson $227,000 to be selected
to administer workers compensation claims for the Arkansas School
Board Association. Wilson gave half the money to Burton L. Elliott,
former director of the state Department of Education, according to
the indictment. In a related scheme, it says that Sedgwick James
conspired with Wilson and Tommy R. Venters, former executive
director of the school board association, to have lawyers
representing school districts pay Wilson $20 an hour for each hour
they billed the state.

In all, the indictment says, Wilson received $1.38 million
through the various schemes, an amount which the government
demanded be repaid. The defendants, charged with a total of 133
counts, will remain free on their own recognizance, Ms. Casey said,
and are expected to be arraigned in mid-May.

Ms. Casey said the investigation was one of the largest public
corruption cases in state history.

"Maybe I grew up on the wrong side of the tracks, but that's an
overwhelming amount of money to me," she said. "Particularly
when you consider the purpose for which that money was originally

130

appropriated: to collect child support and help children and parents who are trying to raise their families. And to have that diverted to a fraud, I think, is particularly egregious."

N.H. Justices in the Balance
As Impeachment Is Weighed
Panel Considers Fate For Members of Court
Cited for Lax Ethics

By Pamela Ferdinand

Special to The Washington Post
Saturday, July 1, 2000; Page A03

BOSTON, June 30 -- In Act II of a magisterial drama that has riveted the Granite State, New Hampshire lawmakers this week began considering whether to bring impeachment charges against members of the state's highest court for the first time in more than 200 years.

House Judiciary Committee deliberations, broadcast live for two days from a legislative office building in Concord, N.H., followed weeks of testimony that exposed a state Supreme Court culture of lax ethical standards and culminated in an abject apology from the prime focus of the inquiry, Chief Justice David A. Brock.

While lawmakers seemed willing to discipline rather than impeach two of Brock's fellow jurists for alleged ethics violations, they questioned Brock's truthfulness and seemed by their words inclined to mete out a harsher recommended sanction for the chief justice, who has presided over U.S. Supreme Court Justice David H. Souter's former bench and set its tone for 14 years.

"It is on a deeply personal note that I say to you today that to the extent that my actions as chief justice on the New Hampshire Supreme Court contributed to the need for this unique historical process and have resulted in the pain, stress, and inconveniences it has produced for all parties, I am sorry and wish to offer my sincere apologies," Brock said.

In concluding remarks Monday before the committee, the white-haired chief justice compared the court to a family and himself to a good father "who keeps missing his child's ball game or who frequently forgets to ask how his wife's day went after she's been home with six children all day." But he denied acting with any malice worthy of impeachment: "I never intended to do anything wrong."

On that point, the 22 members of New Hampshire's predominantly Republican Judiciary Committee must decide by majority vote. They are scheduled to reconvene on Wednesday to issue an opinion either removing (by impeachment or the less complicated Colonial-era "bill of address"), reprimanding or exonerating one or more of the three state Supreme Court judges under investigation. If the state House of Representatives votes to accept an impeachment recommendation, then in August a Senate trial assisted by former Democratic senator George J. Mitchell of Maine would commence--a spectacle not seen in New Hampshire since 1790.

The judicial terrain already has shifted: The associate justice whose divorce precipitated the constitutional crisis resigned, and all three justices, including Brock, stepped aside temporarily. Wayward recusal practices were remedied, and Democratic Gov. Jeanne Shaheen today established a Judicial Selection Commission to screen and recommend new judicial candidates. Yet political and legal observers say the court's reputation for impartiality and fairness has undoubtedly suffered. At stake is the trust between citizens and the court, they say, and the balance between judicial oversight and independence in a state with particularly low tolerance for secrecy and abuse of power.

"Many members of the public have always expressed skepticism about the system, and this probably confirms their worst nightmares," said Richard Uchida, a member of the New Hampshire Bar Association's ethics committee. "The damage is substantial and, in some respects, perhaps irreparable."

The scandal's repercussions could unravel dozens of cases, legal observers said, from the controversial state Supreme Court ruling mandating a new formula for funding public schools to the divorce settlements of judges. The public hearings clearly wearied the state legislators charged with exacting justice from allegedly injudicious justices, one of whom likened the court atmosphere in recent months to a funeral home.

"It's been a tremendous burden," said Rep. Andrew R. Peterson during a television interview. "It's not a job we asked for."

The possibility of judicial malfeasance first surfaced in February when state Supreme Court Clerk Howard Zibel alerted authorities to an incident involving Associate Justice W. Stephen Thayer III. On Feb. 4, Brock told colleagues he had appointed two new judges to a special panel for Thayer's acrimonious divorce. Brock said he did not intend to invite comment from the justices, all of whom were recused from the case, but Thayer stunned them by angrily objecting to one of the selected judges.

In a memo to the state's Judicial Conduct Committee, Zibel accused Thayer of trying to intervene in the panel selection and said Brock tried to dissuade him from reporting the ethical violation. Evidence also emerged that Thayer failed to report a $50,000 loan from a lawyer-friend who occasionally appeared before the bench.

Attorney General Philip T. McLaughlin widened the investigation, accusing the entire court of ignoring judicial rules by continuing to comment on cases from which they disqualified themselves due to conflict of interest. (Recused judges elsewhere typically leave the room.) McLaughlin also accused them of failing to swiftly report misconduct.

In a deal with the state attorney general's office, Thayer resigned to avoid prosecution, and no criminal charges have been filed against any member of the court. Concern about the allegations was sufficient, however, to prompt a legislative inquiry and shift the focus of the investigation from Thayer to Brock.

New Hampshire justices, who are nominated by the governor and approved by a five-member executive council, serve until age 70 unless they retire or are removed. The Judiciary Committee in this case has decided to use a single burden of proof--clear and convincing evidence--to determine whether any justice committed an impeachable offense, cited in the state Constitution as bribery, corruption, malpractice or maladministration.

Among other considerations, panel members are examining whether Brock improperly invited feedback from his peers on the divorce panel appointment and acted on the associate justice's attempts to change it. Lawmakers will also consider the court's two-week delay in reporting Thayer's action to the Judicial Conduct Committee.

Brock testified that he was distracted by other matters--a heavy court docket and his daughter's recent cancer diagnosis--and was hesitant to report Thayer out of compassion for his colleague. "I had to make a judgment about how best to handle the situation and didn't want to do anything to humiliate him or raise the temperature any higher," he said. "My immediate thought was, 'I need time to sort this thing out.' "

The justices reported Thayer's action only after Zibel announced his own intention to do so--a matter of timing that prompted one Judiciary Committee member to comment, "I do wonder if Mr. Zibel had never filed his memo, if we'd ever know about this at all."

The committee also is gauging whether Brock tried to sway a lower court judge in a 1987 contract dispute case involving a state senator who controlled judicial pay raises. More generally, they must weigh conflicting testimony about the court's 50-year tradition of allowing judges to participate in cases from which they were recused.

Brock and others said such participation did not alter the outcome of any case, and the court has since tightened its rules on recusal. Legislators, with days of soul-searching ahead of them, nevertheless remain troubled.

"They're not going to get off scot-free," warned Democratic Rep. Martha S. Solow. "There will be some consequences to be paid."

A Financial Fiasco Is in the Making

By Kelly Patricia O'Meara

Insight
July 30, 2001

"Put your concerns in writing and mail them to me." Click; the line goes dead. The voice on the phone was that of Los Angeles Superior Court Presiding Judge James Basque as Insight pressed him to explain whether the Los Angeles Superior Court Judges Association (LASCJA), of which he is the chairman, has made any attempt to pay 30 years of back taxes to county, state and federal authorities.

It has been more than two years since Insight broke the story of the Los Angeles Superior Court judges earning money off the books by providing minimum continuing legal education (MCLE) classes to attorneys in the courtrooms. The fees collected were deposited into a private bank account that has come to be known as the $100,000 "coffee and flowers" fund (see "Is Justice for Sale in L.A.?," May 3, 1999).

The problem with this arrangement is that, apparently to cover for the fact that the judges weren't paying taxes on this income, whether earned or extorted, the LASCJA illegally used the employer-identification number (EIN) of the County of Los Angeles. In time the county politely asked the learned jurists to stop using that number. But no criminal charges were filed against the judges and no one raised the issue of making good on back taxes. So when Basque abruptly ended that telephone conversation, Insight decided to take another look at the status of that private bank account and to revisit the Los Angeles County Superior Court Finance Office.

Insight put its "concerns" about those back taxes in writing, as requested by the presiding judge, and hand-delivered the formal request to his chambers. Basque neither responded to the questions nor agreed to a meeting, instead deferring to the county's counsel, Frederick Bennett.

Although Bennett says that he "has some background information concerning the [judges] association," not once in his three-page response did he discuss whether the judges have made any attempt to pay what could amount to 30 years of back taxes and penalties. Instead, he obfuscates, rambling on that he is "informed and believes the association has used its own taxpayer's identification number since approximately 1997, when the county auditor [J. Tyler McCauley] indicated that would be the better practice."

For the LASCJA to use its own identification number, as required by law, is a "better practice?" What about it being illegal for the judges to have enjoyed their private income for so many years under the county's EIN? Not a word. But Bennett continues to defend the judges by explaining that "the association does not pay taxes," as he is "informed and believes that it is an organization exempt from taxes."

Bennett provided a copy of the LASCJA's year 2000 federal IRS 990 Form indicating the organization's tax-exempt status but advised that the information he was providing should be verified with the LASCJA's attorney, John J. Collins of the Pasadena law firm of Collins, Muir and Traver.

Collins had less information than Bennett. It appears that Collins can only speak about the LASCJA back to the winter of 1997, when he first began representing the association. Asked if he is aware of any efforts by the judges to pay taxes on these large sums of money earned during the 30-year period, Collins tells Insight: "I can't speak about that because I don't know they made any money."

That assuredly is a lawyerly response, given that Collins admitted to having read Insight's earlier article about the LASCJA which contained details about checks being deposited into the judges' private Bank of America account. It at that time contained a little more than $100,000.

Neither Collins nor the judges have addressed the issue that, based on the bank records, large sums of money may be owed in back taxes. Furthermore, based on correspondence from Collins, it is clear that the association's counsel is much more informed about the status of the account than he lets on.

Since Insight began looking into the "slush fund" of the Superior Court judges and their finance office, requests for information have been submitted by private citizens, including Marvin Bryer, a retired computer analyst in La Crescenta, Calif. He became involved in the Superior Court's financial matters because of problems his daughter was having in a child-custody case. In February 1998, Bryer made a statutory request through Collins to inspect the LASCJA's records. Collins refused, saying LASCJA "is not a public entity nor an exempt organization as defined under this statute." He stated that "the Los Angeles Superior Court Judges Association is a private organization and its documents, including financial records and tax information, are confidential and not subject to disclosure."

While Collins says the LASCJA is a "private" organization, according to California Secretary of State Bill Jones, the association filed for tax-exempt status in December 1997 - well within the time frame of Bryer's request for inspection of the records. When Insight reminded Collins about this correspondence, the lawyer once more stonewalled, saying: "I'm not giving you any opinion on that. That's not part of my function. I'm not telling you what their legal status is. Everything that's out there is a matter of public record. You've got the filings, the informational returns and that's enough for you to come to your conclusions."

Meanwhile, the LASCJA continues to use the county courthouse for its private business. According to documents filed with the California secretary of state, the LASCJA lists the courthouse at 111 North Hill Street as its business address. Then there is a letter from Collins dated November 2000 stating that "the tax returns for 1998 and 1999 have been deposited in Room 119 [the Superior Court Finance Office] of the Central District Court. You should ask for Mr. Alf Schonbach, who is the court administrator of finance and accounting." Despite assurances from county auditor McCauley that the judges no longer were conducting their private business from the court premises, Collins continues to direct inquiries about the LASCJA to the court's finance office.

Schonbach long has been a key player in the oversight of the LASCJA account. And it is Schonbach who was in command of the Superior Court Finance Office when one of his underlings, Gregory

Pentoney, and an attorney friend, Robert Fenton, cooked up a scheme to collect $5 million in unclaimed sums deposited - and long forgotten - in the county's Condemnation and Interpleader [C&I] trust fund. Pentoney and Fenton pleaded guilty to one felony count of taking a bribe and receiving a bribe. Pentoney was sentenced to two years in state prison; Fenton received 16 months. As a result of a series of Insight articles about theft from the C&I trust account, Schonbach was directed to produce a listing of the unclaimed funds and make it publicly available. This currently reflects a balance of a little more than $54 million but does not include the "zero-balance" cases, where principle has been paid but interest still is accruing. Insight's articles also prompted the Los Angeles County Board of Supervisors in September 2000 to request a special audit of the C&I account - at a cost to taxpayers of $18,000 - which eventually was made public last February.

The accounting firm of Vasquez Farukhi & Co. conducted the special audit of the C&I trust account and stated it did not find "any material misstatements in the Condemnation and Interpleader Fund." In other words, the C&I account is in good shape. But is it?

For the purposes of defining the fund Vasquez Farukhi explained that the "SK4 [Condemnation and Interpleader Fund] was established by the County of Los Angeles for the Superior Court of the county to account for four types of deposits consisting of eminent domain [condemnation] deposits, interpleader [deposits for credit relief], nonbondsmen bail deposits and deposits made in compliance with judicial order." Having been advised by Los Angeles County Treasurer Joe Spillane that the county takes in between $400 million and $600 million a year, financial analysts tell Insight it seems odd that the C&I fund audit would reflect a mere $54 million.

Even more odd is that no one in the county government could provide Insight with a bottom-line figure of how much cash was collected through the C&I fund for fiscal 2000 alone. Spillane explained that he had little or no knowledge of the court's finances. He receives a bottom-line figure from the auditor but has no clue about the deposit specifics. "We're not looking," explains Spillane, "for each of the individual deposits for each of the funds. That would be impossible. My function is to account for funds that are

139

in the treasury, balance those to our bank accounts and our investments and have cash available for disbursement." Spillane insists, "The auditor has the detail. I don't know what is in the condemnation fund because it's a fund that we don't maintain." Claiming to have exhausted his knowledge of how the money moves in Los Angeles, Spillane recommended that Insight speak with McCauley, the county auditor - a task easier said than done.

Several weeks passed before McCauley allowed a brief telephone interview and, while the agreed-upon focus of the conversation was to provide a bottom-line figure on the amount of cash being collected at the Superior Court, the auditor said he could provide few specifics. For those, he said, Insight would have to go to Schonbach in the Superior Court Finance Office. And, of course, Schonbach refused to discuss the court's cash collections.

While McCauley could provide little financial information about the courts, he was surprisingly well-versed in the "special" audit of the C&I account conducted by Vasquez Farukhi. Asked why the audit reflected a balance far less than acknowledged by the treasurer, McCauley had his ducks in a row. Recall that Vasquez Farukhi certifies the audit of the SK4 (Condemnation and Interpleader Fund), which it declares includes four deposit items, including nonbondsmen bail and judicial orders. But if the audit includes these deposit items, then the balance reported is far below the amount reported to be collected by the court.

So what is going on here? McCauley tells Insight: "It was just a mistake by the auditor. They should not have included those [nonbondsmen bail and judicial orders]. I have to talk to Alf Schonbach, but I was assured by my staff that no such funds come through the C&I account. I don't know where the contract auditor got that statement he put in the report."

A respected accounting firm states that it has audited a trust fund consisting of specific deposits, then the county auditor claims the contract auditor just made a mistake - that it couldn't have audited those deposits because they're not part of the audited trust fund. And somehow no one in the Los Angeles County government, including the Board of Supervisors that requested the special audit, caught the multimillion-dollar blunder until Insight began asking why the audit as certified was short tens of millions of dollars.

While the county auditor was quick to point out the "mistake" on the part of the contract auditor, Vasquez Farukhi doesn't see it that way.

Lead auditor Lee Waddle tells Insight that the description used in the audit of the C&I fund "would have come out of [the county's] records. It would come out of the L.A. County accounting manual or a form. We just don't dream things up. I'd have to go back and check my work papers."

When Insight asks Waddle to do just that - to clear up the matter by locating the source of the description of the C&I account - he says, "No, we get paid by the hour here and I really can't be spending time on that. I couldn't do it anyway as far as particulars go because we have tight controls from the ethics of the organization. As far as the report goes, it stands by itself. Whatever it says, it says. If you want to know who set up the criteria, you'll have to check with the county."

Check with the county? Spillane, McCauley and Schonbach, the same county officials who either refuse or are unable to answer questions about the court's finances? The officials who say they are unable to provide detailed information about the amount of cash deposited in the Superior Court in a single year? Perhaps taxpayers in Los Angeles will have time to find out what happened to all those millions.

Meanwhile, Insight pressed on trying to obtain a bottom-line figure for cash taken in by the court. McCauley's office finally provided a 37-page computer printout that allegedly reflects the court's cash deposits for fiscal 2000. Although the printout provides a monthly ending balance for credits and debits, the report provides no details about the source and amounts of the debits and credits represent, providing only the unauditable lump-sum transfers.

As one accountant put it, "This is archaic. It's ridiculous to think that a county as large as Los Angeles can't program an accounting system that reconciles the books on a daily basis and [that] also can easily produce specific information about various accounts and provide yearly fund balances. It's just absurd."

****FAULTY NUMBER CRUNCHING****

How could the books for the County of Los Angeles be in such a mess if the authorities there weren't trying to hide something, critics ask. At least some of the problem appears to lay with the computing system. The Countywide Accounting and Purchasing System (CAPS) is a product of American Management Systems (AMS) and has been used in Los Angeles since 1987. IRS Commissioner Charles Rossotti is the founder and former chairman of AMS and remains a major stockholder in the company that provides computing services not only to Los Angeles County but to key federal agencies, including the IRS.

As Insight recently reported, due to severe problems with its AMS accounting system, the Department of Housing and Urban Development (HUD) was unable to balance its books under the recently departed secretary Andrew Cuomo (see "Cuomo Leaves HUD in Shambles," March 5) and, in 1999, was unable to account for $59 billion (see "Why Is $59 Billion Missing from HUD?" Nov. 6, 2000). Not surprisingly, under pressure from Insight, HUD since has decided to scrap the HUDCAPS computer program. But others have had similar problems with AMS finance systems, including the states of Mississippi and Kansas. Then again, as any auditor will be glad to confirm, there is nothing like institutionalized confusion to cover for and invite corruption.

Los Angeles Judge Sued For Money Laundering

Special to The Los Angeles Times by Richard Winton

A Los Angeles Superior Court judge has settled a civil suit alleging that he and others helped launder more than $1.8 million belonging to a wealthy physician friend, attorneys said Monday.

Judge Patrick Murphy will pay no money toward the $525,000 settlement, but his sister, Barbara Parsons Murphy, who allegedly handled part of the missing money, will pay $145,000, said Tracy Green, Murphy's attorney. The settlement will become official when all the defendants pay their portions of the settlement today, attorneys said.

The lawsuit, filed in November 1998 by the Smith Barney and Prudential Securities brokerage firms, accused [Judge] Murphy and several others of helping physician George Taus three years ago to wrongfully launder and conceal more than $1.8 million owed to Taus' creditors and his ex-wife.

The alleged scheme also is the subject of a federal grand jury investigation and a probe by the district attorney's office.

"Judge Murphy is glad to see the case settle," Green said. "We are cooperating with the investigation and we are doing our best to show our client, Judge Murphy, isn't guilty of any wrongdoing."

Green said it was her understanding that the district attorney's office had deferred its investigation to federal investigators, and the next step will be for Murphy to provide evidence to prove his innocence.

Under the civil settlement, none of the defendants admitted any liability, Green said. However, the settlement does not preclude the plaintiffs from asking for more money through restitution if criminal charges are filed.

Taus must foot most of the settlement, paying $271,000, attorneys said.

The rest of the money is coming from Murphy's sister and eight other defendants, who include Murphy's former paralegal and Stephen Alexander, a former Azusa mayor. Alexander could not be reached for comment Monday.

The suit alleged that in 1996, two years after Susan Taus filed for divorce, George Taus withdrew the money from a joint brokerage account and family accounts without her knowledge. The money was invested in a shell corporation, which in turn paid it out as part of a sexual harassment settlement to a ghost employee, the suit alleged.

That employee was a paralegal who once worked with Murphy when he was a private attorney, before his 1992 election to the bench. In a deposition filed in the case, the paralegal, Maryanne Baumgarten, testified that she then moved the money around at Murphy's direction.

The lawsuit alleged that [Judge] Murphy received $330,000 in cash, property and gold coins. It claims that the judge received nearly $14,000 for a new roof on his residence and $1,500 in car repairs. His attorneys have denied that he ever saw any money and claimed that others tried to implicate him to save themselves.

Attorneys for the brokerage firms confirmed the settlement Monday.

Taus could not be reached for comment.

The settlement comes as Murphy is facing possible removal from the bench by the state Commission on Judicial Performance for missing more than 157 days of work on sick leave last year and more than 400 days of work since 1996. The commission oversees the conduct of California judges.

The state investigation was initiated after it was revealed earlier this year that, while on sick leave and collecting his $117,000 salary, Murphy apparently enrolled as a first-year student in a Caribbean medical school. An attorney for Murphy, Edward M. Moses, last month acknowledged that Murphy withdrew from a medical school because of illness.

Murphy last month returned to the bench and was reassigned from the Citrus Court in West Covina, where he had heard criminal cases, to Traffic Court near downtown.

CHAPTER TEN

I did everything I could possibly do and found that Georgia would not protect my children. In July, 2000, after I received word that Judge Wood gave custody of the children to Andy, I sought help outside of Georgia. I called a child advocate in Mississippi, Lydia Rayner, and she introduced me to an attorney, Laurie Caldwell. Laurie convinced me to move to the Gulf coast of Mississippi. She told me that if the girls continued to say they were being abused by their father, that she would ask a highly respected forensic abuse specialist in the area to talk with them. Laurie was certain the State of Mississippi would protect Amanda and Jessica.

I began my move to Mississippi in August, 2000. In September, I took my children to Mississippi over my Labor Day visitation weekend. Prior to the trip they told me over the phone that they had tried to run away from their father's home, and when I asked why, the phone hung up. They were not allowed another phone conversation with me.

I alerted Laurie Caldwell, who then called Dr. Donald Matherne to ask if he would be on standby if we needed him. On the way to Mississippi, I asked Amanda and Jessica why they had tried to run away, and they said, "You know, Mommy." I said, "No, I don't. Tell me." They shared with me again that their father came into their bed at night and fondled them. Amanda said the bed would dip down as he got in bed with her and she pretended to be asleep. She "tried not to cry," she said, because "that made her daddy angry." I called Laurie and told her, and she immediately arranged for Dr. Matherne to meet with us the very next morning.

Dr. Matherne spent the following day talking with me, then Jessica, and then Amanda. Afterwards, he told me that if I returned Amanda and Jessica to their father that irreparable damage would be done. [His report may be found in Appendix F, Exhibit L] At that point I knew I could never send them back again. There was no way that I was going to send them back to be abused again. I love them so much. I would have done anything to protect them. I remember when Laurie and I told them that they would be protected, and that they would not have to go back to their father's home. They were so happy. I believed with all of my heart that finally they were going to be safe. So did Laurie.

The children were to be returned to Andy on Labor Day Monday at 6:00 p.m. We could not get into court until Tuesday the following morning. Laurie told me there was good legal reason not to return them and that I should not call Andy because of the danger that it posed to the children. So I didn't.

Mississippi Protects the Children

Early Tuesday morning Judge J. Walter Teel with the Harrison County Chancery Court of Mississippi looked at Dr. Matherne's report along with the other abuse reports from Dr. Hill, Dr. Brentnall, Dr. Pearce and letters from Dr. Cheatham, Gail Vernon and supervisors. He was convinced that the children were indeed abused and deprived children. The State of Mississippi immediately took emergency jurisdiction of Amanda and Jessica. He ordered that they go to the Children's Shelter until Andy was noticed and an emergency hearing could be held.

I was so glad to be in Mississippi with Amanda and Jessica because finally there were people who were doing what was required by law and what made sense to protect children using sensible and accepted protocol. The State of Georgia and the representatives in the Cobb County Superior Court had failed us terribly and had done so much wrong. I thought that the Mississippi court was going to make everything right and protect us from Andy and his family from ever hurting us again.

The time we spent together in Mississippi was so healing. I began to see the children get better even while living at the shelter, and I began to feel better too knowing that they were safe and that I was with them. Judge Teel allowed me to take Amanda and Jessica from the Shelter everyday from 8:00 a.m. until 5:00 p.m. It was so good to spend the time with them. Lydia had a swimming party with lots of adults and kids. It was so much fun especially for Amanda and Jessica. When Lydia's grandson, Tyler, cried, Amanda would carry him on her arm and rock him as she walked about to calm him down. I was so proud of her. She loved babies, and babies loved her. Jessica was so young and so brave. A little girl at the shelter took her pillow, and Jessica talked with her, but she would not give it back. We had to talk to Ms. Daniels, the shelter supervisor who was able to convince the little girl to return it to Jessica. One of the moms at the shelter was very kind and sewed up a hole in Jessica's doll. Each night was so difficult as I left them, but I knew they were safe and that we had to go through this period of time to bring them safely home to me.

One evening we were in a terrible storm. We were in our car not far from the shelter, when all of a sudden it became pitch black, and it began to rain and hail. We could only see streaks of wind and hail directly on the windshield. All the cars around us had come to a complete stop. We were terrified. As it began to pass, and I could see the light from the Sonic restaurant to the side of us, I drove up under the drive-in area and waited. We found out that windows in three cars around us had been blown out, and a large tree fell down on a car just ahead of us. Even with something so scary as this happening to us, we were so thankful that we were together and away from Georgia, their father and the people who had brought so much pain and suffering.

I picked the children up one Thursday morning. Amanda and Jessica told me that they both had the same nightmare the night before. When they told me about it, I asked them to write it in a journal that they had just started. Jessica complained that she didn't know how to spell yet, but I encouraged her to write her dream anyway and to try to spell each word by the way it sounded. I had forgotten that I asked them to do this. It was not until several months later that I saw what they wrote. It was disturbing to me that they had the same nightmare, and it frightened me.

When we hugged, kissed and said good night at the shelter that night, Thursday, September 14, 2000, I thought I would be seeing my daughters early the next morning. Never did I imagine that I would not see them again for so long. Their nightmare has haunted me since.

My nightmare

Yesterday night I had a nightmare it was about that my dad tooks me and evrybody else and he took us back to Alanta and he wodent let us comto are mom ever ever in are hole life again. he even wodent when we were a old Laty.

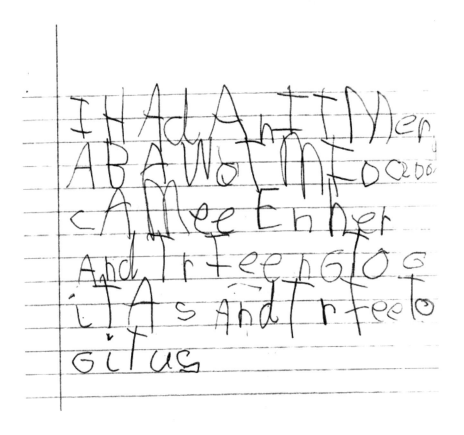

Later on Thursday night, I tried to call the girls at the shelter to say goodnight. The staff told me they had orders that I could not talk to them. I became very alarmed. The next morning, I tried to call again, and I talked with Ms. Daniels who told me the same thing.

I went to court at 9:00 a.m. Friday morning, September 15, 2000. I had a terrible feeling in my gut. Andy was there with his attorney, John Mayoue, and an attorney from Jackson, Mississippi. He also brought with him Diane Woods, Dr. Elizabeth King and Lorita Whitaker. They all stared at me with hatred. Ms. Whitaker whom I had never met locked her eyes on me and stared me cold.

Laurie Caldwell was there to represent me, and Dr. Matherne was there to report to the court. My brothers, Mark and Robin, along with a few other Mississippi friends were also present. I quickly learned that there is jurisdictional law that would not allow Mississippi to hold the hearing. It would have to go back to the original court in Cobb County.

At the urging of Andy and his entourage, Judge Teel ordered that Diane Woods would escort the children back to Georgia, put them in a foster care home until a hearing could be held, and that neither Andy or I could see the girls or talk with them until further order from the Cobb County court. Judge Teel ordered that Dr. Matherne's report was to be given to Judge Bodiford and to the Department of Family and Children's Services, and it was ordered that no one was to talk with Amanda and Jessica about the allegations of abuse.

My heart sank, as I knew that Diane Woods, Elizabeth King, Lorita Whitaker, and Andy's attorneys, would not protect my children. They would return them to their father and bring harm to me.

And that's exactly what happened.

Andy, assisted by his attorneys, Diane Woods, the Cobb County District Attorney's office and the Kennesaw Police Department obtained three warrants for my arrest. Immediately after the hearing in Mississippi on Friday, September 15, the FBI arrested me on a UFAP warrant (unlawful flight from one state to another to avoid prosecution), and they took me to jail, even though I had done nothing wrong and had broken no law. The FBI told me they were sorry, but they had orders. They solemnly walked me to their car. They put handcuffs on me and took me to the Harrison County, Mississippi jail. I could not even say good-bye to Amanda and Jessica. They booked me, searched me, and stripped me naked. I put on orange and white striped pants and shirt and flip-flops. I was taken to an area with about 30-40 other women and was given a cell with one other woman. Cement walls and a cement floor and a cement ceiling surrounded me. I carried my sleeping mat with a worn sheet, a toothbrush, and a roll of toilet paper.

The guards were hateful and treated everyone with contempt. One guard would take her club and knock everything over as she went from cell to cell. She yelled at each person and pounded on the windows and the beds. I was not given a fork for eating and was refused all requests I made for pen and paper, a book to read, and the phone number of my attorney.

The women had not been outside in the sun for many days. We did not go out during the five days I was there either. The male inmates went outside daily.

I started to bleed while I was in jail and asked for menstrual pads. I was told to use my sheet. Laurie Caldwell forced them to finally give me a bag of pads. The guard who gave them to me told me to hide them under my clothing as I took them back to my cell so that no other woman would know. I looked pregnant as I walked back into my cell, and every person there knew I was hiding something. As soon as I received the pads, my bleeding stopped, and I began to distribute them to all the other women. Doesn't God do funny things?

My clothes were bloody, and they would not give me clean ones. But all I could think about was Amanda and Jessica. I felt so numb and so afraid of what was happening to them.

The women in jail began to ask me why I was there. I told them that I had tried to protect my daughters from their father's abuse. I found out during the five days I was there that most of the women in jail had been sexually abused when they were children. They said their mothers had never done anything to help them. They were so angry at the world. As a result, they had acted out criminally. They were so amazed that I had tried to do something for my children, unlike their mothers. They were profoundly affected.

When I was jailed, Diane Woods and Elizabeth King immediately went to the shelter where Amanda and Jessica were and broke the Mississippi court order to which Diane Woods had agreed and had signed. They talked with Amanda and Jessica for over an hour about the abuse. They reunited them with their father for their trip back to Atlanta. Woods wrote a letter September 18, 2000, to the Department of Family and Children's Services and told them that the children's statements to her and Dr. King were inconsistent with what Dr. Matherne had reported, leading DFACS and the court to believe that Amanda and Jessica had not been abused by their father. It was months later that we found out that the girls had in fact told them that their father had sexually molested them.

Cobb County District Attorney Patrick Head refused to agree to a bond so that I could be released. The Mississippi judge said that by law he had to set bond, so Mr. Head told them to set it so high that I could not make bail. The court refused his request and set the bail for $5,000. Finally, after spending five days in jail, Laurie along with my brother, Robin, were able to bond me out. Andy and his group did everything they could to keep me in jail as long as they could. I was released on the evening of Tuesday, September 19, 2000. I happened to hear by fifth hand that a hearing was going to take place in Cobb County early the next morning. There was no way I could be there, nor had they notified me or my attorneys of the hearing.

Unlawful Suspension of My Rights

On September 20, 2000, Judge Bodiford held this emergency *ex parte* hearing called by Diane Woods. Judge Bodiford stated I had asked for a continuance to allow me time to return to Georgia, retain counsel, and appear for the hearing, and he asked Ms. Woods to respond to the motion. Ms. Woods stated, "I cannot agree to a continuance. ...I need a protective order from the court."

My family and friends sat in the courtroom and witnessed what happened. Ms. Woods told the court that the children should be returned to their father and that my family and I should not be allowed to come within 3,000 yards of them or of any of the Titelman family. George Washington, a supervisor with DFACS testified there had been "numerous investigations." He said he had read Dr. Matherne's report and that "there was no information that would overturn the judge's earlier ruling that the custody should be with the father." Judge Bodiford agreed that it was an emergency to give the children back to the father. He ordered that Dr. Matherne's report be sealed from the public, along with all the other Mississippi court files, in Diane Woods's office. He ordered everything that Diane Woods requested. Amanda and Jessica were sent back to their father, and an order was issued to keep me and my family from seeing my children.

The fundamental legal doctrine of due process of law found in the Fifth and the Fourteenth Amendments of the United States Constitution protects our basic rights to life, liberty, and property. It prohibits all levels of government from arbitrarily or unfairly depriving individuals of these rights. Some of these rights are so basic, natural and fundamental that they must be protected with guaranteed enforcement, such as,

- Right to a fair and public trial conducted in a competent manner
- Right to adequate notice of a lawsuit
- Right to be present during testimony
- Right to cross-examine witnesses
- Right to be heard in one's own defense
- Right to be told of the crime being charged
- Right to own property
- Right to freedom of religion
- Right to freedom of speech
- Right to raise one's children

An *ex parte* hearing or conversation occurs when only one party meets with the judge alone. *Ex parte* communication denies one of the fundamental due process guarantees. In *Camero v United States*, 375 F.2d 777, 780-81 (Ct. Cl. 1967), the court held:

[O]ne of the fundamental premises inherent in the concept of an adversary hearing ... is that neither adversary be permitted to engage in an ex parte communication concerning the merits of the case with those responsible for the decision. It is difficult to imagine a more serious incursion on fairness than to permit the representative of one of the parties to privately communicate his recommendations to the decision makers .... We are of the opinion that due process forbids it.

A treatise for judges, *Judicial Conduct and Ethics* § 5.01 states,

Ex parte communications deprive the absent party of the right to respond and be heard. They suggest bias or partiality on the part of the judge. *Ex parte* conversations or correspondence can be misleading; the information given to the judge 'may be incomplete or inaccurate, the problem can be incorrectly stated.' At the very least, participation in *ex parte* communications will expose the judge to one-sided argumentation, which carries the attendant risk of an erroneous ruling on the law or facts. At worst, *ex parte* communication is an invitation to improper influence if not outright corruption.

On September 20, 2000 Judge Bodiford held an *ex parte* hearing after he had several *ex parte* communications with Diane Woods, Patrick Head, and John Mayoue and/or Pamela Gray. I was never noticed, had no attorney representation, was not allowed to cross examine witnesses or present evidence and testimony at this hearing. I learned of the hearing only the night before right after being released from the Harrison County Mississippi jail where I had been for five days because of bogus arrest warrants initiated by Andrew Titelman, Diane Woods, John Mayoue, Pamela Gray, and Detective Craig Chandler. After learning about the hearing, I faxed a letter to Judge Bodiford to get the hearing postponed. Judge Bodiford denied my request. He then issued an *ex parte* order that

I nor any member of my family can come within 3000 yards of any of the Titelman family including my children, Amanda and Jessica. As a federal appellate court stated regarding ex parte communications in the case of *Camero v United States*, "It is difficult to imagine a more serious incursion...." A leading treatise for judges, Shaman's *Judicial Conduct and Ethics*, "[E]x parte communication is an invitation to improper influence if not outright corruption."

The September 20, 2000, hearing was not a legal hearing and the resulting order was not a legal order. Due process never took place. Even though this was pointed out to Judge Bodiford in a subsequent hearing on October 4, 2000, and even though he agreed that it was not proper and that the order would be voided, Judge Bodiford has refused all this time to actually sign an order vacating his illegal order. If Judge Bodiford would simply sign such a decree putting into effect what he said he would do on October 4, 2000, then at least I would be seeing my girls on a regular basis. On October 4, Judge Bodiford decided that I could not visit the children for only a period of two weeks. He called it a "gentlemen's agreement." Even after my subsequent attorney Richard Ducote wrote Judge Bodiford a letter in November, 2001, merely asking him to sign an order simply reflecting what Judge Bodiford decided on October 4, 2000, he refused and accused my lawyer of being unprofessional.

I was devastated by what had happened. I could only imagine how Amanda and Jessica were feeling and the fear they were experiencing. Laurie, Lydia, and Dr. Matherne were appalled, as were all of our friends and family. None of us could understand how something like this could happen.

Laurie and I immediately began to search for an attorney in Atlanta who would represent me. Even though I had been released from jail in Mississippi on bond I still had arrest warrants out for me in Georgia, which meant that as soon as I entered Georgia I would be arrested again. But I also had to go to court there and defend against felony charges they were bringing against me.

It was very difficult finding an attorney. John Mayoue was telling people that I was "paranoid schizophrenic", and many attorneys did not want anything to do with me or the case. Laurie and I found an attorney, Kathy Portnoy, who said she would help me. When I arrived in Atlanta, I drove to the Cobb County jail and told them who I was. They immediately arrested me, as I knew they would. I was in jail for half of the night until my mother was able to bond me out.

CHAPTER ELEVEN

There were now two reasons I had to go to court, first to try to get the children safe from their father and second to defend myself from the criminal charges for which I had been arrested. Judge Bodiford set a hearing for October 2, 2000, for contempt of court charges against me. Kathy Portnoy needed more time to prepare. On October 2, she sent her associate, Brenda Godfrey, to ask for a continuance. On the advice of Kathy Portnoy, I was not there. Judge Bodiford was furious that I was absent. A two day continuance was given and a hearing was set for October 4.

Unknown to Brenda Godfrey, my mother and friends were present for the October 2 hearing. Immediately after the hearing I receiving several phone calls from concerned friends and family. It was reported that Ms. Godfrey stated to the court, "There is no concern about the children because they are in a safe place with their father." It was also reported that John Mayoue, opposing counsel, went to Ms. Godfrey and asked her if he should file a lien on my house for the costs of going to Mississippi, even though his motion for costs had already been dismissed in Mississippi. She told him he should! My mother and friends went to her after the hearing. Ms. Godfrey was shaken when she learned who they were, and she became angry and defensive. She told my family and friends that I owed an apology to the court and that I needed to raise a lot of money.

When I learned of this, I was furious. I called her and confronted her. She attacked me saying that while she was in John Mayoue's office looking at his files, she saw evidence that I had coached the children to say these things. I was appalled when I found out that Ms. Godfrey went to John Mayoue's office and was duped. The "evidence" she saw were "anonymous" letters that indicated I told the children to say these things. She had no idea where the letters came from or who may have written them. These letters, like other anonymous letters surfacing over the next two years, were obviously written by Andy and his family.

I told Ms. Godfrey I did not want her working in my case again. When I addressed this with Ms. Portnoy she acted as though it had not occurred. She stated to me that she would not have

157

taken my case unless she believed me. She also said she needed Ms. Godfrey working with her.

We went to court October 4, 2000. Kathy Portnoy brought Ms. Godfrey to assist her. It had been three weeks since I had seen Amanda and Jessica.

Diane Woods put on a pathetic act in court as she attempted to shed a tear or two and grunted out what was supposed to be a cry. She told the court that when she and Dr. King went to the shelter to see Amanda and Jessica that they found them in a terrible state from the abuse I had inflicted upon them by taking them to Mississippi. She said, "I cannot describe to the Court or the parties in this courtroom the state I found those children in when I got to the shelter and had to tell them what was going on. I don't want them put through any more of this. ... This is serious, Judge. This had impact on those children."

This certainly wasn't the first time Ms. Woods deceived the court. The supervisor at the shelter, Ms. Bajda Daniels, told the jury what really happened when she testified at my criminal trial six and a half months later, as I explain on pp. 175-176.

Kathy Portnoy told Judge Bodiford he had broken the law by doing what he did on September 20th, by having a hearing without giving me any notification and removing my rights to see my children. There were discussions about voiding all the orders from that hearing and giving me my visitation rights back again until we could have a full blown hearing.

After that hearing when I tried to see my children, Andy, his attorneys, Diane Woods, Dr. King, and Lorita Whitaker all said, "No." I was told I would be arrested if I went anywhere near them. During this hearing Kathy Portnoy told the court that we were prepared to dismiss my appeal that I had filed from the final hearing. I couldn't believe my ears. Brenda Godfrey leaned over and told me if I didn't drop the appeal I would never see the kids again. Ms. Portnoy looked at me waiting for my approval. I couldn't understand why this was happening, but felt I had no choice. I didn't know anything about the law and had to depend upon them at the time. They were the legal experts. The appeal was, therefore, dropped. I found out much later from other attorneys that Kathy Portnoy and Brenda Godfrey had played me for a fool. They purposefully lied to me.

The court could not hold me in contempt without dropping the other criminal charges, as it is considered double jeopardy to prosecute someone twice for the same offence. Judge Bodiford stated there may be some gray area that he could punish me in some way. John Mayoue was attempting to get an order for me to pay the Mississippi costs which he said amounted to approximately $56,500 even though by law it had been dismissed in Mississippi and Georgia could not rule on the issue. Andy refused to honor all aspects of the property settlement to which he had agreed and signed in mediation. We had a rental house during our marriage of which Andy was to sign over to me and I was to pay him 50% of the equity from my share of the monies that were to be given to me from the Pension Plan. Judge Bodiford put a stay on the transfer of property from Andy's name to mine even though Andy was in contempt of court for not abiding by the agreement.

These issues were left unresolved even though the law was clearly in my favor. The hearing was reset for November, 2000, but was never held because Ms. Portnoy's husband was hospitalized in intensive care and she wanted another $15,000 from me. I wanted Dr. Matherne to testify before Judge Bodiford to show how serious a mistake it was to have the girls live with their father. I wanted him to tell what the girls disclosed to him. The court had already made decisions without all the facts and was determined to hold me in contempt of court.

For three months I struggled with Kathy Portnoy to try to get her to do the things that had to be done in order to get Amanda and Jessica protected and renew my contact with them. The first month I paid her $15,000 fee. One month later Ms. Portnoy requested $15,000 more, which was paid. Every time it was time to go to court, Ms. Portnoy's office staff would call me and tell me she had to cancel. Then after doing absolutely nothing, $15,000 more was requested, and I was told if I didn't pay it that Ms. Portnoy would not represent me.

I sent the children's new shoes to Ms. Portnoy and asked that they be given to the girls. I sent letters and cards by way of Ms. Portnoy. A Thanksgiving letter was returned to me stating I could make no references to God. I took Christmas presents to her office. I had to give the presents to a courier for delivery to John Mayoue. Later when I received an itemized statement I saw Ms. Portnoy charged me $500 for that action. I was calling her frequently leaving messages and asking why she had not filed the necessary pleadings to get protection for my children. She rarely talked to me, and when she did, she talked in circles.

I asked another attorney, Richard Ducote, to meet with us to determine what the problem was. I then learned that Kathy Portnoy represented men who had been accused of child molestation, and that she, too, used "Parental Alienation Syndrome" to defend them and to get custody of the children for them. Her conflict of interest explained why she was not helping me. In January, 2001, when I fired her and retrieved my files, the shoes, letters and cards I thought had been given to my children were in her files. They had never been sent.

In December of 2000, after my many requests to see the children, Ms. Portnoy received a letter from Diane Woods stating I could see one of my daughters for one hour at the DFACS office under supervision, and the other the following week. We received another letter stating that I could sit across a table from them and play a game. We believed they were setting me up, and that they were trying to convince Amanda and Jessica that I was a dangerous woman. We wrote back demanding that I have the regular visitation to which I was legally entitled. When it was apparent that the only way I was going to be able to see the children was through supervision, we wrote saying we would agree to supervised visitation. Diane Woods then immediately stated she would allow no visitation at all.

During the time Ms. Portnoy was supposed to represent me, she asked Dr. Peter Thomas, another Atlanta psychologist, to examine all the files. I was told to pay him $5,000. He called me and told me that it appeared the children had been abused. He also told me I had to be willing "to play the game" or never see my children again. He said that whether there was abuse or not, we could never mention abuse again, and that if I ever did, the Georgia courts would rule against me. "That's the way Georgia is," he said. He asked, "Are you willing to play the game?" I was appalled.

That night I went to the beach and lay in the sand next to the shore. I beat the sand with my hands and my feet. I screamed out as tears poured from my eyes. My screams were swallowed up in the sounds of the waves splashing against the shore. I angrily sought God and questioned why He was not helping us.

I tried to call Amanda and Jessica many times and left messages on the recorder. Then I no longer was able to get through because the phone had been changed to a non-published number. We continued to try to get permission for me to see the girls per the court order of the final hearing the year before. The answer was always, "Absolutely not."

Justice for Children (JFC), was made aware of the abuse of Amanda and Jessica. After studying the case they became advocates for my daughters. JFC is a national nonprofit organization of citizens concerned about children's rights and their protection from abuse. It was founded in 1987 by Randy Burton, a former Chief Prosecutor of the Family Offenses Section of the Harris County District Attorney's office in Houston, Texas, in response to the inadequacies and failure of child protective systems. Justice for Children's position in cases is recognized and valued by local and national media, legal and medical professionals, child abuse experts, and various other children's rights organizations. It has been featured on many TV news programs and has been recognized by the American Bar Association.

JFC contacted Governor Roy Barnes who told them to contact the official state child advocate, DeAlva Sims. Ms. Sims reacted with hostility towards Justice for Children. Kimberly Stabler, Executive Director of JFC, receives numerous phone calls from Georgia regarding children that are not being protected by the State. But when she tries to talk with the people responsible she is confronted only with anger and defensiveness.

I went to the Cobb County Superior Court Clerk's office and asked to see my file. I found in the file that Diane Woods and Elizabeth King have unlawfully recorded an enormous bogus lien against a property that was to be signed over to me in the division of property settlement. The illegal lien was signed by Judge James Bodiford. Woods and King essentially stole my property. Just prior to this lien, Diane Woods was paid approximately $900 more by me than what the court had ordered me to pay her. This was paid at her request and communicated to me by Kathy Portnoy. I was told I better pay it if I wanted to see my kids.

November, 2000, Officer Burrell with Kennesaw Police Department went to a tenant of the house Andy and I owned in Kennesaw saying he was looking for Wendy Titelman. He told the woman that he and other officers had been perusing the neighborhood often in search of me and not to be surprised if she (the tenant) is stopped again and asked about her identity. He told her it was very serious and that it had gone to a federal level. This was purposeful harassment to intimidate this family into questioning me. The Cobb County Superior Court and police departments knew exactly where I was. I had already been arrested in Georgia, processed and was in their system. There were no warrants for my arrest at that time. The tenants refused to pay another penny in rent and were evicted several months later.

In January, 2001, I hired a different attorney, Randy Kessler. Even though he initially agreed he would do everything I had requested, after he received $10,000, I struggled to have him file the necessary motions. He then demanded more money and refused to file the motions I was requesting.

I had begun to realize that local attorneys were not willing to stand up and fight the system in which they had to work day after day. They were not willing to tell a judge that he was wrong and should be recused for his illegal behavior. They did not want to upset or to get on the wrong side of the guardian *ad litem* and court appointed psychologist with whom they would have to work in the future. They believed to do so would be political suicide, even though it is their ethical obligation to competently and vigorously represent their client.

After the final hearing in June of 2000, I confronted my attorney, Mr. Dupree, and Kyle Broussard, his paralegal. I addressed his weak representation of me, and his failure to present evidence and properly cross-examine those who lied at the final hearing. Kyle responded to my anger by saying, "Well, we are a political organization." There was evidence that was never presented to the court. There were important witnesses that the court should have heard. I requested numerous times that Dr. Frank

162

Pittman and Diane Woods be deposed and that the polygraph tests results be examined by another investigator. Mr. Dupree told me he would take those actions, but he never did. Nor did he object to the use of the polygraph, which is widely known by professionals to be ineffective in a case of sexual abuse.

A house falls when the foundation is weak. Mr. Dupree, who was supposed to uncover the truth and firmly plant our feet on it, totally failed and in the end, refused to do so. I firmly believe that my children and I would not be in this situation today if I had been represented in a competent, honest, and vigorous manner.

My attorney should have objected to the illegal *ex-parte* communications. He should have had the use of "Parental Alienation Syndrome" and "False Memory Syndrome" thrown out on the basis of "junk science." He should have challenged Diane Woods and her unsworn statements and reliance on Dr. Pittman's false claim to know the Titelmans better than anyone else. He should have shown the cover up of sexual abuse by playing Dr. King's own tapes to the court and the video produced by Andy Titelman, and he should have uncovered and presented the phone notes which documented King and Woods having concocted their plans to do interviews and then have an emergency hearing in order to give custody to Andy. He should have done many things that he never did. In his closing arguments, he further "sold me out" when he stated, "I don't believe that anyone is going to sexually molest the children. If they have been in the past, I don't believe it will happen again."

Lydia introduced me to another attorney in the fall of 2000, Richard Ducote. He has a nationwide practice representing victims of sexual abuse and domestic violence and has helped hundreds of abused children across the country. Richard's primary specialization is in cases where courts have granted custody of children to child molesters and domestic violence perpetrators, and he has been an ardent opponent of the bogus "Parental Alienation Syndrome." He has had appearances on Donahue, Oprah, 60 Minutes, CNN, and Good Morning Britain, Leeza and interview quotes in Parade Magazine, Good Housekeeping, Money, and the National Law Journal. The New Orleans Times-Picayune described him in a 1987 feature story as "raising hell for children in courtrooms all over the country."

At the recent 7th International Domestic Violence Conference Richard participated as a Plenary Panel Speaker before 1700 people. He sat next to Ruth Busch, J.D., Associate Professor, University of Waikato, New Zealand. The moderator, Dr. Robert Geffner, told everyone that Richard Ducote was responsible for the first law in America to prohibit child abusers and domestic violence perpetrators from getting custody of their children. Upon hearing this, Ruth Busch became so excited and reported the passage of a law in New Zealand using Richard's law as the model. Now she knew it was Richard that was behind it.

Richard knows what these bad dads do to their children and to their wives, and he does what is necessary to stop it. There are children all over the country who love Richard because of what he has done for them, and I have talked to a few of them.

I first learned of Richard through Judge Sol Gothard with the Louisiana Fifth Circuit Court of Appeal. I called Judge Gothard prior to my final hearing after learning that he has written articles about child abuse and domestic violence. He told me I should contact Richard Ducote. He said he had tremendous respect for him and that he was his protégé. Judge Gothard also told me about the judges manual that warns judges that "Parental Alienation Syndrome" should never be allowed in the courtroom. I asked Hylton Dupree to use Richard as an expert witness, and Mr. Dupree told me that the court would not allow him to testify. I have since learned otherwise.

Richard has spent a lot of time thinking about Amanda and Jessica and considering what to do in light of all the errors and cover-up. He has filed motions and lawsuits to free the children and bring them home to me. He knows that we must have the case heard by someone other than Judge Bodiford, someone who is unbiased and decides on the evidence. And he knows that we have to remove the deceitful and incompetent Diane Woods, Elizabeth King and Lorita Whitaker.

In October, 2001, we learned in discovery that Diane Woods and Elizabeth King are good friends and had planned their scheme before Dr. King ever met the family. Even after the exposure of this corruption, and the *ex-parte* communications and *ex-parte* emergency hearing and severe bias, Judge Bodiford is adamant that they will all stay put.

In a 1915 case, *Nichols vs. State*, the Georgia Supreme Court stated,

> The administration of the law, especially that of the criminal law, should, like Caesar's wife, be above suspicion, and should be free from all temptation, bias or prejudice, so far as it is possible for our courts to accomplish it...[23]

Accordingly, Diane Woods, Elizabeth King, Lorita Whitaker and Judge Bodiford should be recused.

the Criminal Trial

We had to get past the hurdle of my criminal trial, The State of Georgia v. Wendy Jane Titelman. There was no basis for the Federal UFAP warrant, and therefore, the charges were dropped immediately. There were two warrants issued by the State of Georgia, both without basis as well. One was dropped, and the State of Georgia pursued the other.

The trial was finally held April 23-27, 2001. Richard had long before told me I would have to be patient, the wheels of justice move slowly. Outwardly, I have been patient, and I act calmly. Inwardly though, I am dying from the grief of what has happened to our lives.

Richard and I found a local attorney, Michael Hirsh, a wonderful man who is a friend of the Williams' family whom the children knew and adored. Michael defended me in the trial with Richard's help. For one week they worked day and night to present my case to a twelve-member jury.

Judge Robert Flournoy ruled that we could not bring up any evidence of abuse prior to the divorce somewhat limiting our defense. There were numerous reports made by individuals substantiating sexual abuse and other abuse that had been reported to DFACS, Crimes Against Children, the Cobb County Police Department, the Kennesaw Police Department, and the Georgia Bureau of Investigators. Judge Flournoy would not allow us to present any of these witnesses or to allow the jury to hear anything that happened prior to the final hearing in June of 2000. We had to totally rely on Dr. Matherne's September, 2000, report and one taped conversation that Dr. Elizabeth King made with the children.

I was being prosecuted for the offense of interstate interference with custody. The indictment under the statute which I was charged read,

> Wendy Jane Titelman ... in the County of Cobb and State of Georgia, on the 4th day of September, 2000, did unlawfully and intentionally take Amanda Titelman and Jessica Titelman, minor children, away from the individual having lawful custody of said children, to wit: Andrew Titelman, and did remove them from this state, contrary to the laws of said state, the good order, peace and dignity thereof.

The final custody order did not prevent me from taking the children out of the state. On September 1, 2000, we traveled to Mississippi for our scheduled visitation. It was impossible for me to take them out of Georgia on September 4, as we had already been in Mississippi for several days. Under the laws of the state, there was justification in my not returning Amanda and Jessica to their father on September 4 when our visitation ended. The State of Mississippi thought the same and on September 5 took emergency jurisdiction over the children. The State had to prove beyond a reasonable doubt that my actions were not justified. The entire prosecution was bogus.

Francey Hakes, Assistant District Attorney, was the prosecutor. Her witnesses were Andy Titelman, Diane Woods, Elizabeth King and Lorita Whitaker.

Andy's testimony was very short. He testified that he had never read Dr. Matherne's report and was not really interested in reading it.

We learned that Diane Woods has had no child abuse training and is not qualified to the role she plays. She admitted to agreeing and signing the Mississippi court order preventing her and others from conversing with the children about the abuse and preventing contact between the children and their father and mother. But she said she didn't have to follow it.

Lorita Whitaker concocted a story that I tried to feed my children to the alligators during our visit to Alexander Springs in Florida just a few weeks prior to our going to Mississippi. She has never met me or spoken with me, and she admitted that she has no interest in speaking with me. The only other time I had seen her was in Mississippi when she stared at me with hatred in the courtroom. She stated that she is an expert in child sexual abuse, but when asked about classic books and known accepted protocols, she was not familiar with any. She said her training was from "personal experience." She stated that you can identify molesters just by looking at them and that you can spot them on the street.

Ms. Whitaker tried to discredit Dr. Matherne. She said he abused the children when he had them "demonstrate masturbation" using their hand on a closed fist to show what their father did to them. In other words, Ms. Whitaker took the ridiculous position that it was wrong to find out what had happened to the children by asking them to describe it. She also admitted at the criminal trial that the girls love and miss me very much and want to visit me. Yet, during the criminal trial Ms. Whitaker served as the prosecution's "expert witness consultant" and the State's representative to assist Francey Hakes in her cross examination of my expert witnesses. She attempted to help the state convict me, her clients' mother. She testified that she has told the children that I do not want to see them.

During a break, I went up to her in the courtroom and asked if I could talk with her. She immediately panicked, turned and whispered to Francey Hakes. Ms. Hakes loudly and defensively told my attorney that Ms. Whitaker would not be talking with me, and I was not to approach her again. We were shocked that the children's therapist had no interest to talk with their mother and refused to have any communication with me whatsoever.

Since the trial, on March 27, 2002, we deposed Ms. Whitaker. She would not reveal anything in her file or anything about the girls. She did say at her deposition that she will not talk with me, and she stated she has no interest in any evidence that shows that the children have been sexually abused. She said it has nothing to do with her role as a therapist for the girls, and that her loyalty is to Andy.

In the criminal trial, Dr. Elizabeth King was asked about her experience as an expert in child sexual abuse. She admitted to having read most of Richard Gardner's books and using "Parental Alienation Syndrome." She said she has attended workshops presented by Joan Kelly who published with Judith Wallerstein, and one of CRC's founding officials. These are two of Gardner's disciples who promote his PAS and alienation of affection propaganda. When Dr. King was asked about her awareness of nationally accepted published protocol for conducting sexual abuse evaluations, she answered she is aware they exist. However, she could not name even one protocol. Michael asked her if she used any of the protocols. She answered, "I use sort of an informal assessment based on having reviewed several of the protocols that are currently being used and having reviewed some of the literature that's been published." Further, we found out she is not familiar with books that are most notable in her field. This is the woman who claims to be an expert in child sexual abuse. Here are some of the other questions Michael Hirsh asked her and her answers:

Q   Dr. King, are you aware that there are no psychological tests in determining if a man is a child molester if he doesn't confess?

A   Am I aware that there are?

Q   No tests that can determine if a man is a child molester, unless he confesses?

A   I believe that would be accurate, yes.

Q   Okay. Dr. King, is it also true that deliverate false accusations of sexual abuse made in the context of a custody case are rare? Would you agree with that statement?

A   That they are rare?

Q   Yes, that allegations -- deliberate false -- deliberate false allegations of sexual abuse in the context of a custody case are rare is my question?

A   Given that it would be difficult to prove that something were deliberate, that would not surprise me in the least; and given the number of custody cases that are filed, I believe that issues of sexual allegation are a small percentage so that the percentage of deliberately misleading allegations would be, in fact, very small, yes.

***

Q   Isn't it true that, if sexually abused children know they are going to be with their abuser, that they will act in such a way that's trying to please him?

A   I think that happens sometimes.

Q   And would you agree with me that sexually abused children don't necessarily show fear of the abuser? Isn't that also correct?

A   Yes, that's correct, they don't always show fear of the abuser.

***

Q   You'll agree with me, Dr. King, won't you, that child molesters cannot be detected by how they look, speak, their jobs, that kind of thing, isn't that correct?

A   I believe that's correct. Of course, there are certain occupations that are more attractive to pedophiles than others.

Q   All right. And you'll agree with me that there are fathers who, in fact, molest their daughters?

A   Yes.

Q   And you'll agree with me, won't you, that often the vehicle for that molestation comes in the way of playing games to use - to get cooperation from the children, isn't that also correct?

A   Yes, that can happen

Q   Yeah. And sexually abusued children will you - you'll agree with me, won't you, that sexually abused children very often recant their reports of abuse and say the

169

Q   abuse didn't happen because of pressure or threats ... from the abuser?

A   That can happen, yes.

***

Q   ...It's true, isn't it, that there - when there is a divorce, that there tends to be a picking up of sides, particularly in young children, between mom and dad?

A   Sadly, that happens, yes.

Q   And also sadly sometimes they will view, whether rightly or wrongly, they will view one parent as being more advantageous to them than the other, isn't that also true?

A   More advantageous?

Q   ... For instance, one parent might tend to indulge and spoil the child, you can have whatever you want and one might be more strict?

A   That happens, yes.

Q   And it's also true that, isn't it, that some children would feel safer in one house or the other?

A   That's often true.

Q   ...Isn't it also true that they might see an option opening up to be away froman abusive parent when the parents are living separately, isn't that also true, they might - that a child might see that as an option?

A   I think that's possible. I think you would have to look at the ages of the children --

Q   Okay.

A   -- as a factor in that.

Q   Certainly it happens?

A   Certainly it can happen, yes.

While Dr. King was on the witness stand, Michael Hirsh asked her if the girls reported in September of 2000 that they had been abused by their father. Dr. King turned to Judge Flournoy and asked, "Do I have to answer that question? You will get mad at me if I do." Judge Flournoy told her to answer the question. The answer was, "Yes," the girls had told her and Diane Woods that they were being abused. Dr. King went on to say that even if Andy

170

had molested the children, he should still be considered for custody.

Ms. Hakes subpoenaed Judge Bodiford to testify against me. He came into the courtroom, grinning ear to ear, willing to do so. We couldn't believe their gall. Michael Hirsh addressed the court,

> Your Honor, I am trying to think of all the objections that I could interpose right now, and I am running out of fingers. With all due respect, Judge Bodiford, I think this is highly, highly improper. Number one, the appearance of a judge testifying on behalf of the prosecution against -- effectively why she's calling him against the accused is in and of itself improper. Number two, there is a pending, ongoing legal matter in Judge Bodiford's Court and his -- I think that his appearance here even so far is – he should be recused from the -- further in the domestic relations matter. This is highly improper. And third, his what -- in your opinion, what legal -- what order is in effect is a legal opinion. He's essentially being called as an expert witness. In fact, we got the transcript of October 4th. It's and exhibit. It's in evidence. They are going to have it.

After Michael's objection, Judge Flournoy did not allow Judge Bodiford to testify before the jury.

All the individuals who testified for the State led the court to believe that the children were doing fine. However, in discovery we found a phone message from Lorita Whitaker to Elizabeth King on January 11, 2001, four months after the girls were taken from the Mississippi shelter. The message stated, "Amanda has begun writing on the walls with markers and they are both stealing things. ... They stole a checkbook and wallet from one of Andy's employees. She caught them. Also caught hiding credit cards. ... Andy said Jessica stole and found employee's check's in Jessica's purse." An expert told me this indicated to him that the children were trying to get the resources necessary to run away. The message went on to state that Andy told Lorita Whitaker that Jessica told him that "Mommy told her to lie about Daddy doing bad things to her," and Andy is "concerned they can lie with a straight face."

When it was our turn to present witnesses in the criminal trial, Laurie Caldwell, Bajda Daniels, Dr. Donald Matherne, and Dr. Joyanna Silberg testified.

Laurie Caldwell told the court that the children told her about the abuse. She described what she did to get Dr. Matherne to examine the children. She also told about the emergency proceedings in the Harrison County Chancery Court. She testified that Judge J. Walter Teel was very concerned about the children's safety and protection from their father, and that he invoked the emergency provisions of the Uniform Child Custody Jurisdiction Act to help the children. She said that because of the way the UCCJA is written, that the matter had to be heard in Georgia. She said Judge Teel was very concerned, but he felt he had no choice, the law stated that Georgia would have to hear it.

Dr. Matherne testified that he is a clinical and forensic psychologist with over thirty years of experience, a consultant to the courts and the State Attorney General's Office, and works mainly with murder, abuse and personal injury cases. He described his meeting with Amanda and Jessica and me. He explained the methodology that he uses stating, "It has been peer reviewed by other psychologists, guardians *ad litem,* prosecutors, defense attorneys and judges," and "follows a paradigm that they have found to be acceptable and credible."

He stated, "I observed a mother who had a close relationship with her daughters and the two daughters had a close relationship with their mother. Both girls were quite happy and it appeared to me that they had a very effective bond."

He said Jessica described her father as "mean," "who hits her because he gets angry." He said that Jessica pointed to the genital area on a drawing and indicated that this is where she had been touched by her father. She took a pen and circled the area and wrote her name next to it. Dr. Matherne said he asked her to show him with her hands what happened, "I said, take your hand and close it, and I want you to pretend that this is your private area. I want you to take your other hand and show me what happened." He said that Jessica took her other hand and rubbed it across her closed fist and that she referred to her father touching her under her clothing when she was in bed. Dr. Matherne told the court he asked Jessica if she shared this with anyone else, and she told him she told Dr. King, but that Dr. King didn't seem interested. Both children explained that Dr. King changes the subject when they try to tell her about the molestation. He stated that based on what Jessica shared that she was fearful of returning to her father and that intervention was needed to protect her.

He testified about his interview with Amanda. When he asked Amanda if anybody ever hurt her, she said that her father hits her, that he gets mad, screams and yells. He said Amanda also drew a circle around the genital area of the picture and she wrote her name and said that her father comes into her bed at night and touches her under her clothing. She said, "He took his hand and put it under my jammies and he rubbed me on my pee-pee hole." She said to Dr. Matherne, "It makes me feel like he doesn't love me." She demonstrated to Dr. Matherne with her hands by rubbing one hand over the other. Dr. Matherne said, "She said that she told her mother because she wanted, quote, my mom to help me, period, closed quotes."

Dr. Matherne was asked to explain what recantation is. He answered,

Well, what happens is there is an original allegation, an original statement by a child that something has happened. Call that an allegation. And at some point in time, a child then may change their story. I am always concerned when the original allegation is changed and they say, 'No, it didn't happen.' ... Now when it occurs, one can make two assumptions, the original allegation was falsified or the original allegation was truthful and the recanted statement is false. And one has to understand why the statement was recanted. Have there been forces that have occurred that changes the child's belief that it is not in the child's best interest to continue with the allegation? So it's important that when there is a recanting, that the child be seen again to understand what dynamics may have played a part in the child's change of story to help the

> Researchers have reported that children who are not protected do what their abuser tells them to do in order to survive.

Court then arrive at a decision of which statement to accept, either the original or the newer statement.

He told the court that children recant "because of the problems that it causes them," but that the original allegation was true. He also stated, "...falsification of alleged abuse is more likely to occur between the ages of twelve and sixteen in the female population." It was his opinion that Amanda and Jessica had suffered sexual abuse by their father and that any recantation was as a result of their not being believed and protected in the first place.

Researchers have reported that children who are not protected do what their abuser tells them to do in order to survive. "Children who live in homes where there is violence are often recruited into a family conspiracy of hiding the abuse," says the ABA Center on Children and the Law. "Child witnesses quickly learn the family rule requires 'keeping the secret.' Children who break the silence and disclose the abuse often painfully learn that the abuser finds yet a new reason to further harm them or their mother."[24]

Ms. Daniels testified that she is the supervisor at the Harrison County Children's Shelter and that Amanda and Jessica were perfectly fine at the shelter. She told the jury that we had a very close and loving relationship and that the girls were always excited to see me.

Diane Woods had already testified that she found the children in a terrible state and that I had abused them by taking them to Mississippi and having them put in this shelter. Ms. Daniels, however, testified that the children became upset and were crying because Woods and King were taking them from the shelter instead of their mother.

Ms. Daniels was asked by Michael Hirsh, "Did you see how the girls responded to them (Woods and King)?" Ms. Daniels answered, "Yes, when I went to tell the girls to get their things together, they was going home, they was running around getting their dolls and blankets, real excited. Once they walked in the room to see who was there to get them, just something came over them.

So they sat on the sofa together real close together, you know. ... One of the ladies asked them, 'do you remember me, you know?' and she told the name. The children just sort of dropped their head, start looking at the floor. Told them they was going to have to go back to Georgia. They started crying."

Ms. Daniels was asked, "Did Amanda or Jessica say anything?" And she answered, "Jessica said, asked where is my mommy and other than that, that was all that was said. They just sat there with their heads down looking at the floor crying."

Michael asked, "And then these two ladies from Georgia took Amanda and Jessica away?" Ms. Daniels replied, "Yeah, they took them away and told the children we were going to have to go back. And so the children got up. They were still crying when they left out the door." Ms. Daniels became emotional as she finished her answer, "When they passed the window, they were still crying. I just had to almost like suck up the tears because the children were just so sad, you know. I felt like, you know."

As I heard for the first time the whole story of what happened that day at the shelter, I was flooded with so many emotions. I was hurt, angry, furious, and I desperately wanted to comfort my children who had suffered at the hands of these people. They endured so much pain - emotional, physical and sexual abuse that they should never have had to endure. How dare them! HOW DARE THEM!

As I mentioned before, Dr. Joyanna Silberg, a psychologist at Baltimore's Sheppard Pratt Hospital, is internationally recognized for her expertise in child sexual abuse. She examined all of the files from Dr. Elizabeth King, including the raw testing data and audio taped sessions with Amanda and Jessica. She also studied the videotape made by Andy and his girlfriend, Anita, which shows them browbeating the girls to recant their allegations of abuse in February, 2000. She concluded that Dr. King's work was incompetent. She said that Dr. King actually discouraged the children from reporting the abuse to her. This confirmed that the children accurately told Dr. Matherne that Dr. King did not listen to them and changed the subject when they tried to tell her about what their father does to them. Dr. Silberg could not reveal to the jury her findings prior to August 4, 2000, when the divorce decree was signed, because of the courts order limiting our testimony. She was able to tell the court, however, that this was absolutely true. She was able to prove it based on Dr. King's one and only audiotape she had made since the children's return from Mississippi. The tape was played for the jury.

Dr. Silberg testified that Dr. King in her evaluation of Amanda and Jessica used the discredited theories of Dr. Richard Gardner, who "espouses ideas such as that sex between children and parents is a normal activity." She said, "He recommends techniques which are coercive and dangerous to children. He talks about jailing children. He talks about treatment for incest is giving vibrators to mothers so that they can learn how to have orgasms." "His ideas are outrageous," she said. Dr. Silberg stated anyone implementing Richard Gardner's methods in conducting a sexual abuse evaluation, "would most likely have the child be forced to live with the abuser."

> "[T]here "is a phenomenon that is occurring wildly through the United States. There are many professional organizations who are concerned about the fact that children are lately being put in the custody of abusing parents."

Her findings indicated that Dr. King had purposefully covered up the abuse from the very beginning and that the results of the testing that was completed on their father and me had been grossly misrepresented in Andy's favor.

Dr. Silberg testified there "is a phenomenon that is occurring wildly through the United States. There are many professional organizations who are concerned about the fact that children are lately being put in the custody of abusing parents." She said, "I am not the only one concerned about this; Mr. Ducote is not the only one. There are national organizations, APA, the National Institute of Justice, the Association of Juvenile Justices, all of them are looking at this particular phenomenon which is occurring around the country and is of major concern."

Everyone in the courtroom, including the prosecution team, was mesmerized as Dr. Silberg stood at a whiteboard and illustrated how Dr. King had failed in her responsibility to protect the children. I thought as she spoke that she was educating the people in the Cobb County court. But her teaching fell on deaf ears.

After all of the testimony was presented, Francey Hakes began the closing arguments. She argued to the jury that everyone who testified in my behalf had a vested interest because they were being paid by me. She said the only ones who were neutral were Diane Woods, Elizabeth King, and Judge Bodiford.

Michael Hirsh who stands 6'7" countered, "The State says there is no sexual abuse because the children recanted. Recanted. Yes, every one of their witnesses said abused children typically recant when they are not protected after reporting and when they are pressured or threatened by the molester. What did Amanda and Jessica say in Mississippi? 'Mommy, I'm afraid, I'm afraid that daddy will take me back and I'll never see you again. Even when I am grown, daddy won't let me see you.'" "Andy Titelman made good on his threats," Michael went on to say. "But he did it with the help of three people, Diane Woods, Betty King and Lorita Whitaker."

Ms. Hakes in rebuttal began by quoting the Bible, "The Bible says a guilty man fleeith where no man pursue, but the righteous stand bold as the lion." She told the jury that I fled to Mississippi, but that the State had proved beyond a reasonable doubt that I did not believe my children were being molested. Francey Hakes said, "Wendy Titelman has decided that she wants justice when she deserves none." She compared me to Timothy McVeigh and stated that I am a vigilante. She said Justice for Children "are like anarchists" and "they don't accept what governments do." The Cobb County District Attorney's office took the position that the State of Georgia makes no mistakes. However, the truth is that Justice for Children has helped to expose the truth of this case, and the Cobb County District Attorney is threatened by that.

The State of Georgia was trying to imprison me for up to five years because I took my children to professionals who substantiated the abuse reports that they have repeatedly made. I do not have a criminal record, have never abused my children, and have never had any finding of abuse of my children. There was no order preventing me from taking the children with me to Mississippi. Georgia law requires that it is the joint and several duty of each parent to provide for the protection of his or her child until the child reaches the age of majority. I had clearly done everything I could within the law to protect my children.

What does a parent do when the court doesn't allow for that protection? There have been some parents who have taken their children into hiding in order to protect them from harm. Joseph and Mary took their son, Jesus, and hid with him until he was safe. "..an angel of the Lord appeared to Joseph in a dream, saying, 'Arise, take the young Child and His mother, flee to Egypt, and stay there until I bring you word; for Herod will seek the young Child to destroy Him.' When he arose, he took the young Child and His mother by night and departed for Egypt." (Matthew 2:13-14) Was Joseph a criminal? He protected his child, Jesus, from a murderer, the King of Judea, by leaving and hiding.

Francey Hakes, angry with the Mississippi judge's involvement, stated, "The State of Georgia knows best how to protect it's children." Does it now? I am sickened by the arrogance of this statement. Georgia did not and boldly refuses to protect Amanda and Jessica. The state has failed to protect countless other children, many who have died while in the state's custody. How could they make themselves to be superior to all else, especially now that the record proved that those whose opinions this court relied upon were untrained, incompetent, and dishonest.

The jury began their deliberation process. I numbly waited for their verdict. While they were deliberating they requested the picture of Amanda and Jessica that we put into evidence, and they asked the bailiff if Michael Hirsh really has twelve children. Michael had shared with the jury that his family was about as large as the number of children at the shelter in Mississippi. Michael's wife brought birth to their thirteenth child early this year. Michael showed a picture of his family to the jurors after the trial in answer to their question.

It didn't take long; the jury, in record time, came back with a verdict. Michael told me that it wasn't good, because if the deliberation is short, it usually indicates a guilty verdict. When the jurors came into the room one by one they looked grim and did not look at me. Michael turned to me, and under his breath, he said, "We're screwed." A few moments later, he was exuberant, saying,

"No, we're not. It's okay." Someone on the jury gave him a thumbs up. The verdict returned was, "Not Guilty."

After the jury was dismissed, they all stayed and hugged me, cried with me, and talked with Michael Hirsh and Richard Ducote for over an hour. They told them they asked for the girls' picture because they wanted to see if it was torn. They were infuriated at Francey Hakes who during her closing argument picked up the picture and snapped it so hard that we all reacted thinking it was ripped. They said that they wanted to do something to help Amanda and Jessica because the evidence showed Andy was guilty of molestation and that the State of Georgia had failed to protect them. They decided to write a letter to District Attorney Patrick Head and Judge James Bodiford.

The foreperson of the jury, Bryan Wilson, wrote the letter in behalf of all the jurors stating the conclusions they had drawn during their deliberation. [Appendix C] Six of the jurors signed the letter. My understanding is that some of the others were afraid to sign for fear of retribution by individuals in Cobb County who they believed had covered up the abuse of the girls and had maliciously prosecuted me. They wrote,

> ...We were perplexed as to why our State would pursue such a case so diligently when there were obvious errors in the indictment and credible reports indicating sexual and emotional abuse to two small children and the prosecution of the mother who sought to protect them from harm's way.

> We, the jury felt that the "State of Georgia" did in fact, neglect to protect these children and furthermore, did not have the children's best interests at heart. It appeared they wished to cover up blatant miss-steps by an agency (DFACS) that appears to have made several errors in judgment. ... Not only will this save the State of Georgia the expense of prosecuting such flimsy cases, but will also serve to better protect the ones who need it the most, the *CHILDREN* of our State.

***

...The indictment was very poorly written and poorly executed. The dates were inconsistent with the prosecution's effort to paint the mother as a "law breaker and flight risk". Based on the information we received, the dates listed in the indictment were within the legal limits spelled out in the final divorce decree's visitation schedule. It is incredible to believe that our court system would put a decent woman in jail for doing something completely legal during the indictment's window!

***

Based on the evidence presented, we, the jury, were unanimous in agreeing with and supporting Ms. Titlemen in her beliefs that there was probable cause to protect her children. The evidence gave strong indication the children were being sexually molested by their father. Ms. Hakes, the Assistant Prosecutor, in her closing statements called Ms. Titlemen a "zealot" like Timothy McVeigh for wanting to take the law into her own hands and protect her children.

***

...We, the jury, saw Ms. Titlemen as someone desperately trying to use the legal system in Georgia to its fullest extent to protect her children, but to no avail. Then, when discovering more evidence of abuse, was left with no choice but to apply to the State of Mississippi for help. Although Ms. Hakes painted Ms. Titlemen as a manipulator and extremist, we felt that she was justified in using whatever means necessary to protect her children. Ms. Hakes said over and over during her cross-examinations "the State of Georgia knows best how to protect its children". We are not so sure after sitting on the jury and seeing first hand the types of "guardians" and "counselors" that the State of Georgia appoints to protect our most precious resources and future taxpayers. Dr. King admitted under oath, the children told her they were being abused. Why then do the children remain in the custody of the accused when the State does not appear to have proved otherwise?

***

...We, the jury, were horrified when Ms. Hakes told us in her closing statements that Ms. Titlemen didn't deserve justice. What does that mean?! Doesn't everyone deserve justice and aren't we all innocent until proven guilty?

***

...The court appointed Guardians and Counselors were not credible and did all they could not to disclose real findings or intentions. Ms. Woods defied a State of Mississippi court order (within 24 hours) to protect the children from their father until additional hearings could take place and certain evidence be reviewed. Ms. King (a supposed expert) interrogated the children for two and one-half hours without taking any notes, or tapes, etc. She then appeared to try and cover up the disclosure of the sexual abuse to the court when asked in direct questioning. Therefore, we found that there were several disclosures of sexual abuse but little evidence at all of recantations. Ms. Whitaker went so far as to say the children were "abducted"!

***

...The State's witnesses were pathetic in our opinion. They were poorly rehearsed, poorly accredited and overtly biased.

***

...We all agreed that the children were in all likelihood being sexually abused by their father. Also, the custody and well-being of these minor children should be a major concern to Cobb County. A new group of unbiased experts needs to re-evaluate this case... I feel that this jury has served justice, and that the state's mishandling of this case has cost the taxpayers of Cobb County, Georgia a lot of money.

Word spread through the Internet. Friends, family and people I don't even know from all over the country sent letters to Patrick Head and to Governor Barnes and others stating their outrage that

181

nothing was being done to protect Amanda and Jessica even in the face of all the evidence and the findings of this jury. They demanded that the children be protected. I kept thinking they would have to protect the girls now. There was so much evidence, and a jury of twelve peers found there was abuse. But the Cobb County gang dug their heels in and refused to protect the children. And again the devastation and pain of not being able to help Amanda and Jessica or to see them flooded me.

the Cooked Grand Jury "Investigation"

A copy of the jury letter was faxed to us on May 30, 2001. On June 4, I traveled to Atlanta and did three things. First, I filed with the Cobb County Superior Court a petition to disqualify District Attorney Patrick Head from participating in the investigation of Andrew Titelman for the sexual molestation of Amanda and Jessica.

Then I called the foreperson of the grand jury, Barbara Mabary, and asked her if I could bring her a packet of information for the grand jury to review and consider. It was a request to investigate Andy Titelman for sexual molestation along with documentation of abuse and the jury letter. I also stated in the request, "The sexual abuse of my daughters by their father Andrew Titelman has been covered up by the Department of Family and Children's Services, a Cobb County attorney Diane Woods, who was court appointed to 'represent' the children in the custody case with my ex-husband, Dr. Elizabeth King, a Fulton County psychologist, and the Cobb County District Attorney's Office."

Third, I went to the Magistrate Court and asked Judge Laura Austin for a warrant for the arrest of Andrew Titelman for the sexual molestation of Amanda and Jessica.

I believe that Judge Austin wanted to help, but she expressed that she was being put in a very bad position because of Judge Bodiford, Patrick Head, and Diane Woods' involvement. She told me that I would never win in Georgia because I was dealing with the "good 'ole boys who would stick together no matter what." She considered what to do for several hours and then called me to tell me that she would not issue a warrant for Andy's arrest. Instead, she had requested Detective Bishop with "Crimes Against Children," a division of the Cobb County Sheriff's office, to do an investigation of him.

The day after I filed the petition to disqualify Patrick Head, I tried to schedule an emergency hearing before the Chief Judge of the Cobb County Superior Court, but I was given no date for hearing, and no one could tell me where the pleading was. I was furious, convinced that Cobb County was playing games with me. I saw doors close and people whispering and unwilling to talk with me openly. Secretaries sent me on wild goose chases. After several days, I filed another emergency motion.

A couple of weeks later I received an "invitation" in the mail from Patrick Head to testify before the grand jury in the investigation of Andy for the sexual abuse of Amanda and Jessica. I was given less than 24 hours notice to get to Atlanta. I quickly made the expensive last-minute flight arrangements and arrived the next morning. I then learned that Patrick Head was running the show.

I immediately sought out a judge to help me with the petition to disqualify Patrick Head. I received a call from Judge Bodiford's law clerk, stating that Judge Bodiford had been assigned this case and would see me in the courtroom. This was preposterous that Judge Bodiford was assigned this case, and I told him so. I told him he needed to recuse himself. Judge Bodiford refused. He had it and was not going to let it go. He scheduled a hearing for two days later.

The next day, on June 20, I took my friends, Peggy Carlson and Susan Ibarra, with me to the Courthouse where I would testify before the grand jury. We sat in a lobby for what seemed to be hours waiting for me to be called. While sitting there, we witnessed Francey Hakes coming from the grand jury area. As she stood before us in the reception area and got on the elevator directly in front of us, she smiled broadly and said out loud but looking at no one, "I'm not going down, I'm only going to the top."

Tom Weathers, an Assistant District Attorney, finally came and took me into the grand jury room. He simply told me to tell them whatever I wanted. I was greeted with cold peering eyes and silence. I attempted to share everything I could. The jury members began to direct angry questions at me as I saw the sneers and smug looks on their faces. I left knowing that something was grossly wrong.

Peggy and Susan who had been waiting for me all the while shared with me that while I was testifying that Francey Hakes came back and then left with Patrick Head, Diane Woods, Elizabeth King, and Frank Pittman and others from a room next to where I was testifying.

On June 21, the next day, I went to the hearing before Judge Bodiford, I was told for the first time that the disqualification of Patrick Head was "moot" because the grand jury had already completed their investigation and had issued a "no bill," "brought with malicious intent." Judge Bodiford said that never before in the history of Cobb County did they have anything marked "brought with malicious intent."

I argued with Judge Bodiford for several hours that the investigation had been thwarted and blocked by District Attorney Patrick Head. I told him not one of the witnesses evidencing sexual abuse was called, but all of those who had been named by the jurors as covering up the sexual abuse, and whom Patrick Head had used to testify against me in my criminal trial, had been brought before the grand jury to testify. "This is a case of the fox guarding the hen house," I said. I told the Court that D.A. Head in essence, "cooked" the grand jury to get his desired result so that he could protect himself from criticism and accountability. He, therefore, has a personal and political interest in the possible or actual prosecution of Andy Titelman. I argued that he must be disqualified and either the Attorney General or some completely independent private prosecutor appointed as provided in Georgia law to make all decisions regarding this case.

The juror's letter was brought up. Judge Bodiford angrily threatened the jurors for having written it. He accused my attorneys or me of having written the letter or coercing them into taking this action with intent of fraud. He said they may lose their homes and their cars for libeling Andy Titelman by calling him a child molester. He made snide remarks that this was "all a tactic by Ms. Titelman" and that I brought this lawsuit in order "to harass" the parties involved and that "she will never take no for an answer." This was said without hearing any testimony from me, Dr. Brentnall, Dr. Pearce, Dr. Matherne, Dr. Silberg and Dr. Faller, without hearing the evidence that Diane Woods and Dr. Elizabeth King intentionally misled the court and DFACS relative to their interview with the children on September 16, 2000 and the October 6, 2000 audio tape of Dr. King's session with the children and without hearing any testimony from me and without hearing anything from Bajda Daniels, the Mississippi Harrison County Children's Shelter Supervisor whose testimony would directly contradict Diane Woods' statements to the Court October 4, 2000 that the children were traumatized by remaining in Mississippi instead of being traumatized by Ms. Woods and Dr. King returning the children to Georgia.

Bodiford stated, "If the DA is so far out after you, why haven't you been able-why hasn't any judge, why hasn't any grand jury, why hasn't the DA, why hasn't somebody seen it your way? Would you mind explaining that to me? I ain't that smart but let me tell you what, why, if you're so right, why have all these other agencies, why have all these other officials with everything to lose, with everything to lose, including their reputation, and their retirement account, their BMW's and their salaries, their homes, their families, why are these folks against you?"

Every time I tried to answer a question or to address a concern, Judge Bodiford interrupted me and confused the discussion. As soon as I would start to answer a question, he would ask another. He would cut me off every time I tried to express myself, and then he would go into long speeches. Judge Bodiford issued a final order denying my motion and stating it was moot.

On June 28, 2001, Lorita Whitaker, the children's "therapist," hand picked by Diane Woods, sent an e-mail to Bryan Wilson, the foreperson of the jury in my criminal trial threatening him with a lawsuit for writing the letter to Patrick Head and Judge Bodiford. [Appendix D] She tried to mislead him with erroneous information. Richard Ducote responded to her with a return e-mail confronting her for her behavior and inviting her to sue us so that the truth by all means could come out. [Appendix E] He told her, "She [Wendy Titelman] will continue to publicize your errors and incompetence in her children's case. In fact, rest assured that this letter will get broad internet circulation. Have your attorney call me so we can accept service and get to trial immediately. I, and others would relish the opportunity to cross examine you and your associates in this case."

Several months later on October 3, 2001, Richard Ducote took the depositions of District Attorney Patrick Head and Assistant District Attorney Francey Hakes on behalf of me for a malicious prosecution lawsuit filed in the United States District Court in Atlanta (Wendy Titelman v Andrew Titelman, Craig Chandler, John Mayoue, Pamela Gray, Diane Woods). The evidence we found in this discovery proved that the Cobb County District Attorney's office and Patrick Head intentionally manipulated, deceived, and withheld evidence from the grand jurors to protect Andrew Titelman and to conceal the cover-up of sexual abuse by Diane Woods, Dr. Elizabeth King, and the Cobb County District Attorney's Office.

In his deposition, Mr. Head stated that when Ms. Mabary, the foreperson of the grand jury, made him aware of the investigation, Mr. Head told Ms. Mabary that he "would take care of it." Mr. Head certainly did "take care of it," by taking care of himself and his cronies rather than seeking justice and the truth. He admitted that he only "periodically" gets involved in any presentment to the grand jury. Knowing there was an outstanding petition to have him removed from participating in this investigation, he still chose to lead the "investigation," even though he was named in the materials given to the 2001 May/June grand jurors as having a conflict of interest and participating in the cover-up of the abuse by the various agencies and professionals. Mr. Head purposefully took charge of this investigation knowing that his name was at stake as well.

The only time that Patrick Head excused himself from the grand jury room was when I made my presentment on June 20. He stated, "I felt it would be better to have someone in there that Ms. Titelman had not been making accusations about."

Mr. Head revealed that he does not meet with or prepare witnesses prior to a grand jury investigation, and that he "just lets them come in and testify" Yet in a facsimile dated June 12, 2001, found in Mr. Head's files, Patrick Head met with Diane Woods, who was called by Mr. Head as a witness, at a Waffle House to discuss her testimony and to ask her who should be called as a witness before the grand jury. Ms. Woods wrote,

> Thank you for coffee yesterday morning. Follows is my Guardian ad Litem report in this matter dated May 17, 1999. On pages 3-5 you will see an account of my conversation with Frank Pittman, Ph.D. In my discussions with Betty King yesterday, she asked whether or not Dr. Pittman could be of help with the Grand Jury. I told her that I would pass along her comments to you. Dr. Pittman certainly has an extended history with this family and is one of the folks I relied upon when making my preliminary report.

> Let me know if you want to discuss Dr. Pittman further.

Also, to prepare for the grand jury investigation, we learned that Mr. Head asked Lorita Whitaker to videotape the children in a session with her discussing allegations of sexual abuse. This video was made June 12 at SafePath Children's Advocacy Center. Francey Hakes stated in her deposition that Lorita Whitaker confirmed with her that Ms. Whitaker "frequently" talks with Amanda and Jessica about "Mrs. Titelman telling the children what to say and to lie about Daddy and that Daddy never touched them" and "about the incidents surrounding their being taken to Mississippi." Not only is this a highly unethical practice by Ms. Whitaker, but also Mr. Head's request for such a video is evidence of his desire to vindicate Andy from any indictment. This is an extreme abuse of the system.

Francey Hakes admitted that Patrick Head asked for the names and addresses of the State's witnesses in the criminal trial and Dr. Frank Pittman to parade them before the grand jury. Mr. Head admitted that he has not talked to even one of the numerous witnesses that have substantiated the sexual abuse charges against Andrew Titelman nor did he subpoena or invite any of them to speak to the grand jury. Their names and addresses had been submitted to the grand jury with a request that they be called as witnesses by me. Discovery also showed that Mr. Head and Francey Hakes were in communication with Andy's attorney, Pamela Gray, and her office on several occasions. Furthermore, Mr. Head's communications included Diane Woods and Lorita Whitaker, individuals who were named as participating in the cover-up of the sexual abuse. The records also indicate cordial communication with Andy Titelman on several occasions. In a memo dated July 18, 2001, Andy wrote,

> Dear Pat - Joy to the World! How about this? On page 2, it states that Ms. Titelman now lives in Louisiana? Wow, is she on the move! I have no choice. Will be retaining Mr. Cauthorn.

There is evidence of additional collusion between Francey Hakes and Pamela Gray. On June 8, 2001, Ms. Hakes spoke with Ms. Gray by phone and then faxed her the jurors' contact information from my criminal trial and a note that stated, "Let me know if you get any responses."

Assistant District Attorney Francey Hakes admitted in her deposition that she went in and "talked to" the grand jury for an hour at the beginning of their session either "at her or Patrick Head's suggestion." She refused to reveal her role in doing so, stating that she was not a witness nor a legal advisor nor a district attorney prosecuting the case, but was "assisting Pat." It was also discovered that Patrick Head met with Francey Hakes and discussed the "beginning she would have at the opening session of the grand jury." She also stated that Pat Head was the one in charge and that he personally planned how he was going to "present" this case to the grand jury.

We found in Francey Hakes files her notes from a phone conversation with Dr. Elizabeth King on March, 13, 2001, prior to the criminal trial. She recorded Dr. King told her that the children's initial disclosures were through Dr. Lynn Brentnall, but that it was a "leading interview big time." She noted reporting "the second evaluator, Diane Pierce, credentials in question." Dr. King told Ms. Hakes that I talked with her about Faye Yeager and going underground and that I had journal notes regarding taking the children underground. I never talked to Dr. King about going underground, nor did I ever talk to her about Faye Yeager, a rather famous woman who has helped other mothers hide in order to protect their children from abusive fathers when the court has failed. Her own daughter suffered at the hands of the court being forced into the custody of her father whom she alleged was sexually molesting her.

> Patrick Head deliberately withheld from the grand jury a video tape that was produced at the SafePath Children's Advocacy Center by DFACS June 23, 1999, of the interview with Amanda, conducted by Julie Hall and Detective Amy Henderson, wherein Amanda clearly disclosed her father's sexual molestation of her.

Years later, when the child was 16, it was found he had indeed molested her and many other children. Dr. King told Ms. Hakes I had "refused to visit with the children since Mississippi." King also told her Wendy Titelman "will not stop this unless she goes to jail."

Patrick Head generated highly unusual court orders that were signed by Judge Adele Grubbs. Judge Grubbs is a neighbor of Gail and Michael Vernon, who have become my friends over the past couple of years. Several months previously Gail went to Judge Grubbs and talked with her about the girls not being protected. Judge Grubbs said she was a friend of Diane Woods and that Diane Woods and Hylton Dupree were working together to help her be elected as a Cobb County Superior Court Judge. She said she was going to talk to Diane about the case. Later when Gail approached her, she was very abrupt and supported Diane Woods' position, saying there was "no evidence of abuse."

The orders that Judge Grubbs signed were clearly suspect. Patrick Head and Francey Hakes stated in their depositions that prior to this there had never been an order to bar the recording of testimony in Cobb County, nor had there ever been an order sealing the names and addresses of grand jurors and forbidding contact with them, even in the most serious and heinous criminal investigations. Yet, this is what Judge Grubbs signed for Mr. Head. The orders were an obvious attempt to further nail the door shut on my girls.

The Crucial Video They Wanted No One to See

Patrick Head deliberately withheld from the grand jury the videotape that was produced at the SafePath Children's Advocacy Center by DFACS June 23, 1999, of the interview with Amanda, conducted by Julie Hall and Detective Amy Henderson, wherein Amanda clearly disclosed her father's sexual molestation of her. This crucial evidence was concealed by the District Attorney's office in my criminal prosecution as well, despite the demand for the discovery of all exculpatory evidence. It was only in discovery through the federal law suit that Patrick Head was forced to provide this video. It was found in his files sealed with orange tape and marked "Evidence."

This newly discovered evidence, which I was never previously able to obtain or view despite due diligence, proves that Amanda was sexually abused by her father. The tape also shows the dangerous involvement of Diane Woods during Amanda's disclosure of the abuse. At one point Detective Henderson left the room to speak with "Diane," who was watching the interview on closed circuit TV. It became even more abundantly clear that the truth regarding the sexual abuse of Amanda and Jessica by their father was intentionally concealed and suppressed by the district attorney's office for the sole purpose of protecting the district attorney's office and the various agencies that were to protect these children by the laws set forth in and for the State of Georgia from accountability and liability.

I viewed this tape for the first time in October, 2001. I watched my precious child as she nervously and very clearly described her sexual abuse by her father to Julie Hall and Detective Amy Henderson. My heart felt it would explode with grief as her words poured into the wounds already so deep.

In the interview, Julie Hall asked Amanda to tell her about her daddy. Amanda answered, "He's mean." "How's he mean?" she asked. "Try to remember back one time you can remember when he was mean and tell me about it." Amanda answered, "When he hit me." "Okay, tell me about that." "He got really angry at me,"

Amanda replied. "What did he get angry about?" Amanda said, "I don't know." Ms. Hall asked, "Did it hurt or not hurt?" "It did," said Amanda. "Did it leave a mark on you like a bruise or not leave a mark? she asked. Amanda responded, "Yes."

During the interview, Ms. Hall suddenly turned to Detective Henderson and motioned for her to go talk to Diane Woods. In the background it sounded as though someone was knocking on the wall. Detective Henderson left the room and returned a few minutes later.

Ms. Hall drew a picture of a girl and asked Amanda to describe the parts of the body. She asked her, "Is there any place on this girls body that somebody probably shouldn't touch?" "Yes," said Amanda. Ms. Hall asked, "What parts? You can just point to it." Amanda pointed to the part of the body between the legs. Ms. Hall asked Amanda to circle the parts where she had pointed, which Amanda did. "Has there ever been a time that anybody has touched you on these places except the doctor or except your mom helping you give you a bath?" Amanda answered, "Yes." "When was that?" Amanda thought for a moment and answered, "Two weeks ago." "What happened?" Ms. Hall asked. Amanda was wringing her hands. She looked down and answered, "Daddy rubbed it." "Can you show me how he rubbed it? You want to show me on the picture?" Amanda rubbed the picture where she had circled. During this time, Ms. Hall looked towards the camera where Woods was and then Detective Henderson did as well. You could hear a voice in the background. Ms. Hall stated, "Now I noticed that you were using your fingers. Did Daddy use his fingers or not use his fingers?" "He did," Amanda answered. "He did use his fingers? Okay," Ms. Hall said. "Where were you?" Amanda stated, "In my bed."

They had a discussion about where she slept and if she had already gone to sleep and if her eyes were open or closed. Ms. Hall said, "So you saw him, and then what?" "I felt things," Amanda responded. "What did you feel?" "His hand." "And what was his hand doing?" "Touching it," Amanda said. Ms. Hall then asked her to point to the place. Amanda pointed to the spot she had circled in the picture. Ms. Hall asked, "What did it feel like?" Amanda said, "A bug was biting me." "How long did he touch you there?" "For an hour," Amanda responded. "How did you feel about the whole thing happening?" She said, "Angry."

Ms. Hall defined truth and made certain Amanda knew what the truth is. "Now what you told me about dad and the two fingers, was that the truth?" Ms. Hall asked. "Yes," Amanda said.

"Did anybody talk to you about what you should tell me today or anything you should say today? "No," Amanda replied. "Tell me again what your mommy told you, why your mommy told you were coming here." Amanda answered, "Tell the truth." Detective Henderson asked, "Did your mommy tell you what you should tell the truth about?" "Yes." "What did she say?" she asked. "She said tell the truth about the finger."

Ms. Hall asked, "Has anybody ever asked you who you wanted to live with, your mom or your dad?" "Yes," said Amanda. "Who has asked that?" "My mom." "What did you say?" Amanda replied, "I want to live with my mom." "How come?" "Because she's nicer." "Why wouldn't you want to live with your dad?" "Because he does that finger stuff and stuff," Amanda stated. "When your mom asks you who you want to live with, do you feel okay with her asking you that or does it make you feel uncomfortable?" Amanda responded, "Okay." "Has your dad ever asked you?" "Yes." "Do you feel okay with him asking you?" "No," Amanda said. Ms. Hall asked, "What's the difference? Why is it okay for your mom to and not your dad to?" Amanda replied, "Because sometimes daddy tells lies." "Like what kind of lies?" asked Ms. Hall. "That mommy doesn't love me, and he'll get me a different mom," said Amanda. "He says that to you?" "Yes." "How do you feel about that?" "Angry," she answered.

"Has your mom ever told you what you need to say or tell somebody so that you can live with her or has she not done that?" Amanda answered in the same tempo she had answered previous questions, "No." "No? You were really thinking about that. Were you remembering something?" "Yes." "What were you remembering?" "That she will always love me, no matter what."

Assumptions are very dangerous, especially when it concerns the lives of people. To assume that allegations of sexual abuse that arise during a custody battle indicates a vindictive alienating parent is not only incorrect but brings life damaging consequences upon innocent victims. Diane Woods told my attorney, Hylton Dupree, that she was convinced by this interview that I had coached Amanda to say these things. She said because Amanda looked down and away when she answered the question about what her daddy did to her that Amanda was thinking about what I told her to say.

Kee MacFarlane and Jill Waterman, et al, in their book, *Sexual Abuse of Young Children*, in the chapter entitled Child Sexual Abuse Allegations in Divorce Proceedings state the following:

> Evaluators need to be careful of the questions, "Did Mommy [or someone else] tell you to say these things?" Young children tend to be very literal in their thinking, and we have found that an affirmative answer to this question may not always be what it appears. Parents may talk to their children about an upcoming interview in order to reassure them, encourage them, or lessen their anxieties. Sometimes they will say things like, "I want you to tell the interviewer [police officer, doctor, counselor, etc.] what you told me about what Daddy did." To some children, that translates as, "Yes, she told me to tell you this." It does not mean that the child did not report it to her first, and it is crucially different from coaching. Evaluators need to be sure that children understand their questions, and that they understand children's answers. When the meanings of answers are uncertain, questions should be rephrased or the child should be asked to restate the question in her own words.[25]

This crucial evidence was never seen by the court. Dr. King never mentioned it in her report or her testimony. During the custody hearings, it was deliberately and wrongfully suppressed by Diane Woods to protect herself from accountability for her earlier recommendation to place the children in Andy's custody. Undoubtedly had the Cobb County Superior Court believed the children were sexually abused, I would have been awarded sole custody and Andy supervised visitation at the most. Ms. Woods's only reference to that interview during the course of the June, 2000, custody trial is in her closing statement to the court on June 30, 2000:

> When I got in this case and started speaking with therapists and DFACS and school officials and police officers and as time progresses, representative of the district attorney's office and <u>I think one time observed Amanda on a two-way mirror when Julie Hall and Amy Henderson of the Kennesaw P.D. were interviewing Amanda</u>...[emphasis added].

> I did want to add that Ms. Titelman said something that I don't believe was correct, at least from my perspective. I think the statement was made that Amy Hall or Julie Hall and Amy Henderson and I concluded that she had coached the girls. I don't think that was the case. I think what ultimately ended up being the outcome of the two-way mirror was that <u>Amanda was not consistent or credible, at least to the people that were interviewing her and the way I observed it</u> [emphasis added].

Neither Amy Henderson nor Julie Hall ever testified in the custodial case nor have they ever been cross examined, but Ms. Woods offered her statement to the court that these individuals and she discount this important piece of evidence. Observe that Ms. Woods used the term "*I think*" three times, evidencing her wish to forget all about this issue because that tape holds profound consequences for her in light of her previous recommendation supporting Andy as custodian and her prior refusal to believe the sexual abuse evidence. How could she have forgotten the details of this interview?

If I am not coaching the children to report their father's abuse, the only other explanation is that the children are simply reporting what they have experienced. Diane Woods admitted they have been traumatized, but cannot explain why. The circular reasoning and contortions of logic she uses to justify her actions and the incredible risks she takes with the children's lives are again illustrated by her statements at the September 20, 2000, hearing before Judge Bodiford, after Dr. Donald Matherne interviewed the girls in Mississippi and wrote his report, which resulted in the Mississippi protective custody order on September 5, 2000.

After Diane Woods rushed to Mississippi with Elizabeth King, Lorita Whitaker, Andy Titelman, and John Mayoue to secure the return of the children to Andy's custody, despite their detailed complaints of his coming to their beds at night and rubbing their genitalia, Ms. Woods explained to Judge Bodiford why the girls should be again turned over to Andy Titelman:

> So the second point in this is after a full hearing and after a thorough evaluation, I believe by Dr. King and myself - we both recommended that Mr. Titelman should be the custodial parent and my recommendation was supervised visitation. So what we would be asking today in terms of the children, I have talked to the children and Dr. King has talked to the children and I believe there has been a proper evaluation by Dr. King who has seen the children more frequently than Dr. Matherne, who has seen the children once, and Dr. King believes the children are so tainted, as is their testimony, and they have been talked to by so many people that we will probably never have the full story on the children and while no one can say one hundred percent that these children have not been sexually abused, I don't think anybody is qualified to say that they have not just because of the nature of the allegations that have been made, but Dr. King and I believe that it would be in the best interests of the children to return them to their father.

Diane Woods is completely unqualified to evaluate anything; Dr. King's work is likewise incompetent and biased; and Diane Woods and Dr. King are only deciding what is <u>in their own best interests</u>. Diane Woods deliberately concealed from Judge Bodiford and DFACS that after the girls were taken from the Mississippi shelter home by Ms. Woods, they told her and Dr. King that they were abused by their father. It is also established that the videotape of June, 1999, DFACS interview by Amanda proves the sexual abuse at a time before she "talked to so many people." Under Diane Woods's thesis, no children would be protected from sexual abuse because the system requires multiple interviews which are then used to discredit their reports.

An examination of Ms. Woods during the one time when she was under oath - her federal court deposition - reveals the shocking truth about Diane Woods's involvement and the absolute and total mistake made by any reliance on her opinions. In her deposition taken on October 3, 2001, Ms. Woods admits she has no training or expertise in the field of child sexual abuse. She told Dr. King prior to Dr. King's evaluation began that she -Diane Woods- did not believe the children had been sexually abused, thus compromising the objectivity of her friend Dr. King. She never discussed with Amanda or Jessica whether or not they were in fact sexually abused by their father! She has never discussed with the children where they wanted to live! She had essentially no contact with the parties or the two children, yet billed an astounding figure of approximately $22,000 for her "services" as Guardian *ad litem* for Amanda and Jessica. After she learned of the new sexual abuse allegations reported to me and Dr. Donald Matherne, Ms. Woods traveled to Mississippi and did no investigation whatsoever. Instead, she and Dr. Elizabeth King intentionally misled DFACS and Judge Bodiford into believing that their interview of the children on September 16, 2001, undertaken contrary to the Mississippi court order to which Diane Woods agreed, discredited Dr. Matherne's report. To the contrary, the children confirmed to Ms. Woods and Dr. King that their father was molesting them. This is the woman on whose opinion the court placed so much weight, the woman who destroyed my daughters. Below is a segment of her deposition taken in the federal case. It is marked "Q" where Richard Ducote asks her a question and marked "A" for Diane Woods response. Mr. Jerry Gentry is Ms. Woods attorney.

Q   Do you consider yourself to have any degree of expertise in the area of child sexual abuse?

A   Could you define "expertise," please?

Q   Well, a person, as you know, under the law, an expert is defined as a person who, because of knowledge and training and experience, knows more about a particular subject than a lay person would know, to the extent that they would be permitted to give an expert opinion in court.

Mr. Gentry: Are you asking her, could she be qualified as an expert in child sexual abuse?

Q   Well, were she so offered - - I guess if somebody were to offer you as an expert, do you believe that you would have the qualifications and would meet the criteria for such a definition whether, or not the Court would find that it would be procedurally correct for you to be offered as an expert, if that makes sense?

A   No. No.

Q   No what? Because I gave you a couple of convoluted questions.

A   Right. I don't think I would be qualified as an expert in court as to sexual abuse.

Q   Have you had any training whatsoever in the area of determining whether or not a child has been sexually abused?

A   "Training" meaning examining – I don't understand what you mean when you say "training."

Q   Have you had any professional training through any organizations that provide – let me back up a little bit. Are you aware that there is training for attorneys, that there are conferences, seminars, workshops, held for attorneys to educate them on the diagnosis or the legal proof of child sexual abuse?

A   I am aware that there are trainings available for attorneys about the issue of child sexual abuse. I'm not aware that there's trainings available for attorneys to qualify them as experts.

Q   That's not my question.

A   I didn't understand your question.

Q   My question is not for the purpose not for the purpose of qualifying attorneys as experts --

197

A   Right.

Q   -- but for the purpose of educating attorneys so that when they get involved in cases where there are allegations of child sexual abuse that they will be able to do a good job, and know the dynamics, the evidence of sexual abuse, etcetera?

A   Yes, I'm aware of that training.

Q   Have you ever gone to any of that training?

A   As an attorney?

Q   Yes.

A   No.

Q   Have you ever gone to any training in any other capacity that deals with issues of child sexual abuse?

A   In juvenile court, but not as an attorney.

Q   What function or what role did you have for that?

A   I don't recall what function I was in at that time.

Q   Do you recall anything about the training?

A   No

Q   Have you ever read any books written for attorneys that specifically deal with child sexual abuse cases, or cases involving allegations of child sexual abuse?

A   Books?

Q   Yes.

A   No.

Q   Do you own any such books?

A   Books?

Q   Yes.

A   No.

Q   Do you own any articles?

A   Yes.

Q   What articles do you own?

A   I don't recall the titles.

Q   Can you name any of the people or professionals in the country who have written books or articles or treatises for attorneys or mental health professionals on child sexual abuse?

A   I can't name any this morning, no.

Q   Now, do you have a position today as the – without conceding that your status as guardian *ad litem* still remains; that issue had been raised in the custody case before – but do you have a position today regarding whether or not either Amanda Titelman or Jessica Titelman have ever been sexually abused by their father, Andrew Titelman?

A   My position is that I do not believe that they were sexually abused.

Q   And is that based on your own independent investigation?

A   That is based upon the investigation that took place during the trial of the case.

Q   When did you first take the position that Amanda and Jessica, or either one of them, had not been sexually abused by their father?

A   It was probably at the close of Dr. King's evaluation.

Guardians Ad Litem Hurt Kids

In June, 2002, Richard Ducote published a law review article entitled, *Guardians Ad Litem in Private Custody Litigation: the Case for Abolition.*[26] This case is a prime example why Guardians *ad litem* should be abolished. Several quotes from his review of legal literature are particularly relevant to Diane Woods and her conduct as Guardian *ad Litem* and are shared below.

Diane Woods' actions as Guardian *ad Litem* are the product of her conflict of interests, *i.e* the protection of the children vs. protection of herself from accountability for her grossly negligent backing of the abusive Andrew Titelman as custodian. Nancy Moore, in another law review article, *Conflicts of Interests in the Representation of Children*, cogently explained the problem:

Aside from duties to nonclients, lawyers' own interests may impinge on the representation of a client. This is one of the most difficult types of conflict to monitor, as lawyers are understandably reluctant to reveal all of the various ways in which they might be tempted to sacrifice a client' interest for their own. Moreover, while lawyers routinely reveal their own financial interests in the subject matter of representation, they are less likely to disclose other types of personal interests...As with adult clients with disabilities, lawyers can exercise enormous power over clients who are children, and attorneys can use the power to steer the litigation in their own desired directions. Unfortunately, there is very little that is presently done under the rules of professional conduct to monitor these conflicts effectively.[27]

There is no question that the positions taken by Diane Woods during the course of the trial in the custody case in June, 2000, were given great weight by the Cobb County Superior Court. Perhaps the judges perceived the guardian *ad litem* to be a neutral, independent, and competent investigator who could be trusted to provide the Court with the best perspective on the facts of the case.

At the conclusion of the final custody trial conducted before Judge Wood, Diane Woods offered her "closing statement," which consisted of her "purported" expert opinions without expertise, rank hearsay concerning witnesses never called to testify, and her recommendation that Andy be given sole custody of the children. She was not under oath and was never subjected to cross-examination. Nonetheless, her position is premised on the fact that the children have been *"subject to some kind of trauma,"* but that she does not know what it is.

This sort of unbridled, unsworn guardian *ad litem* monologue composed of hearsay, self-inflation and un-expert opinion is routinely condemned by courts and commentators.

Diane Woods' actions in this case reinforce and support the position taken by Professor Martin Guggenheim in his article, *The Right to be Represented But Not Heard: Reflections on Legal Representation of Children*:

Allowing the attorney to present his personal views of the case to the factfinder would not assist the courts' deliberation. The fact that an attorney believes that a certain witness is not telling the truth or that a certain legal rule applies to the case is simply irrelevant to its deliberations...But this partisan advocacy is not simply irrelevant; it is also potentially destructive of our legal process. Allowing the attorney to testify about what he believes to be the appropriate outcome of the case encourages the factfinder to abdicate its responsibilities to the lawyer. Instead of making its own judgments, the factfinder soon comes to rely on the judgment of the attorneys. Instead of independently examining the facts and law, the factfinder asks only what the lawyers think...

* * *

In the hard cases, the judge is most unsure of the appropriate outcome and will be most tempted to rely on the [attorney advocating for a child's 'best interests'] judgment. But for every [attorney] who advocates for a particular result, one can easily find a different attorney who would urge the opposite outcome. In the end, it will be the child's attorney, and not the judge, who decides the case.[28]

In a George Mason Law Review article the authors write,

Furthermore, some individuals thrive in being in a position of power over others. A guardian ad litem can insert herself into a family to structure the interactions among the family members, without having any historic, emotional, financial, or physical commitments and responsibility for the consequences. Without the controls and limits which are inherent in the judicial system and which constrain judges, the guardian ad litem, with or without admirable motives is not accountable.[29]

Without any authority whatsoever for doing so, Diane Woods has required that she personally approve all presents and notes sent to the children by me, has unilaterally suspended my visitation with

> "In order to ensure that the child's voice is heard in court, a representative should be an advocate who will advance the child's position and not make independent judgments of the child's best interest."

my daughters, has "forbidden" Amanda and Jessica to play with long-term playmates in the neighborhood, has unilaterally directed the children's school personnel to avoid all contact with me and to refuse my request for copies of school records, has admittedly disobeyed the Harrison County, Mississippi, Chancery Court September 15, 2000, consent order to which she was a party wherein she agreed that the children would not be interviewed without the prior consent of this Court, *etc.* Furthermore, she threatened me early on in the case that she -Ms. Woods- would put the kids in a foster home and that I would never see the kids again if I ever said anything "negative" about Mr. Titelman.

In a Pennsylvania Law Review comment, the author states,

Ambiguity about the attorney's role in family litigation has emerged as an important issue in recent years. The role of children's counsel is often undefined and consequently, hotly disputed. Should she play the role of a guardian ad litem, who determines what is best for a child, or that of an advocate, who is obliged to present the wishes of her client?...

In order to ensure that the child's voice is heard in court, a representative should be an advocate who will advance the child's position and not make independent judgments of the child's best interest. An advocate, unlike a traditional guardian ad litem, insures that the child's voice is heard with full force in legal proceedings.[30]

the Videotape Produced by Andrew Titelman

Another videotape, one "produced" in more ways than one by Andy in February, 2000, was used by Dr. King and Ms. Woods as "proof" that the children were "coached" to report the sexual abuse. Although the "coaching" theory at this hearing was abandoned by Ms. Woods in her closing statement on June 30, 2000, that "emergency hearing" resulted in my loss of custody, and placement on an outrageous schedule of supervised visitation. It is now known from Ms. Woods's federal deposition that this "emergency hearing" on February 18, 2000, held on a day's notice to me without the benefit of a prior review of Dr. King's report, was tainted by Ms. Woods's advance *ex parte* communications with Judge Bodiford. When Judge Wood, heard the June, 2000, trial, I was still under supervised visitation with my daughters.

This videotape created by Andy Titelman, like the June, 1999, interview with Amanda discovered in the District Attorney's files, was never produced at any trial, and consequently, never seen by the court. If was only after custody had been taken away from me, that I was able to obtain a copy of this tape and see it for the first time.

Both of these videotapes have now been reviewed by Dr. Kathleen Faller, a legitimate, leading international expert in child sexual abuse at the University of Michigan whose extensive curriculum vitae includes the publication of 6 books, 45 articles, 11 book chapters, 2 media productions, 3 research reports, 2 encyclopedia/dictionary entries, 8 book reviews, 3 journal editions, 227 grants, contracts, fellowships and scholarships, a monograph, a dissertation and numerous works in progress. She has acted as a consultant on numerous occasions and has given over 225 training sessions. Dr. Faller's thorough and competent review of these videotapes has resulted in her findings that the first tape establishes that "it is more likely than not that Amanda was sexually abused in a manner similar to what she described." The second Andrew Titelman produced tape is simply documentation of his bullying and coercive attempts to force the girls to recant. One December 11, 2001, Dr. Faller reported,

This appears to be a browbeating session. The father speaks in a loud and threatening voice, standing up while Amanda is sitting at the table and Jessica appears to be on the floor. He is overbearing. He essentially insists his daughters say that they lied when they said he touched them in a sexual way. He also coerces them into saying that their mother persuaded them to make the allegations. They also blame Lynn Palmer for making them lie... When they do not give him the response he wants to hear, he repeats leading questions, coerces, and cajoles them until they do provide the desired response. The girls are obviously uncomfortable. Amanda is avoidant (she has to be instructed to look at her father) and she appears resentful. But essentially they appear to give in to his dominance. It is doubtful they could have resisted his insistent questioning. It is likely that he would have continued in this vein until they said what he wanted to hear.

The father does not give a good impression. Because of the coercive and confrontational nature of his questioning style, one cannot have any assurance in the accuracy of the children's responses. While it is possible that the girls appeared uncomfortable in the confrontation because they had lied about the abuse or because their father is behaving in a domineering way, it is more consistent with Amanda's forensic interview that their discomfort relates to having to recant actual abuse. [Appendix F, Exhibit B]

My young daughters have been placed in the sole custody of their abusive father, and their relationship with me, their protective mother, has been unconscionably curtailed. There is little that could be more destructive to the children's best interest than what has occurred here.

The criminal court jury, which heard the evidence and promptly acquitted me of the bogus criminal charges prompted by Ms. Woods, Andy, and others, aptly and cogently expressed their outrage. Even Judge Robert Flournoy, who presided over my criminal trial, commented to my criminal defense attorney Michael Hirsh, who was arguing that the charges should be dismissed:

> You have very effective witnesses, Dr. Silberg, and you had Dr. Matherne, very effective witnesses to testify that, in their opinion, [Ms. Titelman] was acting very reasonably, did what any concerned mother would do. And actually, I think you've conveyed to the jury that they could draw the inference that, in fact, the Cobb County justice system did shut down on Wendy Titelman and didn't give her redress, et cetera, et cetera.

A time-line of activities that transpired from April 27, 2001, the date that I was acquitted, up to October 3, 2001, the date the deposition was taken of Patrick Head, Francey Hakes, and Diane Woods is detailed below. These activities shown within this time-line found in discovery, clearly demonstrate how Patrick Head and Francey Hakes manipulated the grand jury in order to block the indictment of Andrew Titelman for child molestation.

Furthermore, it shows the Cobb County District Attorney's busy involvement with the State's witnesses from the criminal trial, Andrew Titelman, and his attorney after Patrick Head learned of my request for a grand jury investigation. In light of the fact that Mr. Head almost never participates in such grand jury activities as indicated in his deposition, this time-line shows he has taken much time and energy, and has gone to great measures and expense to involve himself, Francey Hakes, Diane Woods, Dr. Elizabeth King, and Lorita Whitaker in this instance to control and manipulate the grand jury into turning against me, and away from the true evidence. During the course of discovery in the federal case it was found that Patrick Head prepared and presented to each member of the 2001 May/June Grand Jury a bound book, approximately three inches thick, taken from the individuals interested in prosecuting me at the criminal trial. Again, these are the same people my jury named as individuals covering up the sexual abuse of Amanda and Jessica.

TIME-LINE

5/30/01	Letter from the foreperson of the criminal jury was delivered to D.A. Patrick Head and Judge James Bodiford.
6/4/01	a) Petition filed to disqualify District Attorney from participating in any investigation of Andrew Titelman; Grand Jury asked to investigate Andrew Titelman and the cover up of the sexual abuse of Amanda and Jessica Titelman; Wendy Titelman asked for the issuance of a warrant for the arrest of Andrew Titelman.
	b) Judge Laura Austin, late night, orders an unbiased investigation to take place by Detective Bishop regarding child molestation by Andrew Titelman.
	c) Detective Bishop with Kennesaw Police Department talks to Francey Hakes about her talking to Judge Laura Austin and faxes her a note to this effect.
6/?/01	Francey Hakes phones Judge Austin and kills the investigation.
6/?/01	Francey Hakes and Patrick Head meet with Andy Titelman.
6/8/01	a) Christina Firth, Paralegal to John Mayoue and Pamela Gray responds to Patrick Head's request for Dr. Elizabeth King's transcript from the final hearing in June, 2000.
	b) Francey Hakes talks to Pamela Gray about contacting the jurors from the criminal trial and sends to her the list of jurors and asks for the responses.
	c) Anonymous letter addressed to Andy Titelman postmarked 6/8/01 was put in the mail.
6/?/01	Patrick Head and Fracey Hakes talk to Lorita Whitaker about doing a video of Amanda and Jessica at Safe Path.
6/11/01	a) Diane Woods and Patrick Head meet at Waffle House.
	b) Diane Woods talks with Betty King as a result of meeting with Patrick Head at Waffle House.

c) Andrew Titelman faxes Patrick Head and Francey Hakes the anonymous letter postmarked 6/8/01 addressed to Andy Titelman.

6/12/01   a) Diane Woods sends fax to Patrick Head saying that Betty King "asked whether or not Dr. Pittman could be of help with the Grand Jury," and also stated, "Dr. Pittman certainly has an extended history with this family and is one of the folks I relied upon when making my preliminary report."

b) Videotape produced at SafePath of Lorita Whitaker with Amanda and Jessica Titelman about *"Mrs. Titelman telling the children what to say and to lie about daddy and that Daddy never touched them"* and *"about the incidents surrounding their being taken to Mississippi."*

c) For the grand jury investigation, Patrick Head issued subpoenas to the State's witnesses who were called to testify against Ms. Titelman in the trial of The State of Georgia v Wendy Jane Titelman.

d) Letter dated 6/12/01 was prepared to be sent to Ms. Titelman inviting her to present testimony to the Grand Jury.

6/?/01   a) Patrick Head and Francey Hakes talk about what Ms. Hakes "beginnings" would be with the Grand Jury.

b) Patrick Head asks Francey Hakes for the names and addresses of the State's witnesses from the criminal trial.

c) Patrick Head prepares a large notebook of materials from the State's witnesses to be given to each grand juror.

6/20/01   a) Adele Grubbs signs order stating that no recording transcription or other memorialization of Frank Pittman's testimony before the Grand Jury shall be made.

b) Under the presentment of Patrick Head, Francey Hakes talks to Grand Jury for up to an hour for the "beginnings" and spoke and met with witnesses throughout the day.

c) The State's witnesses used in the criminal prosecution of Wendy Titelman are called by Patrick Head as witnesses before the Grand Jury along with Dr. Frank Pittman and Det. Mary Finlayson from Cobb County Crimes Against Children.

d) Francey Hakes and Patrick Head exit the Grand Jury area together with the following witnesses while Ms. Titelman is talking to the Grand Jury: Diane Woods, Elizabeth King, Lorita Whitaker, Frank Pitman and others.

6/21/01   a) Judge Adele Grubbs signs order stating that no one may contact the May-June Grand Jurors and that their names and addresses be sealed from the public.

b) Judge James Bodiford holds a hearing to set up a hearing for the "Emergency Motion for Ruling on Emergency Petition for Disqualification and Appointment of Substitute District Attorney."

6/22/01   a) Restraining orders issued to everyone who testified before the Grand Jury.

b) Judge Bodiford holds a hearing on the "Emergency Motion for Ruling on Emergency Petition for Disqualification and Appointment of Substitute District Attorney," and rules that it is a moot point. He threatens the criminal jurors who signed the letter of May 30, 2001.

c) Jeffrey Bogart, Attorney for Frank Pitman, sent a letter to Patrick Head requesting a copy of the order Judge Grubbs signed.

6/28/01   Lorita Whitaker writes a threatening letter to the foreperson of the criminal jury for writing letter.

7/18/01   Andrew Titelman faxes Pat Head and Francey Hakes communication about Ms. Titelman living in Louisiana and his retaining Mr. Cauthorn, a new attorney who formerly sat as a superior court judge.

Seeking an Unbiased Judge

I filed a motion for new trial and another motion for the recusal of Judge Bodiford. A hearing was held January 28, 2002 regarding Judge Bodiford's recusal and resulted in his stepping aside from this D.A. recusal case. He stated that an order would be issued within 24 hours to the Chief Judge of Cobb County Superior Court and that I would receive a phone call from the Chief Judge's office. I didn't receive a phone call, so I called and spoke with Chief Judge Stoddard's administrative assistant who said the case had been put back on the "wheel of fortune" and that it had been assigned to Judge Nix. I called Judge Nix's office to set a hearing date and spoke with his administrative assistant. I was put on hold, and then Judge Nix picked up the phone and told me that a judge was being assigned from outside the circuit and that I should communicate with the court administrator.

So I immediately called the court administrator, Skip Cheshire, and left a message on his recorder to return my call. On the following day Mr Cheshire told me that he knew nothing about this case and could do nothing without an order from Judge Nix's law clerk. On February 11, 2002, I called Judge Nix's office and briefly spoke with the administrative assistant and left a message for the law clerk to call me regarding Mr. Cheshire's need. I received a call the same day from Judge Nix who left an angry message on my voice mail. He stated,

> Ms. Titelman, The message that you gave my secretary was incorrect. I have checked with Mr. Cheshire. He did not tell you that he was waiting on an order from me. He told you about the procedure which must come from the 7th District Administrator. What you need to do is what I told you and that's you understand that the case is being assigned to a judge who is going to be brought in [sic]. You don't have to do nothing else [sic]. You don't call nobody [sic] except Mr. Cheshire and you don't call my office back. You don't call any other judge. You need to sit still and follow the procedure that we have,

not a procedure that you want. We are going to do things correctly, and you need to sit still until they are done and not to worry people to death. Now your phone call to my office was inappropriate, it was inaccurate, and you stated things to my secretary that did not happen, because I have spoken and I have exact wordage [sic] that was conveyed. So you either misunderstood Mr. Cheshire and you communicated that misunderstanding to my office. I do not sign an order and there is not one waiting for me to sign. So do not call my office back, period! And Mr. Cheshire will have that done in 2 or 3 days, but I suggest you wait until it is done, and quit trying to run the system the way you want it run.

On February 15, 2002 I called Mr. Cheshire who informed me to call Jody Overcash, the Seventh District Court Administrator. I spoke with Ms. Overcash the same day. She informed me that "Cobb County" wanted Judge Arthur Fudger in Dallas, Georgia, to hear the case. She stated that "Cobb County" told her that Judge Bodiford would handle part of the case, Judge Wood would handle part of the case and Judge Fudger would handle part of the case. She also advised me to call the Cobb County Clerk or Judge Fudger's office to set a hearing date.

I then called the Cobb County Clerk to schedule a hearing. She informed me that the case had been closed in June, 2001, and a hearing date could not be set. I called Clerk Jay Stephenson who informed me that he could not set a hearing date or "create new laws for me." I called Mr. Cheshire to ask how I could set a date for hearing. He said he could not help me. I called Judge Fudger's office and spoke with his law clerk. I requested that a hearing date be established and that all the records pertaining to this case be given to Judge Fudger. An hour later, the law clerk called me back and stated he had talked with Judge Fudger regarding my two requests and that Judge Fudger would be calling Ms. Overcash.

I followed the customary procedure established by Cobb County to file motions and to set hearing dates, and I followed the advice given by the administrators. This should have been a simple administrative task. I had to file a motion with the Court to force a hearing to be held. On May 1, 2002, I finally went before Judge Fudger.

I thought we were going to have a hearing regarding the Motion for New Trial to Disqualify the District Attorney from participating in an investigation of Andrew Titelman. Judge Fudger announced this was a hearing only on my motion to recuse Judge Bodiford. Attorneys who examined the record and friends who were present at the hearing before Judge Bodiford months before understood Judge Bodiford recused himself from the case. Now I was having to hear this all over again.

At this hearing I presented all the exhibits attached to the motions in the file and the hearing transcripts, the depositions of Diane Woods, Patrick Head and Francey Hakes as evidence.

Judge Fudger signed an order May 9, 2002. He stated that "this action arose out of a divorce action." He said that a hearing had been set for September 20, 2000 because of problems in custody and visitation, but that Judge Bodiford continued the hearing until October 2, 2000. He said at that hearing "custody was left with the father and Petitioner's visitation was suspended." He went on to state I declined to introduce any evidence. He wrote that Judge Bodiford "in no way threatened or made disparaging remarks about them [the jurors]." He said he has read the entire file and found no indication of any *ex parte* communications or hearings with substantive matters or issues. His final words were,

> This case and all the other related cases have been exhaustively and extensively tried. It is extremely doubtful that either more judges or more criminal actions will help the situation. There does not appear to be any reason to recuse Judge Bodiford or to disqualify District Attorney, it is; HEREBY ORDERED, that Petitioner's Second Motion to Recuse Judge James Bodiford should be dismissed and the same is hereby overruled and denied.

We appealed. The appeal was denied by the Georgia Court of Appeals and the Georgia Supreme Court without comment.

Going Back to Judge Jon Bo Wood

We had previously filed an Extraordinary Motion and Brief for New Trial And/or Motion and Brief to Set Aside; Emergency Petition for Change of Custody, or in the Alternative, Petition for Change And/or Modification of Visitation prior to my criminal trial. This was amended with all the discovery information. We also filed for the recusal of Judge Bodiford, Diane Woods, Elizabeth King and Lorita Whitaker.

Based on the facts a new trial should have been granted. However, when we went before Judge Bo Wood on April 22, 2002, for the Extraordinary Motion for New Trial, he denied the new trial, and stated he would allow no evidence to be put on the record. A petition for discretionary appeal was filed and on July 26, 2002, the Supreme Court of Georgia denied the petition without comment.

Protecting Their Own

I wrote complaints to the Georgia Bar Association, the agency responsible for the ethical accountability of attorneys. Nothing was done. The complaint against Diane Woods was returned to me. The problem was not that I had too little to give them, but that I presented "too much" documentation! I sent it back along with a letter to the president of the Bar Association expressing my concern that evidence of corruption was being refused by the Bar, and I copied it to the Chief Justice of the Supreme Court. I have never received even an acknowledgment of receipt from the Bar Association even when I followed up with another letter. I have since learned that Dr. Elizabeth King sits on the review board of the Georgia Bar Association!

I also sent complaints against Dr. Elizabeth King and Lorita Whitaker to the Secretary of State Licensing Division. The complaint against Dr. King was immediately dismissed. The complaint against Ms. Whitaker has never been investigated, even when I followed up with phone calls and letters. I then learned that Dr. King's partner, Dr. Carol Webb, is on the review board for the Secretary of State.

I wrote to the Judicial Qualifications Committee, which is supposed to hold judges accountable. No one responded. In April, 2002, Richard Ducote called and spoke with Ms. Cheryl Custer who told him that it did not matter what the law says about *ex-parte* communications, because "that's the way they do it in Georgia" and she saw nothing wrong with anything Bodiford did.

Whenever I reported that the law was not being followed, I was told by various people, including Ms. Custer, Sr. Judge Fudger, D.A. Patrick Head, and Superior Court Clerk Jay Stephenson that it didn't matter what the law stated, "that's the way that Georgia does it."

"What a mess," is the common statement I hear when people speak of the "Titelman" case. The only "mess" is the tangled web the Cobb County team wove in their deception. Obviously, this is a case that deserves a lot of examination. The deception has been so great, that the tangled webs must be cleared a strand at a time to see what went wrong. Then the light of truth will disperse the darkness. Only then can justice take place and peace begin.

We have uncovered a great deal of truth, and we have filed the proper pleadings to correct the errors. However, we thus far have found that Laura Austin's words hold true - the "good ole' boys" are sticking together no matter what. Each judge has shut down every motion thus far. We continue to fight in every available avenue.

Seeking Justice at the Federal Court

July 13, 2001, Richard and Michael filed a federal lawsuit against Andy, his attorneys, John Mayoue and Pam Gray, Diane Woods, and Detective Craig Chandler, who were responsible for maliciously having me arrested and pursuing criminal action against me. Judge Owen Forester with the Northern District of the U.S. District Court in Atlanta was eventually assigned the case.

The defendants immediately obtained a stay on discovery from Judge Forester, which delayed our right to uncover additional information pertinent to this case. We asked for a jury trial. However, on August 8, 2002, Judge Forrester issued an order dismissing the lawsuit. He states that I am attempting to "relitigate issues from the underlying divorce and custody proceedings," and that it is "...merely another attempt to introduce her charges of sexual abuse into this litigation."

Clearly, Diane Woods, Elizabeth King, Andy Titelman and others wanted me in jail because of the continued substantiation of sexual abuse, which threatened their professional and personal lives. They want to separate me from my daughters in order to silence them and punish me. Judge Forrester ruled that we cannot use the girls' abuse and the cover up to show these defendants motives. He also stated that the jury who wrote the letter with findings that prosecution was malicious was not empaneled to make that decision. He ruled that "the letter is inadmissible and does not constitute a demonstration of 'maliciousness,'" even though this jury heard the evidence behind my prosecution, was outraged by what they found, and voiced that outrage in a written letter.

Judge Forrester also held that because Judge Flournoy, who heard the criminal trial, denied my motions for directed verdict of not guilty, that act "conclusively establishes that there was probable cause to prosecute Plaintiff," and dismissed the lawsuit saying it is insufficient as a matter of law under the rationale of Monroe v. Sigler, 256 Ga. 759 (1987). He stated we would have to prove that "Judge Flournoy's denials of her motions for a directed verdict were achieved through fraud or corruption."

Richard Ducote filed a pleading in February, 2002, arguing that Judge Forrester's reasoning was incorrect:

In Wolf Camera, Inc. v. Royter, 2002 Ga. App. LEXIS 25 (January 14, 2002), the court affirmed the trial court's ruling that the plaintiff's denied directed verdict motion in the underlying criminal trial did not preclude the subsequent malicious prosecution suit. First, the appellate court observed that O.C.G.A. § 51-7-43 leaves the question of probable cause for the jury alone to decide, under the direction of the court. Next, the appellate court noted that a denied directed verdict motion in the criminal trial, to be efficacious must stand unreversed and untainted by fraud or corruption, citing *Wingster v.*

Huntley's Jiffy Stores, 200 Ga.App. 252, 407 S.E.2d 481 (1991), one of *Monroe's* progeny. Finally, the court held that the determination of the existence of fraud or corruption beneath the directed verdict motion was likewise for the jury to decide in the tort trial, unless the facts regarding probable cause are undisputed. Applying these precepts to the facts before them the court stated:

Here, although the trial court in Royter's criminal trial denied his motion for directed verdict, there was evidence in the malicious prosecution trial, which could support the jury's determination that such denial was obtained through fraud committed by the Defendants. As discussed above, there was evidence which could support a determination by the jury that the Defendants acted in unison to frame Royter and conceal exculpatory evidence. And because the trial court's denial of Royter's motion for directed verdict was based on evidence which the jury found to be disingenuous, it cannot be said that it was procured in the absence of fraud or deceit.

Applying the *Wolf Camera* holding to the instant case, if a jury could find that the defendants jointly committed fraud or withheld exculpatory evidence in an effort to frame Ms. Titelman, the denial of the directed verdict motion is irrelevant. Well, Ms. Titelman's criminal jury has already made that determination. Next, newly found exculpatory evidence, which was concealed by the defendants, has been unearthed through discovery in this case. In late October, 2001, through the deposition of the Cobb County District Attorney in connection with this case, Plaintiff obtained a videotape reflecting an interview by Georgia child protection officials with Ms. Titelman's daughter (then age 7) on June 23, 1999. In the interview, the child clearly discloses the same sort of sexual molestation she later reported to Dr. Matherne in September, 2000. Dr. Kathleen Faller, one of the nation's foremost authorities on child sexual abuse, has examined

215

this tape in comparison to a videotape of Defendant Titelman browbeating the children into retraction, and has concluded that this child was likely molested by her father. Defendant Woods's knowledge of this tape -and guilt in concealing it - is established by her admissions in her statements to the child custody judge on June 30, 2000, conceding her presence there, but misrepresenting the facts of the interview. Furthermore, Defendant Titelman's denial prior to the directed verdict motions that he molested the children was likewise fraudulent and deceitful. It is axiomatic that if Defendant Andrew Titelman would have admitted sexually abusing the two girls, Judge Flournoy would have directed a verdict of acquittal in a heartbeat and would have ordered Mr. Titelman's arrest. Or perhaps, had he admitted the sexual abuse to the county prosecutor, Ms. Titelman would have never endured this outrageous prosecution, period.

Given the current state of Georgia law, as Ms. Titelman argued in her original opposition and now as buttressed by this most recent opinion, the denial of the directed verdicts in the criminal trial do not require the automatic dismissal of this suit under the *Monroe* rationale because: 1) the denials were reversed by the criminal jury letter, 2) the denials were not based on Judge Flournoy's determination that the evidence was sufficient as a matter of law to support a conviction, 3) Judge Flournoy denied the second motion despite acknowledging that it was valid, 4) the State's stipulations at the criminal trial demonstrate the lack of probable cause, and 5) the directed verdict denials were the result of a prosecution in which these Defendants acted fraudulently, without a full, fair and complete disclosure of the facts, and in which exculpatory evidence was concealed.

This lawsuit should have gone before a jury to decide its merits. Judge Forrester prevented that from happening. We are appealing to the Eleventh Circuit U.S. Court of Appeals in Atlanta.

We have received an additional order sanctioning Michael Hirsh and/or Richard Ducote for bringing the lawsuit, and we are expecting large sanctions which will, of course, be appealed.

The Federal Libel Lawsuit

On August 13, 2002, we filed a federal lawsuit against Andy's new wife, Anita Miller Titelman, for libel. Anita wrote a letter to a prominent citizen of Atlanta, Mr. John Sherman, stating lies about Richard and me and accused us of illegal and felony behaviors. As I explain below, this letter from Anita Titelman is consistent with other anonymous letters received in the past. The letters are all very similar in writing style but the person writing presents himself or herself or themselves as a different person each time.

The first letter was received by me approximately July 25, 2000 just after the final custody hearing, immediately after we had received a phone call telling us what the judges verdict was, and ten days before the final judgement was signed and fifteen days before it was entered into the Court record. The letter was not dated and not signed. The writer states she doesn't know me nor my former husband very well, but that she was in the courtroom everyday. She said she knew that I "screwed up" and that I was going to lose my children. This person says she has three children and one stepchild. She wrote, "Mr. Titelman is no child molester, and I don't think that you even believe that. You were a desperate woman and we all knew what was happening." She said, "A few experts have called you mentally ill. It sickens me to know all of this. But yes, you could have easily gotten custody and child support if only you would have admitted that perhaps your ex did not "wrongly touch" the girls. ... You're done. Finished." She went on to say, "Your former husband seems to be a good father, and I know that he has a steady girlfriend that perhaps helped him win this case. ... I looked for her to make an appearance in the courtroom but apparently it was not a good idea. And now you are faced with the prospect that another woman will possibly be 'mothering' your children."

The second letter was written to Laurie Caldwell in Mississippi and received just prior to the hearing that Andy and his entourage

217

attended. This person states she is a friend of mine and that I asked her and others to write a letter of support for me. She said "she knew me for six years through the church of which I now deny." She writes, "Wendy is making up the molestation charges against her ex husband. She tried to make me a part of it in the divorce/custody battle here in Georgia, and she succeeded in getting some of our other friends to go along. ... She told me then that claiming molestation would be the only way to get the children. She said that she could get Amanda and Jessica to say almost anything she wanted them to. When I told her how damaging this would be to the kids, she said that they are young and that once she has custody and has them in church all will be okay. ... Wendy ADMITTED to me that Andy never really touched the girls." She writes further, "My husband and I decided together to let you, the judge, Andy's attorneys, psychologists, etc know her situation. When I sat in that courtroom (here in Georgia) and heard some of the things Wendy said and I KNEW SHE WAS LYING I was scared to death for her. I watched and listened and I KNEW that she was going to loose the kids. ... She has talked about going 'underground' so nobody was that surprised when she kidnaped the girls." She finishes her letter by saying, "I am not signing my name as to the fear that Wendy will read this and I do not want to upset her anymore than necessary."

Laurie told me Judge Teel received a similar letter as well.

On June 11, 2001, Andy faxed a note to Patrick Head and Francey Hakes stating, "To Whom It May Concern: This letter was received in Saturday's mail - There is no signature." The letter that was attached is addressed to Andy and reads,

> Andy, I'm not sure why, but I feel as if I need to warn you about Wendy. She is out to completely destroy you, your reputation, your family and your girlfriend. She and her troop have some pretty scary plans. I don't think that you ever did anything to the girls and in the beginning Wendy didn't either, however I think that now she does believe it. They are talking of going on talk shows, local gatherings, etc. I've been told that they use all means possible to get what they want. I have heard all of this

through a very reliable mutual friend of Wendy's and myself. I will continue to keep you, Wendy, Amanda and Jessica in my prayers.

Richard Ducote received an e-mail August 13, 2001 from, as appears on the e-mail, "John Sherman." This person states she has been trying to get in touch with me and asks Mr. Ducote to pass information on to me. She said she sees the girls "quite often and they are doing great." She writes,

> I want to let Wendy know, maybe she already knows, that there is quite a bit of support going around here for Andy. There are letters like you wouldn't believe! ... There are letters of support from teachers, counselors, old neighbors, new neighbors, babysitters, parents of school friends. ... There are copies of polygraph tests (where Andy passed 2 times and Wendy failed 2 times). There is so much more you wouldn't believe it! I'm not sure who orchestrated this whole thing, Andy said he had no idea, and neither did anyone else I asked, but it does exist believe me.

She ends her letter saying, "(I am not going to sign this letter for the obvious reasons). Thank you in advance for forwarding this to Wendy."

The anonymous letter that was sent by e-mail to Richard was traced, and we found that "John Sherman," the owner of the e-mail address, was unaware of anyone using his address. He was able to uncover that Anita Miller Titelman, the bookkeeper for Park Place on Peachtree in which he lives, had come into his home and used his computer and e-mail address to send this anonymous letter while he was out of the country. He asked her for a written explanation, and he faxed us the letter that Anita wrote to him and a letter that Anita told him that she faxed to Richard. Richard, however, never received anything directly from her.

The letter she wrote to Mr. Sherman states,

This is a very complicated situation. ... First, the attorney, Mr. Richard Ducote, is an attorney for the "Children of the Underground". I'm not sure if you've ever heard of that group before. It is a group that "helps" mothers take their children "underground" and hide when the fathers have been awarded custody of the children. ...The mother had accused him (Andy) of molesting the girls when he filed for custody. She admitted in court that she made that up to stop him from going for custody. She was also said to be mentally ill by 2 different physiologists. Anyway, to make a long story short...she kidnaped them in September of 2000 and took them to Mississippi. They were found after a week and brought back to Georgia. She hasn't been able to see them yet and it's been almost 2 years. She isn't even able to see them in a "supervised" situation. Richard Ducote has been helping her out and trying all kinds of "slick & unlawful" ways to "win.".... But this is not over yet. Mr. Ducote's strategy is to "keep filing lawsuits" for anything that he can. (Isn't my life exciting-just like a TV movie!) ... If you receive ANY OTHER CORRESPONDENCE from Mr. Ducote would <u>you please give it to me and I will immediately give it to the attorneys involved in this case</u>.

She signed her name, "Anita." Mr. Sherman faxed us this letter as well as the letter Anita told him that she faxed to Richard. In the letter to Richard she states,

I sent the letter to you on behalf of someone that didn't have access to a computer (or even know how to use one). This person asked me to forward the letter to you and gave me your e-mail address. Mr. Sherman was out of the country and I was periodically sending him his messages/e-mails. I sometimes had trouble sending his messages from his computer so I would email them downstairs to my computer and then forward them on to Mr. Sherman. I was doing this on my lunch break, so I quickly typed the letter from the handwritten one that was sent to me and most likely was forwarded to Mr. John Sherman's computer along with the others. Mr. Sherman had no knowledge of the letter nor the circumstances surrounding the letter. Neither did Mrs. Sherman.

On September 10, 2002, a note was sent to me through the mail that reads,

> Heads up. … Anita has an uncle that is a Superior Court Judge in Fulton County and he also lives at Park Place Condos where she works. (supposedly that's how she got the job there). She moved in with his family for a while when she left her husband in another state and is said to be very close to him. Just be careful and do some research. This is all I know and it came from a very reliable source. Just thought you needed to know.

On the outside of the card sized envelope my name and address had been cut from another sheet of paper and glued to the envelope. This was like an anonymous note Richard received postmarked May 3, 2002, in that his name and address had been cut out and taped to the envelope, and on the inside was an anonymous message as well.

On September 16, 2002, in the federal libel suit, Anita's attorneys filed a motion requesting that the libel case be transferred to Judge Owen Forrester because of his handling of the malicious prosecution lawsuit. It was transferred immediately, not allowing any time for a response from us. This is not a basis for transfer, and we filed a motion to recuse Judge Forrester. This is an entirely separate case involving different parties and a distinct cause of action. The case was subsequently returned to the original federal judge, Richard W. Storey.

In Anita Titelman's deposition December 19, 2002, Ms. Titelman refused to answer simple, basic questions by stating "I don't remember," "I don't know," "I'm not sure," or "No idea" 258 times. For example, she was asked how she got Richard Ducote's e-mail address, and she answered, "I'm not sure," and "I don't remember." He asked her what was the purpose in sending the John

Sherman e-mail to him. She answered, "I don't know." He asked her, "Where did you get that information from (referring to the content of the e-mail? She said, "I don't know." He asked, "Why would you make fun of somebody you don't even know who it is?" She answered, "I don't know." When asked who she talks to about the things she stated, she answered, "I don't remember." She offered no basis for her libel of us and admitted she knew it to be false. Yet when asked if she wanted to apologize, she said, "No." She went on to say, she would probably say it again.

February 26, 2003, we received from Ms. Titelman her responses to our interrogatories of her. The first question was, "State your name, date of birth, present address, the names and ages of each of your children, your driver's license number and any other names by which you have been known. She answered, "Anita currently resides at with her daughters A.T. (10) and J.T. (8)..." [emphasis added]. This is consistent with all her other behaviors, just simply to hurt me.

the Juvenile Court Petition

We are pursuing other avenues to get protection for Amanda and Jessica. June 10, 2002, I along with 29 other Petitioners asked the Cobb County Juvenile Court to file a "Petition for Adjudication of Deprivation." [Appendix F] Under the Uniform Rules for the Juvenile Courts of Georgia, a petition alleging deprivation "may be made by any person, including a law enforcement officer, who has knowledge of the facts alleged or is informed and believes they are true." It is unprecedented that 30 people from all walks of life have come together demanding the protection of the girls. Usually it is DFACS that brings the petition.

Along with these Petitioner's statements, reports and letters evidencing abuse were attached as exhibits.

The Petition also states: "Furthermore, in an effort to protect himself from accountability for his molestation of the children, and to punish the children for their disclosure of the abuse, Andrew Titelman has vigorously attempted to terminate all contact and relationship between the children and Petitioner, has isolated the children from their long term friends and close relatives, and has terminated their long standing social and extracurricular activities. He has also attempted to terrorize the children by repeatedly telling them that they will be kidnaped if they play at neighbor's homes, that gifts sent by Petitioner may contain bombs, and that Petitioner has in the past attempted to drown them, starve them, beat them, etc. He has also subjected them to threats, intimidation, and browbeating to force them to maintain their silence about their abuse."

Petitioner Jerry Geiger went to the Cobb County Juvenile Court on June 10, 2002, to file the Petition. He was asked to wait and approximately 20 minutes later, the clerk returned it to him refusing to file the Petition. He was informed that Judge Juanita Stedman, Chief Judge of the Cobb County Juvenile Court and part-time Cobb County Superior Court Judge had reviewed the Petition and refused it.

The O.C.G.A. § 15-11-37 states, "A petition alleging delinquency, deprivation, or unruliness of a child shall not be filed unless the court or a person authorized by the court has determined and endorsed upon the petition that the filing of the petition is in the best interest of the public and the child." There is no reasonable reading of the Petition that could possibly suggest that it is not in the best interest of my two little girls or the public for this petition to be filed.

We have attempted to have a writ of mandamus issued by the Court of Appeals and The Georgia Supreme Court to force the Juvenile Court to file the petition. Both denied the mandamus and directed us back to the Cobb County Superior Court. We sought a Writ of Mandamus from the Cobb County Superior Court and set a hearing date for December 12, 2002.

The O.C.G.A. § 15-11-28 clearly states that the juvenile court has exclusive original jurisdiction concerning any child who is alleged to be deprived. The Petition sets forth a plethora of facts and evidence establishing that Amanda and Jessica are sexually abused by their father, and are thus "deprived." Thirty outraged Petitioners, prominent members of the public, who have information that is pertinent to the children's deprivation and abuse, fervently asked that the "Petition for Adjudication for Deprivation" be filed. There is no other legal remedy for the legal rights of Amanda and Jessica. This is *per se* a failure of justice.

The Juvenile Court, through the Cobb County Attorney's Office, moved that the mandamus petition be dismissed. They contend that the Petition is an inappropriate vehicle where other legal remedies are being pursued, i.e., the on-going litigation in the Cobb County Superior Court before Judge James Bodiford.

The Juvenile Court's position that this case has to be handled in the Superior Court in the "custody case" flies directly in contradiction to the Supreme Court's holding in In *Re M.C.J.*, 271 Ga.546, 523 S.E.2d 6 (Ga.1999). There, the Supreme Court rejected the notion that a juvenile court deprivation action brought by one parent against another parent, even where the relief sought includes a custody determination, is simply a custody case within the Superior Court's purview, and beyond the juvenile court's jurisdiction. The fact that other cases exist is of no significance whatsoever, if this petition does indeed assert a valid cause of action for an adjudication of deprivation. There is no authority for the blanket posture that allows child sexual abuse and deprivation cases to be disposed of by "other legal remedy," nor does the law require a deprivation case to be dismissed when there is on-going or pending litigation in another venue regarding the parents of the deprived children.

The sexual abuse of children is conduct reviled in Georgia, as in all civilization, and the law goes to great lengths to punish those responsible so that our children can live safely. The policies of the State of Georgia clearly provide that children should be free of a sexually abusing father and that a mother who knows that her children are being molested has a moral and legal obligation to do everything possible to protect her children from the father. Under § 16-6-4, O.C.G.A., sexual molestation is punishable by 5-20 years in prison.[31] A father like Andrew Titelman who molests his daughters should have his parental rights terminated.[32] A mother, like me, who knows of the father's abuse of her daughters must act to protect them or risk losing her own rights.[33]

The juvenile courts have specialized expertise in child abuse cases beyond that of the Superior Court, and as such the legislature has properly designated the juvenile court as the proper forum for these matters. If sexual abuse of children is indeed condemned in Cobb County, and if the protection of child sexual abuse victims does indeed trump the interests of "the system" in avoiding the uncomfortable admission of its fallibility, the mandamus we have filed will be granted and the motion to dismiss denied.

On December 3, 2002, Judge Robert Flournoy, III - the same judge who seemed sympathetic in my criminal trial - issued a final order dismissing the Writ of Mandamus and circumvented any hearing taking place. Judge Flournoy, erroneously thought the mandamus was asking that he declare the children to be deprived. He states, "This Court could never mandamus the Juvenile Court Judge to find the children to be deprived. This would be nonsensical." The mandamus was simply asking the Superior Court to compel the Juvenile Court to hear the petition, not to make the juvenile court decide one way or the other. We filed an appeal. After hearing nothing back from the appellate court, I called the Georgia Court of Appeals and talked with the clerk. She informed me that the court has not received the record from Cobb County Superior Court, and could do nothing until the record was received. When I asked her what the time requirements were, she told me there is none, that Cobb County could sit on it for years and most likely would

the Right to Free Speech

Richard Ducote wrote a four-page letter on April 29, 2002, to the peers of Diane Woods and Elizabeth King telling them what they have done in this case and asking them to hold Ms. Woods and Dr. King accountable. [Appendix G] Approximately two hundred letters were sent out. The letter also invites Ms. Woods and Dr. King to sue him if the information is defamatory.

No lawsuit has been filed. We received several responses from attorneys in Atlanta who said this was not the first time this had

> "[T]he purpose of the free speech protection is to enable every citizen to bring the government and any person in authority to the bar of public opinion by just criticism upon their conduct."

happened by this duo, but there had been other cases involving children that Diane Woods and Elizabeth King acted in concert to put the children with the abuser.

Andy's attorneys are asking the Cobb County Superior Court to disallow Richard from representing me because of this letter that was sent out. Our right of free speech is protected by the First Amendment of the U.S. Constitution and Art. 1, § 1, & 5 of the Georgia Constitution. In *Wood v Georgia*, the Supreme Court held that the purpose of the free speech protection is to enable every citizen to bring the government and any person in authority to the bar of public opinion by just criticism upon their conduct.[34] Richard nor I have broken any law or ethical rule, and we have not libeled any person. They are furious that someone is actually fighting to protect the girls and exposing the evil things this court has done. We continue to speak the truth and seek justice. It is our hope that the public, upon learning what has happened here, will also voice their criticism and hold these people accountable.

People must be held accountable for their bad deeds. Otherwise, these crimes will continue and attorneys, guardians *ad litem*, court appointed psychologists, court appointed therapists and judges will continue to make money off a very sick system that destroys the lives of women and children and ultimately destroys a society.

CHAPTER TWELVE

A day or two prior to my criminal trial, Francey Hakes called some of my witnesses and screamed at them, demanding to know where I got the money to fight this. If it were not for the generosity of many people as well as my attorneys, Michael Hirsh and Richard Ducote, standing behind me, I would be in jail now. It sickens me to know that the State of Georgia knew they had broken me financially and thought there was no way I could fight what they were trying to do to me.

My mother has made it possible for me to go to court so many times to fight. It costs a lot of money, more than most people ever have in their life, and she has given it freely hoping that it will bring Amanda and Jessica protection and our being able to be with them again. I am greatly indebted and very thankful for her and many others who have given of their resources of time, money and prayers.

This gross injustice has affected many. Some adults have told me they awake troubled in the middle of the night and feel a great urge to pray for us. It has caused many to feel anger and grief. It does not make sense to anyone and is very confusing and frightening to all. It has caused them to question the integrity of our courts and justice system.

The children who used to play and study with Amanda and Jessica are frightened by what has happened to them. Many of the kids ask regularly when they will see the girls again. They do not understand why Amanda and Jessica cannot live with their mother. They are troubled that there are people keeping them from even seeing me. They remember me as a loving and caring mom. They remember Amanda and Jessica being upset because they were forced to return to someone they did not want to be with or live with, someone who they said was hurting them. They remember the children saying they want to live with their Mommy, but that no one will let them. The Carlson children refuse to go to sleep each night until they have prayed for my girls. The children feel unsafe.

Friends have told me about times they have seen the children from a distance. Susan Ibarra told me she saw them with Andy at CC's pizza restaurant in Kennesaw while she was there with her children. She went up to say hello, and Andy told them (Amanda and Jessica's friends) to get away. The girls sat silent with their heads hung.

A child advocate, Vicki Pierce, went to Andy's home to serve papers on him, but only a nanny and the children were there. The nanny told Vicki there was something very wrong with the mother who did not want to see her children.

I sent certified letters to the children, but most of them came back to me refused or unclaimed. Now I send letters by regular mail hoping that the girls might get at least one of them. I sent Halloween, Thanksgiving and Christmas presents through Andy's attorney, who then sent them to Diane Woods. But well after Christmas a friend of the girls told me that Amanda and Jessica had received no gifts or letters from me at all.

At one point I hired an investigator, Kevin Tidwell, to deliver Valentine gifts to Amanda and Jessica. He lives just a few blocks from where Andy lived at the time. He went to Andy's house frequently at different times of the day and night, but he never found anyone home. He concluded that no one lived there anymore. Then about a week before my criminal trial late in April, 2001, he found them at the house. The girls were there, and Kevin told Andy in in the girls' presence that he had brought gifts for them from their mother, Wendy Titelman. Andy told the investigator to get off his property and to take the gifts with him, that he did not know anyone by the name of Wendy Titelman!

I sent some of Jessica's birthday presents by Federal Express. I sent Easter baskets to the girls by certified mail in c/o Andy Titelman at AAMCO Transmissions. Susan, Andy's secretary, signed for them.

On another occasion Jan and Jerry Geiger, tried to deliver birthday presents to Amanda. Andy refused the gifts saying that there might be a bomb in one of the packages. He told them to get off his property and to take the presents with them. The girls were there, and Jan was able to at least wave at them. A couple of days later Andy called the Geiger's home. I was there visiting that day, and I answered the phone. Andy thought I was Jan, and when he found out it was me, he immediately hung up. Jerry received a letter from Andy the next week saying that any gifts to be given to the girls had to go through Diane Woods first and that they should give the gifts to her.

Gail and Michael Vernon have tried to deliver gifts to the girls several times, but rarely find anyone at the house. Last Christmas Michael separated the gifts I sent into five bags, two for Amanda, two for Jessica and one for both of them. Michael and his father went to Andy's house on Christmas day. Michael went to the door with two of the bags of gifts and left the others in the car. Anita answered the door. She immediately took the children into the kitchen and Andy went to the door. Michael told him that he had gifts for the children from their mother. Andy told him he had a choice. He could give the gifts to Diane Woods or he could leave them with him, but he would open every one of them first to see if they were appropriate. Michael left the two bags of gifts with Andy and took the other three bags home believing that the children would never receive any of the gifts. There have been other occasions they have left gifts at the door because they could never find anyone home, and once they left presents with the next-door neighbor hoping the children might receive them.

It wasn't long after that a detective with the Cobb County Police phoned Gail and ordered her to cease delivering gifts from me to the girls. When Gail challenged him saying there was nothing in any order that stated that I could not give my children gifts, he told her that the order was being changed to include this. When Gail shared this with me, I told Richard Ducote, who called the detective and left a message asking him to call back. He also stated in the message that the *ex-parte* order was illegal and any supposed change being made to it was totally bogus. The detective never called Richard back.

The children's great uncle, Dan, has also attempted to see the children and to give them gifts. He traveled from Huntsville and went to their home several times throughout a day and never found anyone home. He and his family routinely call me and are very distressed over what has happened.

My brother, Mark, is talking with as many people as he can all over the country, hoping to find answers, and to express his outrage. He has been a speaker on the subject in Washington, D.C. He has found other mothers who are going through the same turmoil, and he has become an advocate for the movement to make changes in the family court system that would allow this kind of atrocity to occur. He has cared so much about what has happened to his nieces and to me and is building a file of documentation for Amanda and Jessica. The day will come when he will be able to share with them what really has happened. This is a speech Mark gave at a rally in Washington to protest these national problems.

ROCK AMERICA 2001 SPEECH
By Mark Evans

Good Morning everyone. My name is Mark Evans. I'm honored to have this opportunity today to speak to you about this important issue of Justice for Children in Family Court. My talk is about how normal loving moms are losing their children in divorce.

First I'd like to tell you a bit about me and why I came to talk to you today. I'm a dad with three children (two daughters and a son) ages 19, 17 and 16. Six years ago, unfortunately, they suffered the trauma of divorce. Divorce, in itself, is a devastating event for children and parents. The lawyers in our case almost made it worse by trying to turn our divorce into a custody contest. I nearly fell for it. Better sense prevailed, however, and in a Plano, Texas parking lot using the back of an envelope, my ex-wife and I outlined a divorce agreement in which I relinquished physical custody of my children to her.

I reached this painful decision by asking my children which parent they preferred to live with and honored their wishes to be with their mom. My attorney told me I was making the worst mistake of my life. Well, the jury is still out on that self-serving assertion. I share this to let you know that I understand very well the pain a dad can experience losing daily contact with his children in a divorce. I also learned a lesson about how some attorneys will encourage conflict between divorcing parents that of course results in more money in the attorneys' pockets and the pockets of all the other bottom feeders of divorce court.

This reminds me of why lawyers can't go to the beach. It's because cats will come along and try to bury them in the sand. :-)

All kidding aside (they're not all bad), my children were very fortunate in that my ex-wife and I did not fight it out in court. You could say that we escaped falling through the vortex of the black hole of family court, that seems designed to strip everyone who enters of their wealth and dignity and in some cases their children. My sister, Wendy Titelman, has not been as fortunate. The traumatic forced separation of Wendy from her children Amanda and Jessica is the real reason I am here today.

It might help to know a little more about me to understand my motivation. My educational background is in psychology and computer science. I have done doctoral studies in social psychology and masters level study in computer science. My first job as a psychology research assistant at Georgia State University was with Dr. Josephine Brown, a developmental psychologist who had a grant to study mother-infant interaction and how general patterns of interaction are affected when the baby is born premature. The study was conducted at Atlanta's Grady Memorial Hospital. I was one of four observers who watched and recorded mother and infant behaviors such as vocalization, touching, burping, smiling, etc. I observed in the neighborhood of fifty mother-infant pairs in that study. I came away with a great appreciation for the bond between a mother and her newborn baby. The moms here know better than I that, with rare exceptions, this bond never ceases.

After nearly completing the course work for a PhD, I switched career direction from the chaos of psychology to the predictable world of computer software, predictable some of the time at least. For the past 21 years, I have worked as a software designer in the telecommunications industry.

Family Court never appeared on my radar screen until my divorce six years ago and only then as a place to be avoided. However, with my sister Wendy's divorce last year in Cobb County, Georgia, our faith in the scales of justice was shattered and I was propelled into the world of Internet activism with the aim of learning as much as possible about the dark labyrinths of Family Court. As we all know, knowledge is power. I hoped to one day have the power to help Wendy and her children.

As I began to network, I learned that Wendy's case is not unique. She is but one of a growing number of moms who have been erased from their children's lives as punishment for trying to protect their children from abuse. I know that sounds crazy, but it is true. Some very strange, Third-Reichian theories are being used in family courts across the nation to switch custody from the protective parent to the parent the child has identified as an abuser.

On the drive here from Plano Texas, I stopped in Atlanta to visit my esteemed professor Jim Dabbs from Ga. State University and his charming wife Mary. Mary introduced me to her friend Jenny Richardson who authored the book "Diaries of Abuse, Diaries of Healing." Jenny was interested in learning about this ROCK America march and about my motivation for attending. After I told her about my sister, she told me the story about how she became a storm chaser. In 1992, Jennie narrowly escaped death when a tornado leveled the house in which she sought shelter in Dahlonega, Georgia. For three days, she was trapped by rubble in the crawl space under the old house. Soon thereafter, she became a storm chaser. Later on, it occurred to me that following family courts is a lot like storm chasing. Tornadoes and family courts have one big thing in common: They are both good at ripping things apart!

If only we had more storm chasers keeping watch over the family courts that so often operate in secrecy behind closed doors. Most people either don't care or are unaware of the atrocities that occur in family courts each week. It's only human nature to care only when we or a loved one are affected directly. Many victims of injustice are left wondering, "Where's the outrage?" "How can they get away with these atrocities?" The answer, some suggest, is that legal abusers do what they do because 1) no one's watching and 2) they can get away with it. Except for a few brave journalists and whistle-blowing attorneys, the news coverage of the dark culture of family court is non-existent. A few exceptions come to mind such as the whistle-blowing story on July 4th by WFAA News in Dallas about a judge who played solitaire behind the bench on his computer while he was supposedly hearing child custody cases, and more troubling, the judge assigning lucrative Guardian Ad Litem cases to a crony who did free legal work on the judge's mother's estate. Susan Goldsmith of the L.A. Times also comes to mind with her excellent stories about Idelle Clarke and Irene Jensen. These stories are a step in the right direction, but need to be multiplied a hundred or a thousand times to expose how the courts truly operate. Unfortunately, most news organizations treat this as a taboo subject.

You may be wondering about this race number (2020) pinned to my shirt. By happenstance, I got this number when I ran the Houston Marathon this past January. I'm big on symbols and want you to remember these two: 1) 2020 is the vision we must have to see the truth of what's going on in family courts; and 2) that we must go the distance, no matter how far or how long it takes, to right the horrific wrongs of these family courts.

To wrap up my introduction, I would like to relate one other visit I had in Atlanta with my mother's neighbors, Rick and Mary Thompson.* Rick is a retired business owner and former associate pastor of a church in Atlanta. I have known Rick and Mary all my life. They are like Godparents to my siblings and me. A few weeks ago Rick and Mary attended a court hearing in Cobb County involving my sister Wendy. As Wendy tried to present her case in the hearing, the judge repeatedly interrupted her with tirades berating her character and her sanity. The judge's rage became so extreme that his DA friend interrupted and asked him to stop talking to avoid being quoted on the Internet and having that come back to haunt them. Rick and Mary were both appalled and saddened by the judge's vitriolic, unprofessional behavior. If only such court proceedings could be videotaped for all to see. As we said goodbye, Rick asked me to speak loud and clear at this march about the deplorable state of affairs of the family court in Cobb County. (HEY RICK, CAN YOU HEAR ME?)

I leave you with these two questions:

1) Who's keeping watch over the family courts of America?

2) How do we get people to care?

With your indulgence now, I want to share a brief essay I wrote, entitled "Twelve Steps for a Mom to Lose Her Children in Divorce" that I have distilled from observing my sister and other moms who have been stripped of their children.

The following are steps for a mom to follow in Cobb County Georgia and many other locales across the USA to lose her children in divorce:

1. Marry a charming business man (whom we shall call Jack) who comes from a wealthy family. You are impressed with Jack's love of children. Jack spent over $140,000 to win custody of a daughter from a previous marriage. Of course, Jack would never do this to you. Jack says his finest qualities are loyalty and honesty. Hmmm.

2. Give birth to two daughters and survive a close brush with death due to complications with your second pregnancy. Give up your career to be a stay-at-home mom.

3. To help you sort out the strains and conflicts of a blended family, record your deeply private thoughts in a diary that Jack can later steal and use against you.

4. Strive to make God and church the bedrock of your life, especially if Jack is an avowed atheist. Participate in church activities and take Bible study classes so that you can be branded a religious fanatic.

5. Home school your children because of concerns with the quality of the local public school system and because you want only the best for your children. For this you will be branded an anarchist.

6. Contract a serious lingering illness with Multiple-Sclerosis-like symptoms so that as household chores slide while you convalesce, Jack can say you are a hypochondriac, sloppy housekeeper, and lousy entertainer for his friends visiting from abroad.

7. As your daughters begin to mature (ages 4 and 6) take note of things they say that suggests that daddy likes to play with more than just the rubber duck while bathing with the

girls, that daddy plays games that he does not want mom to know about.

8.   Follow your natural maternal urge to protect your children by having them evaluated by a forensic psychologist. When the psychologist tells you the girls have been sexually abused, proceed to the threshold of family court hell -- the Department of Family and Children Services (DFACS, CPS, etc.) -- where you file charges of sexual abuse against Jack.

9.   When you select a lawyer for the ensuing divorce, choose someone nice with a good reputation in the Christian community who will turn the other cheek when the other side accuses you of fabricating evidence of sexual abuse, of parental alienation, of being vindictive, hysterical, and insane.

10. You discover your lawyer also represented Jack's first wife, ineffectively, in divorce court (what a small world). Since you've gone so far with this lawyer, ignore the advice of family members to get a new lawyer. They are probably wrong anyway because to change lawyers makes you look unstable.

11. Disregard that for every dollar you spend on a lawyer and psychiatric professionals, Jack's family will spend three. Disregard that the legal system is more concerned with money and influence than with doing the right thing for children.

12. During the two years leading up to a custody trial in which temporary custody is switched to Jack and his new girl friend because you have been branded an alienator, vindictive and insane, continue with all your heart to fight for your children. Exhaust all your resources and borrow from friends and family for mounting legal bills, even a therapist for yourself to prove that you are not insane.

(Unfortunately, your sanity became suspect when you married Jack in the first place.) The more you try to protect your children and prove yourself worthy, the deeper the court appointed "professionals" (Guardian Ad Litem, Psych, etc.) will be pitted against you while all the time billing you for their services! It's like being robbed and then having to pay the robber. Note that it is not necessary for you to engage in adultery, prostitution or nude dancing, to abuse drugs or alcohol, to abuse or neglect your children, or engage in other immoral, unethical or illegal behavior. To lose your children, just follow these twelve steps. This is the general pattern by which moms in Georgia and in family courts across the USA are being stripped of their children and all their parental rights. The children are deprived of their mom's love and daily guidance. And the Jacks of the world are free to repeat the cycle again and again. As the children you once nursed and nurtured place their little hands on their hearts and pledge, "One nation under God, indivisible, with liberty and justice for all," will they think of themselves and their mom and wonder if they got justice?

Love Takes on a Deeper Meaning When Facing Evil

It is so very difficult to express how it feels not to be able to see Amanda and Jessica, to hold them, kiss them, hear their laughter, heal their wounds, or to be able to do anything for them. The pain has been great, and my nightmares have been many. When the courts failed us, I experienced a deep despair. The grief and pain that followed cannot be fully put into words.

My heart is more than broken, my body aches with pain and exhaustion, my mind is filled with despair and unrest, and my spirit has been beaten and broken.

My loss is great. We will never be able to get back what we have lost. No one can take the pain away that has deeply pierced us for so long. No one can give us the minutes, hours, days, weeks, and years of time, energy and life that have been robbed from us. No one can give Amanda and Jessica their young years back that they should have had the protective arms of their mother around them, and I can never go back and put my arms around the children whom I have not even seen for over two years now. This time is lost forever. The separation of Amanda and Jessica from me has caused me to distrust humankind. The evil that has permeated our lives by others has deeply wounded us and robbed us of great treasures.

The grief that mothers like myself experience is far greater than if we had lost our children to death. Like an open and infected wound that is constantly being irritated and contaminated, we cannot heal. Everyday we are faced with the knowledge that our children continue to be abused, not only by their father, but by court order. The damage done robs and destroys life, even though the breath in our children's lungs continue.

The long-term effects of this will be immense. Not only are these children going to have to endure the effects of sexual abuse, and distrust of people for their failure of protection and refusal to believe them, but they will suffer for the rest of their lives because of the absence of their mother over these years.

Experts say, like scar tissue, the effects of sexual abuse never go away. Some children never share with anyone and keep the abuse a secret either because they don't have the language to describe it, they have been frightened to keep the secret, or they are afraid no one will believe them. Many articles and books say abuse can cause problems of depression, anxiety, guilt, fear, sexual dysfunction, withdrawal, dissociation, and acting out with hostility. Other effects may include regressive behaviors such as thumb sucking or bed-wetting, sleep disturbances, eating disorders, and non-participation in school and activities. Adults who were sexually abused as children can have self-destructive behaviors, such as alcoholism or drug abuse or physically abusive relationships and sexual promiscuity. The list goes on to include self-hatred, suicidal behavior, post traumatic stress disorder, disassociation, multiple personality disorder, repeat victimization, running away, criminal behavior, prostitution and on and on and on.

Diane Woods's disregard for the well being of Amanda and Jessica has brought serious consequences. Her philosophy that "they are already damaged kids; what's a little more damage," reeks of hateful disregard for human life.

If God had not given me the ability to reason, I do not know how I would have responded to those who are doing this to us. The natural instinct of a mother is to protect her young at all costs. A bear would have gone into combat with whoever was hurting her babies. I have been in combat for a very long time with Andrew Titelman and his family, his attorneys B Pam Gray and John Mayoue, Diane Woods and her friends - Dr. Elizabeth King, Lorita Whitaker, Judge James Bodiford, Detective Craig Chandler, and District Attorney Patrick Head. I have fought within the law with all of my might, using every tool and resource that God in His infinite wisdom has given to me. It has taken a very long time, and has taken quite a toll on me.

Amanda and Jessica are innocent of what their father has done to them and to me. It is an evil and unlawful act when a father seduces a daughter. A child should never be put in the position of having to say, "No," to their parent's sexual desires. It has caused Amanda and Jessica confusion, embarrassment and much suffering. It is not their fault, and they have done no wrong.

The nightmares Amanda and Jessica had in September, 2000, which they recorded that their father and everyone else was going to take them from Mississippi back to Atlanta and that their father would never let them see me again, were obviously a result of the threats of their father should they ever tell anyone again. I'm sure the children believe we will never see each other again because of their dreams, what their father tells them, and Ms. Whitaker's telling the children that I don't want to see them.

Even though all this seems so grim, I have hope. I believe in God's words, "I know the plans I have for you, plans for welfare, not for evil, to give you hope in your final outcome" (Jeremiah 29:11). "Eyes have not seen, ears have not heard. Neither has it entered into your heart what I have prepared for you" (Isaiah 64:4). God is not finished yet. I believe that He wants to accomplish something greater through all of this. All the hurt and pain that we have had to endure can be used for the good of others. If they are willing, God will use Amanda and Jessica in a mighty way like he did with Joseph in the book of Genesis. And God will bless them, as He blessed Joseph.

Even though I understand the cycle of human suffering and deprivation of love that occur in every life and the damage that it does which causes people to react and respond to life in many different ways, I still cannot comprehend how individuals can be so cold and uncaring about other people's lives, especially the lives of children - not to just be uncaring, but to purposefully bring harm.

Dr. Viktor Frankl, a psychiatrist who was tortured and suffered under Hitler's regime, wrote about his experience in a concentration camp in his book, *Man's Search for Meaning*. Dr. Frankl writes that when he tells his story, most people do not believe these things ever took place even though pictures and testimony have well documented these atrocities. Those who experienced it went through shock, then apathy and then for many, death. He made some important discoveries during this time, and he wrote,

> The way in which a man accepts his fate and all the suffering it entails, the way in which he takes up his cross, gives him ample opportunity - even under the most difficult circumstances - to add a deeper meaning to his life. It may remain brave, dignified and unselfish. Or in the bitter fight for self-preservation he may forget his human dignity and become no more than an animal. Here lies the chance for a man either to make use of or to forgo the opportunities of attaining the moral values that a difficult situation may afford him. And this decides whether he is worthy of his sufferings or not."[35]

Maturity is seen by the manner in which one responds to situations and whether one makes good or bad decisions, especially during difficult times. It is not a question of whether we will suffer or not. We all will suffer at some point in time, some much more than others. It is during these difficult times that we can grow and develop inner beauty, or we can choose to morally decay wreaking havoc on mankind.

Dr. Frankl grasps a great truth as he states,

A thought transfixed me: for the first time in my life I saw the truth as it is set into song by so many poets, proclaimed as the final wisdom by so many thinkers. The truth - that love is the ultimate and the highest goal to which man can aspire. Then I grasped the meaning of the greatest secret that human poetry and human thought and belief have to impart: The salvation of man is through love and in love.[36]

One who understands the depth of God's love and that he has a purpose here on Earth, becomes more aware and filled with God, and consequently, he is able to face adversities with grace and dignity. As a result of this filling up with God's love, one is able to love others in a meaningful way.

Love takes on a deeper meaning when facing evil. There are times when one must boldly stand against that which is wrong and demand that which is right. It requires one to be very shrewd, wise and knowledgeable.

The love I have for Amanda and Jessica has sustained me during these years of uncovering the truth and making it known to as many as possible in order to force justice to prevail. Depending on their own will to survive Amanda and Jessica can recover. It is also possible that they may never recover from the abuse they have had to endure. They will never be the same. I will never be the same. But we have to make decisions regarding our losses and how we are going to allow it to affect our lives. Each one of us individually must make choices that will cause us to grow into either a stronger, more courageous and loving person or an angry, bitter and hateful person. Many people choose the latter and display the deep and buried pain and anger in many ways. I pray that my children will choose to live a life filled with love even during the most disturbing times of their lives. It is only then that one can experience satisfaction, purpose, and fulfillment.

God said, "The truth will set you free." It has been Richard Ducote's motto throughout this fight. I know that together, with time, we may heal. We will need to talk a lot about what has happened. And every time we want to hide something deep inside of us and not tell anyone because we are afraid or embarrassed or feel guilty or hurt too much from it, that is the time we need to open up and share what it is, and receive acceptance and love in its place in order to heal completely. As Amanda and Jessica heal they will grow to be powerful young women who will be capable of setting this world on fire because of what they have had to endure as children. To begin to heal they will have to be freed from the bondage they are now in and know they are safe and loved.

God has given me strength through the love of others who support me and hold me up. I have prayed that He has done the same for Amanda and Jessica. I pray that He keeps them from harm, that He guards their heart, their mind, their spirit, their soul and their body. I pray that He puts people in their lives who love them and tell them the truth. I pray that He blesses them, indeed! And that He increases their understanding and make them wise. I pray His hand is upon them, and that He walks with them and guides them. May He keep them from evil so that they cause no pain. I pray He brings Amanda and Jessica back home to me soon. I pray for justice to prevail!

CHAPTER THIRTEEN

The headlines in the Atlanta Journal Constitution recently read "State Needs to Get Serious About Fighting Child Abuse." Other recent headlines have read: "State Must Do More to Protect Children," "Abuse Claims Usually True." Jane O. Hansen reported in December, 1999, "State Law Mandates That Doctors, Teachers and Others Report Child Abuse, But They Can't Find Out What The State Does About It." These are serious headlines that tell us the truth about what is happening.

The problem is exacerbated as a result of those who choose to believe that a father would never do such a thing to a child, much less his own. Some are in denial in the face of overwhelming evidence, similar to the bishops who have covered up the sexual abuse of children by their priests. Behind every child molester there is a mother or a friend who supports them because they see other qualities in them that they love. It is very dangerous to deal with issues by ones emotions, especially those in the legal profession where facts and evidence are crucial to bring out truth and justice. A very relevant caution is sounded in MacFarlane and Waterman, *Sexual Abuse of Young Children*:

> There even appears to be a danger that some parents, particularly mothers, may automatically be regarded as paranoid, hysterical, or perverted in their thinking for simply suspecting their ex-husbands of such a thing as child sexual abuse. It is a reflection of society's longstanding refusal to acknowledge the widespread existence of incest. For divorcing mothers, the assumptions made about their motives can serve as an insurmountable barrier to getting help. This bias may be so strong that their reports to others of what their children have told them can actually jeopardize their own positions as future custodians of their children. This form of double jeopardy will only serve to reinforce the silence that already surrounds this problem, and to endanger children further. Very young children are not prone to fantasizing about molestation and are rarely capable of describing or

243

re-enacting things about which they have no knowledge or experience.

We must guard against our own unconscious motives for participating in this bias. We must recognize that it is much easier and more in accordance with our images of the world to regard a mother as crazy or hysterical than to recognize an otherwise seemingly rational and caring father as capable of the behaviors described. Beyond that, such a view may serve to reinforce our own denial of what we, like most people, would rather not see.[37]

The court, the various investigation agencies, attorneys and the community at large are implored to heed this warning.

What has happened to Amanda and Jessica and other children across the country will continue to happen to others in the future as long as there is no accountability. The family court has become very dysfunctional and does not protect children and mothers. Biased and/or corrupt judges, attorneys, and psychologists must be exposed in order to stop them.

> A judge's signature can bring peace or perpetuate family turbulence.

The courtroom belongs to the people. We must become more empowered and take control of what is ours. We have entrusted our courts to judges. We must hold them accountable for the administration of justice for which they were elected or assigned to do. A judge's signature can bring peace or perpetuate family turbulence. We must do everything in our power to ensure that the laws of our country are being followed and that the decisions judges are making are sound, rational and are consistent with the welfare of the people.

My brother, Mark, posed two very good questions: Who's keeping watch over the family courts of America? How do we get people to care?

Many are angry that this is happening but don't know what to do about it. So I've talked to some experts in the field and asked them, and this is what they have to say.

244

At the recent International Domestic Violence Conference the following press release went out. It outlines what experts across the country say needs to happen.

SAN DIEGO, CA, SEPTEMBER 27, 2002 - Family violence experts from all over the nation have called for sweeping changes in the child protective system to ensure that children are not placed in abusive situations. The recommendations are part of a report resulting from a think tank, which last month explored the impact of court awarded custody to parents who have been physically or sexually abusive to their children or who have committed acts of domestic violence on a non-offending parent, even resulting in murder, in some cases. The initial think tank was held as part of the "6th International Conference on Family Violence: Working Together to End Abuse," hosted by the Family Violence & Sexual Assault Institute in San Diego and Children's Institute International in Los Angeles. The follow up has been occurring as part of the 7th International Conference on Family Violence September 24-28, 2002 in San Diego.

As a result of the think tank and follow up discussions, participants released the following Declaration:

"Children have a fundamental human right to a safe environment, and to be protected from all forms of physical, emotional and sexual abuse, violence and exploitation. Despite the best efforts of many good people, there remain serious problems that too often result in children being denied these basic human rights in our juvenile and family courts."

Among the think tank's key recommendations are development of national standards for child custody evaluations, appointment of competent counsel for children at risk of abuse, and barring the use of "parental alienation syndrome," a pseudoscientific theory that has resulted in placement of children in the custody of abusive parents, in judicial proceedings. "We can't let these children down. They've already been let down by an abusive parent. We have to change the child family and dependency court systems, so they do not do additional harm," says Dr. Steve Ambrose, Vice President of Programs for Children's Institute International. "The courts are sadly failing to protect too many children who have been exposed to family violence in their homes."

According to the National Clearinghouse on Child Abuse and Neglect, there were an estimated 826,000 victims of maltreatment nationwide in 1999, which is equivalent to a rate of 11.8 victims per 1,000 children.

High profile cases such as the OJ Simpson custody hearings mirror the difficult and heart-wrenching decision courts must make as a matter of course on behalf of children. Former victims of abuse and experts in the fields of child abuse, child advocacy and research, and family violence discussed ways to improve the system in order to avoid further endangering the well being of abused children.

The panel concluded that appointing legal counsel for children is critical, for courts to have a greater likelihood of protecting children who are truly at risk of serious abuse if the children involved in those cases are provided competent counsel who are required to act like real lawyers. With counsel, the children's well-being is more likely to be addressed by the courts.

"Despite the well intentioned efforts of many dedicated court professionals, we believe that there are far too many children who are not being adequately protected by our family and juvenile dependency courts," says Dr. Robert Geffner, President of the Family Violence & Sexual Assault Institute and Chair of the think tank. "Too often, decisions are made on children's behalf based on unsubstantiated theories like 'parental alienation syndrome,' without adequate representation from the children themselves and relying on biased court evaluations by mental health professionals. In the worst cases, placement and visitation orders are rendered that place children in physical and/or psychological jeopardy."

To ensure that children are appropriately protected by our family and juvenile dependency courts, the think tank recommended the following reforms:

1. In light of the fact that "Parental Alienation Syndrome" is not a bona fide disorder or condition, and is neither a valid nor reliable means of determining whether child sexual abuse or domestic violence has occurred, it should be deemed inadmissible in any judicial proceedings. Despite the fact that PAS does not meet the tests set forth in either the Frye or Daubert decisions, its widespread use by custody evaluators, guardians *ad litem,* and judges often results in children place in the custody of abusive parents.

2. More research and development, including reliable and valid instruments to screen and assess domestic violence in custody cases and follow-up studies on the outcomes of child custody decisions in high conflict cases.

3. Implementation by all states of the model code of conduct for appointed counsel for children as approved by the American Bar Association Board of Governors.

4. Holding accountable under the law any professional whose gross negligence causes harm to a child.

5.   Development of national standards for child custody evaluations, including: creation of child custody panels based on education, experience and training; selection of evaluators in individualized cases; review of evaluation reports including content and timeliness; and removal and oversight of panel members.

6.   Uniform selection, training and evaluation standards for first responders and child protective agency workers in cases involving family violence, child abuse and domestic relations/family law courts. Training must be expanded to focus on skill development in situations that most closely replicate the complexities of domestic violence cases.

Results of the think tank are being compiled in a white paper and will be distributed in the coming months to organizations that serve children and families at risk for abuse and neglect, as well as key decision makers and policy makers.

"We hope this begins serious efforts by organizations to change policies and create new policies and standards so that victims of domestic violence will be assured of their safety and well being," says Dr. Steve Ambrose, Vice President of Programs at Children's Institute International. "We will continue to work to ensure that children are not placed in abusive situations by courts, social service agencies and child protective services."

What You Can Do

The voice and demands of many change the face of a nation. It is by choice of action that change occurs. Here are some suggestions that we all, the community at large, can act upon:

1. Establish court watch programs where volunteer citizens actually sit in the courtroom and monitor the conduct and rulings of the family court judges.

2. Push for legislation abolishing guardians *ad litem* and instead provide attorneys that actually represent the wishes of the children in custody cases.

3. Make issues and questions about child abuse and domestic violence a part of every forum and debate for our judicial candidates.

4. Enact legislation that provides an automatic appeal of custody and visitation cases if a party desires one.

5. Enact legislation that limits the options that judges have in the face of evidence of child abuse and domestic violence in custody and visitation cases.

6. Enact legislation that requires child abusers and domestic violence perpetrators to pay all costs and attorneys fees incurred by the parent attempting to protect the child.

7. Enact legislation to ensure that bogus junk science such as the "parental alienation syndrome" is banned from all use.

8. Advocate with the licensing boards lawyers, physicians, and mental health professionals to hold accountable professionals who violate their duties to children by using incompetent and bogus approaches to the problems of abuse and domestic violence.

9. Work with your state supreme court to require all judges to complete mandatory training on the issues of domestic violence and child abuse, and ensure that such educational programs are conducted by competent responsible experts.

10. Finally, meet with your local prosecutor to ensure that parents attempting to protect their children from abuse and violence do not themselves end up being prosecuted for their reasonable and responsible actions taken in response to system failure.

Bill and Nadine Youngblood along with other juvenile court petitioners who are familiar with my girls and their abuse are fed up with the system failure in Georgia and the refusal of the various agencies and the court to protect them. They took action. Bill, who is the past Chairman and CEO of Financial Network Corporation in Atlanta, Georgia, wrote a letter to Governor Barnes December 2, 2002, in behalf of the 30 petitioners and others in the community. He asked the governor to issue an emergency order pursuant to O.C.G.A. Section 45-12-29-34 and the Constitution of the State of Georgia Article 5, Section 2, Paragraph 1, directing that the law enforcement authorities, DFACS, the State Child Advocate and the Attorney General offices do whatever is necessary to protect Amanda and Jessica. Bill received a letter in response dated December 9, 2002, from DeAlvah Simms. She writes,

> As recently as May 3, 2002, the Governor asked for the Titelman case to be reexamined because of the continued allegations of possible sexual abuse of Amanda and Jessica Titelman. The Office of the Child Advocate reviewed available documentation and made contacts with the parties involved with this investigation. Collateral contacts were also made with agencies outside the scope of OCA authority. However, some participants were unable to speak with us due to a federal lawsuit that was pending on the case at the time of this review.

> Since the Office of the Child Advocate has the primary responsibility for the oversight of DFCS performance, a review of their records was completed. Some concerns were found with documentation requirements from the first referral in 1999 and recommendations were made to Cobb DFCS based on those findings.

> A meeting was also scheduled with the Cobb County District Attorney's office to review their participation and actions over the course of these allegations. We found the law enforcement response to these allegations to have been both thorough and professional. Cobb County authorities have responded to Ms. Titelman's allegations at every opportunity, even to the extent of having a Grand Jury investigate her complaints. After hearing the evidence and giving Ms. Titelman the opportunity to present her case, the Grand Jury found her allegations to have been maliciously brought.

These allegations have been thoroughly investigated and just as thoroughly reviewed on many more occasions.

We were very glad to get her letter because it documents the lack of investigation they have done. Bill and others wrote her back and sent copies to many officials in Georgia who are involved in child protection. This is some of what Bill had to say:

...I find it hard to believe that you have done anything more than recycle the misinformation provided by Cobb County. With all due respect, your letter does nothing more than defend the acts and omissions of these Cobb County agencies and officials. What, Ms. Simms, about the children? They are the issue.

Why do you think I wrote my letter? These are children who are victims of abuse and neglect and they need your help. The county system has failed to protect them. You are entrusted with the authority to protect and care for them. I am asking you to do your job.

Your letter states that your office reviewed documentation, made contact with the parties involved and made collateral contacts with agencies outside the scope of OCA authority. It is very difficult to comprehend this assertion. Let me provide a list of people whom you failed to contact or interview:

- Wendy Titelman
- Amanda Titelman
- Jessica Titelman
- Dr. Donald Matherne, the forensic psychologist and abuse specialist who documented the abuse in September, 2000.
- Dr. Lynn Brentnall, the first psychologist to have spoken with Amanda and Jessica and documented the abuse in March and in June of 1999.
- Dr. Diane Pearce, the abuse specialist who saw Amanda and Jessica and documented abuse in September, 1999. She was contacted as a result of Diane Woods' refusal to talk with Dr. Brentnall or believe her report of abuse. Dr. Brentnall believed if someone else had the same conclusions as she, Diane Woods would then have listened.
- Gail Vernon, who personally witnessed sexually inappropriate behavior by Andrew Titelman with Jessica Titelman.

251

- Dr. Kathleen Faller, one of the nation's leading authorities in child sexual abuse, who has reviewed the June, 1999, DFACS interview with Amanda Titelman and the February, 2000, tape of Andrew Titelman browbeating the children into recanting. I have available Dr. Faller's curriculum vitae, her affidavit, and a copy of the interview of the videotape of Amanda Titelman's interview, wherein she clearly discloses the abuse by her father, consistent with the ongoing abuse she reported to Dr. Matherne.
- Dr. Joyanna Silberg, an internationally renowned sexual abuse expert psychologist from Shepherd Pratt Hospital in Baltimore, reviewed the evidence in this case and testified in Ms. Titelman's criminal trial. She exposed Dr. Elizabeth King and proved she was determined to discourage the children from disclosing their father's molestation.
- The jurors who heard the evidence in April, 2001, and wrote a scathing letter to DA Patrick Head and Judge Bodiford documenting the abuse and the cover-up by DFACS, Woods, and King. I have enclosed their letter.
- Lynn and Jim Palmer, who are witnesses to the children's behavior and to whom the children disclosed that their father was abusing them.
- Lisa Curtis, to whom the children disclosed that their father was abusing them.
- Janice Morgan, whose children played with Amanda and Jessica, went to Wendy Titelman with concerns about Jessica, saying that she believed Jessica was being sexually abused.
- Jan Geiger, who has known the family and children since they were born, witnessed behaviors that led her to believe that Amanda and Jessica were in danger of abuse by their father.
- Karyn Covington and Joyce Saye, Supervisors from A-Plus Services, who were assigned by Diane Woods to supervise Ms. Titelman while visiting with her children, made reports of the children's disclosures of abuse and bizarre behavior of Andrew Titelman.
- Dr. James Cheatham, Diplomate, American Board of Psychiatry and Neurology and Addiction Psychiatry, examined all the records pertaining to the Titelmans and concluded that Andrew Titelman is unfit to serve as a

parent/guardian of the children and believes him to be a sexual predator.

- I am enclosing a video that was made 6/23/99 by DFACS of an interview with Amanda Titelman. In this video, Amanda disclosed sexual abuse by her father. The video was found in October of 2001 in DA Patrick Head's files. It had been sealed with tape and kept undisclosed. It was never presented to the grand jury, was never turned over during the criminal trial, and was never presented during the custody hearings.

The documentation of these facts, testimonies, reports, affidavits and a videotape have all been available to you and should have been reviewed. They have been filed repeatedly in the Cobb County Superior Court. ...

This list of individuals is the same whom DFACS refused to contact or interview because Diane Woods told the caseworkers that there was no abuse to investigate. ...

Finally, I must respond to your comments regarding the grand jury. Again, had you spoken to anyone outside the Cobb County group, you would know the facts. On April 27, 2001, Ms. Titelman was resoundingly acquitted of criminal interstate custodial interference charges. A scathing letter was written to Judge Bodiford and District Attorney Patrick Head by the jury clearing her (copy enclosed). Ms. Titelman herself asked that the Cobb County Grand Jury investigate the specific issues and charges made in the jurors' letter. She also asked the court to appoint a special prosecutor since Patrick Head had an obvious conflict of interest. Disregarding Ms. Titelman's request, the grand jury appointed Patrick Head in charge of the investigation. At no small cost to the taxpayers, Mr. Head presented his usual cast–Diane Woods, Andrew Titelman, Elizabeth King and Francey Hakes. ...Not one witness listed in this letter was ever presented to the grand jury. Ms. Titelman (who lives out of state) was given one day's notice to come and "speak" to the grand jury. Patrick Head controlled the entire unbelievable show.

At this point, I must ask you to re-read the statement in your letter to me. Have these allegations been thoroughly reviewed and investigated? I think not. There has never been a thorough investigation of these charges, and any review performed has been like yours, deficient and shamefully inadequate. When will the laws of Georgia be used to protect these children?

Bill Youngblood and Dan and Jeannette Adkins received a letter back from Bobbi Nelson. In her letter dated February 3, 2003, she states, "Due to your letter, the Office of the Child Advocate is again, looking into the Titelman case." However, February 28, 2003, she had attempted no investigation other than to receive a phone call from Dr. Joyanna Silberg and to discuss the abuse with her.

Bill also received a letter from Robert Grayson, who provides legal services to the Cobb County Department of Family and Children Services as a Special Assistant Attorney General. He told Bill he forwarded Bill's letter to DFACS for "whatever action may be deemed appropriate." Catherine Anderson, the Cobb County DFACS Director, wrote to Bill in a letter dated February 7, 2003, the following:

> While we are very concerned about the welfare of every child that comes to our attention we cannot investigate a family unless there are current allegations. From a review of the record it appears that the last investigation concerning these children was completed in February 2000. Since we do not have current allegations alleging abuse or neglect of these children at this time, we do not have the authority to open an investigation.

This news was quite extraordinary. The February, 2000, investigation was an investigation of me for cruelty to children prompted by Dr. Elizabeth King based on her parental alienation syndrome conclusions. There was nothing in their records to indicate any investigation of Dr. Donald Matherne's report in September, 2000. Yet, George Washington, Supervisor of Cobb County DFACS testified regarding this report at the September 20, 2000, *ex parte* hearing. Dr. Joyanna Silberg's report, Dr. Kathleen Faller's report, nor the juror's letter was ever investigated. Ms. Anderson admitted in her letter that a copy of the juror's letter was in their file. There is now hope, as another major hole has been found, that an independent investigation will be conducted through DFACS.

We also learned February 28, 2003, that bills have been introduced by both the Senate and the House to grant qualified immunity to guardians *ad litem* against any civil liability arising out of performance of his or her duties in this function. Diane Woods is attempting to get the Georgia legislature to make certain that Amanda and Jessica can never sue her for her destruction she has caused "in their behalf." As the law now reads, Georgia is one of the few states providing a means for children to sue their guardians *ad litem*. Everyone helping on my case will attempt to stop Woods's legislative scheme from happening.

I love Amanda and Jessica with all of my heart and with every breath I take. They fill my every thought and my every step. All my goals and desires are centered on them. Their home is ready for them. Their dolls and stuffed animals, pillows and covers, and lots of hugs and kisses and holding and talking and laughing and crying are awaiting them. I am anxiously looking forward for them to come home. My arms are open wide, and every moment that passes that I am not with them, is a moment too long.

I will never stop fighting for them and praying blessings over their life even when I am an old lady. I will continue every moment of my life to do everything possible to work towards the goal of bringing my children home to me and protecting them. My faith filled words will come to pass. They will come home to me.

When they come they will enter our home and see all their belongings as if they were here all along. They will meet our dog, Tobey, who will immediately know them from the scent of their belongings. He will lick them and be so happy to see them. As we go upstairs to their room they will see covering the floor all the presents still wrapped for them and all the letters that were returned and never opened. We will go for walks with Tobey at the Audubon Park and ride our bikes, and skate, and laugh and play together. We will reunite with old friends, and we will make new friends. We will bask in the joy of being together once again.

I have been and am presently walking in a valley as dark as death. Amanda, Jessica, and I have been robbed of life, liberty and justice. I implore the Cobb County Superior Court to LET MY CHILDREN GO!

DIRECTORY OF KEY INDIVIDUALS

Judge Laura Austin - Part-time Cobb County Magistrate Court Judge who refused to issue a warrant for the arrest of Andrew Titelman for the molestation of his daughters even in the face of abundant evidence. She said, "You will never win in Georgia. You are dealing with the good 'ole boys who stick together no matter what." She futilely ordered an investigation to be done by Detective Bishop.

Detective Bishop - A detective with Kennesaw Police Department who did no investigation of Andrew Titelman for the molestation of Amanda and Jessica after being requested to do so by Judge Laura Austin. He asked Assistant DA Francey Hakes to call her and tell her about "the criminal matter." He then did no investigation.

Robin Blankenship - Amanda and Jessica's Suzuki Piano Teacher who called Wendy Titelman with concern after a piano lesson that Andy Titelman attended with the girls. She stated that she believed that there was something very wrong and unnatural between Andy Titelman and his daughters and said the lesson was a total waste of time because the girls could not concentrate at all. She testified at the final hearing before Judge Jon Bo Woods.

Judge James Bodiford - Cobb County Georgia Superior Court Judge presiding over the Titelman custody case. He gave custody of the girls to Andrew Titelman in an emergency hearing with one day's notice, and put Wendy Titelman on supervised visitation. He is also presiding over the Disqualification of Patrick H. Head, District Attorney, from the investigation of Andrew Titelman for the molestation of his children.

Lynn Brentnall, Ph.D. - Psychologist, who was the first to assess the children psychologically and academically, and who substantiated abuse. She reported to the Department of Family and Children's Services (DFACS) in June, 1999, that the children were molested by their father. Diane Woods told others she is a "quack" and a "hired gun." Diane Woods refused to meet with Dr. Brentnall.

Kyle Broussard - Paralegal for Hylton Dupree who, when confronted by Wendy Titelman for the law firm's failure to represent her fully stated, "Well, we are a political organization."

Laurie Caldwell - Mississippi Attorney representing Wendy Titelman in the Chancery Court of Harrison County, Mississippi who advised her to move to Mississippi. She testified at the criminal trial of The State of Georgia vs. Wendy Titelman.

Margaret (Peggy) Carlson - Friend of Wendy Titelman whose children used to play with Amanda and Jessica and are now unable go to sleep at night until they pray for them. She witnessed Francey Hakes going in and out of the grand jury area and at one point leaving with Patrick Head, Diane Woods, Elizabeth King, and Frank Pittman and others from a room next to where Wendy Titelman was testifying during the sham "investigation" of Andrew Titelman for the molestation of Amanda and Jessica. She is also a petitioner in the juvenile court Petition for Adjudication of Deprivation.

Detective Craig Chandler - Detective with Kennesaw Police Department, who maliciously sought the arrest of Wendy Titelman, and first secured a warrant for her arrest through the FBI under fictitious charges. He testified at the criminal trial of The State of Georgia vs. Wendy Titelman and is a defendant in the malicious prosecution lawsuit.

James Cheatham, M.D. - Psychiatrist who, at Wendy Titelman's request, saw her numerous times between March, 2000 through June, 2000 to evaluate her mental condition. He concluded that there was nothing wrong with Wendy Titelman and, after examination of all the records, believed that Andy Titelman is a sexual predator. He advised Diane Woods and Dr. Elizabeth King of his findings and testified at the final custody hearing before Judge Jon Bo Woods.

Karyn Covington - Supervisor with A-Plus Services appointed by Diane Woods to supervise Wendy Titelman's visits with her daughters from March, 2000 through June, 2000. She witnessed and reported the children's reports of sexual and physical abuse by their father, and Andrew Titelman's paranoid and other strange behaviors. She testified at the final custody hearing before Judge Jon Bo Wood. Her testimony included that Amanda shared with her that her father "tickles me in my privates"... "at night - a lot."

Lisa Curtis - Friend of Andy and Wendy Titelman who became alarmed with Andy's behaviors. She investigated the Sterling Club to which Andy belonged and was appalled at what she learned. The children told her their father was hurting them. After careful questioning she determined he had sexually molested them. She reported the abuse to DFACS, Crimes Against Children, Cobb County Police Department, Kennesaw Police Department, and Dr. Elizabeth King. The various agencies never called her back.

Bajda Daniels - Supervisor, Mississippi Harrison County Children's Shelter where Amanda and Jessica lived during the first two weeks of September, 2000. She testified at the criminal trial of The State of Georgia vs. Wendy Titelman and directly contradicted Diane Woods' statements to the Court October 4, 2000 that the children were traumatized by Wendy Titelman taking them to Mississippi. She testified that the children became upset and were crying because Woods and King were taking them from the shelter instead of their mother.

Alton Davis - Friend of the Evans family and beloved "Poppy" to Amanda and Jessica. He is also a petitioner in the juvenile court case.

257

Richard Ducote - Attorney who has extensive national experience in child custody and visitation cases involving child sexual abuse and domestic violence, and who is responsible for the enactment of laws, both nationally and internationally, to protect children and protective parents. He represents Wendy Titelman in the Cobb County Custody case since June, 2001 and the federal malicious prosecution lawsuit. He assisted Michael Hirsh in the criminal trial of the State of Georgia vs. Wendy Titelman, and signed the Petition for Adjudication of Deprivation of Amanda and Jessica. He wrote a letter to the Atlanta professional community exposing Diane Woods and Dr. Elizabeth King's cover-up of the sexual abuse of Amanda and Jessica, inviting Woods and King to sue him. He is a co-plaintiff with Wendy Titelman in the federal libel lawsuit against Anita Miller Titelman.

Hylton Dupree - Attorney for Wendy Titelman in the custody case from October, 1998 through the final hearing in June, 2000.

Frances Evans - Mother of Wendy Titelman, Grandmother of Amanda and Jessica, and witness to abusive behaviors of Andy Titelman with Amanda and Jessica. She is also a petitioner in the juvenile court case.

Mark Evans - Wendy Titelman's brother who traveled to Mississippi to attend the emergency hearing. He has since become an advocate and spoke at Rock America in Washington, D.C. He is also a petitioner in the juvenile court case.

Robin Evans - Brother of Wendy Titelman who along with his wife shared with her that he believed Andy was molesting Katie Titelman and was concerned for Amanda and Jessica. He traveled to Mississippi for the emergency hearing and helped to get Wendy out of jail.

Kathleen Faller, Ph.D. - Leading international expert in child sexual abuse at the University of Michigan whose extensive curriculum vitae includes the publication of 6 books, 45 articles, 11 book chapters, 2 media productions, 3 research reports, 2 encyclopedia/dictionary entries, 8 book reviews, 3 journal editions, 227 grants, contracts, fellowships and scholarships, a monograph, a dissertation and numerous works in progress. She has acted as a consultant on numerous occasions and has given over 225 training sessions. She reviewed two video tapes, a DFACS interview of Amanda wherein she disclosed her sexual abuse by her father and another tape produced by Andy Titelman. She concluded, based on these two video tapes, that the children were most likely sexually abused by Andy Titelman and that the children had been brow-beaten by their father to recant their allegations of sexual abuse.

Judge Robert Flournoy, III - Cobb County Superior Court Judge who presided over the criminal trial in April, 2001, and who commented to criminal defense attorney Michael Hirsh: "You have very effective witnesses, Dr. Silberg, and you had Dr. Matherne, very effective witnesses to testify that, in their opinion, [Ms.

Titelman] was acting very reasonably, did what any concerned mother would do. And actually, I think you've conveyed to the jury that they could draw the inference that, in fact, the Cobb County justice system did shut down on Wendy Titelman and didn't give her redress, et cetera, et cetera." He is also the judge who in November, 2002, dismissed the Writ of Mandamus to compel the filing of the juvenile court Petition for Adjudication of Deprivation.

Judge Owen Forrester - Federal Judge, United States District Court for the Northern District of Georgia, Atlanta Division, who in August, 2002, dismissed the malicious prosecution lawsuit and ordered sanctions against Richard Ducote.

Judge Arthur Fudger - Georgia Superior Court Senior Judge who in May, 2002 presided in the recusal hearing of Judge James Bodiford in the case of the Disqualification of Patrick H. Head, District Attorney, in the Investigation of Andrew Titelman for the Molestation of Amanda and Jessica Titelman.

Jan Geiger - Friend of Wendy Titelman who believed Andy was molesting Katie and that Amanda and Jessica were next in line. She met with Wendy Titelman to discuss her concerns and was not surprised when Wendy called her in tears after Amanda had shared that her father had sexually molested her. She reported her observations to DFACS and Crimes Against Children and was never contacted by anyone. She accompanied Wendy Titelman to the Kennesaw Police Department and spoke with the Chief of Police, Chief Dwaine Wilson. She along with her husband unsuccessfully tried to deliver gifts to Amanda and Jessica. She also signed the juvenile court Petition for Adjudication of Deprivation.

Jerry Geiger - Friend of Wendy Titelman who tried to deliver gifts to Amanda and Jessica. He is also a petitioner who tried to file the juvenile court Petition for Adjudication of Deprivation and was refused by Judge Juanita Stedman. His concern for what has happened to Amanda and Jessica has led him to plan a second career, after retirement, as an attorney performing pro bono services in similar situations. Among other diplomas he holds a law degree from Oklahoma City University.

Pam Gray - Attorney for Andrew Titelman in the custody case who attacked Wendy Titelman's faith and values. She is also a defendant in the malicious prosecution lawsuit.

Judge Adele Grubbs - Presided as the Cobb County Superior Court Judge over the May-June, 2001 Grand Jury. She signed orders that were not only highly unusual but also had never been ordered in Cobb County before even in the most serious and heinous criminal investigations. She signed an order stating that no recording transcription or other memorialization of Dr. Frank Pittman's testimony before the Grand Jury shall be made; another order was signed sealing the names and addresses of grand jurors and forbidding any contact with them.

Julie Hall - DFACS Social Worker who interviewed and taped Amanda Titelman in June, 1999, as she disclosed the abuse of her by her father.

Francey Hakes - Cobb County Assistant District Attorney and Prosecutor for The State of Georgia vs. Wendy Titelman. During the criminal trial she stated, "Wendy Titelman has decided that she wants justice when she deserves none." She compared Ms. Titelman to Timothy McVeigh and stated that she is a "vigilante." She said Justice for Children "are like anarchists" and "they don't accept what governments do." She tried to put Wendy Titelman in jail for up to five years for having substantiated the sexual abuse of her daughters by a Mississippi psychologist and for attempting to protect them through the Mississippi Harrison County Chancery Court. She assisted DA Patrick Head in assuring that the May-June, 2001 Grand Jury would bring a "no bill, brought with malicious intent" in order to protect Andy Titelman, the district attorney, herself, and others from accountability.

Patrick Head - Cobb County District Attorney who covered up the abuse of Amanda and Jessica, and who "cooked" the May-June, 2001 Grand Jury to bring a "no bill, brought with malicious intent" in order to protect Andy Titelman and himself and others from accountability. He met with Diane Woods at a Waffle House to scheme who should be presented to the Grand Jury. None of the professionals who had substantiated abuse nor any of those who called DFACS, Crimes Against Children, the Cobb County Police Department, or the Kennesaw Police Department were called to testify. Those that Patrick Head used to try to convict Wendy Titelman were called before the grand jury. Francey Hakes at either her or Patrick Head's suggestion led the Grand Jury for the "beginnings" for up to one hour. During discovery in the federal malicious prosecution lawsuit, the DFACS tape of the interview of Amanda disclosing abuse was found in the DA's files sealed with orange tape and marked "evidence." This tape was also never presented to the grand jurors and was never turned over during the criminal trial as required despite the demand for the discovery of all exculpatory evidence.

Detective Amy Henderson - Detective with Kennesaw Police Department who was present for the interviews of Amanda and Jessica with DFACS social workers. She refused to contact doctors and others who had substantiated sexual abuse and was angry at Wendy Titelman because she complained to her superior that Detective Henderson was not properly conducting the investigation. Afterwards, she talked to a small number of individuals to conclude her "investigation" and complained to them that Wendy Titelman tried to have her fired.

Zoe Hermanson - Friend of Wendy Titelman who allowed Wendy, Amanda and Jessica to live in her home during a transitional period from the sale of her marital home to the move to another home that was not ready, and who felt threatened by

Andy Titelman during his visits to her home which caused her to contact an attorney.

Jacqueline Hill, Ph.D. - Psychologist, who along with Dr. Lynn Brentnall, interviewed the children during the period of initial disclosures of sexual abuse. She testified at the final custody hearing before Judge Jon Bo Wood that Dr. Brentnall followed an accepted protocol and asked appropriate non-leading questions in determining the children had been abused. She described to the court results of the psychological testing which was completed prior to the allegations of abuse and which revealed an issue of secrecy with the children and that they were either being abused or being set up to be abused. Diane Woods refused to meet with Dr. Hill.

Michael Hirsh - Stands six feet, seven inches tall in more than one way. He is the father of 13 and the attorney who defended Wendy Titelman in her criminal case. He took the case shortly before trial and after talking with the witnesses determined for himself that Andy Titelman is guilty of sexual molestation. He has been committed since to do whatever he can to get the children free from their abuser, even though the system has attempted to punish him for representing Wendy Titelman. Following the criminal trial he has served as the local attorney in the federal malicious prosecution lawsuit and in the custody case.

Susan Ibarra - Friend of Wendy Titelman whose children and she saw Amanda and Jessica at CC's Pizza and was told to get away from them by Andy Titelman. She witnessed Francey Hakes going in and out of the grand jury area and at one point leaving with Patrick Head, Diane Woods, Elizabeth King, and Frank Pittman and others from a room next to where Wendy Titelman was testifying during the sham "investigation" of Andrew Titelman for the molestation of Amanda and Jessica.

Martin Inman - DFACS Social Worker who interviewed the children at their school with Detective Henderson after Dr. Diane Pearce made a report to DFACS. The children disclosed to Mr. Inman and Detective Henderson that their father dressed up like a girl in a purple dress and makeup. He dismissed the allegations of abuse after scheduling a meeting with Andy Titelman at his home and seeing no evidence of a purple dress.

H. Elizabeth King, Ph.D. - Court appointed psychologist, who with Diane Woods deliberately covered up the sexual abuse of Amanda and Jessica and who used the junk science of "Parental Alienation Syndrome" and "False Memory" to give custody of the children to their abusive father. She testified at the criminal trial that even if Andy Titelman had molested his children, he should still be considered for custody. She refused to sue Richard Ducote after he mailed letters to scores of her colleagues accusing her of the cover-up. She hired a prominent criminal defense attorney to block her deposition in the malicious prosecution case.

Stephen King, M.D. - Pediatrician who saw Amanda and Jessica. After talking with Wendy Titelman about the allegations of abuse, he talked with Amanda who disclosed to him that her father was rubbing her in the vaginal area. He called DFACS to report the allegations of abuse.

Barbara Mabary - Foreperson of the May-June, 2001 Grand Jury. Wendy Titelman called Ms. Mabary and then took a packet of information to her asking that the grand jury conduct an investigation of Andrew Titelman for the molestation of his daughters. She was given the letter from the criminal jury and was told the abuse "has been covered up by the Department of Family & Children Services, Diane Woods, Dr. Elizabeth King, and the Cobb County District Attorney's Office." Ms. Mabary went to District Attorney Patrick Head for advice on how to handle the investigation. The District Attorney told her he would "take care of it."

Donald Matherne, Ph.D. - Highly respected Mississippi clinical and forensic psychologist with over thirty years of experience, a consultant to the courts and the State Attorney General's Office who works mainly with murder, abuse and personal injury cases. He testified in the criminal case about his meeting with Amanda and Jessica and Wendy Titelman in Mississippi in September, 2000. He described the methodology that he uses in determining whether children have been abused has been peer reviewed by other psychologists, guardians *ad litem,* prosecutors, defense attorneys and judges, and "follows a paradigm that they have found to be acceptable and credible." He stated, "I observed a mother who had a close relationship with her daughters and the two daughters had a close relationship with their mother." Jessica described her father to him as "mean," "who hits her because he gets angry." Amanda told him that her father "hits her, that he gets mad, screams and yells." Both girls separately described what their father did to them and pointed to the genital area on a drawing and indicated that this is where each of them had been touched by her father. Jessica reported that her father touches her under her clothing when she was in bed. He told the court that Amanda said her father comes into her bed at night and touches her under her clothing. She said, "He took his hand and put it under my jammies and he rubbed me on my pee-pee hole." Dr. Matherne stated, "She said that she told her mother because she wanted, quote, my mom to help me, period, closed quotes." Dr. Matherne asked Jessica if she shared this with anyone else, and she told him she told Dr. King, but that Dr. King didn't seem interested. Both children explained that Dr. King changes the subject when they try to tell her about the molestation. He stated that based on what Jessica and Amanda shared that intervention was needed to protect them. He told Wendy Titelman and wrote in his report that if the children were returned to their father "irreparable damage would be done."

John Mayoue - Andrew Titelman's attorney in the custody case. Defendant in the malicious prosecution lawsuit. In his closing statement June 30, 2000, in the final custody hearing he stated that the only people whose judgment could be deemed reliable and trustworthy were Diane Woods, Elizabeth King and Judge

Bodiford. He also falsely led the court to believe that there had been 14 investigations for the allegations of sexual abuse all proving Andy Titelman was innocent of child molestation. In the court papers he has filed since August 4, 2000, he has never stated that his client did not molest the children.

Judge Kenneth O. Nix - Cobb County Superior Court Judge whom Wendy Titelman called to schedule a hearing for the recusal of Judge Bodiford. He called Wendy Titelman and left an angry message stating, "...You don't call nobody except Mr. Cheshire, and you don't call my office back. You don't call any other judge. You need to sit still and follow the procedure that we have, not a procedure that you want. We are going to do things correctly, and you need to sit still until they are done and not to worry people to death. ... So do not call my office back, period! ... [A]nd quit trying to run the system the way you want it run."

Lynn Palmer - Friend of Wendy Titelman who allowed Wendy, Amanda and Jessica to live with her and her family after the girls had disclosed the sexual abuse by their father, and who acted as a supervisor for over a month to Wendy Titelman at Diane Wood's request. She witnessed the children's fear of their father, disclosure of abuse and abusive behaviors of Andy Titelman. She reported the abuse to DFACS, Crimes Against Children, Kennesaw Police Department, and Dr. Elizabeth King, and accompanied Wendy Titelman to talk with District Attorney Patrick Head to get protection for the girls. She also signed the Petition for Adjudication of Deprivation of Amanda and Jessica.

Jim Palmer - Friend of Wendy Titelman who along with his wife, Lynn, allowed Wendy, Amanda and Jessica to live with him and his family after the girls had disclosed the sexual abuse by their father, and who acted as a supervisor for over a month to Wendy Titelman at Diane Wood's request. He witnessed the children's fear of their father, disclosure of abuse and abusive behaviors of Andy Titelman, and he reported the abuse to DFACS, Crimes Against Children, Kennesaw Police Department, and Dr. Elizabeth King; He is also a petitioner in the juvenile court case.

Shirley Parsons, Ph.D. - Psychologist who saw Andy and Wendy Titelman for 93 visits during the major course of their marriage and reported to Dr. Elizabeth King and to Diane Woods Andy Titelman's bizarre behaviors.

Diane Pearce, Ph.D. - Specialist in child abuse and psychotherapist who substantiated the sexual abuse of Amanda and Jessica in September, 1999. Reported to DFACS the details of abuse including sexual fondling, statements made by the children, and pictures that were drawn describing their father dressing up like a girl with a wig, dress, nail polish and make-up. She shared that Amanda reported that "her daddy's bottom looks like he has a dragon's tail in the front." She testified at the final custody hearing before Judge Jon Bo Wood. Andy Titelman and Diane Woods accused her of being a friend of Wendy

Titelman who attended her church. Diane Woods told others that Dr. Peace is a "quack" and a "hired gun."

Frank Pittman, M.D. - Friend of Andy Titelman's family and prominent Atlanta psychiatrist specializing in family crises, men's issues, marriage, and infidelity. He saw Katie, Andy and Wendy Titelman ten times during the first six months of their marriage and twice after their divorce was filed seven years later. Diane Woods falsely reported in a letter to Judge Bodiford that he had seen Wendy and Andy Titelman for over eight years and knew them better than anyone else. After a subpoena was issued to him requesting the dates of his visits, he admitted in a letter that he had not seen Wendy Titelman for seven consecutive years out of the supposed eight year time period. He testified before the May-June, 2001 Grand Jury at the request of Woods and Head and had his testimony sealed from any recording and any release of information to anyone outside of the jury. He has authored three books, written advice columns for New Woman and Psychology Today, lectures worldwide and frequently appears on television and radio shows. He has made pro-pedophile statements such as the statement made in Psychology Today, Jan., 1999, Beware Older Women Ahead. He writes, "Matings between women who have been around and boys who have not are generally portrayed as acts of generosity and mercy, rather than as child molesting. As long as the older women don't expect the liaison to be permanent, they won't frighten boys who want to be sexual but aren't ready yet to be grown-up." He has befriended other pro-pedophiles such as Warren Farrell whose statements include , "When I get my most glowing positive cases, 6 out of 200, the incest is part of the family's open, sensual style of life, wherein sex is an outgrowth of warmth and affection. It is more likely that the father has good sex with his wife, and his wife is likely to know and approve - and in one or two cases to join in." (Warren Farrell, interviewed in Penthouse, December 1977, "Incest: The Last Taboo" by Philip Nobile) He has also aligned himself with individuals involved with Ralph Underwager's False Memory Syndrome Foundation.

Kathy Portnoy - Attorney for Wendy Titelman in the custody case after the final hearing, late September, 2000 through January, 2001. She made apparent to Judge Bodiford during a hearing October 4, 2000, that his *ex parte* order barring Wendy Titelman and her family from seeing Amanda and Jessica was illegal. She improperly advised Wendy Titelman to dismiss her appeal. She refused to file the motions that Wendy Titelman and Laurie Caldwell had originally discussed with her in order to get protection for the children. It was later discovered that she had a conflict of interest which interfered with her representation of Wendy Titelman, as she represented abusive men and used "Parental Alienation Syndrome" to get custody for them. She charged Wendy Titelman an astounding $30,000, appeared in court for approximately one hour and, without the approval of Wendy Titelman, filed a simple two and a half page pleading that had no substance.

Joyce Saye - Supervisor with A-Plus Services appointed by Diane Woods to supervise Wendy Titelman's visits with the girls from March, 2000, through June, 2000. She reported that Amanda and Jessica shared with her that their father often made them say untrue things, and that when she asked them for an example, Amanda stated, "like when he touches us wrongly." She reported finding bruises on Jessica's wrist shaped like a hand print, and was told by Jessica that her father did it. She was accused by Andy Titelman and Diane Woods of being a friend of Wendy Titelman and of attending her church. She testified at the final custody hearing before Judge Jon Bo Woods.

Joyanna Silberg, Ph.D. - Internationally renowned psychologist; coordinator of Trauma Disorder Services for Children at Sheppard Pratt Hospital in Baltimore, Maryland, and past president for the International Society for the Study of Dissociation. She examined all of Dr. Elizabeth King's files regarding the Titelmans, listened to Dr.King's audio tapes of her sessions with the girls, and concluded that Dr. King's work was incompetent. She played the King tapes and testified in Wendy Titelman's criminal trial that King had purposefully ignored the children's attempts to tell her about the abuse. She explained to the jury that Richard Gardner's "Parental Alienation Syndrome", which King had used to discredit the children's reports of abuse, was discredited and pro-pedophile.

DeAlvah Simms - Child Advocate and attorney for the State of Georgia whose office was created by the Legislature to "provide independent oversight of persons, organizations, and agencies responsible for providing services to or caring for children who are victims of child abuse and neglect," "to act independently of any state official, department, or agency," to "identify, receive, investigate, and seek the resolution ...of complaints made ...on behalf of children concerning any act, omission to act, policy, practice, or procedure of an agency or any contractor or agent thereof that may adversely affect the health, safety, or welfare of the children," to "request an investigation by the Georgia Bureau of Investigation of any complaint of criminal misconduct involving a child," "to communicate privately, by mail or orally, with any child and with each child's parent or guardian." She is mandated under O.C.G.A. 15-11-170 to "provide children with an avenue through which to seek relief when their rights are violated by state officials and agents entrusted with their protection and care." Ms. Simms received a letter from Richard Ducote regarding the cover-up of child sexual abuse by Diane Woods, Esq. and Elizabeth King, Ph.D. and a copy of the jurors letter expressing their outrage for cover-up of sexual abuse by Cobb County officials and court appointed representatives. Wendy Titelman attempted to contact her on several occasions. Ms. Simms has refused to talk with Ms. Titelman and has dismissed all allegations of abuse. She responded by letter to Bill Youngblood, a petitioner in the Juvenile Court case, who wrote to Governor Roy Barnes asking him for his intervention. She told him that the office of the governor was in transition and had forwarded his letter to her and that after talking with the Cobb County District Attorney, she found that "the response to these allegations to have been both thorough and professional." She also told him,

"Cobb County authorities have responded to Ms. Titelman's allegations at every opportunity, even to the extent of having a Grand Jury investigate her complaints." After receiving another letter from Mr. Youngblood outlining all the witnesses who her office had never contacted, another investigation was opened.

Kimberly Stabler - Executive Director of Justice for Children who contacted Governor Roy Barnes, Georgia State Child Advocate DeAlvah Simms and Chief Dwaine Wilson with the Kennesaw Police Department regarding the abuse of Amanda and Jessica and other abused children in Georgia. She was treated with hostility. During the criminal trial, Assistant DA Francey Hakes said Justice for Children "are like anarchists" and "they don't accept what governments do." JFC is a national nonprofit organization of citizens concerned about children's rights and their protection from abuse in response to the inadequacies and failure of child protective systems to protect abused and neglected children. Justice for Children's expert opinion is recognized and valued by local and national media, legal and medical professionals, child abuse experts, and various other children's rights organizations. It has been featured on many TV news programs and has been recognized by the American Bar Association. A tireless advocate for abused women and children harmed by the failure of the legal system.

Peter Thomas, Ph.D. - Psychologist who told Wendy Titelman she must be willing "to play the game," that she must never mention the word abuse in Georgia again whether the children were abused or not, because if she did, she would never see her children again. He said, "That's the way Georgia is."

Kevin Tidwell - Investigator who tried for over two months to deliver Valentine presents to Amanda and Jessica from their mother. He was told by Andy Titelman to get off his property and take the presents with him.

Andrew (Andy) Titelman - Father of Amanda and Jessica whom he has physically, spiritually, and emotionally abused and sexually molested. He has been protected from prosecution by Diane Woods, Elizabeth King, Lorita Whitaker, DA Patrick Head, and others. Judge James Bodiford and Judge Jon Bo Wood gave him full custody of the children ignoring the evidence of abuse. Defendant in the malicious prosecution lawsuit. Orchestrated the mailing of "anonymous letters" designed to discredit Wendy Titelman.

Katie Titelman - Daughter of Andy and Sydney Titelman.

Gail Vernon (pseudonym) - Witness to Andy Titelman repeatedly sliding his daughter, Jessica, over his groin while singing, "touching, touching, touching," while sitting in Ruth Mitchell ballet waiting area during the Spring of 2000. She called Crimes Against Children and Cobb County DFACS to report this incident and was never contacted for an investigation. Testified at the final custody hearing before Judge Jon Bo Wood in June, 2000. Since, she and her husband

Michael tried to deliver gifts to Amanda and Jessica on several occasions and was contacted by the Cobb County Police department and told to stop. When she stated there was nothing in any order preventing the children from receiving gifts from their mother, the detective told her the court order was being changed. She is also a petitioner in the juvenile court case.

Michael Vernon (pseudonym) - Husband of Gail Vernon who tried to deliver gifts to Amanda and Jessica on several occasions. He is also a petitioner in the juvenile court case and a resident of Cobb County who is very concerned with his government and their lack of protection of Amanda and Jessica.

George Washington - Supervisor at Cobb County DFACS who testified at the ex parte hearing in September, 2000. He stated there had been numerous investigations, and that he had read Dr. Matherne's report and that "there was no information that would overturn the judge's earlier ruling that the custody should be with the father." Even though Judge Teel with the Mississippi, Harrison County Chancery Court ordered the report to be given to DFACS, Dr. Matherne's report cannot be found in the DFACS file and there is no recording of any investigation.

Tom Weathers - Cobb County Assistant District Attorney who dismissed all allegations of sexual abuse based on the reports of Diane Woods, Dr. Elizabeth King and Detective Amy Henderson. He was present for Wendy Titelman's testimony to the grand jury in June, 2001.

Lorita Whitaker - Court appointed therapist for Amanda and Jessica who during the criminal trial served as the prosecution's "expert witness consultant" and the State's representative to assist Francey Hakes in her cross examination of Wendy Titelman's expert witnesses, attempting to help the state convict Wendy Titelman, her clients' mother. She told the court that she has told the children that their mother does not want to see them and accused her of trying to feed the children to the alligators. Sent an e-mail to Bryan Wilson, foreperson of the criminal jury, threatening him for having written the letter to DA Patrick Head and Judge James Bodiford. In her deposition for the custody case she refused to answer any questions about the children and stated her loyalty was to Andy Titelman. She said she has seen no reports, videos or tapes regarding the abuse of Amanda and Jessica and is not interested in seeing any. She said it has nothing to do with her role as therapist to the girls. It was reported by Asst. DA Francey Hakes during her deposition that Ms. Whitaker talks frequently with the girls about, "*Mrs. Titelman telling the children what to say and to lie about daddy and that Daddy never touched them*" and "*about the incidents surrounding their being taken to Mississippi.*" She refuses to talk with Wendy Titelman.

Bryan Wilson - Foreperson of the criminal trial jury who wrote a letter in behalf of the jurors to District Attorney Patrick Head and Judge James Bodiford expressing their outrage over the malicious prosecution and treatment of Wendy

Titelman, the State's failure to protect the children, and the cover up of sexual abuse by the District Attorney's office, DFACS, and court appointed representatives. He has courageously maintained his interest in spite of threats from Lorita Whitaker and suggestions from Judge Bodiford that the jurors should lose their homes and automobiles for writing the letter. He has stated he is concerned for the welfare of the children.

Judge Jon Bo Wood - Walker County Superior Court Judge who presided in the final custody hearing in June, 2000, and after hearing evidence of the sexual abuse of Amanda and Jessica by their father, Andrew Titelman, he awarded full custody to Andrew Titelman.

J. Diane Woods - Attorney and court appointed guardian *ad litem*. Her duty was to represent the interests of Amanda and Jessica in the custody case. She convinced Judge Bodiford and Judge Wood to ignore the abundant evidence of the girls' sexual abuse by Andrew Titelman, and to put the children in his custody. She has deliberately covered up the children's sexual abuse to protect herself from accountability for her actions. She has now admitted under oath in a deposition that she has no expertise in child sexual abuse and never spoke to the girls about the abuse allegations. Billed approximately $22,000 for her "services" and seized Wendy Titelman's interest in her home. Urged Judge Bodiford to bar all contact between the children and their mother, and their mother's relatives. In Wendy Titelman's criminal trial she was exposed as incompetent and a liar. Strongly criticized by the criminal jury in their letter to Patrick Head and Judge Bodiford. Refused to sue Richard Ducote over his letter accusing her of the deliberate cover-up. She is a defendant in the federal malicious prosecution lawsuit. Ms. Woods bears more responsibility than any other individual for the destruction of Amanda and Jessica. She is now attempting to get Georgia law changed so that she cannot be later sued by Amanda and Jessica.

APPENDICES[i]

Appendix A   Letter from Elizabeth King to Wendy Titelman stating she could not intervene in behalf of Amanda and Jessica

Appendix B   Elizabeth King's telephone notes with Diane Woods recording the strategy they would use to take custody of the children away from Wendy Titelman

Appendix C   Letter from the criminal jury to District Attorney Patrick Head and Judge James Bodiford expressing outrage for what they witnessed

Appendix D   E-mail from Lorita Whitaker to Bryan Wilson threatening him for writing the juror's letter[ii]

Appendix E   E-mail from Richard Ducote to Lorita Whitaker confronting her for her threats to the jurors and inviting her to sue Wendy Titelman

Appendix F   Juvenile Court Petition for Adjudication of Deprivation of Amanda and Jessica Titelman[iii]

---

[i]

All documents in the appendices are photostatic copies of the originals unless otherwise indicated.

[ii]

A name and phone number was removed from the end of the e-mail.

[iii]

The petition has been retyped from the original for the purposes of this book. Pseudonyms have been used for the names of my children and several individuals. Other alterations include the removal of two church names, the address of Andrew Titelman, and the addresses and phone numbers of the

Exhibit A   Dr. Lynn Brentnall's report
Exhibit B   Dr. Kathleen Faller's report
Exhibit C   Dr. Diane Pearce's letters and Amanda's drawings
Exhibit D   Lynn Palmer's letter to Dr. King
Exhibit E   Jim Palmer's letter to Dr. King
Exhibit F   Jan Geiger's letter to Dr. King
Exhibit G   Lisa Curtis' letter to Dr. King[iv]
Exhibit H   Janice Morgan's letter to Dr. King
Exhibit I   Supervisor's reports
Exhibit J   Gail Vernon's letter
Exhibit K   Dr. James Cheatham's letter
Exhibit L   Dr. Donald Matherne's Report[v]
Exhibit M   Jury Letter

Appendix G   Open letter from Richard Ducote to the peers of Diane Woods and Elizabeth King asking that they be held accountable and inviting Woods and King to sue him.

---

petitioners. Also omitted from the exhibit in the book is Wendy Titelman's affidavit, Dr. Kathleen Faller's affidavit and her resume' which alone fills 32 pages. The exhibits have been altered to reflect the pseudonyms and pseudonym signatures have been replaced.

[iv]

Attachments regarding Justin Sterling and the Sterling Club are not included.

[v]

The anatomical drawings included here are copies of the originals, except the children's pseudonyms have replaced their true names in the same style and placement as the true names appear on the masters.

Appendix A

Peachtree Psychological Associates

1819 Peachtree Road, Suite 600
Atlanta, Georgia 30309
(404) 352-4348
(404) 352-4334 fax

Ann Hazzard, Ph.D.
H. Elizabeth King, Ph.D.

Cal VanderPlate, Ph.D., ABPP
Carol Webb, Ph.D., ABPP

November 11, 1999

Ms. Wendy Titelman
2179 Shillings Chase Drive
Kennesaw, GA 30152

Dear Ms. Titelman:

I am in receipt of your letter of November 07, 1999. It would be quite helpful if the people who have approached you, if they feel comfortable, would write me a note about their observations of the children at ballet. I appreciate you sending their names and phone numbers and I may be making phone contact with them as well.

I can appreciate your anxiety about the children particularly given the comments they are making to you and the changes in behaviors others have noticed. Given my role in the situation, i.e. a custody evaluator, I cannot intervene on their behalf. We have an appointment scheduled for me to administer the Rorschach to you. I will complete the testing of you and Mr. Titelman as quickly as possible and I have made appointments to see the girls again. My intentions are to do a thorough investigation of the situation particularly regarding your concerns and to bring my assessment to a conclusion as quickly as possible.

Sincerely,

H. Elizabeth King, Ph.D.
Clinical Psychologist

HEK/mab

cc: Diane Woods, GAL
   Hylton Dupree, Jr.
   Pamela Gray

Appendix B

9/30/99

Titlema
    Diane Woods.. phone call
Serious round of serious allegation
Dr. Van Horn - christian counselor..
        Police Officer will call -- Out of her case
if - consistent for several months... 2 investigators
DF +

        alternating weeks..

        Got into fight at Police Chief office
→   Katie - Wendy + her Daddy had an incestus
relationship
                Henderson the Detective
        Amy - Warrant for Cruelty to
Children -
                Interview - Emyzn Heary
        Kids said they lied to the police
office...

        Straight custody eval
            Jackie Hells crew... ST is guy in
We suspect ... they report.

Appendix C

Bryan Wilson, Jury Foreperson
State of Georgia vs. Wendy Titlemen

Dear Honorable Judge Bodiford and Mr. Pat Head:

My name is Bryan Wilson and I recently served as a juror on a trial (Apr 23-27, 2001) in the Cobb County Superior Court of Georgia. Several members of the jury have requested that I write a letter summarizing our thoughts and concerns pertaining to the case we heard; State of Georgia v. Wendy Titlemen. To understand why this case even made it to trial was a question each of us had to ask while we were deliberating on Friday. We were perplexed as to why our State would pursue such a case so diligently when there were obvious errors in the indictment and credible reports indicating sexual and emotional abuse to two small children and the prosecution of the mother who sought to protect them from harm's way.

We, the jury felt that the "State of Georgia" did in fact, neglect to protect these children and furthermore, did not have the children's best interests at heart. It appeared they wished to cover up blatant miss-steps by an agency (DFACS) that appears to have made several errors in judgment. I would like to take an opportunity to summarize these areas of concern. I sincerely hope that action can be taken to correct these situations in the future. Not only will this save the State of Georgia the expense of prosecuting such flimsy cases, but will also serve to better protect the ones who need it most, the CHILDREN of our State.

Conclusions
1. The "Indictment". The indictment was very poorly written and poorly executed. The dates were inconsistent with the prosecution's effort to paint the mother as a "law breaker and flight risk". Based on the information we received, the dates listed in the indictment were within the legal limits spelled out in the final divorce decree's visitation schedule. It is incredible to believe that our court system would put a decent woman in jail for doing something completely legal during the indictment's window! Very poorly written indictment in our opinion.

2. The charge of "Fleeing Justice". Based on the evidence presented, we, the jury, were unanimous in agreeing with and supporting Ms. Titlemen in her beliefs that there was probable cause to protect her children. The evidence gave strong indication the children were being sexually molested by their father. Ms. Hakes, the Assistant Prosecutor, in her closing statements called Ms. Titlemen a "zealot" like Timothy McVeigh for wanting to take the law into her own hands and protect her children. I believe the majority of us on the jury have children. It was also unanimous that had we felt there was reason to believe our children were being abused or neglected in any way, and when seeking help, found the state (who is supposed to protect our children) unwilling to review the evidence in an unbiased light, would have reacted in similar ways.

3. "Taking the law into her own hands". We, the jury, saw Ms. Titlemen as someone desperately trying to use the legal system in Georgia to its fullest extent to protect her children, but to no avail. Then, when discovering more evidence of abuse, was left with no choice but to apply to the State of Mississippi for help. Although Ms. Hakes painted Ms. Titlemen as a manipulator and extremist, we felt that she was justified in using whatever means necessary to protect her children. Ms. Hakes said over and over during her cross-examinations "the State of Georgia knows best how to protect its children". We are not so sure after sitting on the jury and seeing first hand the types of "guardians" and "counselors" that the State of Georgia appoints to protect our most precious resources and future taxpayers. Dr. King admitted under oath, the children told her they were being abused. Why then do the children remain in the custody of the accused when the State does not appear to have proved otherwise?

273

4. **"Does Not Deserve Justice!"**. We, the jury, were horrified when Ms. Hakes told us in her closing statements that Ms. Titlemen didn't deserve justice. What does that mean?! Doesn't everyone deserves justice and aren't we all innocent until proven guilty? For the Assistance Prosecutor to openly say that a citizen doesn't deserve justice is an outrage and an insult to our justice system.

5. **Court appointed zealots.** The court appointed Guardians and Counselors were not credible and did all they could not to disclose real findings or intentions. Ms. Woods defied a State of Mississippi court order (within 24 hours) to protect the children from their father until additional hearings could take place and certain evidence be reviewed. Ms. King (a supposed expert) interrogated the children for two and one-half hours without taking any notes, or tapes, etc. She then appeared to try and cover up the disclosure of the sexual abuse to the court when asked in direct questioning. Therefore, we found that there were several disclosures of sexual abuse but little evidence at all of recantations. Ms. Whitaker went so far as to say the children were "abducted"! This accusation further alienated the jury by displaying such blatant bias against the mother, Ms. Titlemen.

6. **"Paid Expert Witnesses"**. Ms. Hakes was very careful to point out numerous times that the defense had hired "expert" witnesses who were paid for their services. Where is this wrong? We all got paid for doing what we considered our civil duty. Ms. Hakes gets paid, the state appointed guardians and counselors get paid, the judge and court employees get paid, so why did she feel this was such a big deal? Ms. Hakes tried to make it a huge deal by claiming the defense had "hired guns". The State's witnesses were pathetic in our opinion. They were poorly rehearsed, poorly accredited and overtly biased. At one point, Ms. King, when asked a direct question about the children confiding to her that they had been abused by their father, turns to the judge and says, "I don't want to answer that, they may get mad at me". Would the State really get "mad" if she told the truth under oath?

In conclusion, the jury collectively felt that the divorce of Wendy and Andy Titlemen contained deep dividing issues. It was our wish that more information could have been disclosed to assist our decision. We all agreed that the children were in all likelihood being sexually abused by their father. Also, the custody and well-being of these minor children should be a major concern to Cobb County. A new group of unbiased experts needs to re-evaluate this case and bring closure regarding visitation that satisfies all parties if appropriate. It has been an honor to serve as the foreperson of this jury. I feel that this jury has served justice, and that the state's mishandling of this case has cost the taxpayers of Cobb County, Georgia a lot of money.

Regards,
Bryan E. Wilson
Bryan Wilson, (bryanewilson@email.com)
Foreperson

Donna M. Kimball
Donna M. Kimball

Ann E. Klueter
Ann E. Klueter

Vicki L. Croft
VICKI L. CROFT

Kimberly J. Savransky
Kimberly J. Savransky

Cynthia P. Winter
Cynthia P. Winter

Appendix D

Subj: **FW: Titelman case; letter from Whitaker to jury foreman . . . interesting.**
Date: 6/28/2001 7:38:17 AM Pacific Daylight Time
From: mrhirsh@netzero.net (Michael Hirsh)
To: ducotelaw@aol.com (Richard Ducote)

——Original Message——
From: Sunpm
[mailto:sunpm@imcingular.com]
Sent: Thursday, June 28, 2001
9:23 AM
To: Mrhirsh@netzero.net
Subject: Fw: Titelman case

Fyi. Should I worry?
——Original Message——
From: Lorita Whitaker
<lbwhitaker@mindspring.com>
Subject: Titelman case
Mr. Wilson - As I am sure you
are aware, I testified in the
Titelman case on which you
served as a juror. I deeply
regret that you, the jury,
have been innocently pulled
into this case.
For your information, the
Grand Jury heard all evidence
last week on this case,
including over 2 hours of
testimony by Wendy Titelman.
They voted 19-0 in favor of
Andy Titelman and found
Wendy's prosecution to be
"malicious". Had you the jury
heard all the evidence, I am
certain you would have had a
more complete understanding of
a very complex situation that
has, in fact, developed over a
period of years. Please
understand that we were
forbidden to refer to any
events prior to Aug. 4, 2000,
the date of the final divorce
decree. Literally volumes of
evidence was withheld from you
because of the nature of the
criminal case.
I hope that you are also aware
that you are being quoted
(including on internet sites)
as stating that I have
conspired to cover up sexual
abuse and am incompetent. I
do not blame you because I
know the power of the
individuals that are involved

in this case.
However, these quotes have now
come back to me from a number
of sources in the community,
including some of my patients
that have inadvertently
crossed paths with members of
your jury. I am now seeking
legal advice concerning a
possible lawsuit for slander.
You may want to consult a
neutral attorney of your own
choosing concerning the risk
that all of you are placing
upon yourselves.
I wish for all of you the best
and that you will be able to
move forward with your own
private lives.
Sincerely,

Lorita Whitaker, MSW
Ga. Licensed Clinical Social
Worker

------------------- Headers -------------------
Return-Path: <mrhirsh@netzero.net>
Received: from rly-zd01.mx.aol.com (rly-zd01.mail.aol.com [172.31.33.225]) by air-zd05.mail.aol.com
(v78_r3.8) with ESMTP; Thu, 28 Jun 2001 10:38:16 -0400
Received: from integrity.com ([63.251.172.27]) by rly-zd01.mx.aol.com (v79.22) with ESMTP id
MAILRELAYINZD14-0628103751; Thu, 28 Jun 2001 10:37:51 -0400
Received: (qmail 15373 invoked from network); 28 Jun 2001 14:36:55 -0000
Received: from unknown (HELO michaelh) ([208.187.151.59]) (envelope-sender <mrhirsh@netzero.net>)
     by smtp.integrity.com (qmail-ldap-1.03) with SMTP
     for <ducotelaw@aol.com>; 28 Jun 2001 14:36:55 -0000
From: "Michael Hirsh" <mrhirsh@netzero.net>
To: "Richard Ducote" <ducotelaw@aol.com>
Subject: FW: Titelman case; letter from Whitaker to jury foreman . . . interesting.
Date: Thu, 28 Jun 2001 10:44:48 -0400
Message-ID: <000001c0ffe0$e1fec020$3b97bbd0@michaelh>
MIME-Version: 1.0
Content-Type: text/plain;
     charset="iso-8859-1"
Content-Transfer-Encoding: 7bit
X-Priority: 3 (Normal)
X-MSMail-Priority: Normal
X-Mailer: Microsoft Outlook 8.5, Build 4.71.2173.0
Importance: Normal
X-MimeOLE: Produced By Microsoft MimeOLE V5.00.2314.1300

Appendix E

Subj:	**Your letter to Bryan Wilson re: Wendy Titelman**
Date:	7/2/2001 9:34:05 PM Pacific Daylight Time
From:	Ducotelaw
To:	lbwhitaker@mindspring.com
CC:	Mrhirsh@netzero.net, bryan.wilson@sun.com, defender4aj@yahoo.com

Dear Ms. Whitaker,

    I am one of the attorneys representing Wendy Titelman in the custody case in Cobb County. Your letter to Bryan Wilson, the foreperson of the criminal jury which quickly acquitted Ms. Titelman on April 27, 2001, has been forwarded to me. Apparently Diane Woods and Dr. Elizabeth King have selected you as the "point man" to attempt to undo the damage done to the three of you by your own actions in this case, because they perceive you as being the least vulnerable. It is interesting that the jury letter addressed to Pat Head and Judge Bodiford does not mention you by name, although Dr. King and Ms. Woods are named and vehemently criticized in the letter. Yet, you are the one now attempting to bully Mr. Wilson and the other jurors who correctly analyzed the situation here by threatening to sue them for what are obviously privileged and immune communications on their part. If you want to sue someone, sue Wendy Titelman. She has, and will continue to state publicly that your work on this case was incompetent and that you are coveringup the sexual abuse of the girls. She would welcome your suit, as she would welcome suits by Dr. King, Ms. Woods, and Andy Titelman. Be my guest. If you believe that she fabricated the sexual abuse allegations, please have the courage to state so. You will then be promptly sued and a jury can sort it all out. Let's examine your letter to Mr. Wilson, point by point:

    1) "The grand jury heard all of the evidence last week and voted 19-0 in favor of Andy Titelman and found Wendy's prosecution to be malicious." The grand jury inquiry was led by Pat Head, despite a motion brought by Ms. Titelman to recuse him because of his conflict of interest. Pat Head "cooked" the grand jury just the way he wanted them. He, you, Andy Titelman, Diane Woods, Dr. King, etc. all got together and planned the grand jury presentation. None of the evidence presented at the criminal trial in Ms. Titelman's defense was presented to the grand jury. No Dr. Matherne, no Laurie Caldwell, no Bajda Daniels, no Dr. Silberg - and very importantly, none of the Pat Head/Diane Woods/Betty King/Andy Titelman team had to be cross examined!!! So you guys went to the grand jury with hours of your "cover your rear" testimony, and the Wendy Titelman is malicious and crazy slander, and since you were not challenged by anyone, you pulled it off. Mr. Head was very clever in instructing the grand jury to avoid taxing Ms. Titelman with costs, despite the finding of "maliciousness" because under the law, she could then expose everything presented to the grand jury by you guys to defend the financial assessment. Ms. Whitaker, your own testimony proved your incompetence: A) The absolutely foolish "Wendy was feeding the kids to the alligators" opinion, B) Your complete ignorance of the standard professional sexual abuse treatises, which you thought were "self-help books," C) Your opinion that you could spot molesters by looking at them, D) Your bizarre criticism of Dr. Matherne because he discussed their reports of abuse with the children, D) You, as the children's therapist, acting as Ms. Hakes's assistant, E) Your refusal to speak to Ms. Titelman, Dr. Matherne, etc., and on and on. In summary, your presentation was shockingly pathetic. The continual cover-up for the benefit of Ms. Woods and Dr. King is illustrated by the very unusual step taken by the court in not requiring Dr. Pittman's grand jury testimony to be transcribed, and by ordering Ms. Titelman (and all of the witnesses for the appearance of equal treatment) not to contact the grand jurors, which is otherwise her right. Also, the names of the grand jurors are now sealed, despite the fact that such is public record.

    2) "No evidence prior to August 4, 2000, was allowed." I accurately predicted that this defense would be used by you guys. You all know that it was Pat Head, Francie Hakes, Diane Woods, and Andy Titelman who had Judge Flournoy rule that nothing prior to August 4 could be presented in the criminal trial. Ms. Titelman strongly opposed that ruling, and tried at every step of the criminal trial to open all of the facts to the jury. So, it is a bit disingenuous to use this line. In fact, the reason you all opposed the pre August 4 evidence is because it explains why Ms. Woods and Ms. King in their minds had to lie about the children's disclosures to themselves and Dr. Matherne in order to protect themselves for their early positions that Andy Titelman should have custody. Why would Dr. King and Ms. Woods refuse to let the jury know that they were the ones who were responsible for the children being with their father, despite the children's reports and the independent eye witness testimony of others in community proving the sexual abuse prior to August 4?

    3) "Power of the individuals involved." This is indeed the most paranoid thing I've heard in this case. To whom are you referring? The only power here, Ms. Whitaker and company, is the truth- your only enemy.

    I think the criminal jurors should get legal assistance so they can sue you immediately upon your continuation of your baseless hostility against them. I doubt that you can find an attorney to sue any of them. But, by all means, feel free to sue Ms. Titelman. She will continue to publicize your errors and incompetence in her children's case. In fact, rest assured that this letter will get broad internet circulation. Have your attorney call me so we can accept service and get to trial immediately. I, and others, would relish the opportunity to cross examine you and your associates in this case. Finally, as Robert Burns, the great poet once observed, "O, wad the power the giftie gie us, to see ourselves as eithers see us."

Sincerely yours,

Richard Ducote
Attorney at Law
731 Fern Street
New Orleans, LA 70118
(504) 314-8400
(504) 314-8600 [fax]

APPENDIX F

IN THE JUVENILE COURT OF COBB COUNTY
STATE OF GEORGIA

IN THE INTEREST OF:)
AMANDA TITELMAN, *a child*)
     and   )   No._____
JESSICA TITELMAN, *a child*)
_____)

PETITION FOR ADJUDICATION OF DEPRIVATION

The Petitioners - Wendy Titelman, Richard Ducote, Timothy G. Schafer, Nadine Youngblood, Bill Youngblood, Doreen Buben, Ray Buben, Margaret Carlson, Mark Evans, Gail Vernon, Paul Vernon, Cathy J. Dishman, Jan Dahlin Geiger, G.A. Geiger, Deana Williams, Lynn Williams, Rick Thompson, Mary Thompson, William D. Adkins, Janice Morgan, Jim Palmer, Lynn Palmer, Denise Savely, Wayne Savely, Lisa Curtis, Robin Blankenship, Frances Evans, Alton Davis, Jane Reibel, and James Reibel, on behalf of Amanda Titelman and Jessica Titelman, respectfully pray that the children be adjudicated deprived children within the purview of O.C.G.A. § 15-11-2, *et seq.*, and thereafter the children be placed in the sole legal and physical custody of Petitioner Wendy Titelman, subject to supervised visitation by the Respondent father Andrew Titelman, conditioned on his successful completion of a specialized sexual offender program, for the following reasons:

1) The Petitioners are as follows:

    a.   Wendy Titelman, mother of Amanda and Jessica, has diligently attempted to protect her daughters. She was the children's primary caretaker for most of their lives. The children were placed in the father's legal custody despite evidence of on-going sexual abuse. Ms. Titelman lives and works in New Orleans, Louisiana, c/o 731 Fern Street, New Orleans, Louisiana 70118.

    b.   Richard Ducote is an attorney at law, residing in and licensed to practice in Louisiana, and has served as counsel *pro hac vice* for Wendy Titelman in the Cobb County Superior Court proceedings (Docket #'s 98-1-5890-33/00-10-8035-33). He appears here as an outraged public citizen petitioner familiar with all of the evidence and facts generated by the witnesses. For 24 years he has been a nationally recognized child advocate specializing in the protection of abused and neglected children. Prior to his admission to the Louisiana Bar, he served as a juvenile probation officer. Within his first year of admission to the Bar, he started the first program in Louisiana providing attorneys for abused and neglected children, and wrote the grant which created the Tulane School of Law Juvenile Law Clinic. In 1981 he created one of the first statewide legal offices in the country dedicated solely to freeing foster children for adoption, and in that capacity served as a special assistant district attorney in 19 Louisiana parishes (counties), trying termination of parental rights cases in 40 Louisiana courts. Since that time, he has appeared in courts in over forty states advocating for abused children and their protecting parents. He has written legislation in Louisiana to protect abused children in custody cases, and those laws have become models for many states. He regularly trains psychologists, social workers, judges, attorneys, and guardians *ad litem* nationwide at the request of courts, the American Bar Association, the National Council of Juvenile and Family Court Judges, The Northern Plains Tribal Institute, and other professional and governmental agencies. He has been honored by the American Bar Association, the Louisiana Foster Parent Association, the National Association of Social Workers, and the LSU School of Social Work for his achievements on behalf of victims of child abuse and domestic violence. He is considered one of the foremost authorities in the country on protecting sexually abused children and domestic violence victims in family courts.

c.   Timothy G. Schafer, a person of majority, who is domiciled in the Parish of Orleans, State of Louisiana, has been a member of the Louisiana State Bar since 1963, and has employed Wendy Titelman as his law firm's office manager for a period of eleven months, appears as a petitioner to represent that: he is familiar with Wendy Titelman; he has observed her as an honest, intelligent, sincere individual who is dedicated to the protection of her two daughters; he has reviewed documents pertaining to the custody proceedings in Cobb County, Georgia and has been appalled at the failure of those, who are charged with the duty of protecting minors, to fulfill their obligation to these children.

d.   Nadine Youngblood is married and has grown children and young grandchildren. She is a former office manager and administrative assistant. She comes as a petitioner for the following reasons: Nadine has been a friend of Wendy Titelman for several years. She met Wendy through her daughter. For the last 3 years, she has followed the situation with Amanda and Jessica very closely. Ms. Youngblood has concluded that these girls have been abused and are not being protected. This conclusion came after diligent research. She is committed to doing everything possible to see that these children are rescued.

e.   Bill Youngblood is Chairman and CEO of Financial Network Corporation in Atlanta, Georgia. He is married and has grown children and young grandchildren. He comes as a petitioner in behalf of Amanda and Jessica for the following reasons: Bill became involved with Wendy's case through his daughter and his wife. Because the family had a personal relationship with Wendy, Mr. Youngblood elected to do his own research and investigation into the situation. He did not want to make decisions based on an emotional viewpoint. He wanted to decide based on facts and documentation. In conclusion, Mr. Youngblood believes that the claims of child sexual abuse are valid. He is greatly concerned about the future and welfare of the children. He is actively supporting Wendy Titelman in her efforts to protect her children.

f.   Doreen Buben is a wife, the mother of four children and a school teacher.

She and her husband, Ray, reside in Cobb County. Ms. Buben comes as a petitioner for the following reasons: Doreen has been a friend of Wendy and her daughters for many years. Her children played with Amanda and Jessica and were close to them. Ms. Buben and Wendy home schooled their children and were in the same home school group for a period of about two years. Doreen has followed Amanda and Jessica's case from the beginning. She read documentation and has watched with disbelief as each event happened and the children were ignored in their pleas for help. She couldn't believe this was happening in her county. She has made a commitment to help Wendy and the girls so the terrible injustice done here will be corrected.

g.   Ray Buben is a builder in Cobb County. He is married and has four children. Mr. Buben comes as a petitioner for the following reasons: Ray's wife and children were friends with Wendy and her daughters for several years. As the facts came out, Ray could not believe that these children were not being protected in the county where he lives. He is appalled by the whole situation.

h.   Gail Vernon is a licensed physical therapist and the mother of 4 children. She is very interested in this case because she saw Andy Titelman slide his daughter, Jessica, up and down over his private area with his legs open while saying "touching, touching, touching." This occurred while they were in the waiting area at Ruth Mitchell Ballet and while their daughters were in ballet class. It stresses her greatly that there is an over-abundance of evidence that the children should be removed from their father's custody and placed with Wendy Titelman, but they remain in his home. Ms. Mattson believes the children's statements that their father "tickled their private parts," and it makes her sick and sad that he has full custody of these girls.

i.   Michael Vernon is the husband of Gail Vernon. He believes that his wife saw Andy Titelman holding his daughter between his legs and sliding her up and down while saying "touching, touching, touching." He believes her as he has not known her to be capable of lying in the 14 years he has known her. Also, after reading the letter written to Judge Bodiford and D.A. Patrick Head by the jury from Wendy Titelman's criminal trial, where they found her totally innocent of custodial interference, Mr. Vernon is confident that justice is not being served in this situation. He is totally disgusted with the fact that a probable child molester is living with his children while the mother who has committed no crime is not allowed to even see them.

j.   G. A. (Jerry) Geiger is the President and CEO of Geiger Financial Group, a financial services consulting firm based in Atlanta, GA. Prior to founding GFG, Mr. Geiger served for 15 years as a senior vice president and senior manager of Financial Service Corporation, a SunAmerica company and subsidiary of AIG. Mr. Geiger has been in the financial services industry since 1967. During his 35 year career, he has been a branch manager and regional manager for New York stock exchange firms including Merrill Lynch and A. G. Edwards. Additionally, Mr.

Geiger served 28 years in the United States Naval Reserve, retiring in 1995 with the rank of Captain. Mr. Geiger received a bachelor of engineering from Youngstown State University; a master of science degree in engineering from University of Arizona; a masters of business administration from Arizona State University; and a juris doctorate from Oklahoma City University. Mr. Geiger's concern for how our legal system disenfranchises many children, such as Amanda and Jessica Titelman, has led him to plan a second career, after retirement, as an attorney performing pro bono services in similar situations. Mr. Geiger has 3 grown children, 2 stepsons whom he has been actively involved in raising, as well as three grandchildren. Mr. Geiger has known Wendy Titelman for ten years, since shortly after the birth of her elder daughter, Amanda, in 1991. Mr. Geiger has known Wendy as a very loving and caring mother, having seen her interact with her children on many occasions during the last 10 years. Also, approximately a year ago, he observed Amanda and Jessica react to him when he attempted to deliver birthday gifts for Amanda from their mother at their father's house. It was clear to him that both girls were acting under some sort of fear of talking to anyone. Specifically, he approached Jessica outside the house when he drove up to deliver the gifts. While he felt that Jessica recognized him, she was very reticent to look at Mr. Geiger or engage in any conversation. Mr. Titelman refused the gifts telling Mr. and Mrs. Geiger to get off his property. It is Mr. Geiger's firm belief that the current custody arrangement has impacted the mental and social well being of Amanda and Jessica negatively. He prays the court will make a change in custody and protect the girls from apparent abuse.

k. Jan Dahlin Geiger is a Certified Financial Planner, practicing in Atlanta, Georgia. She works primarily with high net worth individuals and closely held business owners. Prior to becoming a financial planner, Ms. Geiger was a corporate lending officer with several banks, including a position as Vice President with Citicorp (now part of Citigroup). Prior to her work in corporate banking, she was an officer in the United States Navy, last serving as an Assistant Aide and Flag Lieutenant to a navy four star admiral, the Atlantic Fleet Commander (CINCLANTFLT), in Norfolk, Virginia. Ms. Geiger has an undergraduate degree from Washington University in St. Louis as well as a masters in business administration in accounting and finance from Georgia State University. Additionally, she received her CFP designation from the College for Financial Planning in Denver, Colorado in 1988. She is the mother of two sons and has three stepchildren and three step-grandchildren. Ms. Geiger has been close personal friends with Wendy Titelman for about 11 years, since before she married Andy Titelman and long before her children were born. After her kids were born, she became a full time stay at home mom and seemed to enjoy it immensely. Ms. Geiger is absolutely convinced that this petition is valid and necessary for the protection of Amanda and Jessica, who have not heretofore been protected.

l.   Cathy J. Dishman has been a close friend of Wendy, Amanda and Jessica Titelman since 1989. She works as a homemaker in Hampton, Georgia and is married and the mother of five children. She 'volunteers as Education Coordinator and leader of the Children's Ministry Program, and serves on the Missions/Outreach Committee for New Hope United Methodist Church where her family attends regularly. She served as PTA Secretary at Kemp Elementary during the 2001-2002 school year. She was asked to serve as President for the 2002-2003 school year and declined this invitation because of her busy schedule with many other commitments. She also has a four year old son with Down Syndrome who enjoys a great deal of her time and attention. Ms. Dishman is joining this petition requesting the release of Amanda and Jessica Titelman into the custody of Wendy Titelman because Amanda and Jessica have been denied the justice that two innocent children deserve. She is appalled that not a single person who was "investigating" the allegations of sexual abuse against Andy Titelman ever contacted her in any way, for information *of any kind* as it related to this case. She personally believes that these children have been abused by their father. Having known Wendy Titelman for more than ten years, she's never known her to be anything less than a loving and caring mother who's risked everything to protect her children. She also believes that the system of Cobb County has so far failed to protect Amanda and Jessica in the worst sort of fashion. These innocent girls told person-after-person about the shameful, hurtful, and depraved things that were happening to them at the hands of their father. Children are taught by authority figures and their parents what "inappropriate" touching is. They're also taught why they should tell another adult, no matter who the person is that's touching them or what they tell them will happen if they tell. These children did exactly as they were told to do if they were ever touched "wrongly". Their voices fell on deaf ears. Amanda and Jessica have suffered at the hands of the same system that is sworn to protect them. Ms. Dishman respectfully requests that Amanda and Jessica Titelman who have suffered more than anyone during the course of these events be returned to the custody of their mother and protected from their abusive father.

m.   Mark Evans is a brother of Wendy Titelman and uncle of Amanda and Jessica Titelman. Mark is an honors graduate of Georgia State University, with a bachelors degree (1973) and a masters degree (1976) in psychology. In 1977, while Mark was a doctoral candidate in psychology at GSU, he seized an opportunity to be a visiting psychology student at the University of Texas at Austin. At UT, Mark became interested in Computer Science and was accepted into the masters program in the summer of 1978, the coursework for which he completed in 1980. In 1980, Mark accepted an offer from Bell Laboratories in Holmdel, New Jersey and was a member of the technical staff until 1985 working on human factors and software design of voice/data terminals. Since 1985, Mark has been a manager and a software design engineer with DSC

Communications Corporation and the Hewlett Packard Corporation (Tandem/Compaq Telecom division) in Plano, Texas. Mark is married with a son and two daughters from a prior marriage. His oldest daughter is an honors student at Texas Women's University, son is a Marine recruit, and youngest daughter a senior in high school and member of the track and cross-country teams. Mark's fondest memories of raising his children are of him coaching several of their sports teams (soccer, baseball, basketball) over the course of several years. Mark is an avid soccer player, swimmer and marathon runner. Wendy Titelman has been a good person all her life, nice, honest and upright to a fault, well-liked by school mates and employers, a good mom adored by her children, and should not have to endure the persecution and torture of being separated from her children solely for attempting to protect them from their father's sexual abuse. Mark Evans, as a result of his efforts to protect Amanda and Jessica from this abuse, now works with Moms Against Abuse, National Association of Family Court Justice, Mother's Rights, and Women United. Mark believes that the same dynamics that have long protected pedophile priests are in play with his sister's case. Hardly a day passes that he does not grieve for his nieces and sister. He heartily joins this petition to let the record show his support of his sister and nieces and to demand an end to their torture and persecution.

n.   Rick Thompson is retired from the Engineering Department of Atlantic Steel Company in Atlanta, Georgia and served as Minister to Single Adults from 1976-1990 at a prominent church in Atlanta. He is presently serving in Pastoral Ministry at a rapidly growing church in Dunwoody, Georgia.

o.   Mary G. Thompson, Rick Thompson's wife, was Corporate Secretary of ThompsonMade Wood Products, Inc. in Chamblee, Georgia for 26 years. She also served as a Sunday School and church worker for many years. Mr. and Mrs. Thompson have known Wendy Titelman since she was two years old, as a neighbor and a friend. The Thompson's have seen that a terrible miscarriage of justice has occurred in the lives of Amanda and Jessica and they are interested in seeing that corrected.

p.   William D. Adkins is a resident of Huntsville, Alabama and a great uncle to Amanda and Jessica. He is retired after having spent three years in the U.S. Army, then working for the U.S. Air Force and the National Aeronautics and Space Administration for approximately 32 years. He has known Wendy since her birth and has never known her to tell a lie and has always been an outstanding woman and mother. He has been kept informed of the unbelievable things that have happened to Amanda and Jessica. He attended several days of the criminal trial against Wendy where the jury recognized that she was being improperly prosecuted and that the children's father was more than likely guilty of child molestation. In addition they also stated that the state of Georgia has failed to protect the children. Mr. Adkins agrees that the state of Georgia has failed to protect these children, and that they not only deserve to be protected from molestation, they deserve to be returned to their mother's care and protection immediately.

q. Jim Palmer is President of Envision International Marketing and has marketed specialized building products and energy technologies on an international basis for 11 years.

r. Lynn Palmer, is a freelance artist and the wife of Jim Palmer. Mr. and Mrs. Palmer are friends of Wendy, Amanda and Jessica Titelman. In 1999 Wendy, Amanda and Jessica lived with the Palmers for about six weeks while Wendy made arrangements for a permanent place to live. This was a temporary arrangement that was necessary because of the danger the children were in as a result of their father's verbal and apparent sexual abuse of the girls. They saw that the girls were obviously scared of their father as evidenced by their screaming and crying when they knew they would be forced to be taken by him when the guardian *ad litem* refused to admit that the girls were being molested in the face of overwhelming evidence. They recall that she called for an emergency hearing by the judge to require Wendy to relinquish the girls against their will to their father. How she could do this after being an eye witness at DFACS to Amanda describing sexual abuse by her father is incomprehensible and in the Palmer's opinion criminal. When Amanda and Jessica would return to the Palmer's home after being with their father, they were obviously withdrawn and unusually quiet and sad for about a day and then they would begin to return to their happy, joyful behaviors which they saw as further evidence of the abuse and relief of feeling safe again when they were away from him. Jessica and Amanda both confided in Mrs. Palmer and told her that their father was touching them inappropriately on a regular basis each time they were forced to stay with him. This happened while the girls were staying with them and took place during the forced visitation by Andy Titelman. On one occasion, Andy pounded on the Palmer's front door and stood in their driveway screaming at the top of his lungs. Mr. Palmer called the police and filed a report of this occurrence, but after the officer met with Andy, for some unknown reason, he changed the report to reflect harassing phone calls as the complaint which was not why he called the police. When Mr. Palmer contacted the Kennesaw police department at a later time to find out why the report was filed inaccurately, they told him the officer was no longer on the police force and nothing could be done about it. The Palmers are appalled with the manner in which these precious girls have been treated by the court, the guardian *ad litem*, DFACS and the judicial system. There is considerable evidence of abuse, and therefore, they join this petition to put an end to the perhaps irreversible damage being done to these innocent girls. In their opinion, it is the court's responsibility and sworn duty to rescue these innocent victims from a life of torturous abuse by their father and for justice to be done finally in protecting them from further destructive harm.

s. Lisa Curtis received her B.A. from Emory University in December 1991 with majors in French and Religion. She received a Fulbright Award after publishing a study comparing video versus textbook methods in The French Review, and she taught English to high school students in Poissy, France. Ms. Curtis has worked with children on many levels and over the years, her volunteer experience has included tutoring children in a homeless shelter and working in and coordinating the curriculum for a weekend afternoon program for inner-city children. Lisa Curtis met Wendy and Andy Titelman and their children in 1997. She grew to love Amanda and Jessica as she spent some long weekends with them in their home and occasionally babysat them. In November 1999, Amanda and Jessica shared with Ms. Curtis that their father was molesting them. She immediately reported this abuse to every agency she thought could be of help. Lisa Curtis joins this petition because she is appalled that no one in a position of power has helped Amanda and Jessica Titelman, and she desperately wants to see these girls rescued from the abusive situation in which they live and returned to their loving mother. Ms. Curtis wants to see Amanda and Jessica have a chance to experience some happy childhood and healing.

t. Janice Morgan was a certified teacher in the State of Florida. She taught 2nd, 3rd and 4th grades in the Osceola County School District in Kissimmee, Florida. She taught from 1989 until 1994. Now, Janice is a "stay at home" Mom and is currently very involved in her children's school. She is the Co-President of the PTA, for the second year, at their school. Being involved in such a huge child advocacy organization as the PTA, Janice is very aware of the protection that precious school children have the right to receive. She serves in the position to be an advocate for children locally and statewide.. Ms. Morgan joins in this petition with a deep desire for the protection of Amanda and Jessica and states that it is imperative that these children receive the protection they deserve and get out of their father's abusive environment. Ms. Morgan was one of the first to identify a possible sexual abuse situation many years ago. As testimonial and professional information has been released it is obvious that her original claim exists and these children are being sexually abused continually. Therefore, she feels it is her duty as an advocate for children to join in on this petition.

u. Robin Blankenship is a piano teacher with over twenty years experience of working with children and their families. She taught piano to Amanda and Jessica for several years. She joins in bringing this petition because the court system has not acted in the interest of protecting these children.

v. Margaret Carlson is a homemaker in Cobb County. She has personal knowledge of the girls and the petitioner, Wendy Titelman, as she and her children used to play and meet with Amanda and Jessica and Wendy on a regular basis. She witnessed the close nurturing relationship between Wendy and her daughters. She also has knowledge that there were evidences of abuse that were never acted upon. Since the children have been in the custody of Andy Titelman, her children have had no contact with Amanda and Jessica who had been good friends with her children. Ms. Carlson's children will not go to sleep at night without first making sure that they pray for Amanda and Jessica. Ms. Carlson has witnessed a tremendous injustice and petitions this court to protect these children from further harm.

w. Jane Reibel is a student and the mother of two children and resides in

Brooklyn, Michigan.

x.   James Reibel is in the business of building construction and is the husband of Jane Reibel. Mr. & Mrs. Reibel come as petitioners to see that Amanda and Jessica are removed from their father's home. They are speechless that the children have not been heard or listened to and that nothing has been done to protect them. They have known Wendy Titelman since 1988, as she was their next door neighbor in Manchester, Michigan. Many times Wendy took care of their 2 girls and is the Godmother to the youngest. During visits with Wendy when she lived in Atlanta, they observed the joy on her face while interacting with Amanda and Jessica and the patience she had with Amanda and Jessica, after waiting so long to have kids. They petition the court because Amanda and Jessica were very bright loving girls and deserve better than what has been done.

y.   Frances Evans is the mother of Wendy Titelman and grandmother of Jessica and Amanda Titelman. She has never witnessed such injustice that has been done and finds it unbelievable how things like this can happen in our beloved country. When she attempted to visit the children at their father's home on October 11, 2001, to just see the children, to hug and kiss them and tell them how much they were loved, Mr. Titelman's girlfriend closed the door in Ms. Evans face. Within a very short time 3 police cars arrived and Andy Titelman showed up and demanded that Ms. Evans be arrested and insisted that her car be towed away from the street. Amanda waved to her from inside the house until Andy's girlfriend shoved Amanda out of sight. Ms. Evans could understand if her daughter had done something wrong and was immoral. Instead she has witnessed Wendy being the most loving caring mother there could ever be. No words could ever tell how heart wrenching it was for Ms. Evans to see the children cry and cling to their mother begging her not to send them to Andy Titelman. During this grievous time Ms. Evans has had 2 heart attacks - what has happened to her grandchildren has almost been unbearable. She recounts the terrible deeds Andy Titelman has done to his children: threatening them that they will go to children's jail and he will hurt their mother and they will never see their mother again if they do not do what he says, allowing no contact with life long friends, removing them from long term activities - ballet, piano, Spanish classes and gymnastics. She remembers her daughter helplessly standing and watching 4 ½ year old Jessica locked in the car with her father screaming at her because she told her mother what her father had done to her while her mother and Amanda were at the store. Ms. Evans will do everything possible to help her grandchildren in every way. Her home and worldly possessions are theirs at any time. Frances Evans wants something done to alleviate this injustice, and therefore, joins in bringing this petition.

z.   Alton Davis has known Wendy Titelman 25-30 years. She is just like his daughter, and she calls him her step-father. He believes she is the finest and most upstanding person you will ever meet. Jessica and Amanda call him Poppy. He was privileged to see the children almost every week from the time they were born. It was Mr. Davis with her mother that carried Wendy to the hospital for the birth of Jessica and helped her mother take

287

care of Amanda. He found it odd that Andy Titelman did not care enough to take his wife or even call about her even though he knew she was going to the hospital and they were going to have to take the baby early because she was so ill with high blood pressure and toxicity. Mr. Davis cannot stress enough the love Wendy has for her children and they for her. He appears here as a petitioner because it is unbelievable how something like this has or is happening. He will continue to support Wendy and Amanda and Jessica through thick and thin.

aa. Lynn Williams has worked with the United States Postal Service for many years and was a neighbor of Wendy, Amanda and Jessica Titelman for 18 months.

bb. Deana Williams, the wife of Lynn Williams, is a homemaker and the mother of 4 children. During the 18 months that Mr. and Mrs. Williams lived right next door to the Titelmans, they got to know them very well and were very disturbed at what they saw and what was happening in the children's lives. They come now as petitioners requesting the court to take Amanda and Jessica away from their father who is causing them great harm and return them to their mother.

cc. Denise Savely, wife and mother of two, comes as a petitioner for the following reasons: Denise has known Wendy for almost four years and knows that she is a person with outstanding character, a loving and devoted mother, a caring and loyal friend, and a hard worker. She has followed Wendy's case involving her two daughters about two years and is appalled at the things that she's seen happen and the way her case has been mis-handled by Cobb Superior Court. It is her hope that this petition will result in Wendy regaining custody of Amanda and Jessica and that they will be protected from further abuse.

dd. Wayne Savely is a District Manager for AT&T. He is married and the father of two children and comes as a petitioner on behalf of Amanda and Jessica for the following reasons: He has observed the injustice in this case over the last few years as Wendy has fought to protect her two precious girls, Amanda and Jessica. He is appalled at the manner in which the system has placed these two girls in harms way. It is frightening to see how this travesty has unfolded despite the overwhelming evidence that has been presented. Ms. Titelman is an outstanding mother who has fought steadfastly for the rights of her two daughters to be free from abuse. Others would have grown weary and tired after all the effort and resources she spent on her case. But every day she wakes up more determined than the day before to see justice for her girls. Her resolve and the overwhelming evidence will not permit any of us to give up hope that justice will be done in this case.

2) It is in the best interest of the children and the public that this petition be filed and the proceeding be brought.

3) Amanda Titelman, a female, was born May 26, 1992 and is 10 years old.

4) Jessica Titelman, a female, was born March 30, 1994 and is 8 years old.

5) Amanda and Jessica reside with their father and legal custodian, Andrew Titelman. They were placed in his sole legal and physical custody by the Cobb County Superior Court on August 4, 2000, in Case No.98-1-5890-33.

6) The children have been sexually, physically, and emotionally abused by Respondent Andrew Titelman, as is set forth herein.

7) In June, 1999, Amanda Titelman disclosed to Dr. Lynn Brentnall, psychologist, that her father "rubbed her a lot and it happened when they were in bed together." When asked to show what her father did to her, Amanda rubbed a doll in the vagina/genital area, which she did repeatedly. Amanda shared that her father told her that this was "their secret and she was not to tell." He told her several times not to tell. Amanda said she was afraid of her father, and she did not like him rubbing her. [Dr. Brentnall's report is attached as Exhibit A.]

8) On June 23, 1999, a video tape was produced by the Cobb County Department of Family and Children's Services wherein Amanda clearly describes her sexual abuse by her father. Dr. Kathleen Faller, who is a nationally recognized child sexual abuse expert, made a thorough and competent review of this videotape and finds that the interview establishes that it is more likely than not that Amanda was sexually abused in a manner similar to what she described. She also stated that Amanda's statement that "it felt like a bug biting" suggests sexual contact under the clothing and inside the labia and that there have probably been multiple incidents which are characteristic of incest. Dr. Faller also examined a video tape which was produced by respondent Andrew Titelman over the course of two days, February 13-14, 2000, and she finds this tape is documentation of his bullying and coercive attempts to force the girls to recant. She states, "this appears to be a browbeating session," as he "speaks in a loud and threatening voice, standing up" and over the girls. "He is overbearing. He insists his daughters say that they lied when they said he touched them in a sexual way. He also coerces them into saying that their mother persuaded them to make the allegations." "When they do not give him the response he wants to hear, he repeats leading questions, coerces, and cajoles them until they do provide the desired response." "They appear to give in to his dominance," and "it is doubtful they could have resisted his insistent questioning." She further states, the second Andrew Titelman tape is more consistent with Amanda's forensic interview that their discomfort relates to having to recant actual abuse, and is absolutely no evidence whatsoever that the girls were not sexually abused. [Dr. Faller's report is attached as Exhibit B.]

9) At the urging of Dr. Brentnall, another doctor examined the children to determine if the conclusions were the same. Dr. Diane Pearce, an abuse specialist, saw the children and concluded that the abuse was more serious than originally thought. Amanda disclosed that Andrew Titelman would "tickle her bottom in her private parts, sometimes under clothing" and "cause her to hurt." Amanda said she would "try not to cry"..."because he might get mad if I cried when I asked him to stop." When asked to stop, Amanda said, "he would act like he didn't hear me." Amanda said that her father "dressed up like a girl with a wig, dress, nail polish and make-up," and "Daddy's bottom looks like he has a dragon's tail in front." Pictures were drawn to describe what she saw and what happened [see attached letters from Dr. Pearce along with Amanda's drawings in Exhibit C].

289

10) In June, 1999, Lynn and Jim Palmer, friends of the children heard disclosures by Amanda and Jessica that their father was touching them in their privates. They witnessed the children's fear of their father, as they were crying and hiding when they were told they would be returning to their father [see attached Exhibit D and E, letters from Lynn and Jim Palmer].

11) Jan Geiger, friend of Petitioner Wendy Titelman, has known the family and the children since they were born. Ms. Geiger witnessed and heard about behaviors that led her to believe that Amanda and Jessica were in danger of abuse by their father (see attached letter from Ms. Geiger, Exhibit F].

12) In December, 1999, Amanda and Jessica disclosed to Lisa Curtis, friend of the children, that their father was hurting them with his fingers on their privates [see attached letter, Exhibit G].

13) Janice Morgan whose children played with Amanda and Jessica and who was trained to recognize child sexual abuse, went to Wendy Titelman with concerns about Jessica, saying that she believed Jessica was being sexually abused [see attached letter, Exhibit H].

14) Karyn Covington and Joyce Saye, supervisors with A-Plus Services, were assigned to supervise petitioner from February 2000 through July 2000 during limited visitation with Amanda and Jessica. Ms. Covington reported that on March 2, 2000 Amanda was picked up from her father's residence and wore no under-clothes and had a bad odor from her vagina. On another visit Amanda shared with Ms. Covington that her father "tickles me in my privates,"..."at night - a lot." Ms. Saye reported that Amanda and Jessica shared with her that their father often made them say untrue things. When asked about what, Amanda said, "Daddy makes us lie...like when he touches us wrongly." The supervisors reported that the children masturbated when sitting still. Jessica had a bruised arm, which appeared to be a thumb and two fingers around the wrist. She reported, "Daddy did it." It was also reported that the children stated numerous times they did not want to go back to their father's house and made physical gestures against returning [see supervisor reports attached as Exhibit I].

15) While sitting in Ruth Mitchell Ballet waiting area, a mother of one of the ballet children, Gail Vernon, witnessed Andrew Titelman repeatedly sliding Jessica over his crotch and softly singing, "touching, touching, touching" [see attached letter, Exhibit J].

16) Amanda and Jessica repeatedly told Ms. Titelman their father was rubbing and hurting them in their privates. Amanda and Jessica repeatedly said they did not want to go back to their father.

17) James Cheatham, M.D., Diplomate, American Board of Psychiatry and Neurology and Addiction Psychiatry, examined all the records pertaining to the Titelmans and concluded that Andrew Titelman is unfit to serve as a parent/guardian of the children and believes him to be a sexual predator [see attached letter from Dr. Cheatham, Exhibit K].

18) Dr. Donald Matherne, forensic abuse specialist, examined Amanda and Jessica on September 2, 2000. Jessica shared with Dr. Matherne that her father "reached under and touched me there." She pointed to the genital area in an anatomical drawing. She

said it would happen when she had been asleep in bed and that when she felt herself being touched "it would wake me up." Amanda stated that her father has touched her under her clothing on her genital area usually when she is in bed. Amanda said, "He thinks I am asleep, but I am pretending. He comes in my room." Independent of each other, Amanda and Jessica drew a circle around the area on an anatomical drawing where they alleged that their father touched them. They both circled the genital area and put an "X" over the opening of the vagina indicating the exact location where they alleged that their father had touched them. Independent of each other, Amanda and Jessica demonstrated how they were touched, by making a fist and pretending it was their genital area. Jessica took her left hand and rubbed it across the top of her closed fist over the opening into her fist. Amanda took her left hand and rubbed it across her closed right fist and said, "He thought I was asleep." Amanda said she told her mother, because she wanted "my mom to help me." Amanda said that this touching of her by her father has happened since the last school year. Dr. Matherne reported that the children are "in immediate danger of irreparable harm and/or further sexual abuse if they return to the custody of their father." [Dr. Matherne's report is marked Exhibit L.]

19) In response to Petitioner's efforts to protect the children from his abuse, Respondent Andrew Titelman attempted to criminally prosecute Petitioner Wendy Titelman for "interstate custodial interference." On April 27, 2001, Petitioner was promptly acquitted of the charges [Docket No. 01901898-40 Cobb County Superior Court], and the jurors were so outraged by Petitioner's prosecution that they wrote a letter to Patrick Head, the District Attorney, and Judge James Bodiford, the judge assigned to the custody case, expressing their shock at what has happened to the children [Jury letter, Exhibit M].

20) Furthermore, in an effort to protect himself from accountability for his molestation of the children, and to punish the children for their disclosure of the abuse, Respondent Andrew Titelman has vigorously attempted to terminate all contact and relationship between the children and Petitioner, has isolated the children from their long term friends and close relatives, and has terminated their long standing social and extracurricular activities. He has also attempted to terrorize the children by repeatedly telling them that they will be kidnaped if they play at neighbor's homes, that gifts sent by Petitioner may contain bombs, and that Petitioner has in the past attempted to drown them, starve them, beat them, etc. He has also subjected them to threats, intimidation, and browbeating to force them to maintain their silence about their abuse.

21) Notwithstanding all of this evidence, the children have not yet been protected from their father's sexual abuse, and still remain in his sole custody.

22) All of Respondent's actions have caused the children grave and permanent physical, emotional, and psychological harm, and as such render the children deprived under Georgia law, and thus within this Court's jurisdiction.

WHEREFORE, PETITIONERS PRAY that, after all due proceedings, the Court adjudicate the children Amanda Titelman and Jessica Titelman deprived children, and award sole legal and physical custody to Petitioner, subject to supervised visitation by the Respondent father, Andrew Titelman, conditioned on his successful completion of a specialized sexual offender program.

IT IS ALSO PRAYED THAT the Court issue such immediate protective orders as are appropriate under the circumstances for the protection of the children under **O.C.G.A. § 15-11-11**, including the immediate removal of the children from the Respondent's home for placement in the home of responsible relatives or friends of the children who are not connected or related to Respondent, pending the completion of these proceedings.

Respectfully submitted,

[ORIGINAL SIGNED BY ALL 30 PETITIONERS]

Wendy J. Titelman
Richard Ducote
Timothy G. Schafer
Nadine Youngblood
Bill Youngblood
Jan Dahlin Geiger
G. A. Geiger
Gail Vernon
Michael Vernon
Margaret Carlson
Robin Blankenship
Deana Williams
Lynn Williams
Ray Buben
Doreen Buben
Rick Thompson
Mary Thompson
Wayne Savely
Denise Savely
Janice Morgan
Frances Evans
Alton Davis
Jane Reibel
James Reibel
Jim Palmer
Lynn Palmer
Mark Evans
William D. Adkins
Lisa Curtis
Cathy J. Dishman

June 16, 1999
Wednesday
Titleman v Titleman

Quite late Tuesday night Wendy Titleman left a message on my voice mail concerning A.T. and J.T. She indicated that A.T. had done considerable masturbation over the weekend and for several days and had just revealed to her that her father had been sexually abusing her.

Before calling Wendy, I phoned her attorney Hylton Dupree. Mr. Dupree and I discussed the situation and I reminded him that I had an appointment with the Titleman's on Thursday. Because Wendy had, for a long time, felt a discomfort between Andy Titleman and his daughters Mr. Dupree and I discussed the seriousness of these allegations with Wendy Titleman. We both brought to her attention the frequency of allegations in a divorce situation. We reminded her that this happens as false allegations most of the time and that frequently children are coached by parents. Mrs. Titleman was told the typical circumstances in cases where false allegations of sexual abuse are brought.

The Titlemans came in for a regularly scheduled session on Thursday, June 17. Wendy Titleman made it very clear to me that she was aware of false situations, but she did not believe this to be false. She reiterated the situations and frequency of masturbation by A.T. and some by J.T. and told me again that A.T. reported to her that Andy Titleman was rubbing her genitals.

I brought A.T. (dressed in sister dress with J.T.) into my office. We talked about what she'd done that week while with her mother and then I approached A.T. with the sexual issue. I asked her if there were occasions when her father touched her in private areas. A.T. told me that Andy had touched her many times. Using the anatomically detailed dolls, I had A.T. show me what her father did. A.T. took the daughter doll and began rubbing her in the vagina\genital area, which she did repeatedly. I took the doll's panties off and asked if her father rubbed her without her panties on and she told me he did not. Using my finger I penetrated the doll and A.T. told me that her father had not penetrated her.

A.T. told me that her father rubbed her a lot and it happened when they were in bed together. She said that Andy would get in bed with her to read her a story, but that instead he would rub her, sometimes reading, sometimes not. A.T. said that this would happen in the morning or at night. When I asked her where J.T. was, she told me she was not sure. Maybe she was in another room or maybe she was asleep. I asked A.T. if her father rubbed her anywhere else and she told me he rubbed her face and hair. A.T. told me that her father told her that this was their secret and she was not to tell. He told her several times, not to tell.

I asked A.T. how she felt about her father and she told me she was afraid of him. She did not like him rubbing her. I told A.T. that he should not rub her and touch places on her that were private and that no one should do this. I also told her that if this happened with her father or anyone that it was not a secret and that she should tell someone. We also discussed that she would likely have to tell about these times with her father to other people and to people that she did not know. We

Exhibit A

talked about this being scary and difficult, but A.T. felt she could tell someone else

I asked A.T. if she wanted to see or spend time with her father and she indicated that she did. She told me that her father and moved into a new house and that he told her when she came to visit him again he would have new toys for her.

L. Bentall

6/18/99

Reported to Defacs
6-18-99
6-19-99

THE UNIVERSITY OF MICHIGAN
SCHOOL OF SOCIAL WORK

FAMILY ASSESSMENT CLINIC
555 S. Forest Avenue
Ann Arbor, MI. 48104-2531
Phone 734-998-9700
Fax   734-998-9710

DATE: December 11, 2001
TO: Richard Ducote, Attorney at Law
FAX: **504 314 8600**
FROM: Kathleen Coulborn Faller, Ph.D. *Kathleen Coulborn Faller*
             Professor, School of Social Work
             Director, Family Assessment Clinic
RE: Titelman

I have reviewed the below described videotapes on the Titelman case. I have not reviewed any other records, and know minimal history of the case. In addition, statements in the forensic interview of A.T. indicate there was a forensic interview of J.T. immediately after A.T.'s, but I did not have an opportunity to review it. Below are my observations about the videotapes.

Forensic interview on 6/23/99 by two interviewers
The forensic interview of A.T. conducted on the above date is a fairly good interview. A.T. is interviewed by a woman interviewer. There is another interviewer in the room, who leaves briefly and also asks A.T. some questions at the end of the interview.

The interview follows a structure. There is minimal rapport building. At the beginning of the interview, A.T. is asked why she is there, and responds "because of daddy." A.T. respond to a follow-up query by saying he is "mean," and when asked specifically how he is mean, goes on to describe her father hitting her on her arm. The interviewer gathers detail about this incident. The interviewer asks about other things about Dad. Then asks about things A.T. likes about Dad. Following this line of inquiry, the interviewer asks comparable questions about Mom.

Focused questions about Dad and Mom do not elicit any allegations of sexual abuse. These come later, after a body parts inventory, during which the interviewer draws a Gingerbread Drawing. After the body parts inventory, the interview asks A.T., if there is "any place on this girl's body that people probably shouldn't touch?" A.T. points to the vagina (for which she says she has no name), the nipples, and the buttocks. After a discussion of appropriate touching of private parts, the interviewer asks if there has "ever

Exhibit B

been a time that anybody has touched you in these places except the doctor or except when your mom is helping you in the bath?"

A.T. responds yes and goes on to provide information about fondling behavior by her father. The actual abuse that A.T. discloses is a single incident of fondling by her father over her clothing. However, her statement that it felt "like a bug biting" suggests sexual contact under the clothing and inside the labia. Another important issue regarding her accuracy is that probably multiple incidents, rather than a single incident, are more characteristic of incest.

The information A.T. provided includes a number of contextual details. She indicates this happened at night, after she was in bed. Her sister sleeps in the same room, but in a different bed. Her sister was asleep. A.T. was wearing her pajamas. She kept her eyes closed, as though pretending to sleep. In response to a question about how she felt when he did that, A.T. responds, "Nervous."

There are also a number of null findings. A.T. indicates her father didn't say anything to her when he was molesting her; she did not say anything to him; and later on he didn't say anything related to the abuse.

The interviewer uses no leading questions. There are very few direct questions. Much of the information is elicited using focused (non-leading) questions or "wh" questions. There are, however, a number of multiple choice questions.

The interviewer follows the principle of eliciting information from the child, rather than asking the child direct questions to get her to confirm information the interviewer already has. The interviewer uses both verbal communication and demonstration, asking the child to show on a gingerbread drawing where and how she was touched.

No questions are asked to elicit information about activities other than the fondling the child describes, nor are there any questions about other potential abusers.

After the information is elicited, the interviewer assesses A.T.'s capacity to differentiate the difference between truth and a lie. When A.T. has demonstrated this knowledge, she is asked if "what you told me about dad and his fingers, is that the truth?" to which A.T. responds affirmatively (that it is the truth).

There are a number of probes to see if the mother has programmed A.T., to which she responds her mother told her to tell the truth, and this is "tell the truth about the fingers." However, it appears that the initial disclosure was to her therapist, Lynn.

There are also probes to see if her mom has told her to say her father sexually touched her in order to live with her mother. A.T. does not provide any information indicating her mother programmed her. She says she wants to live with her mother because she is "nicer" and does not want to live with her father because "Daddy tell lies, like you mom doesn't love you; he'll get me a different mom."

2

Impression

In my opinion, it is more likely than not that A.T. was sexually abused in a manner similar to what she described.

2/13/2000   Video session of Amanda **and** Jessica **with father's girlfriend:**
This session involves a rather young woman, who evidently is the father's current girlfriend, and J.T. and A.T. They are seated at a table.

The father's girlfriend asks direct questions, most of which the girls respond to with short replies: "No", "I don't know," and most of the responses essentially confirm what the girlfriend says makes her happy—that their father is not touching them.

The girlfriend appeals first to J.T. and then to A.T. not to lie anymore.

Jenny responds by saying, "The truth is he's not touching anymore." When asked if he ever has, J.T. says no. A.T. also says no, her dad isn't touching. However, she is less compliant and at one point gives the girlfriend a baleful look, which elicits a query from the girlfriend, "What's wrong?" A.T. gives her another look and says, "Nothing."

The girlfriend wants to know why they would makes these allegations, and A.T. says, "I guess I want to be with mommy." However, she denies that her mother has told her to say this.

The girlfriend tells them several times how "really happy" she is they are telling the truth now and rewards them with desert. At several points, they attempt to avoid her questions by diverting attention to the drawings and cards they are making.

The girlfriend does not tell the girls she is videotaping them and lies to them when A.T. notices the camera is on. She tells her that she is just charging the battery on the camera.

Impression
Because of the beseeching quality and leading structure of the girlfriend's questions, the impression one gets is that J.T. and A.T. are just telling her what she wants to hear.

2/13/2000   Confrontation of Amanda **and** Jessica **by their father**
This is appears to be a browbeating session. The father speaks in a loud and threatening voice, standing up while A.T. is sitting at the table and J.T. appears to be on the floor. He is overbearing. He essentially insists his daughters say that they lied when they said he touched them in a sexual way. He also coerces them into saying that their mother persuaded them to make the allegations. They also blame Lynn Palmer for making them lie (I believe she is their therapist.) When they do not give him the response he wants to hear, he repeats leading questions, coerces, and cajoles them until they do provide the desired response. The girls are obviously uncomfortable. A.T. is avoidant (she has to be

3

instructed to look at her father) and she appears resentful. But essentially they appear to give in to his dominance. It is doubtful they could have resisted his insistent questioning. It is likely that he would have continued in this vein until they said what he wanted to hear. As with the girlfriend, J.T. is more compliant than A.T. is.

Impression

The father does not give a good impression. Because of the coercive and confrontational nature of his questioning style, one cannot have any assurance in the accuracy of the children's responses. While it is possible that the girls appeared uncomfortable in the confrontation because they had lied about the abuse or because their father is behaving in a domineering way, it is more consistent with A.T.'s forensic interview that their discomfort relates to having to recant actual abuse.

2/14/200   Video session with Katy, A.T. and J.T.

Katy appears to have a good relationship with J.T. and A.T. Although she probably was asked to do this videotape, she appears well intentioned and evidently believes that nothing has happened to A.T. and J.T. Most of this videotaped session involves very appropriate interaction between an older sister and younger sisters. I will focus on the portions that address the sexual touching allegations.

Katy prefaces her queries by saying she wants to assure the girls' best interest and make sure they are OK. She then asks the girls about things they are saying, apparently about to sexual abuse by their father, although she does not clarify that this is the topic. Their responses could refer to their abuse allegations or to their recantation. A.T. shakes her head, "no" when asked if anything is happening. Katy then asks if everything is OK with them, and they affirm it is. When asked if what they have been saying is true, they deny.

Katy asks suggestive questions indicating her view is that the children have made these false allegations because they are afraid otherwise they will not be allowed to see or live with their mother. They acknowledge they are worried that they won't be able to see their mother; that their father won't let them visit her. She tells them their father could go to jail because of their allegations.

Katy asks if their mother has told them to say this and J.T. says yes. Alex said that her mother didn't but rather Lynn Palmer. Katy asks "Who is Lynn Palmer?" A.T. responds in a negative tone, "I don't know."

Impression

It is not clear in this exchange whether the children are talking about the abuse allegations or the recantation, nor is there ever any clarification whether what they said, when they alleged sexual touching, was true or false.

4

Final confrontation of A.T. by her father

At the end of the session with Katy, J.T. , and A.T. , the father comes in. First he obscures the view of the girls by standing facing the video camera. Then he turns and says to A.T. that earlier that day she admitted that the statements she made were false an were fostered by Lynn Palmer. A.T. looks somber, then sullen, and uncomfortable. Her father gets her to affirm that Lynn Palmer told her "a lot, a lot" to lie and that her mother was there and must have known that Lynn Palmer told her to lie. He then turns off the video camera.

Impression

Both A.T. 's evident discomfort and the coercive nature of the father's questions mean one cannot have any confidence that A.T. 's acquiescence is supporting actual facts.

5

Caring for People First

1770 The Exchange / Suite 150
Atlanta, Georgia 30339
Telephone (404) 916-9034
Fax (404) 916-9030

Adrienne R. McFall, Esquire
170 Gibbons Way
Athens, GA 30605

Dear Ms. McFall,

This letter is in response to a request made by your client, Wendy Titleman. She has requested that I send to you a summary of my treatment and evaluation of her daughters, Amanda and Jessica. I spent a total of 4 sessions with either one or both of the Titleman girls. Those sessions were on 9/9/99, 9/20/99, 10/4/99 and 11/2/99. During that time I concluded that both girls were suffering from tension and anxiety related to their parents realtionship, sepeartion anxiety from the lack of contact with their mother, and feelings of guilt and helplessness which is most commonly associated with childhood trauma. Based on the circumstances that the oldest child reported to me, I believe that this trauma was due to sexual abuse. Those circumstances were as follows: the girl's father allegedly would "tickle their bottom and private parts, sometimes under clothing; allegedly he would cause them to hurt, but the oldest child would work at not crying, and would try to act as if she were "thinking about something", because "he might get mad if I cried"; when she would ask him to stop, he would "act like he didn't hear me"; the oldest girl reported that her "daddy's bottom looks like he has a dragon's tail in the front"; the youngest girl allegedly would have to take bath's with her father; and that sometimes (allegedly) their father would dress up like a girl with a wig, dress, nail polish and make-up.

On 9/9/99, I reported allegations of abuse to the proper authorities, Dept. of Fam. and Children Services. I spoke with Anita King on that date. On 9/17/00 I wrote a letter of follow-up to Valarie McKenzie due to the fact that I did not receive any response from Ms. King or the detective working the case, Any Hendersen, after many attempts to contact via the phone for follow-up. On 9/30/99, I received a phone call from Martin Inman following up with me on the 2nd investigation. Martin was inquisitive about how I came to know of Wendy Titleman and what my impression of her was. He seemed to have a bias in his conversation at that time.

If you have any further need of information, please do not hesitate to contact me.

Respectfully Submitted,

M. Diane Pearce, Ph.D.
Psychotherapist

Exhibit C

300

Therapy Services, Inc.

Caring for People First

1770 The Exchange / Suite 150
Atlanta, Georgia 30339
Telephone (404) 916-9034
Fax (404) 916-9030

September 17, 1999

Cobb County Department of Family And Children Services
Valerie McKenzie
325 Fairground Street
Marietta, Georgia 30060

Dear Ms. McKenzie,

This letter is to acknowledge your notice to me regarding a report that I made to your office of possible sexual abuse to a minor on the date of 9-9-99. This report was made to Anita King via phone and in regards to Amanda Titleman.

I am concerned that after placing phone calls to Detective Amy Hendersen and Anita King, I have not yet received responses from either. I placed phone calls to both individuals regarding this investigation.

It was my intention to address the child's apparent reluctance to speak candidly with a male investigator regarding her report of sexual fondling from her father. My experience has been that 7 year old females are embarrassed and withdrawn regarding all discussion involving their private parts. My experience has been that most children are extremely guarded in discussing such matters with people that are unknown and/or of the opposite sex. In today's society most parents teach their children to avoid these kinds of situations. Therefore it is not surprising to me that a 7 year old child after being pulled from her classroom in school, would not describe intimate details of a situation that would be traumatic to recall. It is my opinion that her reluctance would be intensified by the fact that the person asking the personal questions is someone with whom she is not familiar with. It is also my opinion that having an adult of the opposite sex present would further complicate the likelihood of disclosure.

At the present time the mother of the child is unaware of the details of my report to Anita King. It is my desire that the trauma this child has experienced thus far be treated without incurring further trauma as a result of the investigation. It is my understanding that the investigation of the report that I made on 9-9-99 has been closed. Please understand that as I continue to treat this child, if the patient should disclose to me any additional information than what I have already reported, I consider it my responsibility to report and contact Anita King with such information.

If you can assist me in contacting the investigators in this case, it would be greatly appreciated. In addition if you should have any further insights into this case that may be of assistance to me, please do not hesitate to contact me. My direct Voice-mail is #770-594-4354. Our office number is #770-916-9020.

Respectfully Submitted,

M. Diane Pearce, Ph.D.
Co-director Alpha-Care Exchange

privates
white

He wears
main purple
Dress.

pink shoes
Make-up
and painted Nails

'me'
not covered

curved
pans

- wears a wig, looks like a girl.
- plays a game

Clothes   little shirt
           big shirt

Lynn Palmer
3925 Collier Trace
Kennesaw, Georgia 30144

November 29, 1999

Dr. H. Elizabeth King
Peachtree Psychological Associates
1819 Peachtree Road, Suite 600
Atlanta, Georgia 30309

Dear Dr. King:

This letter is to inform you of my relationship and experience with A.T. and J.T. Titelman and the mother, Wendy Titelman. I have been friends with them for a few years and have been acquainted on an intimate level.

I approached Wendy, along with another one of her close friends in 1998 and we made a long list of specific concerns that caused us to suspect Andy was probably having inappropriate sexual relationship with his daughters. Wendy and Andy were in the process of divorce but still shared the same household. In my ongoing discussions with Wendy I suggested that her girls should be instructed about having appropriate sexual boundaries even though they were 4 and 6 years old at the time. Wendy was very hesitant about this because she did not want to communicate anything that would steal their innocence. She also was very guarded for fear of harming their relationship with their father in any way. I believe she erred in the opposite direction of what she has been accused of by Andy and his attorneys.

I have seen her be consistently concerned that she not harm her daughters by implying anything negative about their father. Believing there was molestation came with great difficulty and pain for Wendy. Finally, after A.T. began talking voluntarily about her experiences with Andy "touching her wrongly" Wendy has taken all the possible steps to get the girls protection.

Shortly after A.T. 's claims Wendy came to my house June 20, 1999, to protect the girls from Andy knowing where they were. DFCS was notified by Dr. Lynn Brentnall and on June 24, I accompanied Wendy and A.T. for A.T. to speak with Julie Hall at DFCS, and the following day, Diane Woods demanded the girls be returned to their father because she did not believe A.T. 's statement since A.T. had "hesitated and looked down" before answering the question of what her father was doing to her. This was appalling to me since A.T. was speaking with a perfect stranger about something traumatic and embarrassing. Was she supposed to be comfortable and at ease in telling this terrible truth? The day before, (the 23rd of June) A.T. had acknowledged to me personally that her "daddy rubbed her in her private area." When she said it, it was with shyness and embarrassment.

Exhibit D

305

The evening the girls were handed back over to Andy was a gut wrenching, emotional experience to watch. A.T. clung to her mother crying and begged her, "no mommy, don't make us go with him." J.T. hid behind a wall and acted equally terrified.

The following week the girls returned to Wendy at my house with my husband and I being in the position of court designated supervisors. On July 3rd I was sitting with the girls and painting pictures and observed J.T. masturbating. (I had also observed the girls masturbating when they were riding in the car and on other occasions when they were sitting still.) She then said out of the blue, "daddy rubs A.T. wrongly." I asked, "has that happened to you too, J.T. ?" She nodded her head up and down and said, "I think, I think, I think." A.T. then told J.T. , "It's O.K., J.T. ; she knows. I told her." Then J.T. just nodded her head again. A few days later when the girls were due to return to their father, they both told me they did not want to be with him; they were afraid of him. They said they did want to get the toys he had promised them and then they didn't want to have to be with him. They said he gets angry and yells at them. The following week when they returned, they were so distressed and their bodies were hyper tense, they would not even have eye contact or respond when spoken to, especially J.T. I observed them being far more whining, demanding and complaining, but they always would improve after a few days with their mom. This was the case every week they were in my home.

On another occasion, I was visiting the girls and Wendy on August 8. After just coming from Andy's, the girls told me again that they were still being touched wrongly by their father despite the supervision, and they were afraid of going to children's jail if they called 911 or told anyone because their father had threatened them this way. This occurred during the time he was still at his mother's home for supervision with them.

Dr. King, I am a mother and a grandmother of 3 little girls. I also have extensive knowledge of child development and the dynamics of childhood abuse. I have every reason to believe A.T. and J.T. have not manufactured any of the things they have told me. Tragically it appears everything they have said has been dismissed on the contention that Wendy is a vindictive personality, wanting to use her children as weapons. This assumes that she cares nothing about stripping them of their innocence and tarnishing their minds. I along with many of Wendy's friends, all of whom are women of respectable integrity, find this to be outrageous and deplorable and without any shred of evidence. If anyone bothered to investigate her character by talking to those who know her, it would be established that the opposite is true! Can you afford to dismiss these children's testimony based on what the father and a step-daughter who has been bitter throughout the marriage has purported about the mother or based on the Guardian-Ad-Litem's remarks, while she has systematically refused to speak with key people like me and my husband? We are the only people that had six weeks of first hand observations with the mandate that we spend all waking hours with these children and their mother. We tried to report on this to Diane Woods, and she never would return our calls.

My husband and I also observed Andy and his daughter, Katie, and Wendy working through family issues at a psychotherapist group meeting and workshop in 1997. We had not even been introduced to the Titelman's at that time, but were able to observe very sick relational dynamics with Andy and Katie siding against Wendy. This situation gave us some impressions that were later verified after establishing a close friendship.

The impression that Katie was a very disturbed child with a dangerous level of anorexia and absolutely no boundaries with her father made us question his parental abilities. Later, as a result of my friendship with Wendy, I learned how A.T. and J.T. were being caught in the middle and were frequently subjected to rage and intolerance from Andy and Katie.

These are a few of many things that have been complicating factors. I have never seen such a poorly handled investigation from the authorities involved in this case. There are people, however, who have stood with the girls to try to intervene. Dr. Brentnall and Dr. Pierce are reputable psychologists who are convinced that these little girls are being sexually abused. They are also victims of the judicial system. I have spoken personally with two other parents who lost children to abusive parents with Diane Woods handling (or mishandling) their case and refusing to speak to people that were acquainted with the facts. I anticipate that these injustices will eventually be exposed, and I appeal to you to listen to these children and the advocates involved. Diane Woods has refused to even meet with the other psychologists, so I am hoping and counting on your professional reputation and objectivity to provide justice for these children. I love them the way I do my own granddaughters. I hate the suffering I see.

Sincerely yours,

Lynn Palmer

Lynn Palmer

JIM PALMER

3925 Collier Trace   *Kennesaw, GA 30144 USA*

Friday, December 10, 1999

Dr. H. Elizabeth King
Peachtree Psychological Associates
1819 Peachtree Road
Suite 600
Atlanta, GA 30309

Dear Dr. King,

I am writing to you out of great concern for A.T. and J.T. Titleman. My wife has been a close friend of Wendy's for several years and more recently we hosted Wendy, A.T. and J.T. as house guests during a very difficult time for them. As I am sure you know, Wendy had become concerned about the safety and welfare of her girls after the girls had confided to their mother that Andy was touching them inappropriately in their "private area". During their stay in our home Lynn and I were asked to provide supervision 24 hours a day which we were willing to do in an effort to protect the girls from being with their father unsupervised.

While they were with us we observed how happy the girls were until the day the court ordered them turned back over to their father. These little girls were terrified. We all tried to comfort them but it was clear they were being turned over to someone they were terrified of. Both girls were crying beyond the normal crying you would expect from children being passed back and forth between parents. This was traumatic for all of us knowing what these girls would be exposed to when they were with their father.

I saw how the girls were when they came back from being with their father. They were not the same happy little girls I had known when they were with their mother. I have a grown daughter that I raised who now has three beautiful daughters. If any of them looked the way A.T. and J.T. looked after being with someone that supposedly loved them and cared for them I could reach only one conclusion. They had been abused. These children have been abused in the worst possible way. Not only have they been abused sexually by their father, according to their own testimony but they have had to confide this information numerous times to professionals that have done absolutely nothing to stop it from happening and in fact have been responsible for them being put back with the perpetrator for more of the same abuse.

I sat in agony listening to these girls tell my wife what their father had done to them. Why would anyone doubt these precious innocent victims?

The accusation has been raised by Diane Woods that Wendy is a vindictive wife that has forced her daughters to make up lies about their father. This is the farthest thing from the truth possible. Why Diane Woods has taken this posture is beyond me. If she or anyone would take the time to talk to people that have known Wendy for years, they would find out that Wendy has done

Exhibit E

everything to preserve the girl's opinion of their father. We never observed at anytime while they were under our roof for over six weeks of any attempts on Wendy's part to instruct the girls to do anything but tell the truth.

Two years ago, my wife and another friend of Wendy's went to her to confront her about their and my concerns about the girls and Andy's behavior with Katie. My wife has recounted to you in her letter the details of this meeting. The friend in reference had observed Andy's interaction and touching of Katie that resembled two lovers interacting rather than a father and daughter. I observed in a group counseling setting what appeared to me to be an incestuous relationship at the very least on an emotional level if not physical. I remember feeling sickened by Andy's obvious preference for his daughter over his wife in the counseling session. All of this transpired before I ever knew the Titleman's in fact this was my first introduction to them. Later my wife became a friend with Wendy.

Having raised my daughter as a single father then marrying my wife, I understand first hand the dynamics of blended families. There were many tensions between my wife and daughter but never did these tensions divide my wife and I in favor of my daughter. This would have been unthinkable to me. I required my daughter to show respect for my wife and not allow any problems to get between my wife and I. I supported my wife and my daughter knew this and respected my wife as a result. My wife is my daughter's "real mother" according to my daughter as a result of the healthy decisions made to mutually support one another as parents. What I observed with Andy Titleman and his daughter Katie was one of the most unhealthy displays of parenting I have ever witnessed and it led me to wonder if there was more to the story than met the eye. Andy acted like a man caught in an affair trying to appease his lover and rebuff his wife.

All this to say. It must be obvious to you after meeting with these precious little girls that someone has abused them severely. I am not a trained professional such as you and it is blatantly obvious to me. I am writing to you to ask that you do whatever possible to relieve their suffering and this horrible abuse. You can be instrumental in protecting their physical and psychological well being. If there is anything I can do to help in this situation, I will do it. Just let me know how I can help.

The abuse must stop before these girls are damaged any further. Please take whatever action necessary to prevent further abuse. If you even have the slightest concern about this, please put a stop to the visitation with their father until this can be fully investigated.

I remain available to discuss this with you further at anytime. Please feel free to contact me at 770-794-1348.

Best regards,

Jim Palmer

Jan Dahlin Geiger
3405 Barrington Pass
Marietta, Georgia 30062
770-579-8200
jjgeiger@mindspring.com

December 1, 1999

Dr. Elizabeth King
Peachtree Psychological Associates
1819 Peachtree Road
Suite 600
Atlanta, Georgia 30309

Via Fax: 404-352-4334

Dear Dr. King:

I am writing this letter on behalf of my good friend, Wendy Titelman. I have many reasons to believe that her daughters are being sexually molested by their father and I wanted to provide you with the information that leads me to this conclusion.

Wendy and I have been friends for about eight years. We met when she was employed as an office manager for a company that hired me for several months of full time consulting work. (I have an MBA in finance and accounting and am a Certified Financial Planner, and have approximately 25 years experience in corporate banking and financial planning.) After a few weeks at the company, I learned that Wendy was the person to go to with most of my questions as she was very well informed, very intelligent, and got things done quickly. Our relationship was almost entirely business the first few months we knew one another. I grew to have a very high personal regard for her.

After a few months, a personal friendship began to grow, which grew even further after I finished my consulting project for the company. About this time Wendy began dating Andy and married him some months later. My children and I attended their wedding. The following year I was married and Wendy and Andy and their then – year old daughter Amanda came to the courthouse with us as my "witness" to our elopement. In the following year we had dinner at Wendy and Andy's house several times.

When I would ask Wendy how things were going, she was always very guarded about what she said. It was clear she was in distress in her family situation but was not free in sharing a lot, other than to say her husband had such a strong bond with his then- eleven year old daughter that she often felt like the daughter was the wife and she was an intruder who was mostly there to cook the meals, keep the house clean, and act as chauffeur to the daughter. On the occasions we had dinner with them, Andy reminded me of the divorced dads who rarely see their children, so when they do, they focus all their attention on the child. It was hard to believe that Andy and Wendy had full time custody of Katie since Andy paid so much attention to her. It was easy to see what Wendy was talking about when she said she felt like the intruder and Katie was the center of attention in the family.

When we discussed this, we talked of the hope that time would help smooth things out and that Andy would gradually be able to treat Wendy more like a wife and less of an intruder.

There was nothing at this time that I witnessed that suggested that Andy was molesting his daughter Katie. However, it did seem like his relationship with her was really strange and very enmeshed. He seemed

Exhibit F

to treat her more like a romantic girlfriend than a daughter. She seemed to be the absolute focus of his attention, very much to the exclusion of Wendy or anyone else around.

After Wendy had been married to Andy a while, we did not see each other often and maintained our friendship with an occasional phone call. Then about two years ago our friendship began to grow rapidly again when Wendy joined me for my annual birthday celebration and we had a long conversation about the challenges going on in our lives. We decided to form a women's group to meet together weekly to study Biblical principals to help us all grow to become more godly women, more godly mothers, and more godly wives.

Since that time, rarely a week has gone by that Wendy and I have not spent time together, either in person or on the phone. I would consider her one of my closest friends and someone I know intimately and someone who knows me intimately. Particularly as a result of our women's group and all the time we have spent praying together, we have no secrets and no pretenses with one another.

Without hesitation, I can say Wendy is one of the finest people I have ever had the pleasure to know. In addition to the first things I saw in the office eight years ago, such as her intelligence, her organizational skills, her ability to get things done capably and quickly, I have seen her skills as a mother, as a seamstress, as a homemaker, as a group facilitator, as a photographer, as a person dealing with working through life's emotional hurts, and as a friend.

The one common theme that emerges in my mind about Wendy is simply that she is good at everything she does. There is nothing half hearted about Wendy. If she is going to do anything, regardless of what it is, she will learn how to do it well or she simply won't do it al all.

She is one of the rare professional women I have known who has been able to give up a career and throw themselves into full time motherhood with total delight. While I have complained to her at times of certain aspects of full time motherhood that I don't appreciate, she has always responded by enumerating all the things she enjoys about being home full time, particularly being able to home school her children and not having to leave them in the care of others for extended periods of time.

I say all this because these are the reasons I hold Wendy in high esteem. The notion that she is somehow coaching her daughters to say they are being abused by their father is completely ridiculous. It is completely out of character with who Wendy is. I know from the many phone calls with Wendy when she tells me the things her daughters have reported to her about their abuse that she is at wits end to put a stop to it. There is no way she could be a good enough actress to put on the distress I have witnessed in her in the past year.

Many things that Wendy has told me over the years have raised red flags for me in the area of sexual exploitation of her daughters. I was sexually molested as a child by an adult cousin who lived with my family for a number of years. As an adult, I have had extensive counseling in the area of "Incest recovery." In conjunction with this counseling, I have read dozens of books about incest, sexual abuse, and sexual addiction.

Two years ago, I began telling Wendy that many of the things she had mentioned about Andy closely fit the pattern of men who were sexual abusers. At first, Wendy would recoil from my comments and insist that none of what I was saying could possibly apply to Andy. Some time ago, she and I had a lunch where we actually wrote out a list of things she had observed, particularly with Andy and Katie, that clearly pointed to sexual abuse in my mind. I was adamant in telling Wendy that she needed to be worried that once Katie went to college, Amanda and Jessica would be next in receiving inappropriate sexual attention from Andy.

About 18 months ago, I was at the Titelman's house one evening around dinnertime, picking up something that Wendy had fixed for me. Andy came home from work while I was there. Katie was there as well. I was very struck by how odd Andy's behavior was around Katie. She would walk out of the room and Andy would go chasing after her almost like a jilted lover who had just had an argument with his sweetheart. When

2

311

she walked through the room, Andy's attention would be riveted on her as if something momentous was about to happen. I am having a difficult time describing the situation – it was just mostly really weird, like what in the world is going on here that is causing all these powerful undercurrents?

I also have observed radical changes in Amanda and Jessica since Wendy and Andy's separation. The caseworker from DFCS said any changes in the children can be attributed to the stress of the divorce. However, I don't agree. My children went through the stress of a divorce with none of the severe behavior changes I see in Wendy's girls. Amanda has become very withdrawn, as if she has retreated into her own world where she does not connect with other people. Jessica has become hyper active and a compulsive talker, very unlike the child she was a year ago.

Many of the other things that point to sexual abuse I have not witnessed personally, but have heard about from Wendy. Frequent masturbation, fear of going to the bathroom alone, fear of sleeping alone, severe stomachaches are just a few. The most wrenching was hearing of Jessica's breaking into tears when Wendy went to apply medicine to her bottom when it had a rash. The tears rolled down her face as she begged Wendy not to put her finger in her "hole". I cannot fathom how Jessica would know someone was going to put a finger in her "hole" unless someone was doing that to her.

This sexual abuse has to stop! Please help!!

I would welcome your call at 770-579-8200 if you care to discuss any of this further.

Yours sincerely,

Jan Dahlin Geiger

2705 Wynford Avenue
Marietta, GA 30064
December 17, 1999

Dr. Elizabeth King
Peachtree Psychological Associates
1819 Peachtree Road, Suite 600
Atlanta, GA 30309

Dear Dr. King,

I am writing to you out of tremendous concern for A.T. and J.T. Titelman, whose case you are currently investigating. I want to provide you with information I have obtained directly from the girls as well as knowledge I gained and observations I made as a friend of the Titelman family.

You may remember me from interactions you and I had regarding the Lokey girls when I was their nanny. Remembering the support you offered them, I now cling to the hope that you will be able to help rescue seven-year-old A.T. and five-year-old J.T. from the abuse they currently suffer on a regular basis.

I met the Titelmans in the spring of 1997 when Andy, Wendy, and I were learning a process to enable us to experience more love in our lives. I do remember several topics and interactions Andy and Wendy had with Dr. Van Horn during therapy sessions that were part of the "lifestyle of love" Dr. Van Horn was teaching us. That information might be relevant to the case you are investigating, and I would be willing to share that given any necessary legal approval or disclaimer that would allow revelation of information obtained in such a confidential setting.

During the summer or fall of 1997, I began spending a significant amount of time with the Titelman family (i.e., Andy, Wendy, A.T. and J.T. , as well as Katie when she was with them). Frequently, I stayed in their home over long weekends. Andy and Wendy were wonderful hosts to me. Wendy prepared delicious meals, far more nutritious than my normal fare, and Andy picked fresh berries from their yard and made excellent pina coladas for us. Whenever we went out to dinner, Andy insisted on paying for my meal too. One weekend when I was there, Andy even surprised me by washing my car! A.T. and J.T. enjoyed my sharing my Beanie Baby collection with them and their mother, and sometimes, the four of us would pile into Wendy's van and head out for Beanie Baby hunting and trading. Sometimes Andy would drive us to a fish store in Buckhead. We also went to a bird breeder's house to visit the newborn exotic bird the family had selected. At night, I helped put A.T. and J.T. to bed. After that, Andy, Wendy, and I often played games like "Trivial Pursuit." In short, they treated me like a member of the family. At one point, Wendy told me how pleased she was that I had bonded so well with her and Andy and the girls; as she was dealing with a mysterious

Exhibit G

313

illness whose symptoms were similar to multiple sclerosis, she commented to me how comforting it was to have me around to help.

My weekend visits to the Titelman home continued until late fall, when Wendy told me that Andy had complained to her about my being there. Although she questioned him about this (because he had always agreed to and seemed happy about my coming over), Andy would say nothing more than that I interfered with "their privacy." About this time, Andy became involved in an organization called the Sterling Club for Men, or the Sterling Club of Relationships. I remember Wendy telling me that Andy was going somewhere in New York State for some kind of men's retreat. He told her the name of the group and that he would be going with his brother, and he left an emergency contact number but would say nothing more. The secrecy was bizarre. Wendy and I both had suspicious and concerned thoughts. I began searching the internet for information on the Sterling Club, and for hours of searching and cross-referencing, I found little to nothing. Eventually, I called the emergency contact number to see where it would lead me. A hotel answered, and I asked to speak with a manager. I asked him if he could tell me anything about the Sterling Club meeting at his hotel. He told me the group was holding their meetings at another location called "The Armory" but resisted saying *anything* more. The manager said that Sterling did not like any information given out, and he almost sounded fearful about saying anything. The whole situation triggered great concern in me, so I continued to search the internet for information on Sterling. Eventually, I found pieces of information that led me to more.

I found some information on a website run by a private investigator named Rick Ross. He had been hired to investigate numerous cases in which family members and friends had serious concerns that a loved one was involved in a cult. One such cult he had encountered was the Sterling Club of Relationships. Information that I found on his website was corroborated by further information that I located on other websites and particularly in newsgroup postings. All information that I found triggered tremendous concern in me. I am attaching information found recently on the internet. Unfortunately, I no longer have the documents that I pulled off the internet two years ago. I had given Wendy numerous documents I printed from the internet. Wendy informed me that the entire folder of information disappeared from the Titelman's home on Velma Drive. Apparently these documents were only some of the papers that eventually turned up missing. I can only presume that Andy found them and took them. In the documentation attached, you will note teachings of Justin Sterling, the group's founder and leader, which include hostility toward and derogatory language regarding women. Descriptions of group retreats strike me as classic examples of brainwashing and other symptoms of a cult. There are references to Justin Sterling's involvement (frequently under the name of Michael Santangelo) in the production of hardcore pornography. As if all of this information were not disturbing enough, there are even allegations that Justin Sterling molested his own young daughter.

In my research, I found no information that in the least mitigated my concerns about my friend Andy's involvement in the Sterling organization. I was confused, because earlier in the year, Andy had professed his faith in Christ, and what I read about

Sterling was so antithetical to what I thought were beliefs Andy shared with me and with Wendy. Upon reading multiple accounts of Justin Sterling's teachings regarding women, I became very concerned for Wendy, A.T. and J.T. . After Andy's attending the Sterling Retreat, he never returned to any of Dr. Van Horn's group meetings, where we frequently saw each other. This, coupled with the fact that Andy no longer welcomed me to the Titelman home, resulted in my significantly falling out of touch with the Titelman family. From that time (December, 1997) up until last month (November, 1999), I have spoken with Wendy once every few months, and at some point in the past few months, Andy happened to come into the bookstore where I now work. I knew from speaking with Wendy that she and Andy were in the process of a very sticky divorce, and when I saw Andy, the few minutes we had to speak were filled with nothing but his telling me how terrible Wendy had been.

Last month Wendy called and asked if I would be willing to write a letter documenting any memory I had or observations I had made during those months in 1997 when she and Andy and I had attended Dr. Van Horn's groups and spent so much time together. I was alarmed, to say the least, when Wendy told me that over the past few months A.T. and J.T. had been reporting that their father was molesting them.

You may remember, Dr. King, that I love children. I was a nanny for three years to the Lokey girls, whose mother had moved across the country to remarry and had left them in the custody of their father; as the girls' nanny, I essentially functioned as a surrogate mother. (During one of their mom's visits, she even took them to get a Mother's Day card for me!) I worked for Friend of the Family as a registered caregiver I have also taught two-year-olds and three-year-olds in Sunday School, high school students in France, and college students at Emory University.

I can tell you that I have a very special place in my heart for A.T. and J.T. . I asked Wendy if I could see the girls and talk to them myself. A few days later, I went to visit Wendy, A.T., and J.T. . I was pleased to find that although A.T. and J.T. had not seen me for quite some time, we obviously had bonded enough that they remembered and seemed happy to see me. I read the girls a story, and they gave me a tour of their bedrooms. I encouraged Wendy to go ahead and run an errand to the store so that I could have some time alone with the girls. When it was just the three of us alone in the house, I sat on the kitchen floor with A.T. and J.T. , and I asked them, "Is someone hurting you?" They told me, "Yes." I asked them, "Who is hurting you?" They both answered, "Daddy " I asked them, "How is Daddy hurting you?" Almost helping each other complete broken phrases, they said, "He is touching us in wrong places." I asked them, "Where is Daddy touching you?" Seeming embarrassed they eventually said, "Our privates." "Can you point to where he is touching you," I asked them. J.T. pointed to her pubic area, and A.T. nodded in agreement. "Okay," I said. "A.T., when is the last time that Daddy did this to you?" She responded, "a long time ago." I asked her if it had happened the week before when she was with her dad. She said, "No, but he did it to J.T. " I asked her if it had happened to her the time before that. She said, "No." "When did he stop doing it to you?" I asked. "When I started telling people," she responded "Has it happened to you since Thanksgiving?" I asked, and she said, "No, but he did it to J.T. ." J.T. interrupted, "No, not last time." "Yes it did," A.T. disagreed. "He did it to you while you were asleep." "Has it happened to you since Halloween?" I asked A.T. She said, "No". "Has it happened to you since school started this year?" (I was trying to give her time markers she might remember.) And A.T. told me that it had happened to her since school started.

I turned to J.T. . "Did it happen to you time before last when you were with your dad?" I asked her. She nodded her head, yes. My heart just sank for the two of them. "Thank you for talking to me," I said to the girls. "I know this is hard to talk about. I am going to write letters and talk to some people. I am going to try to help you." I got the girls something to eat, and then asked as an afterthought, "Does Daddy tell you not to tell anybody that he is doing this to you?" "Yes," they answered in unison. "Does he tell you something bad will happen if you tell people?" I asked them. "He says we will go to jail," A.T. replied. "Do you know that's not true?" I asked the girls. J.T. piped up, "Mommy told us it's not true, and I believe Mommy." I told her that was good. I did explain to the girls that the police might come to Daddy's house or to school sometime, and that the police might even take them in the police car. But I assured them that if the police took them in the police car, it would be to take them to someplace safe not to a bad place. The girls chimed in, "They would take us to Mommy." I told them that the police might take them to Mommy, or that they might even take them to another place until Mommy could be with them, but again I assured them that it would be a place where they would be safe.

When Wendy returned from the store, it was time for all of them to get dressed for a party. While the three of them were getting ready in the master bath, J.T. announced that she needed to go to the bathroom, and she asked her mom to come with her to the bathroom down the hall. She apparently did not want to go to the bathroom in front of all of us, but she clearly was fearful of going to another bathroom alone. Wendy and A.T. were busy getting ready, so I asked J.T. if I could take her to the bathroom. She said yes. When we reached the door, which was only a few yards down the hall, J.T. went in, and I asked her if she wanted me to come in with her. She shook her head no. I asked her if she wanted the door open or closed and she said closed. "Do you want me to stay here right outside the door?" I asked, and she nodded yes. Dr. King, this sweet little five-year-old girl is afraid to go alone to the bathroom in her own home!

We all left the house together. As I was driving home I could hardly believe that I had been so calm in having that very disturbing conversation with A.T. and J.T. . I felt ill and experienced a sense of urgency to do something to protect them as I realized that in a few short hours they would be back with their father, subject to another week of abuse no child should ever have to experience. When I got home, I pulled out the telephone book and scanned the blue pages for names and phone numbers of any agency I thought might have the authority to help. Between that day (Sunday) and Tuesday of the same week, I called the Department of Children and Family Services, Crimes Against Children, Child Protective Services, and the Cobb County Police. I offered each of these the details of my most recent conversation with A.T. and J.T. A couple of the places took down my report. The indication from each place was that my report would wind up in the office of the Kennesaw Police, who would have jurisdiction in this case I knew from talking with Wendy that in two separate incidences the Kennesaw Police had ended up with A.T. and J.T. 's case and, to my appall, they had dismissed it.

Dr. King, I am severely concerned for A.T. and J.T.   I have found it very troubling and very difficult to understand that although the girls have reported not only to their mother and friends but also to doctors and police that their father is sexually abusing them, *every other week* they are forced to return unprotected to the home of their abuser. I am shocked and sickened to discover that I live in a state that does not give two small children the benefit of the doubt to avoid even the *possibility* of their harm. I do not know who else I can call to report this atrocity. I do not know where else to turn. Sad does not even begin to describe how I feel when I think about what is happening to A.T. and J.T.   and when I think of finding myself in a position of having to report someone I once counted as a dear, treasured friend as a sexual abuser of his own children. It is the kind of awful situation no one would ever want to face.

I implore you. Dr. King, to take each and every measure possible to remove A.T. and J.T. Titelman from unsupervised visits with their father, Andrew Titelman. Please do not let another week go by when A.T. and J.T. are prey to their father's abuse. Please let me know if you are aware of anything I can do to help protect them.

With Deepest Concern,

Lisa M. Curtis

Lisa M. Curtis

A MOTHER'S JOURNAL

December 3, 1999

Dr Elizabeth King
Peachtree Psychological Associates
1819 Peachtree Road
Suite 600
Atlanta, Georgia 30309

Dear Dr. Elizabeth King,

I am writing to you about my deep concern about A.T. and J.T. Titelman. I am a certified Elementary school teacher in the state of Florida with years teaching 2nd, 3rd and 4th grades. I taught these grades prior to moving to Georgia almost 4 years ago. I have three daughters. My oldest, Samantha, and A.T. are friends. My second daughter Stephanie, was in ballet class with J.T. for two years. We frequently had all the girls play together, attend birthday parties, talked on the phone and carpooled to different activities together

About two years ago I picked up J.T. at pre-school and brought her home to play. Wendy had a field trip to the Governors mansion with A.T. J.T. was at our house for approximately 5 hours and did not speak at all. The only way she communicated with my daughter was through smiles and head gestures. Stephanie even questioned me about why J.T. didn't talk. With my prior educational expereience I became concerned over this behavior.

On a second occasion I brought J.T. home with us from ballet and I had to run an errand at Eckerds on the way home. While in the store, J.T. had soiled her underwear and didn't tell me. It was my daughter, Stephanie, who came up and told me that J.T. had an accident. When I asked J.T. if that really happened she nodded her head "no" I took her to the potty and realized that this in fact happened and then I helped clean her up. This really began to send up a red flag in my mind that J.T. was suffering some kind of abuse. The way her behavior was all day it made me wonder what was really going on in that sweet little head of hers. She wasn't a carefree, happy child. Something was darkening her spirit.

Over the next months I continued to watch J.T. weekly at the times our children were together. I still was concerned and confused over her excessively shy behavior. I had only heard her say the word "bye". I knew she could talk because I would hear her talk to her Mom but it baffled me why she was beyond "shy" with others.

My suspicions continued to grow, especially when J.T. was very obviously uncomfortable with the idea of using our potty. My years of educational experience made me suspect that some kind of abuse going on with J.T. , most likely sexual ,because of the strange bathroom habits. I kept quiet because I didn't want to offend J.T. 's Mom. Wendy It is hard to go up to a friend and ask, "Is your child being sexually abused?" It is not a normal conversation between friends. One day while the children were playing outside my neighbor walked up and I told her my concerns over J.T. as well.

Time went by and I went to pick up my daughters at Wendy's house when Wendy and I finally had a quiet moment to talk. We were talking about the girls and it was then I asked Wendy if there was any chance of any kind of sexual abuse going on. She said that I was the second person to ask her that. That made me feel better that I wasn't the only one who had picked up these signals. Wendy then shared with me some other strange occurances that also sent red flags up.

Please evaluate these girls closely. I really feel that they are suffering abuse because I saw it a long time ago, before it was really uncovered. Please re-open this case so that the real truth can surface. These girls are crying out for help. Please be the one to intervene for them.

Sincerely,

Janice Morgan

Exhibit H

318

A-Plus Services, Inc.

1990 Wingate Road
Chamblee, Ga 30341
Ph. 770-455-4574
Fax 770-455-8731

March 2, 2000   Supervised Visitation of Wendy
                       Titelman with daughters A.T. and
                       J.T. , 6:20 p.m.-8:20 p.m., (Supervised
                       by Karyn Covington)

We picked up the girls late because I got lost and arrived
at 6:15. Went back to mom's house. We all went next door to
look at gerbils. We went to Golden Corral to eat dinner. The
girls had a guest over and she went to dinner as well. (This
extra child, a girl about 8 years old, was at Mr. Titelman's
home at pick-up time and was sent along on the visit.) The
neighbors went also. The 2 girls had prayer together. Each
person had a prayer to say if they wanted to. They called it
a prayer chain.

A.T. had on a dress and tights but no under-clothes and the
dress was a summer dress with no sleeves. It was cold that
evening and she had a smell (a bad odor)
from her vagina (as if she had a period.) She is too young
so must not be washing properly.

A.T. also was laughing continuously (inappropriately). When
asked, "Why are you laughing so much" she said she doesn't
get to laugh alot when she is at home. The girl that was
visiting with the children continued to state that Mr.
Titelman said it doesn't matter if we were late, we had to
be back by 8:00. I told her that everything had been taken
care of. I found this to be strange that he would have
discussed this in front of the children and especially in
front of a visiting child. I had talked with Mr. Titelman
and asked if we could be 15 minutes late. He stated that's
fine.

The girls had a great appetite. They had a good visit. No
other problems to note at this time.

Exhibit I

319

A-Plus Services, Inc.

1990 Wingate Road
Chamblee, Ga 30341
Ph. 770-458-4574
Fax 770-455-6731

March 5, 2000

Supervised Visitation of Wendy
Titelman with daughters A.T. and
J.T. , 10 a.m.-6 p.m. (Supervised
by Karyn Covington)

Wendy and I went to pick up the children at their fathers
house, but he was not there. I went to the back of the house
and there were the children. They ran saying "mama is here"
and a man and woman walked up to me and I introduced myself
and they did as well. After they told me that their names
were Alec and Ann, I asked them who they were, and Ann
stated she was their Aunt and Alec was her husband. This was
very uncomfortable because I was not told that someone else
would be there with the children. These people were not very
friendly and they didn't speak to Wendy nor Wendy to them.
The children stated they had been to the Waffle House to eat
breakfast with Ann and Alec.

We came to Mom's house and Mom read them some stories as
they drank their tea.

Later their friends came over to visit and play. We all went
to the park. At lunch the girls had a good appetite. They
played some more games with these friends. They say they
miss them very much.

A.T. was very tearful today. Everytime her mother would ask
her something, she would cry and I asked A.T. would she like
to talk with me and she said yes, so we went down stairs to
talk. I asked A.T. , "Why are you crying? Are you sad?" She
stated that she wants to play with her friends, she stated
she was not happy at home and I asked why she was not happy
at home and she stated the following:

1) My dad yells at me
2) He calls me dumb
3) He calls me stupid (and she said, " I call him
   stupid back")
4) He locked me in my room so I couldn't see my
   mother.
   She was bringing me my medication, but he didn't
   open the door.
5) My dad tickles me in my privates.
   (A) when I'm washing my hands
   (B) at nite - alot
6) He hits me, Why? I don't know why.

At this time it was time to go and I told A.T. if she ever needed to talk to never be afraid and we could talk again when we had more time.

We returned the girls at 6:05 p.m. to Dad's home.

TITFLMAN PAGE 2, 3-05-00. K Covington

March 20, 2000   Visit of Wendy Titelman with A.T. and
J.T. , 6:00 PM until 8:00 PM, supervised by
Joyce Saye

I got to Wendy's house a few minutes early and we were at Andy's house by five minutes until 6:00. J.T. was in the yard and ran to get A.T. when we arrived. I went to the door to say to hello to Andy, if he came to the door. He did. Andy asked me to come in and insisted that the girls leave us alone, sending them out to Wendy's car. I was surprised because he has been adamant that they not be alone for even a moment with Wendy . We were in the entrance hall and Andy closed the door. He was visibly agitated. He said the girls were coming home saying that upsetting things were happening on the visits. I asked what things. He said their mother was trying to make them tell lies about him and was speaking with them inappropriately. He said that she was taking one girl into the bathroom on the pretense of needing to wipe her bottom for her and pressing her to say bad things about him.

I assured Andy that nothing like that had happened on my visits. Andy said well maybe it was not during my visits but they had told him it had happened. Next Andy went into a long speech about Wendy's having lied about him and caused him to have to have visits supervised by his mother during which he could not even take them for a walk unless she came too. He said they had then discovered that everything Wendy had said about him had been lies and that is when they ordered her to have supervised visits instead.

Andy told me was that he had heard Wendy say inappropriate things to the girls on the phone and had signaled them to stop talking to her about whatever those things were. He said that he monitors all of her telephone conversations with the girls and has the authority to cut those contacts out entirely if he does not like what he hears.

Andy said he thought that compared to what he had been through, we at A-Plus had become lax with Wendy. He said she appears to be a nice person but underneath that, she isn't. I assured Andy again that none of the things he mentioned had happened on the few occasions when I had been with the family. I told him that I would be very attentive tonight.

Actually, the only times Wendy and either child have been out of my hearing have been once in Andy's driveway when they ran back to the car after he did not meet them at the door (I stayed by the door, looking for Andy) and once when Wendy was running beside J.T. 's bicycle so it would not fall as J.T. rode. J.T. was squealing all the way so I am sure no subrosa conversations were going on.

I went out to the car at 6:07 and the four of us went back to Wendy's house. Georgia was there when we arrived. Each time I have been with the family, some or all of the four kids next door (Lindsay, Georgia, Calvin and the other brother) have been there for all but the last thirty minutes or less of each visit.

Visit of Wendy Titelman
Supervised by J. Saye   3-20-2000

The last two visits, another little girl, Erin, was also there, but not tonight. Only Georgia was with us at the beginning of the visit tonight but her other siblings all joined us by seven-thirty.

Wendy made vegetable soup and corn bread for dinner . After eating, Georgia, A.T., J.T. , Wendy and I went downstairs where the girls filled plastic jewelry pendants with colored sand. Then we went back upstairs. The other kids had arrived and everyone wanted to play flashlight-tag . It was seven-twenty-six but Wendy agreed that they could play until seven-thirty-five. Everyone went outside.

At seven-thirty-five, the kids from next door went home. A.T. and J.T. thought it would be fun to play flashlight-tag inside but Wendy suggested they turn off the lights and light a candle in the living room and tell scary stories instead. The girls were delighted. A.T. told a funny ghost story but that was the only one anybody could come up with among us.

J.T. asked Wendy for something from the kitchen and I said I needed a few minutes to talk with the girls while Wendy went to fetch it. Wendy said "Fine." While she was gone, I told J.T. and A.T. that I had just a few questions and they said "Okay."

I told J.T. and A.T. that I liked both of their parents, but I wanted them to know that I was just there for them. They said they knew that. I said that I always wanted to know if anything at all did not seem okay to them. They said "Okay." I asked them if anything had happened on any of the visits that bothered them , even if they didn't think it was important. They said "No." I asked if they felt okay about all of the people from A-Plus or if some of the supervisors were not quite as good as others. They said they liked everybody fine and about the same. They said nobody had let anything happen that didn't feel comfortable to them. I asked if they would tell me if anything had. They said "Yes." I asked if they sometimes felt pressured to talk about everything that happened when they were with one parent or the other parent. They said "Yes.". I asked where they felt pressured. They said "At Daddy's house." I asked them to remember to say something to me if they ever felt something should not be happening.

Wendy came back a little later. She and the girls sat together on the sofa talking for a few minutes. She told her daughters that she had something important to tell them. They looked attentively. Wendy said "I love you very much." J.T. and A.T. fell into their mother's lap laughing and hugging her. Wendy told the girls we had to go.

We drove back to Andy's house. The girls gave their mom hugs and J.T. almost couldn't let Wendy go. Wendy sent her along and I went toward the

p. 3

Visit of Wendy Titelman
Supervised by J. Saye

3-20-2000

front door with her. A.T. had already gone in. Andy was waiting at the door and waved good-night to me.

Wendy drove back to her house and I changed into my car and left at 8:14 PM.

Joyce Saye

March 26, 2000   Visit of Wendy Titelman with A.T. and
                                  J.T. , 10:00 AM until 6:00 PM, super-
                                  vised by Joyce Saye

This visit followed a week in which Andy had reproached me because he
claimed that we had been negligent and then complained to A-Plus that I was a
member of Wendy's church, was defensive, and that he did not want me to
supervise Wendy's visits again.. There is not a word of truth in anything Andy
said, except, presumably, that he does not want me to supervise Wendy's visits.
Today, I was concerned that he might refuse to let the girls go with us because
he had been so opposed to my presence.

When we reached Andy's house, I went to the door and he answered it. I think it
would be accurate to say that we were each reserved, or even cool toward each
other. I wanted to avoid being lectured by him again or addressing any of the
things he had said. Fortunately, I didn't have to. The girls came out without
incident. We left and drove back to Wendy's house.

This visit was remarkably similar to all of the others I have supervised even
though this one was eight hours long and the others have been two hours. The
difference was that when we first arrived, Wendy sat the girls down at the
kitchen table, gave them some fruit, tea, and biled eggs, and read two one
page stories to them out of a book of children's Bible stories: one about the
camel and the eye of the needle and one about how women got along in Bible
times, particularly explaining that women in the Hebrew community were
honored. A.T. and J.T. were fairly inattentive and often distracted by other
thoughts. Wendy was patient and let them play.

After reading the stories, A.T. called Erin. The girls went outside to swing and
Erin soon joined them. A.T. left a message for Georgia to come over as soon
as she got home.

We went back inside and Wendy made lunch: salmon patties, squash, corn,
and green beans. We all had lunch. Soon Georgia came and we set off to take
the dog, Teddy, to the pet store where he is being acclimated to other people.
All six of us went. The store was closed but we walked around the shopping
center for a little while. Wendy saw a huge beautiful green moth that appeared
to be almost dead, flapping around on the sidewalk. She scooped it up for the
girls to take to school. The moth sat in her handbag for about five minutes, then,
to everyone's surprise, flew away like a brand new butterfly.

Wendy took us to a small farm at the foot of Kennesaw Mountain where they
have exotic animals the children can see. Teddy ran and played with the
children. J.T. talked a lot about Andy's girl friend and from the amount of
information attributed to her, I would guess she must be living with them now.

p 2. Titelman 26:00

Everything was very pleasant about that. J.T.   just said things like Anita had said she thought Wendy was a nice person and asked whether Wendy liked Anita. Wendy said she had not met her so she didn't know.

Back at the Titelman house, the girls went on playing. We went to a neighborhood park, again all six of us, plus the dog. The girls played until 4:30 when Wendy said it was time to go back home.

When we got back that time, Georgia had to leave but the other three girls played for a long time. Among other things, they discovered a patch of clover that had four leaf clovers for the picking. Each child gathered a bunch. Back at the house, Wendy ironed them between sheets of waxed paper for each child.

Finally at 5:30, Wendy said it was time for her to spend a half hour with her daughters. Erin went home. The girls, Wendy and I sat at the kitchen table. The girls thought of a dozen things to do, like see ten minutes of a movie, etc. but Wendy asked them to just spend that time with her. They planned to do some of the other things they thought of the following evening. Each child sat briefly in her mother's lap and talked about ordinary things. Wendy asked the children how they were. They said they were well.

A.T. said twice on this visit that she did not want to go home to Andy's house: once when Wendy was getting ice cream for them and once when it was time to go. J.T.   proffered that she wanted to live with her mommie this morning when Wendy was trying her best to read Bible stories. All Wendy said was that she wished they could too.

The visit was a play day for the girls with their friends, bounded by two short Bible stories in the morning and thirty minutes of quiet time late in the afternoon. It was much like the two hour visits I have supervised. Wendy and the girls were never out of my hearing together. The girls handled their own bathroom visits, no one said anything to upset them or raise any issue with their father or his household, no one was infantalized, the children had a wonderful time. The time I have spent with the Titelmans has been so ordinary that I only list the things that did not happen to reassure those who need to know that I would say so if they did.

We left for Andy's house at 5:55 and arrived at 6:01. I took the girls to the door. They went in and I looked inside to be sure adults were present and knew of their arrival. Andy was standing at the back of the front hall. He greeted the girls. Since no one else was near it, I reached in to close the front door and said good-night to Andy. He said good-night and came to close the door behind me. Wendy drove back to her house and I left at 6:12.

April 6, 2000   Visit of Wendy Titelman with A.T. and
                                 J.T. , 6:00 PM until 8:00 PM, supervised
                                 by Joyce Saye

This was a difficult visit. Wendy told me when I arrived that Andy's lawyer is saying money from the escrow account cannot be used for supervised visits at a cost beyond $2000. According to Wendy, that amount has already been spent. She is fearful that her visits with the children will be terminated immediately. She says she has no money to pay for the supervision if the escrow account cannot be used. Wendy expressed deep concern but her affect was calm.

The next problem is that we have had to inform the family that Georgia cannot visit with the children because there have been allegations that she has said unacceptable things to them. A.T. is very unhappy about this. I had to intervene several times because A.T. was seeking ways to get around the ban. She and J.T. went back to the issue over and again, asking why and trying to negotiate some latitude. I wanted to avoid leading A.T. and J.T. into a debate about something they could not change. In different ways, it often comes up with these two children that it is best to tell the truth so I wanted to do the same for them as well as I could. I said that there must be some worries about what Georgia might be saying. The girls protested that Georgia never said anything wrong at all. Wendy said that she thought it would be good for the girls to tell Dr. King whatever they had to say about the matter. A.T. said that Dr. King already knew and that Dr. King was actually crying about it when they talked. She said she saw tears in the doctor's eyes.

Wendy made dinner and we tried to keep the children inside for a while. By seven they could hold still no longer and went outside to fly kites with Calvin. The neighbors' other son, and Lindsay came too. Lindsay asked carefully whether she were allowed to come before joining us. Georgia stationed herself on the porch, waved and watched the others playing. That elicited efforts from A.T. to break through the communication barrier. She tried sending messages back and forth through another child but Wendy and I caught on and stopped that.

Then A.T. decided to write letters. Wendy thought that might be okay. I said I really was not so sure. I said that if someone felt worried about what was being said, I thought the same person might be worried about what was being written. For tonight I agreed that letters were okay if A.T. would be willing to read them to me. The girls exchanged letters saying they were best friends and missed each other and would be best friends forever. That was all they said.

The children played outside until 7:40 when I asked them to come inside. It had become a little too complicated with Georgia playing with kites in her own yard but not communicating with the Titelman children, the other neighbor children playing with kites across yards, etc.

All of the Titelman family visits I have supervised in the past have been full of merriment and fun. During this visit, there were shadows. At dinner, Wendy asked the girls things about their everyday lives like what they were doing on spring break, what they had done that was fun, what they dreamed about. A.T. popped up with a story about a recent dream of being at a bowling alley where her father was bowling. She said that she was standing in the lane and the ball he bowled killed her.

The next shadow came when I asked the girls to come inside at 7:40. Of course they did not want to come in and A.T. opened again the question of why access to Georgia was being blocked. She said that whatever anybody had said had been untrue. I said I did not know and that all I thought we could do was tell the truth ourselves.

On the ride back to Andy's house, A.T. said sometimes she had to say things that were not true. I asked her when that happened and she said her father often made her say untrue things. I said I hoped she would tell that, and anything else that she needed to let people know, to the grown ups like Dr. King who were there to help her.

As we turned the corner to Andy's street, A.T. piped up again, saying to me that her daddy made her lie. I looked back at A.T. and said it was okay to tell me what she needed to say. She said, it was ". . . like when he touches (them) wrongly." A.T. and J.T. sat there as solemn as two little girls could be, looking back with old eyes. I said "Does that happen?" A.T. said, "Yes. Daddy makes us lie about it." J.T. just looked straight at me.

The children got out. I asked each if she were okay. Each said she was. I asked if they were upset or afraid. They said they were not. I went to the door, A.T. ahead of me, J.T. lagging behind, hanging onto Wendy. A.T. flew back out of the house with a toy to show Wendy. Andy came behind her with his ever-present telephone at his ear. I went back to the car to shepherd the children back to the front door. Andy asked if they had a good visit. I evaded and said it was fine.

A-Plus Services, Inc

199C Wingate Road
Chamblee, GA 30341

Phone 770 458-4574
Fax 770 456-8731

May 7, 2000

Supervised Visitation of Wendy
Titelman with J.T. and A.T.
10:00 A.M.-6:00 P.M. (Supervised
by Karyn Covington)

I arrived at Wendys at 9:55 A.M.. She made iced tea for the
children to drink in the car, and prepared a picnic lunch to
go to Red Top Mountain.

Picked up the children at their fathers. They were glad to
see their mother, gave her hugs and kisses. Wendy told them
that we were going on a picnic at Red Top Mountain and they
were very excited.

We got to Red Top Mountain, parked and took the food down to
the tables. The girls played at the play ground while Wendy
prepared the food. We had sandwiches, chips, vegetables,
drinks, snacks and fruit. Everything was wonderful and
peaceful.

After we ate we went to the beach for the girls to swim.
This was not the plan and they played in the water with
their clothes on. They really did enjoy their time there.

A.T. had to go to ballet in Marietta at 2:00 P.M. so we left
to get ready. We were there for 45 minutes. A.T. was trying
out for next year's classes.

After that we went to Marietta Square for the Arts and
Crafts show. A.T. and J.T. and some of their friends were
jumping on the rides that were there and drinking lemonade.
We left at 4:30 P.M. and headed back to Wendy's house. The
girls played out side until it was time to go.

The girls had a good visit. We took them back to their Dad's
and dropped them off and we went back to Wendys home, and I
went home.

(XC) KARYN told me that J.T. had
A bRUISED ARM which Appeared to be
A thumb & 2 fingers Around her
WRIST. She told Karyn that
Daddy did it but said "don't
tell A.T. -"

329

A-Plus Services, Inc.
1990 Wingate Road
Chamblee, Ga 30341
Ph. 770-456-4574
Fax 770-455-6781

Supplement to visit of Wendy Titleman
on May 7, 2000, 10:00 A.M.-6:00 P.M.
(Supervised by Karyn Covington)

I noticed that J.T. had a bruise on her right wrist and
asked her what happened. She stated that her Daddy did it. I
asked, "What did he do?". J.T. said, "He grabbed my arm."

Wendy took pictures of her arm on the front porch and when
A.T. came up J.T. jumped up. I asked her why she jumped.
She stated that A.T. would tell Daddy. I said, "Tell Daddy
what?" J.T. said, "That Mommie was taking pictures."

Wendy took more pictures after A.T. left the porch.

May 8, 2000

Visit of Wendy Titelman with A.T. and J.T. 6:00 until 8:00 PM, supervised by Joyce Saye

I met Wendy about five minutes late due to very slow and heavy traffic on Stilesboro Rd. We went for the girls. At Andy's house, there was no sign of life outside. A.T. and J.T. are usually in the yard waiting for Wendy. Something looked different too and I am not sure why. It may just have been that the grass was uncut and there were weeds in the usually perfect lawn. I went to the door and knocked. I could see J.T. in the kitchen through the side lights. A.T. ran to the door and told me that they were with their baby sitter, their father was not at home. I called J.T. and we all went to the car. I called to the baby sitter too to be sure she knew we were leaving.

Wendy told the girls that she wanted to spend time with them first tonight and then they could play with their friends. A.T. complained as she sometimes does if her time with the neighborhood children is shortened at all. Wendy held her ground. She brought the girls into the living room for a mom and daughters talk. Wendy asked the children about their day and about school and everything they were doing in their lives. Unfortunately, this line of conversation bores J.T. and A.T. who are so active they can hardly hold still for a ladies' talk. After ten or fifteen minutes at most, Wendy said they could play with their friends. A.T. and J.T. flew out to find Erin, Olivia, and some of the Williams children.

Only a few minutes later, the pizza man arrived with dinner and we called the girls back in. With Wendy's permission, they brought Erin along. We all had pizza with watermelon for dessert.

J.T. excused herself to go to the bathroom. She called Wendy. Wendy and I went to the door. J.T. wanted some clean panties. Wendy went upstairs and got them and brought them back. She handed them to J.T. and closed the door. Wendy and I went back to the kitchen.

After dinner, Wendy tried another conversation with her daughters and they were as lively and active as before. A.T. began the time doing some contortions on the floor. J.T. ran back and forth to the dining room with her gerbil. Wendy asked A.T. how her stomach had been. A.T. said it had been fine all day. Wendy asked why she thought it had been okay today. A.T. said "Probably because I have hardly even seen Daddy." A.T.'s eyes dart to me and quickly away whenever she says something negative about Andy. Her expression changes from her usual one of merriment to one that looks like fear to me.

Wendy mentioned to me that J.T. had a bruised arm and said that Karen had examined it and reached the same conclusion she reached: that it was a hand print. I looked at J.T.'s arm and there were bruises, including one prominent one. The pattern resembled a thumb and some fingers. I asked her how she got it. She said "I don't remember." I said "It looks like a hand." J.T. laughed and pulled her arm away from me.

331

May 11, 2000

Visit of Wendy Titelman with A.T.
and J.T. , 6:00 until 8:00,
supervised by Joyce Saye

Wendy and I drove to Andy's house to pick up the girls. They were with a babysitter, Holly. Andy was out.

At Wendy's house, she asked the girls to come inside first and visit with her before going outside to play with the neighborhood children. The girls agreed and ran inside. Wendy tried to spend some time talking together but, as usual, the girls were anxious to run and play. They did talk about going to school and going swimming. Then the girls went outside while Wendy made dinner.

A.T. and J.T. came in long enough to eat but, as soon as they could, they were ready to go back out and play. Tonight, the children were skating. A.T. borrowed Calvin's skates. J.T. had some at Wendy's house. The children spent the rest of the time sailing around on their roller skates in the beautiful summer evening. They just seem to be joyful and full of energy and fun when they are at Wendy's house. I hope this is how their lives are all of the time.

When we took the children home, Andy was there. A.T. said goodnight to her mom and went to the door where her father was waiting. J.T. clung to Wendy and did not want to let go. A.T. ran back to the car and clung to her mother as well. We were able to urge them on to the house but their reluctance to leave Wendy was more pronounced tonight than usual. They often tell her that they want to live with her but this is the first time, during a visit I supervised, that they have made a physical gesture against returning to Andy after the visit ended.

332

Supervised Visit of Titleman
A.T. age 8, J.T. age 6

Supervisor: Karyn A. Covington
May 29, 2000 4 pm-8pm

I met Wendy at her home, she was getting ready for the picnic today. At 6:55pm we went to pick up the girls. We arrived at 4pm the girls came running out with their First Aid Kits and hugged their mother and then ran to their father again and hugged him. He acted if he was surprised that they came back to hug and kiss him. A.T. licked her father's face when he picked her up again to say good-bye.

Wendy asked the girls," It seems that things are going better for you. It seems that you are more loving with your dad?" And J.T. stated, "Daddy said if you don't hug me, you can't get into the car." And A.T. stated, "Daddy tells then that they had to hug him when he opens the door and if you don't, then I'm going to do something." J.T. said, "I'm afraid that Daddy is going to find out what I told you. And when he finds out he will yell at me." I told her, "I have to report what you tell me, and not to be afraid."

When we got back to the house we got things together for the picnic. We loaded the van and went to Lost Mountain Pool. We had a good time. we had hot dogs, potato salad, baked beans, chips, brownies, and soda.

There were a lot of families there. Wendy and A.T. swan while I watched. J.T. got into the water; she waded in the water and put her head under the water. She said it was too cold. So, she got out of the water and wrapped up with her towels and laid with her mom.

J.T. said that she didn't feel so good, so Wendy gave her some Tylenol. She went downstairs to play on the computer. A.T. had one of her friends over, Erin and her little brother.

They played downstairs until it was time to go back to Dad's house.

Wendy took them back to their dad's, they had a good visit.

Mr. Titleman appeared to be upset because J.T. went swimming, he stated that the doctor told him for J.T. not to go swimming and I told Mr. Titleman that if he needed for the children to do something or not to let the supervisor know ahead of time.

End of visit.

June 8, 2000   Visit of Wendy Titelman with A.T. and   J.T. ,
          6:00 until 8:00, supervised by Joyce Saye

Wendy and I drove over to pick up A.T. and J.T.   at Andy's house. Our visit began with Andy accusing me of questioning A.T. and J.T. and upsetting them. He insisted that the girls said so. I must have tired of Andy's accusations because I did not try to reassure him. I said that I ask questions when children tell me about abuse and I need to be sure I understand correctly. Andy said he didn't know what my rights were but he did not want anyone asking the girls questions.

I got into the car with Wendy and the children and I saw that the girls were wide-eyed and silent. When anyone spoke, they interrupted and warned each other not to talk about this or that. For example, the girls had the flu recently and had told Wendy and me that they thought they got it from Katie who got sick first. Tonight, the girls were better and Wendy asked if Katie also felt better. One child said that Katie had to go to the hospital but the other cut her short, saying they were not supposed to tell Wendy that. Wendy asked why not and the girls said that it was "the divorce." Their concern over saying something wrong was pervasive and virtually ended communication between the children and Wendy for the entire visit.

At Wendy's house, A.T. and J.T.   wanted to go straight outside to play with neighborhood children. A.T. went out first and played with Erin. J.T.   stayed a little while but she was a little bit feisty to Wendy, I think because she under some kind of pressure. She went outside too. Then Wendy told me that she felt frightened by the things they said tonight. I too felt the impression was chilling.

The children had supper and played with the neighbors until time to go home. Wendy brought them in just before time to leave. She held each child and told her that she loved her very much. The girls told their mother that they loved her too. We took them back to Andy's house. Andy said nothing further to me at that time.

I called A-Plus to talk with Kay about Andy's accusation and learned that Andy had called her to complain again. I do not know why Andy focuses his suspicions on me but I do know that months of unfounded accusations leave me very wary of Andy's perceptions.

June 12, 2000   Visit of Wendy Titelman with A.T. and J.T. ,
                                 6:00 until 8:00, supervised by Joyce Saye

I met Wendy just at 6:00 and she told me we were going out to dinner tonight with the children. We went to Andy's house to pick up J.T. and A.T.. Andy came out and spoke.

Andy decided long ago that I was an imposter who is a personal friend of Wendy's and a member of her church. Last week, he complained that I was asking his children inappropriate questions. He says the children told him these things. I just don't think so, unless they were led. Tonight I wondered again if their claims and memories are being manipulated.

We went to Rafferty's, near Town Center Mall. The children talked freely about day camp and all the things they were doing there. Wendy asked which camp they were going to. They said that it was the Kennesaw Summer Camp near Adams Park. The children were relaxed and happy, distinctly unguarded compared particularly to last week. Without the distraction of neighborhood children, they sat at the table with us, enjoyed their dinners and talked continually with their mother. There was merriment and easy chatter at our table.

A.T. suddenly popped up with rapid-fire questions to Wendy. "Did you throw things at Daddy?" and "Did you hurt Daddy?" Wendy said she had not thrown anything at anyone and didn't remember if she cried. I said to A.T. that the grown ups were trying to figure everything out so she did not have to . . . but J.T. took over for her sister and repeated the same questions in different words: "Did you throw things at Daddy?" "Did you cry when Daddy pushed you?", "Did you hurt Daddy?" Wendy affirmed that she had not thrown anything at anyone and said she did not remember whether she cried, then we both redirected the girls' attention.

In recent weeks, the children have sometimes seemed fearful of talking to Wendy about everyday things. Last week, they were plainly afraid to talk to either of us, repeatedly interrupting each other with tense warnings not to talk about that, e.g. Katie's bout with the flu. Tonight, I wondered if they are being coached at Andy's house to believe in a past that discredits their mother, a past not founded in their own memories.

The children took our guidance and went back to having a good time. After dinner we went to a Garden Ridge store. Wendy bought some candles. She said she likes to keep a three-wick candle burning as a symbol of her prayer that she and her daughters will be reunited. A.T. and J.T. loved the store. I had not been shopping with the Titelmans before and I did not know what enthusiastic shoppers these two girls are.

As we left the store, we drove up to Adams Park and saw the sign for the Kennesaw Summer Camp Program. J.T. asked Wendy to come to the camp to meet them but Wendy explained that she could not, but it made her feel better to know where they were spending their days. The girls asked Wendy to plan a trip with them. J.T. said she wanted it to be to Hawaii. They had fun talking about hoping they could make a trip like that together someday.

Page 2

We drove to Andy's house and let the girls out. Andy came out to meet them and Wendy and I left at a minute or two after eight.

To whom it May Concern:

I write this with the most gravest of concern not understanding how two girls could be taken away from a loving, caring mother.

My child took ballet with Jessica Tittleman for three years. In early Spring of 2000 one Tuesday we were slow getting out after ballet. The waiting room was empty, other than myself and three children, Andy Tittleman and Jessica, and two other mothers deep in conversation. As I was getting Moriah's shoes changed I glanced up and observed the following:

Exhibit J

Jessica was sliding down her father's body. He was sitting with his legs spread apart allowing Jessica rub groin area repeatedly. I turned back around to continue what I was doing then I heard Andy Titleman singing softly "Touching, touching, touching..." I looked up again and he was singing this to Jessica.

Personally I felt very uncomfortable and would not in my opinion quantify this behavior as normal. I felt that I ought to bring this incident to Wendy Titleman's attention.

On June 24, 2000 I testified this incident in court yet the judge gave the father custody of the two girls with the mother only getting the girls every other weekend.

Thank you,
Gail E. Vernon

James S. Cheatham, M.D.
Diplomate, American Board of Psychiatry and Neurology
Added Qualifications in Addiction Psychiatry

To whom it may concern:

Re: Wendy Titleman

This is to advise that Ms. Titleman has been under my care since February, 2000. She is a very intelligent woman who is deeply concerned about the well being of her children She has been under considerable stress for the past several months due to the fact that her husband was granted custody of the children. In my judgment, the husband is unfit to serve as a parent guardian of the children. In fact, I believe him to be a sexual predator.

In my opinion, the custody of the children should be with Ms. Titleman. If there are questions regarding custody please feel free to contact me.

Sincerely,

James S. Cheatham, MD

Exhibit K

2265 Roxburgh Drive - Roswell, Georgia 30076 - (770) 475-8739 Fax (770) 664-8721

REPORT OF PSYCHOLOGICAL CONSULTATION

INTERIM

NAME: Jessica Titelman

REFERRED BY: Wendy Titelman

EXAMINER: J. D. Matherne, Ph.D.

DOB: March 30, 1994

DATE TESTED: September 2, 2000

AGE: 6 Years

EDUCATION:

BACKGROUND INFORMATION:

Jessica Titelman was referred for psychological evaluation by her mother, Wendy Titelman. Specific information is requested concerning the allegation that Jennifer has been sexually abused by her father, Andrew Titelman.

Information is requested to assist in providing information concerning the child's diagnosis and possible need for counseling.

This clinician was provided extensive background information concerning prior evaluations related to the custodial placement of Jessica and her sister, Amanda . Both children were seen for a child custody evaluation during this past year. In reviewing the background information, a question exist concerning whether or not this child has ever been seen for a specific evaluation regarding the allegation of sexual abuse. For the purpose of the interim report, a detailed review of the prior reports will not be discussed at this time.

CLINICAL INTERVIEW AND BEHAVIORAL OBSERVATIONS:

Jessica was seen during the mother's weekend visitation. This is a four day visitation from Friday until Monday, because of the Labor Day holiday on Monday. The mother was interviewed to obtain supplemental background information. Again, the specifics of this interview will not be noted at this time, as this represents an interim report rather than a complete report of the psychological findings. It is noted that the children are in the primary custody of their father, Andrew Titelman, with the mother being granted visitation.

Wendy Titelman stated that her children have indicated to her on prior occasions that they have been touched by their father in a sexual inappropriate manner. The mother is attempting to obtain protection for her children so they will no longer be exposed to the alleged sexual abuse by their father.

Exhibit L

341

TITELMAN, JESSICA

J. DONALD MATHERNE, PH.D.
SEPTEMBER 2, 2000

After completing the interview of the mother, Wendy Titelman, this clinician returned to the waiting room and requested that Jessica accompany the clinician from the waiting area into the consultation office. It was noted that Jessica was well behaved in the waiting room. It was also noted that the child interacted well with her oldest sister, Amanda and also interacted well with her mother.

In questioning Jessica about her relationship with her parents, she noted that she relates well with her mother, but not as well with her father. She describes her father as "yelling at me and Amanda He has hit me on the arm with his hand because he gets angry." She expresses a preference to live with her mother, because her mother is nicer and does not yell at her nor does her mother hit her like her father hits her. From the information provided, it does not appear that the physical discipline used by the father meets the criteria for physical abuse, as the child stated that her father typically does not leave a mark on her when he hits her. Jessica was also questioned concerning any history of sexual abuse The methodology used was consistent with the methodology that has been used in this clinician's appointment as an expert witness for both the Harrison County Youth Court and the Jackson County Youth Court.

The child was shown Figure 9 of the Anatomical Drawings published by Forensic Mental Health Associates. This anatomical drawing depicts the front view of a grammar school female child. Jessica stated that her father has touched her on prior occasions under her clothing on her genital area. She stated that there has never been any digital penetration or penial penetration. She also denies that there has been any history of oral sex. She indicated that when her parents were not living together this physical touching occurred when she would stay with her father. She said that her father "reached under and touched me there." She said that he would reach under her clothing and touch her on her genital area. When shown Figure 9, she pointed to the genital area in the drawing. She was asked to draw a circle around the area in question. She was also asked to put an X exactly at the location in question. She was then asked to write her name for the purpose of authenticity. A copy of this drawing is enclosed for further review. She said that this would typically happen when she had been asleep in bed. She said that when she felt herself being touched "it would wake me up." She believes that her father was under the impression that she was asleep and not aware that she could feel him touching her in this manner. Jessica claims that she had provided this information to Dr. Elizabeth King, a psychologist on prior occasions, but Dr. King did not seem interested in this situation. The child denies that anyone had told her to make up this situation. She claims that her mother only tells her to tell the truth. This child was questioned concerning her awareness of the difference between the truth and a lie. It is very apparent that Jennifer does know the difference between the truth and a lie. This child indicated that she was telling the truth.

The child was asked to make a fist with her right hand and to think of her hand as her genital area. She was then asked to take her left hand and to show the clinician how she was touched. The child took her left hand and rubbed it across the top of her closed fist over the opening into her fist. As indicated, there was no indication using this demonstration of any digital penetration. The child's

2

TITELMAN, JESSICA

J. DONALD MATHERNE, PH.D.
SEPTEMBER 2, 2000

behavior does indicate that she did experience physical contact involving her father touching her under her clothing on her genital area based upon what is alleged by this child.

SUMMARY AND RECOMMENDATIONS:

As this is and interim report, the clinician is not providing the comprehensive findings based upon the review of the extensive background reports and is also not providing the entire report of information obtained during this consultation. It is apparent from the information obtained at this time that the child is alleging that her father did touch her in a sexual inappropriate manner on multiple occasions, typically when he did not realize that she was awake and aware of this physical contact. The child does not appear to have been prompted. The child knows the difference between the truth and a lie. The child emphatically states that she is being truthful about having been touched in this manner. She is not wanting to return to live with her father for fear of what may happen in the future. She expresses a very definite preference to remain in the care, custody and supervision of her mother. She feels safer in this environment.

Overall, this clinician is of the opinion that this child if returned to her father is in immediate danger of irreparable harm and/or further sexual abuse. This opinion is based upon the child's allegation of having been touched by her father in a sexual inappropriate manner under her clothing on her genital area. The child indicates that this has happened before her parents separation as well as since she has been living with her father. This clinician is of the opinion that the allegation of sexual abuse is substantiated. It would certainly be advantageous that this child remain in a protective environment, in the custody with her mother, Wendy Titelman.

It is further recommended that the child be involved in outpatient counseling preferably with a therapist who specializes in the treatment of children with histories of alleged sexual abuse.

DIAGNOSTIC IMPRESSION:

AXIS I: ALLEGATION OF CHILD SEXUAL ABUSE, SUBSTANTIATED
            BY HISTORY

3

TITELMAN, JESSICA

J. DONALD MATHERNE, PH.D.
SEPTEMBER 2, 2000

TESTS ADMINISTERED:

Wide Range Achievement III
Anatomical Drawings Published by Forensic Health Associates

J. Donald Matherne, Ph.D.
Clinical Psychologist

JDM/eht

4

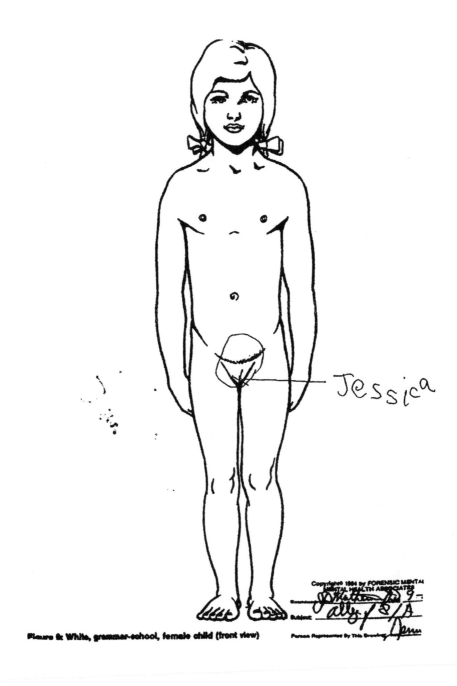

Figure 8: White, grammar-school, female child (front view)

REPORT OF PSYCHOLOGICAL CONSULTATION REPORT

INTERIM

NAME: Amanda Titelman

DOB: May 26, 1992

AGE: 8 Years

REFERRED BY: Wendy Titelman

EXAMINER: J.D. Matherne, Ph.D.

DATE TESTED: September 2, 2000

EDUCATION·

BACKGROUND INFORMATION:

Amanda Titelman was referred for evaluation to investigate the allegation that this child and her sister, Jessica were sexually abused by their father, Andrew Titelman. Both Amanda and her sister were transported to this clinician's office by their mother, Wendy Titelman. The mother has moved to the Mississippi Gulf Coast. She previously resided in Georgia. A final Decree of Divorce was issued in August granting primary custody to the father, Andrew Titelman and visitation to the mother, Wendy Titelman. As this is an interim report, detailed information concerning background information, prior evaluation reports and clinical interview information will be provided in the final comprehensive report. As this represents an interim report, only pertinent information will be provided.

Amanda and her sister was seen separately on this date to obtain information concerning the allegation of sexual abuse. There was a prior child custody evaluation report, which was court ordered. This prior custody evaluation report did not involve a specific sexual abuse investigation. The allegation of child sexual abuse has been made to a number of various professionals and has been an issue of concern for the past one to two years. This clinician is not aware of a specific investigative consultation to address the issue of sexual abuse.

CLINICAL INTERVIEW AND BEHAVIORAL OBSERVATIONS:

Wendy Titleman, mother of Jessica and Amanda was interviewed at length to obtain background information. Wendy Titelman provided the clinician with a three-ring binder that contains extensive information concerning her two children. This clinician had an opportunity to review this information in formulating an opinion concerning the allegation of abuse.

This clinician spoke initially with Jessica and then spoke individually with Amanda. No one else was physically present during this consultation. Amanda is an eight year old child and stated that she is in the third grade. She has performed well in school, but has had a problem with mathematics. She was administered an educational evaluation to obtained specific information concerning

347

TITELMAN, AMANDA

J. DONALD MATHERNE, PH.D.
SEPTEMBER 2, 2000

her educational functioning.

This child stated that she has a very close, loving relationship with her mother. She has had somewhat of a problematic relationship with her father. She did indicate that when her parents lived together they had problems in their relationship. She was questioned concerning which parent she would prefer to live with. She said that she wanted to live with her mom, because "she is so much nicer. She does not yell at me. She takes me places." She said that when she is living with her father he has her stay with his girlfriend, Anita. Sometimes she and her sister have to go to work with her father, who picks them up after school.

Amanda was questioned specifically concerning the allegation of abuse. She was questioned initially about the issue of physical abuse. She said that her father hits her and her sister on their arms with his hand. She describes her father as someone who gets "real mad. He screams and yells." She claims that this situation makes her feel bad and she is scared of her father. She is afraid of him hitting her when he gets angry. She admits that he usually does not leave a mark on her when he hits her with his hand. She was also questioned concerning the issue of sexual abuse. She was shown Figure 9 of the Anatomical Drawings published by Forensic Mental Health Associates. This depicts the front view of a grammar school female child. This procedure is consistent with the methodology used by this clinician in the investigation of alleged sexual abuse as a consultant to the Harrison County Youth Court, Jackson County Youth Court, Stone County Youth Court and Hancock County Youth Court.

Amanda stated that her father has touched her under her clothing on her genital area, which has made her feel very uncomfortable. This usually has happened when she is in bed and "he thinks that I am asleep, but I am pretending. He comes in my room." She said this happened "when my mother was not living in the home." She said that when her father touches her in this manner, "it makes me feel like he doesn't love me." She was questioned concerning whether or not she was of the opinion that this touching was accidental or on purpose. In her opinion, her father has touched her in a sexual manner on purpose. She was questioned concerning whether or not she understands the difference between the truth and a lie. She was very consistent in indicating an understanding of the difference between the truth and a lie. She is insistent that she is telling the truth. She was asked to draw a circle around the area on the anatomical drawing where she alleges that her father touched her. She circled the genital area and put an X over the opening of the vagina indicating the exact location where she alleges that her father had touched her. She was asked to write her name for the purpose of authenticity. A copy of this anatomical drawing is enclosed for further review.

This clinician used the fist demonstration to more specifically depict the alleged abuse. Amanda was asked to close one hand and think of this as her genital area. She was then asked to take her

2

other hand and think of this as her father's hand. She was then asked to show specifically what she remembers having happen to her. She took her left hand and rubbed it across her closed right fist. She said "he thought I was asleep." She said that she told her mother, because she wanted "my mom to help me." She was asked how she specifically felt about what had happened. She said, " I just didn't like him anymore because he did that." She was asked if she had provided this information to anyone else. She said that in her conversations with Dr. Elizabeth King, she had made mention of this, but Dr. King "didn't ask me questions about this. I mentioned it to her, but she was not interested in talking about it." She was then asked why she thought that Dr. King was not interested. Amanda's response to this question was "because she was more interested in going on to another subject immediately!"

She claims that this touching of her by her father has happened a couple more times since the last school year. She said that this has happened as recent as this summer. She said it occurred at home when she was in bed. She was specific in indicating that the room was dark, but "I knew it was him because he is really, really, really, really hairy. I peeked. He had a blue shirt on that said Amoco." She was asked if it was possible that her father had touched her in an accidental manner. She said "no because he took his hand and put it under my jammies. He rubbed me on my pee pee hole." She was asked if she thought that this would happen again. She said she is afraid that it will happen again because "if I was alone with him, probably" it would happen again. She was asked if anyone had told her to make up a lie about this situation. She stated no one had asked her to say this because "it is not made up, because what happened to me really happened."

SUMMARY AND RECOMMENDATIONS:

Based upon the information obtained in this consultation, this clinician is of the opinion that the alleged sexual abuse of this child by her father, Andrew Titelman is substantiated. This opinion is based upon a review of the background information, clinical and behavioral observations and the consultation with this youngster.

It is this clinician's clinical opinion that Amanda is in immediate danger of irreparable harm and/or further sexual abuse if she returns to the custody of her father at this time. It is recommended that she remain in the custody of her mother until there is an opportunity for the allegation of sexual abuse to be specifically substantiated through the court of jurisdiction.

It would be advantageous that Amanda, as well as her sister and mother be seen in outpatient counseling to address issues concerning the parents divorce and the issues related to the alleged sexual abuse of both children.

3

TITELMAN, AMANDA

J. DONALD MATHERNE, PH.D.
SEPTEMBER 2, 2000

A comprehensive report will be provided concerning the findings of this psychological consultation. The information provided at this time only represents an interim report of the psychological consultation.

DIAGNOSTIC IMPRESSION:

AXIS I: ALLEGATION OF CHILD SEXUAL ABUSE, SUBSTANTIATED BY HISTORY

TESTS ADMINISTERED:

Anatomical Drawings Published by Forensic Mental Health Associates

J. Donald Matherne, Ph.D.
Clinical Psychologist

JDM/eht

4

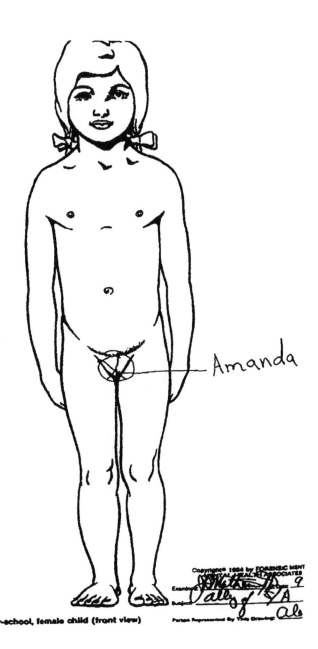

Amanda

Figure 8: White, grammar-school, female child (front view)

A MOTHER'S JOURNAL

Bryan Wilson, Jury Foreperson
State of Georgia vs. Wendy Titlemen

Dear Honorable Judge Bodiford and Mr. Pat Head:

My name is Bryan Wilson and I recently served as a juror on a trial (Apr 23-27, 2001) in the Cobb County Superior Court of Georgia. Several members of the jury have requested that I write a letter summarizing our thoughts and concerns pertaining to the case we heard; State of Georgia v. Wendy Titlemen. To understand why this case even made it to trial was a question each of us had to ask while we were deliberating on Friday. We were perplexed as to why our State would pursue such a case so diligently when there were obvious errors in the indictment and credible reports indicating sexual and emotional abuse to two small children and the prosecution of the mother who sought to protect them from harm's way.

We, the jury felt that the "State of Georgia" did in fact, neglect to protect these children and furthermore, did not have the children's best interests at heart. It appeared they wished to cover up blatant miss-steps by an agency (DFACS) that appears to have made several errors in judgment. I would like to take an opportunity to summarize these areas of concern. I sincerely hope that action can be taken to correct these situations in the future. Not only will this save the State of Georgia the expense of prosecuting such flimsy cases, but will also serve to better protect the ones who need it most, the *CHILDREN* of our State.

Conclusions
1. **The "Indictment"**. The indictment was very poorly written and poorly executed. The dates were inconsistent with the prosecution's effort to paint the mother as a "law breaker and flight risk". Based on the information we received, the dates listed in the indictment were within the legal limits spelled out in the final divorce decree's visitation schedule. It is incredible to believe that our court system would put a decent woman in jail for doing something completely legal during the indictment's window! Very poorly written indictment in our opinion.

2. **The charge of "Fleeing Justice"**. Based on the evidence presented, we, the jury, were unanimous in agreeing with and supporting Ms. Titlemen in her beliefs that there was probable cause to protect her children. The evidence gave strong indication the children were being sexually molested by their father. Ms. Hakes, the Assistant Prosecutor, in her closing statements called Ms. Titlemen a "zealot" like Timothy McVeigh for wanting to take the law into her own hands and protect her children. I believe the majority of us on the jury have children. It was also unanimous that had we felt there was reason to believe our children were being abused or neglected *in any way*, and when seeking help, found the state (who is supposed to protect our children) unwilling to review the evidence in an unbiased light, would have reacted in similar ways.

3. **"Taking the law into her own hands"**. We, the jury, saw Ms. Titlemen as someone desperately trying to use the legal system in Georgia to its fullest extent to protect her children, but to no avail. Then, when discovering more evidence of abuse, was left with no choice but to apply to the State of Mississippi for help. Although Ms. Hakes painted Ms. Titlemen as a manipulator and extremist, we felt that she was justified in using whatever means necessary to protect her children. Ms. Hakes said over and over during her cross-examinations "the State of Georgia knows best how to protect its children". We are not so sure after sitting on the jury and seeing first hand the types of "guardians" and "counselors" that the State of Georgia appoints to protect our most precious resources and future taxpayers. Dr. King admitted under oath, the children told her they were being abused. Why then do the children remain in the custody of the accused when the State does not appear to have proved otherwise?

Exhibit M

352

4. **"Does Not Deserve Justice!".** We, the jury, were horrified when Ms. Hakes told us in her closing statements that Ms. Titlemen didn't deserve justice. What does that mean?! Doesn't everyone deserves justice and aren't we all innocent until proven guilty? For the Assistance Prosecutor to openly say that a citizen doesn't deserve justice is an outrage and an insult to our justice system.

5. **Court appointed zealots.** The court appointed Guardians and Counselors were not credible and did all they could not to disclose real findings or intentions. Ms. Woods defied a State of Mississippi court order (within 24 hours) to protect the children from their father until additional hearings could take place and certain evidence be reviewed. Ms. King (a supposed expert) interrogated the children for two and one-half hours without taking any notes, or tapes, etc. She then appeared to try and cover up the disclosure of the sexual abuse to the court when asked in direct questioning. Therefore, we found that there were several disclosures of sexual abuse but little evidence at all of recantations. Ms. Whitaker went so far as to say the children were "abducted"! This accusation further alienated the jury by displaying such blatant bias against the mother, Ms. Titlemen.

6. **"Paid Expert Witnesses".** Ms. Hakes was very careful to point out numerous times that the defense had hired "expert" witnesses who were paid for their services. Where is this wrong? We all got paid for doing what we considered our civil duty. Ms. Hakes gets paid, the state appointed guardians and counselors get paid, the judge and court employees get paid, so why did she feel this was such a big deal? Ms. Hakes tried to make it a huge deal by claiming the defense had "hired guns". The State's witnesses were pathetic in our opinion. They were poorly rehearsed, poorly accredited and overtly biased. At one point, Ms. King, when asked a direct question about the children confiding to her that they had been abused by their father, turns to the judge and says, "I don't want to answer that, they may get mad at me". Would the State really get "mad" if she told the truth under oath?

In conclusion, the jury collectively felt that the divorce of Wendy and Andy Titlemen contained deep dividing issues. It was our wish that more information could have been disclosed to assist our decision. We all agreed that the children were in all likelihood being sexually abused by their father. Also, the custody and well-being of these minor children should be a major concern to Cobb County. A new group of unbiased experts needs to re-evaluate this case and bring closure regarding visitation that satisfies all parties if appropriate. It has been an honor to serve as the foreperson of this jury. I feel that this jury has served justice, and that the state's mishandling of this case has cost the taxpayers of Cobb County, Georgia a lot of money.

Regards,
Bryan E. Wilson
Bryan Wilson, (bryanewilson@email.com)
Foreperson

Donna M. Kimball
Donna M. Kimball

Ann E. Klueter
Ann E. Klueter

Vicki L. Croft
VICKI L. CROFT

Kimberly Savransky
Kimberly J. Savransky
Cynthia P. Winter
Cynthia P. Winter

IDW 2001-0073536-CV Page 309

353

APPENDIX G

THE OFFICE OF

Richard Ducote
Attorney & Counselor at Law

731 Fern Street . New Orleans, Louisiana 70118

504.314.8400 . 504.314.8600 Fax . Ducotelaw@aol.com

April 29, 2002

To: Members of the Cobb County Bar
      Metro Atlanta Mental Health Professionals

Re: The cover-up of child sexual abuse by Diane Woods, Esq. and
      Elizabeth King, Ph.D.

A clear lesson to be learned from the current scandal in the Catholic Church is that the cover up of child sexual abuse by those entrusted to stop it or prevent it exacerbates this terrible problem and compounds the extensive damage suffered by the victims. You undoubtedly will find this letter unusual- but it is very necessary.

I represent Wendy Titelman, formerly a resident of Cobb County. I have handled child sexual abuse and domestic violence cases fighting for victims in over 40 states. I served as a special prosecutor for termination of parental rights cases in 40 Louisiana courts. By invitation of courts and professional organizations, I regularly conduct child sexual abuse and domestic violence training for judges, attorneys, mental health professionals, guardians *ad litem*, and custody evaluators nationwide. I have been honored for my work by the American Bar Association, the National Association of Social Workers, The Louisiana State University School of Social Work, and others. My successful cases include *Ankenbrandt v. Richards*, 112 S.Ct. 2206 (1992), which allows child sexual abuse victims to sue their abusive parents in federal court where diversity jurisdiction exists. The Harvard Law Review and the National Council of Juvenile and Family Court Judges have praised my groundbreaking legislation enacted to protect abused children in custody cases.

In the Titelman case (Cobb County Superior Court Nos. 98-1-5890-33 and 00-10-8035-33), Diane Woods, a Marietta attorney, was appointed guardian *ad litem* for two young girls. In May, 1999, after a brief investigation, the facts of which she misstated to the court, and despite some emerging evidence of possible sexual abuse by the children's father, Ms. Woods

April 29, 2002
Re: Woods and King
Page 2

recommended that he be granted custody. However, in June, 1999, the children began revealing more details of their molestation by their father, and Ms. Woods then began sabotaging the DFACS and police investigations of the abuse by telling the authorities that the allegations were false. In a recent sworn deposition, Ms. Woods admits that she has no training or expertise in child sexual abuse. Yet, because of her frequent guardian *ad litem* appointments and her association with SafeHouse, Ms. Woods was able to derail official efforts to protect the children from their father's abuse. In August, 1999, Ms. Woods's good friend Dr. Elizabeth King was appointed as the "custody evaluator," and Ms. Woods "assured" her that the sexual abuse allegations were false. However, Woods refused to speak to the children's therapists who documented the molestations, and to the other adults who either heard the children discuss the abuse, witnessed inappropriate sexualized behavior between the father and one child, or witnessed sexual acting out evidencing molestation. Dr. King disregarded the children's reports to her of their father's fondling them.

Woods and King then arranged for an "emergency hearing" on February 18, 2000, for which Ms. Titelman had one day's notice of the hearing and one hour's notice of the purpose of the hearing. At the "hearing", Woods and King convinced the judge to give the father sole custody and to restrict Ms. Titelman to professionally supervised visitation. When the children continued to complain to the visitation supervisors that their father was "tickling" their "privates"at night and touching them "wrongly," Woods asserted that the supervisors were not doing their job and stopped Ms. Titelman's visits. The final custody trial was heard in June, 2000. In closing argument, John Mayoue, Esq., the father's attorney, implored the trial judge to ignore the abundant evidence of the sexual abuse and to simply listen to Woods and King:

> It is difficult to come in here and have somebody say that everybody is wrong and I fully accept the premise that no one knows what happens behind closed doors. That is why we have professionals because you weren't there and I wasn't there. And

April 29, 2002
Re: Woods and King
Page 3

> we don't know what to do other than to rely upon those with professional expertise in this area and, you know, lawyers and with all due respect, judges don't have the kind of training that these people have and I am talking about Dr. King and I am talking about Diane and I am talking about DFACS and I think we have to go a tremendous way to say that we are going to substitute our goals and ideas for theirs.

Woods and King carried the day, and on August 4, 2000, the trial court awarded the father sole custody, but restored Ms. Titelman's unsupervised visits. However, soon the children told their mother about more ongoing instances of their father coming to their beds at night and fondling their genitals. As Ms. Titelman had taken the girls to the Mississippi Gulf Coast for the Labor Day weekend- which she was absolutely allowed to do under the custody decree- she had them examined by the forensic psychologist who routinely performs the sexual abuse evaluations for the courts there. Based on his belief that they indeed were being molested by their father, the Harrison County, Mississippi, Chancery Court placed the children in protective custody. During their evaluations, the girls told Dr. Matherne, the Mississippi psychologist, that they tried to tell Dr. King about their father's abuse, but that she would change the subject. In response to the Mississippi court order, King, Woods, Mayoue, and the father immediately traveled to Mississippi in order to force the children's return to their father in Georgia. On September 15, 2000, as a result of bogus criminal charges of "custodial interference" instituted by the father, his attorney John Mayoue, with the assistance of Woods and King, Ms. Titelman was arrested and jailed. She has neither seen nor spoken to her daughters since that date. They still reside with their father. Despite Woods signing a Mississippi consent order that the girls would not be interviewed without a subsequent Georgia court order allowing such, Woods and King "interviewed" the girls on September 16 or 17. Despite the fact that the girls confirmed the molestation in the interview, Wood inferred to DFACS and the custody judge that the girls stated otherwise.

April 29, 2002
Re: Woods and King
Page 4

On April 23, 2001, Ms. Titelman's trial for "interstate interference with custody" began in the Cobb County Superior Court (No.00-9-4681-40). In the criminal trial, the actions of Woods and King were exposed as they testified for the State. King was forced to produce her one audiotaped interview with the girls (curiously, she had other interviews, but only taped one), and it clearly illustrated that the girls accurately described her changing the subject when they tried to inform her of the abuse. After a quick deliberation, the jury promptly acquitted Ms. Titelman. The jury was so outraged that they wrote the attached letter to Judge Bodiford, the custody judge, and DA Patrick Head condemning the prosecution of Ms. Titelman and decrying Woods and King's conduct.

Diane Woods and Elizabeth King have covered up the sexual abuse of these children to protect themselves from accountability for their negligent placement of the children in the abusive father's custody in the first place. Many ongoing efforts are underway to correct this tragedy. But the sunshine of truth, as well as professional peer accountability and scrutiny, are indeed necessary to prevent other children from experiencing this same calamity. As Dr. King and Ms. Woods continue to give seminars, testify in court, and affect young lives through the mistaken perception of their infallibility, I, for one, cannot stand by quietly.

I wholeheartedly invite Ms. Woods and Dr. King to sue me if this information is defamatory. I will gladly accept service of the suit, and I say, as I have said in the past, let us get all of the facts before a jury.

It is the truth that will set these two girls free.

Thank you for your attention.

Richard Ducote

357

ENDNOTES

1. Richard A. Gardner, *True and False Accusations of Child Sex Abuse*, 1986, pg. 585.

2. Ibid, pg. 117.

3. Ibid, pg. 195.

4. Ibid, pp. 34.

5. Ibid, pg. 80.

6. *Violence and The Family, Report of the American Psychological Association Presidential Task Force on Violence and the Family*, 1996, pg. 40.

7. Phyllis Chesler, *Mothers On Trial*, 1986, pp. 66-92; The American Judges Association, *Domestic Violence & The Courtroom Understanding The Problem...Knowing The Victim.*

8. Nancy Thoennes & Patricia G. Tjaden, *The Extent, Nature, and Validity of Sexual Abuse Allegations in Custody/Divorce Disputes, Child Abuse & Neglect 14*, 1990, pg. 153.

9. Http://www.rickross.com/reference.html.10.

10. Ibid.

11. Http://www.lukeford.com/stars/male/justin_sterling.html.

12. Lawrence M. Rudner, *Scholastic Achievement and Demographic Characteristics of Home School Students in 1998*, ERIC Clearinghouse on Assessment and Evaluation College of Library and Information Services, University of Maryland, College Park.

13. Governor Zell Miller, *By the Governor of the State of Georgia in A Proclamation on Home Education*, Jan., 1998.

14. Frank Pittman, M.D., *Psychology Today, Beware Older Women Ahead*, Jan., 1999.

15. Warren Farrell, interviewed in *Penthouse, Incest: The Last Taboo* by Philip Nobile, Dec., 1977.

16. Theodore P. Cross and Leonard Saxe, *A Critique of the Validity of Polygraph Testing in Child Sexual Abuse Cases, Journal of Child Sexual Abuse*, Vol. 1(4) 1992, pp. 19-31.

17. *Paidika: The Journal of Paedophilia*, Vol. 3, No. 1, Issue 9, Winter, 1993, Netherlands.

18. Http://familycourts.com/default2.html.

19. *Gender and Justice in the Courts: A Report to the Supreme Court of Georgia by the Commission on Gender Bias in the Judicial System,* 8 Ga. St. U .L. Rev. 539, 1992.

20. *Violence and The Family, Report of the American Psychological Association Presidential Task Force on Violence and the Family,* 1996, pg. 40.

21. *The American Judges Association, Domestic Violence & The Courtroom Understanding The Problem...Knowing The Victim.*

22. Http://nafcjcal.org.

23. *Nichols v. State,* 17 Ga.App.593, 606, 87 S.E. 817, 1915.

24. *A Judge's Guide: Making Child-Centered Decisions in Custody Cases,* ABA Center on Children and the Law, pg. 112.

25. Kee MacFarlane, Jill Waterman, et al, *Sexual Abuse of Young Children,* Guilford Press, 1986, pp. 126-127.

26. Richard Ducote, *Guardians Ad Litem in Private Custody Litigation: the Case for Abolition, The Loyola University New Orleans Journal of Public Interest Law,* Vol. 3, No. 2, Spring, 2002, pp. 106-151.

27. Nancy J. Moore, *Conflicts of Interests in the Representation of Children,* 64 Fordham L. Rev. 1819, 1996, pg. 1843.

28. Martin Guggenheim, *The Right to be Represented But Not Heard: Reflections on Legal Representation of Children:*[1] 59 N.Y.L.Rev. 76, 1984, pp. 102-106.

29. Raven C. Lidman and Bestsy R. Hollingsworth, *The Guardian ad Litem in Child Custody Cases: The Contours of our Judicial System Stretched Beyond Recognition,* 6 Geo.Mason L. Rev. 255, Winter, 1998, n.211.

30. Kerin S. Bischoff, *The Voice of A Child: Independent Legal Representation of Children in Private Custody Disputes When Sexual Abuse is Alleged, 138 University Pennsylvania Law Review,* May, 1990, pp. 1383, 1391-1392.

31. *Odette v State,* 273 Ga. 353, 541 S.E.2d 29, 2001; *Jones v State,* 240 Ga.App. 484, 523 S.E.2d 73, 1999.

32. *In re R.E.,* 207 Ga. App. 178, 427 S.E.2d 542, 1993; *In Re J.E.L.,* 223 Ga.App.269, 477 S.E.2d 412, 1996.

33. *In re S.G.,* 182 Ga.App.95, 354 S.E.2d 640, 1987; *In re B.J.,* 220 Ga.App.144, 469 S.E.2d 313, 1996, 53 A.L.R. 5th 499.

1

34. *Wood v Georgia*, 370 U.S. 375, 82 S.Ct. 1364, 8 L.Ed. 2d 569, 1962.
35. Viktor E. Frankl, *Man's Search for Meaning, an Introduction to Logotherapy*, Third Edition, 1984, pg.76.
36. Ibid, pp.48-49.
37. Kee MacFarlane, Jill Waterman, et al, *Sexual Abuse of Young Children*, Guilford Press, 1986, pp. 149-150.